Parks in Transition

Parks in Transition

Biodiversity, Rural Development and the Bottom Line

Edited by
Brian Child

The World Conservation Union

London ● Sterling VA

First published by Earthscan in the UK and USA in 2004

ISBN: 1-84407-069-7 paperback
1-84407-068-9 hardback

Production Management by the Clyvedon Press Ltd, Cardiff, UK
Indexing by Indexing Specialists (UK) Ltd
Printed and bound in the UK by Cromwell Press Ltd
Cover design by Danny Gillespie

For a full list of publications please contact:

Earthscan
8–12 Camden High Street
London, NW1 0JH, UK
Tel: +44 (0)20 7387 8558
Fax: +44 (0)20 7387 8998
Email: earthinfo@earthscan.co.uk
Web: **www.earthscan.co.uk**

22883 Quicksilver Drive, Sterling, VA 20166-2012, USA

A catalogue record for this book is available from the British Library

Library of Congress Cataloging-in-Publication Data

Parks in transition : biodiversity, rural development, and the bottom line / edited by
Brian Child.
    p. cm.
  Includes bibliographical references and index.
  ISBN 1-84407-069-7 (pbk.) — ISBN 1-84407-068-9 (hardback)
        1. National parks and reserves—Africa, Southern—Management. 2.
  Biological diversity—Africa, Southern. 3. Rural development—Africa, Southern. I.
  Child, B. (Brian)

  SB484.A36P37 2003
  333.78'3'0968–dc22

                                                                    2003017506

Earthscan publishes in association with WWF-UK and the International Institute for
Environment and Development

Printed on elemental chlorine-free paper

Contents

List of Tables

List of Figures

List of Boxes

List of Case Studies

List of Authors

Ivan Bond. Senior research associate on the International Institute for Environment and Development's Forestry and Landuse Programme, based in London, UK. Before moving to the UK, Ivan worked for WWF's Southern African Regional Programme Office (SARPO) in Harare, Zimbabwe, as a resource economist and project executive. While with WWF, he completed a PhD on the Communal Areas Management Programme for Indigenous Resources (CAMPFIRE). Ivan has extensive practical and applied research experience of natural resource management in Zimbabwe, Namibia, and Zambia, particularly within the communal lands. He also has ongoing research interests in the importance of transaction and management costs in natural resource management and organizational development.

Brian Child. Chair of SASUSG, worked for wildlife departments in Zimbabwe for 12 years, supported park management and CBNRM in Luangwa valley for six, assisted with restructuring of ZAWA, and has worked with the wildlife sector in some capacity in Uganda, Kenya, Namibia and South Africa.

Graham Child. Former Director on National Parks and Wild Life Management in Zimbabwe (1971–1986) and a former Vice Chairman of the MUNC Committee of SARCCUS. He is a wildlife biologist by training and guided Zimbabwe to the forefront of both wildlife and park management, before retiring in 1986 to become an international consultant on all continents except Antarctica and in all biomes from the arctic to the tropics, specialising in wildlife biology, economics and tourism, and institutional development.

David Cumming. Working in wildlife research and conservation in Zimbabwe and southern Africa since the 1960s. After graduating at Rhodes University in South Africa, he started in fisheries research but soon joined Zimbabwe's Department of National Parks and Wildlife Management. After 12 years at the Sengwa Wildlife Research Institute (where he did his doctoral research) he headed the Branch of Terrestrial Ecology before taking early retirement as Deputy Director of National Parks. In 1988 he started the WWF Multispecies Animal Production Systems Project in Zimbabwe. This later grew into the WWF Southern African Regional Program, where he was Program Director until early 2001 when he became an independent consultant and a research associate in the Tropical Resource Ecology Programme at the University of Zimbabwe. His current research interests are in ecology and management of large mammalian herbivores, and resilience of social–ecological systems in southeastern Zimbabwe. Invertebrates remain an abiding interest, and he works with his wife studying termites and spiders.

Derek de la Harpe. Chartered accountant (Zimbabwe), currently serving as the Executive Director of The Malilangwe Trust. The Malilangwe Trust is a non-governmental organization working in wildlife conservation and rural development. It owns and manages a 40,000 hectare game ranch in Zimbabwe and has rehabilitated the wildlife habitats and populations on the property so that they can be used for tourism and other production. Previously, Derek spent 18 years working for Price Waterhouse throughout southern and eastern Africa. He worked mainly as a management consultant and for the last nine years there was partner in charge of the firms' wildlife, tourism and environmental consulting practice.

Brian Jones. Senior CBNRM Technical Advisor to USAID in Namibia, and formerly an independent consultant in the environment and development sector. He has also worked as a Namibian government official, coordinating the CBNRM programme of the Ministry of Environment and Tourism. He has 14 years' experience in implementation, policy development, and research in CBNRM in Namibia and southern Africa.

Marshall W Murphree. Born in Zimbabwe and educated at university in the United States and Great Britain. He was director of the Centre for Applied Social Sciences at the University of Zimbabwe from 1970 to 1996 and is now Emeritus Professor of Applied Social Science. He was chairman of Zimbabwe's Parks and Wildlife Board from 1992 to 1996.

Acronyms and Abbreviations

ABSA	Amalgamated Banks of South Africa
ADMADE	Administrative Management Design Project
AENP	Addo Elephant National Park
ANC	African National Congress
ANGAP	Association Nationale pour la Gestion des Aires Protegees
BWMA	Botswana Wildlife Management Association
CAMPFIRE	Communal Areas Management Programme for Indigenous Resources
CASS	Centre for Applied Social Sciences
CBD	Convention on Biological Diversity
CBNRM	community-based natural resource management
CBO	community-based organization
CCA	community conserved area
CCTA	Technical Cooperation Commission for Africa South of the Sahara
CEESP	Commission of Environmental, Economic and Social Policy
CEO	chief executive officer
CFU	Commercial Farmers Union
CHA	controlled hunting area
CIFOR	Center for International Forestry Research
CITES	Convention on International Trade in Endangered Species of Wild Fauna and Flora
CMPA	co-managed protected area
CSIR	Council for Industrial and Scientific Research
DDT	dichlorodiphenyltrichloroethane
DNPWLM	Department of National Parks and Wild Life Management
EU	European Union
GAAP	Association Nationale pour la Gestion des Aires Protegees
GAENP	Greater Addo Elephant National Park
GDP	gross domestic product
GNP	Gorongosa National Park
GEF	Global Environmental Fund
GMA	game management area
ha	hectare (1 ha = 2.54acres = $10^4 m^2$)
IASCP	International Association for the Study of Common Property
ICA	intensive conservation area
IDPM	Institute for Development Policy and Management
IUCN	International Union for the Conservation of Nature
KANTIPO	Kafue Anti-Poaching Company Limited

KWS	Kenya Wildlife Service
KZN	KwaZulu-Natal
LIFE	Living in a Finite Environment Project
LIRDP	Luangwa Integrated Rural Development Project
MUNC	Management and Use in Nature Conservation
NGO	non-governmental organization
NLCP	North Luangwa Conservation Project
NORAD	Norwegian Agency for Development Cooperation
NPB	Natal Parks Board
NPWS	National Parks and Wildlife Service
NRMP	Natural Resources Management Programme
OECD	Organization for Economic Cooperation and Development
PA	protected area
PDL	poverty datum line
PLAAS	Programme for Land and Agrarian Studies
PWMA	Parks and Wildlife Management Authority [Zimbabwe]
RDC	rural district council
SADC	Southern Africa Development Community
SANParks	South African National Parks
SARCCUS	Southern African Commission for the Conservation and Utilization of the Soil
SARPO	Southern African Regional Programme Office
SARS	severe acute respiratory syndrome
SASUSG	Southern Africa Sustainable Use Specialist Group
TANAPA	Tanzania National Park Authority
TAWICO	Tanzania Wildlife Investment Company
TFCA	transfrontier conservation area
TILCEPA	Theme on Indigenous and Local Communities, Equity and Protected Areas
UGD	Uganda Game Department
UNEP	United Nations Environment Programme
UNP	Uganda National Parks
UWA	Uganda Wildlife Authority
VAG	village action group
WCPA	World Commission on Protected Areas
WCC	World Conservation Congress
WDPA	World Database on Protected Areas
WILD	Wildlife Integration for Livelihood Diversification Project
WMA	wildlife management area
WPC	World Parks Congress
WWF	World Wide Fund for Nature
ZAWA	Zambia Wildlife Authority

Acknowledgements

We acknowledge the generous financial donations from NORAD and the Ford Foundation, the help and support of the South African National Parks, and the members of SASUSG for their many voluntary efforts.

Preface

For many years, southern Africa has played a key role in rethinking the objectives and approaches that should guide the future management of protected areas. The Vth IUCN World Parks Congress, held in Durban, South Africa, in September 2003, provided the global conservation community with an opportunity to reflect on many of the lessons learned and on the changing paradigms in conservation which are presented through the lens of 'real life on the ground' in this book.

Since the 1960s, southern Africa has embarked on a search for more inclusive approaches to conservation, with the aim of increasing the contribution that private and community landholders make to protecting land and species. Incentive-led conservation has generated real successes, but has also transformed the political economy of conservation from a situation where governments held exclusive jurisdiction over the resource, to one where decisions should increasingly be made by the actual – that is, local – resource managers who, in turn, are increasingly guided by markets.

These experiments suggest that the so-called trade-offs between conservation and development may have been exaggerated, and that the synergies and potential alignments have been underemphasized. Large areas of land are becoming economically more productive through the promotion of wildlife conservation as a significant land-use enterprise. In the communal areas of southern Africa, in particular, this has catalysed significant advances in conservation and in the process of economic transformation. It has also opened our eyes to the inevitable social and institutional changes that are implicit in a market-based approach where transparency, accountability, and democratic decision making are essential to ensuring that economic benefits are accrued by local resource managers.

In some places the economic impetus provided to conservation has begun to transform the way that conventional protected areas are managed. This ranges from individual experiments like Madikwe in South Africa, to the growing number of policy reforms that are transforming protected-area departments into self-funding and semi-autonomous agencies. Whereas the latter has tended to focus on such matters as performance management and commercialization, it has also become evident that these reforms will only succeed if they revisit the relationship between protected areas and society as well.

Who are parks for? If they are common property regimes accountable to society, and if these societies prioritize jobs and economic growth above wilderness and outdoor recreation, does it then follow that parks that respond to these demands and the precondition of ecological sustainability are not only politically more legitimate but also socially and economically more sustainable?

These questions take the debate about protected areas into a new realm in which questions of accountability become paramount. The question of who parks are for leads to a re-evaluation of what they are for. At a high level, this requires a renegotiation of the contract between protected areas and society, including the question of whether all protected areas should be managed by the state, and also the respective role of the state in regulating or managing them. In terms of the performance of protected-area agencies, we will also need to address significant questions about performance accountability. At one level, these agencies need to be held accountable for a combination of conservation and development objectives. On the other hand, the accountabilities need to be clearly and precisely defined.

IUCN's Southern African Sustainable Use Specialist Group comprises largely scholars and practitioners working with or for wildlife agencies, communities, non-governmental organizations, and the private sector across the southern Africa region. Following a philosophy that emphasizes the primacy of the landholders and incentives, this group has been involved in the rehabilitation and transformation of protected areas, in the development of community-based natural resource management (CBNRM), and in studying and promoting incentive-based landholder conservation and sustainable use. The linkages between this intellectual enquiry and policy change have been particularly strong because of the convening power of the group and the strong membership of key government-protected-area policy makers over many years. However, in the search for new answers, it is easy to neglect the need for documenting experiences, much of which remains within an oral network or in the grey literature of reports and project proposals. At times this results in the phenomenon that local discourse is only documented through reports of outside observers, thereby losing some of the specific context that can explain so much of what happens in a region such as southern Africa.

I very much welcome the commitment of the Southern African Sustainable Use Specialist Group in embarking on a process of facilitating scholars and practitioners in southern Africa to document their experiences. Currently, 100 members are writing and editing over 50 case studies, ranging from the rehabilitation of protected areas in Mozambique, to contractual parks in South Africa, and CBNRM programmes in Namibia. The authors are people who have been actively involved in the field and who continue to analyse these initiatives. A companion volume, which will be a compilation of these case studies, is planned for publication in 2005.

This book is a first product in providing a synthesis of these experiences. It offers all of us a fascinating journey through the complex and increasingly contested terrain of paradigms that explain the status quo of protected areas in Southern Africa. Most importantly, it begins to form conclusions about how the governance and relationships between protected areas and society might be improved, and how protected areas can act as engines of rural economic growth and entry points for the expansion of a conservation economy across the landscape.

Achim Steiner
Director General, IUCN
April 2004

Chapter 1

Introduction

Brian Child

In 1903, the president of the US, Theodore Roosevelt, dedicated a monument on which is written: 'For the benefit and enjoyment of the people – Yellowstone National Park, created by an Act of Congress, March 1, 1872'. Thus was born the modern concept of a national park. Managed by national agencies, national parks are set aside for the benefit of people, and their importance has been repeatedly emphasized by such landmark events as the London Convention of 1933, which also defined the purpose of national parks,[1] and more recently by criteria established through the International Union for the Conservation of Nature (IUCN). National parks are seen as the cornerstone of the world's conservation efforts, with a target that each nation sets aside 10 per cent of its land in this manner.

However, national parks are latecomers to the protected-area movement. For thousands of years people have been setting aside and protecting areas of natural value. Some Arabian hemas are more than 1000 years old, as are sacred groves and the temples of Asia. These protected areas are not usually managed by national agencies, nor is use prohibited in them. Indeed, they are usually set aside by local communities to conserve environments of value to them – fodder for droughts, animals for hunting, habitats for bees – or are sanctified for their beauty or calm.

With the colonization of southern Africa, a model of conservation based on strictly preserved national parks and the prohibition of commercial use of wildlife outside them was imposed, not only on traditional communities but also on a more pragmatic conservation ethos based on the wise use of the soil, forest and their products (see Chapter 4). This may have been a reasonable short-term response to the excess of the frontier period, characterized as it was by unfettered open-access predation of natural resources, leading to the slaughter of millions of head of game, often to subsidize the building of nations or farms. However, this response misaligned and undervalued incentives in the less dramatic, but even more damaging, period of settlement that followed exploration: the land was cut up into farms, and wildlife, which damaged crops and threatened or competed with livestock, was insidiously but effectively annihilated by land-use practices that did not value wildlife legislation that prevented all commercial use and controlled hunting. This legislation no longer addressed the central problem. It is highly appropriate to quote the Southern Africa Sustainable Use Specialist Group (SASUSG; 'sausage' as it is called) (1996) conclusions: 'A common perception is that unsustainable exploitation (overuse) is the greatest threat [to wildlife]. We argue that, in terrestrial situations, the greater threat lies in natural systems being replaced with other land uses.'

Forty years ago, the realization dawned that the real threat to wildlife was not illegal or commercial hunting, sensationalist as this is, but wildlife's inability to compete economically with alternative uses of the land. It was being replaced by the plough and the cow, even in areas where one would expect a diverse and robust spectrum of indigenous animals to have a comparative advantage. Thus began a search for solutions that in many ways brought us back to the concepts underlying ancient protected areas – that wildlife and natural resources must usually be locally managed and be of local benefit to survive.

Often originating in national park agencies, but sometimes from persons interested in the health of the soil or agricultural diversification, experimentation began when private landholders were given the rights to manage and benefit from their wildlife in the early 1960s. This effectively denationalized wildlife, and this transformation from a national to a private resource breathed new life into wildlife conservation. Thus was born the 'new' paradigm of incentive-led, inclusive conservation, and the numerous innovations that it spawned. Tens, and then hundreds and now thousands of landholders have replaced normal agricultural activities in whole or in part with natural systems and wildlife, sometimes merely for the pleasure and because they are proprietors, and sometimes for profit. When economists and ecologists demonstrated that this was better for the land, better for the wildlife and provided more jobs and more profit, a movement was born that attempted to transfer this success to communal lands. With the economic advantages of wildlife developed and demonstrated on private land, the commercial model was easily transferable. The next challenge was the complexity of organizing remote rural communities into common-property management units, giving rise to fascinating experimentation and literature on governance, organizational and political theory within the community-based natural resource management (CBNRM) movement. While the World Bank's cutting-edge literature (World Bank, 2002) advocates the theory that the best way to encourage development is to provide poor people with truly discretionary financing, the CBNRM movement has already experimented with cash distribution and wildlife dividends and shown just how powerful fiscal devolution and discretionary financing can be. Governance and democracy are critical issues to the CBNRM movement which also faces the reactionary forces of 'aborted devolution' as those in authority recognize the grass-roots power that these experiments can release.

With this reinvention of ancient wisdom have come great strides in conservation, wildlife, land and economic development, albeit sometimes with strident opposition to the commercialization and use of wildlife and to inclusive, devolutionary processes (in other words the democratization of control). This movement has now come full circle. The performance of private, and in some cases community, conservation are showing up national parks. They are creating more benefits, and usually foster as much and often more conservation than national parks, yet are costing the national treasury nothing. Many national parks are also losing favour with national constituencies, and their funding and superstructures are crumbling from neglect. The paradox is that many national parks are doing particularly badly at just the time that it has been demonstrated that conservation, at least of Africa's spectacular megafauna, has within itself the economic seeds of its own perpetuity. This poses several critical questions for national parks, which this book sets out to identify and begin to answer or at least to draw out.

The first of these is the central political economic question of power and accountability: who are these parks to serve? The national park movement has been highly centralized, even hegemonic, and has so prevented experimentation and evolution that our answers can only be tentative. There are not enough national parks managed privately, by communities or deliberately to encourage economic benefit or local control. Nevertheless, the few indications that we have point to the advantages of a return to the ancient wisdom where protected areas primarily benefit and are integrated with the locality and local people, and where they are deliberately managed to provide benefits with the condition that no irreversible ecological damage is caused. In the context of transitional socio-economies, and recognizing the importance of aligning protected-area goals with the needs of their legitimate constituencies, we investigate this shift of primacy from biodiversity conservation to economic benefit. This suggests that maximizing economic value also maximizes conservation benefits, a conclusion that is counter-intuitive only when conservation is viewed as a narrow biological problem, but not when sustainability is seen as having social, political and economic, as well as biological, roots.

By changing the question of 'who' park conservation is for from global to local, we also radically alter the question of 'what' national parks are for. In this, perhaps, was the biggest surprise to us all. While we did not expect to find that the goals for national parks that adequately took into account the social, economic and political realities of societies in developing countries, what began to emerge was of integrity and commitment derailed and ineffective park management for lack of clearly defined objectives. National park agencies had so many demands they did not know what to focus on and, as Drucker (1973, p144) says, nothing is ever accomplished unless scarce resources are concentrated on a few priorities. Because we cannot manage for something we cannot describe, we therefore need to discuss what exactly conservation should be, so that we can outline the performance accountability of public park conservation agencies.

In southern Africa, we are just touching the beginnings of a new paradigm that aligns protected-area management more closely with the needs of non-affluent societies. Some new ideas are emerging. First, is the starting point that national parks are a common pool resource set aside on behalf of society. Our societies, like many in the world, are in transition from poverty and central planning to, hopefully, sustainable livelihoods and democratic governance. To bring alignment with their constituencies, parks must provide what societies need, which in this context are usually values more tangible than normally associated with parks – namely jobs and economic growth. As we shall continually emphasize, this does not mean, and should not mean, a sacrificing of ecological productivity or diversity. Second, we need to make national parks accountable for their performance. On a political level, we need to learn how to make parks answerable to society while avoiding the problems of elite predation. Managerially, accountability requires that we set and quantify goals far more precisely than in the past. Third, park agency structures are inefficient managerially. They also represent mechanisms that are structured to parks rather than ordinary people. This presents opportunities to develop management systems that are significantly more effective with issues such as the localization of parks, decentralization and performance management emerging as important.

In writing this book we draw on the collective experience of some 100 southern African conservationists, and a great deal of experimentation across the region, some led by remarkable people and others that are a force of circumstances – hungry people sometimes have to find solutions. SASUSG, a regional network of people working in government agencies, non-governmental organizations (NGOs), communities and the private sector, has been privileged to be a part of this learning process. In the past, SASUSG has largely been an advocate of the rights of people to benefit from their resources, in the belief that conservation is best served by internalizing as many of the benefits of wildlife as possible. SASUSG and its members have collectively developed, and are still developing, a variety of conceptual tools to guide and improve resource use: the economics of wildlife, and particularly the impacts of proprietorship (especially the lack of it), taxation and perverse incentives; governance, democracy and equity as it relates to the socio-economic uplift of rural communities; the political economics of shifting power and benefit from the central techno-bureaucratic authorities to thousands of rural people, and the like. Indeed, SASUSG's core belief and experience is that conservation will be most effective when placed in the hands of landholders made responsible by sensible institutions that empower landholders and align and internalize costs and benefits at the level of land units.

In the past two decades, much of the focus has been on private conservation and, particularly, on CBNRM. The management of national parks has been woefully neglected. This book is the first step in redressing this imbalance. It began as a collective effort to bring together many of the experiences from across this diverse region, most of which remain undocumented and unanalysed. We are concerned that this oral knowledge is entering the formal literature largely through secondary or tertiary papers prepared by outsiders, not by the people who initiated and managed these innovations. Therefore members from across the region were tasked with bringing together their experiences in a series of case studies, some 50 of which will comprise volume 2 of this initiative. Using these experiences, individuals volunteered or were persuaded to synthesize these experiences into what has now become Volume 1, this book. Many of these issues were discussed at a workshop in Skukuza, South Africa, in April 2003. At this workshop, it was also decided that SASUSG should progress from advocating sustainable use towards improving the mechanisms that make use sustainable. SASUSG's contribution to the evolution and conceptualization of the paradigm of landholder responsibility and sustainable use would be best served by working with landholders, and especially national agencies, to develop mechanisms for the self-assessment of conservation performance that also provide performance measures to support a process of peer review and learning. But this is for the future.

As the Skukuza workshop demonstrated to us, we are at the beginning of a learning experience where new ideas are rapidly formed, some to be rejected. This book is written to learn from the experiences of southern Africa, and to share lessons with many conservationists around the world who are also dealing with the unprecedented speed of change. What we offer is a compilation of a huge variety of experiences from almost First World South Africa to war-recovering Mozambique, from dry or empty countries like Namibia and Botswana to crowded Malawi, and to a wide range of governance experiences. What makes this region special is its experimentation, born of both desperation and inspiration, and fuelled by the growing value of wildlife and the determination to harvest this value for conservation. With landholders and communities now managing conservation as a business, there is far more experimentation and innovation than when responsibility was monopolized centrally. The learning experience is further improved by the diversity of disciplines that SASUSG and others represent: conservation biologists, wildlife economists, social and political scientists, trying to understand power and property rights and, more recently, emerging experiences with political intuitions and organizational and management theory. Although truly a hotchpotch, in this complexity lies conservation progress.

In Chapter 2, Graham Child, who represents the generation that built parks and laid the first seeds of private and community conservation, presents a historical perspective of the changes and driving forces behind conservation in southern Africa. This, like all the other chapters, draws on inputs and case studies from many other members of SASUSG. The first major innovation was private sector conservation, the theory and results of which are described by Ivan Bond (Chapter 3). Brian Jones and Marshall Murphree (Chapter 4) summarize the performance and principles of the CBNRM experimentation across the region. We have intentionally included both community- and privately conserved areas in a book about protected areas. Not only do they represent a return to ancient concepts, but in many ways their dynamism and experimentation is both an inspiration and a challenge to more conventional protected-area conservation. Moreover, most of the growth in protected-area coverage lauded at the World Parks Congress is in these categories of protected areas.

In Chapter 5, David Cumming assesses the performance of parks in the region against ecological and socio-economic goals. Assessing performance proves remarkably difficult, partly for lack of data and also partly because there is not yet available to us a clearly articulated conceptual foundation against which to measure park performance. In ecological terms we have not defined whether we are conserving ecological process and health or ecological diversity; nor have we clarified the relationship between ecological and economic objectives. Thus we tend to conform to western anthropocentric norms such as not killing animals, so privileging subjective value-sets and recreational interests over ecological and economic imperatives. We subsidize recreational activities. We spend little money monitoring true common value in the form of biodiversity. And we consequently allow the charismatic megafauna, to which we so closely relate, to damage long-term ecological processes that are of ultimate importance to our parks and planet.

Leading on from this Brian Child (Chapter 6) provides some conceptual background as to why centralized park agencies are prone to burgeoning mandates and, consequently, to underperforming. Using case studies, he describes the trends of distancing park agencies from central government towards commercial management systems, and draws out some of the managerial lessons from these emerging parastatals. This is complemented by Chapter 7, which assesses the budding partnerships between state conservation agencies, communities and the private sector, and Chapter 8, where Derek de la Harpe discusses the commercialization of park agencies.

In Chapter 9, Marshall Murphree describes the great changes that are occurring across the region and, in returning to the 'who' question, emphasizes how much more robust is conservation that is centred on local management and benefit.

However, having so long centralized conservation, we need to challenge the mindsets that are threatened by local control, as well as the mechanisms of getting local control to work properly.

As before, the 'who' leads to the 'what', and Chapter 10 discusses what values parks should provide if they are to serve their constituency (that is, society in emerging or transitional economies), and also makes a preliminary attempt to define conservation goals within a framework that is amenable to performance management.

The conclusion also emphasizes why experimentation is so important to the evolution of conservation, as well as re-emphasizing the concerns that parks must serve their societies, and must be accountable to them. It suggests that there is a strong case for managing parks deliberately to create more value, and suggests possible control mechanisms. Building on the evidence of earlier chapters, it challenges the concept that parks should be economic black holes fenced off from their neighbours, returning wealth to the capital city and responding to instructions from the centre. There is indeed a strong case that parks can play an important role as bridgeheads for promoting economic development and landscape integration, and even for acting as rural development agencies, provided their mandate is clearly defined. As with community and private conservation, there is a strong case for devolved management even within conventional protected-area agencies. In advocating that southern Africa should extend these lessons, we end by emphasizing the importance of further, bold experimentation. This needs to be deliberately structured as a learning process, whereby progress is monitored against clearly defined indicators, and innovation and learning occurs through positive competition and peer review.

We hope that the ideas and experiences in this book will help to take forward and widen the debate on why we conserve protected areas, and how we can do it better.

NOTES

1   The 'Convention Relative to the Preservation of Fauna and Flora in their Natural State' held in London in 1933 had a major influence on the concept and development of parks in Africa, and compared with the USA's Washington Convention of 1940, emphasized biological conservation as a prime function of National Parks. Thus African National Parks emphasized public control, the propagation, protection and preservation of fauna and flora (and other features) for the benefit, advantage or enjoyment of the general public, and the prohibition of hunting. The US definition accentuated superlative scenery, flora and fauna, public control and public enjoyment (Cumming, 1990).

REFERENCES

Chase, A (1986) *Playing God in Yellowstone. The Destruction of America's First National Park*, Harcourt Brace Jovanovich, San Diego, New York and London

Cumming, D H M (1990) 'Wildlife conservation in African parks: Progress, problems and prescriptions', WWF Multispecies Animal Production Systems Project, Project Paper no 15, WWF Programme Office, Harare

Drucker, P F (1973) *Management: Tasks, Responsibilities, Practices*, Harper Collins, New York

SASUSG (1996) 'Sustainable Use Issues and Principles', Southern African Sustainable Use Specialist Group, IUCN Species Survival Commission

World Bank (2002) *Linking Poverty Reduction and Environmental Management: Policy Challenges and Opportunities*, The World Bank, Washington, DC

Chapter 2

Growth of Modern Nature Conservation in Southern Africa

Graham Child

Introduction

This chapter examines the growth of nature conservation in southern Africa and the lessons it holds for preserving the human environment at home and abroad. It also outlines the origins of this conservation, its growth and its achievements. It attempts to understand what has shaped the perceptions that have driven nature conservation and the way it has been applied in the region since the early 19th century, because knowing where we are and how we got there is a logical first step towards developing a strategy for the future.

Much of this book is concerned with measures to make nature conservation increasingly relevant to the societies in which we live in southern Africa and beyond, a perception that has *coloured* wild resource conservation in the region from an early date. It was initiated by a concern to protect the resource value of forests as a source of useful timber and from the outset reflected the pragmatism of conserving resources so that they could be used.

Early Colonial Innovation

In 1656, within four years of establishing the Dutch East India Company station, Jan van Riebeeck gave instructions to regulate hunting at the Cape (Brynard, 1977). Early measures were introduced to conserve the southern Cape forests around Plettenberg Bay from 1811 because of their value to the British navy. By the 1830s rapid deforestation in the British colonies in India, Africa and Mauritius was leading to more broadly based conservation awareness (Grove, 1987). By the mid-19th century there was an active and influential conservation community in the Cape. Besides hunting and forests it was concerned with the soil and the veldt, and brought about what were in effect the first state game reserves in Africa, in the Knysna and Tsitsikamme forests in 1886.

The Cape, more than any other part of southern Africa, established the traditions for renewable resource conservation that have led the region. From the mid-19th century conservation thinking was often ahead of that in Europe and North America and the emphasis differed in important ways. From the beginning the Cape tended to be more holistic and pragmatic. A tradition emerged early that tended to view the soil, the veldt and animals as part of a single continuum that should be protected for the good of people on the land.

Natal took the lead from the Cape after the report of a 'Commission to enquire into and report on the extent and condition of forest lands in the colony' (Natal, 1880, quoted by Grove, 1987). This report was a conservation masterpiece for its time and, among other things, had the foresight to note that modernizing Zulu agriculture would necessitate giving individual Zulus security of tenure over their landholdings. The land tenure issue was largely ignored, but the report led to improved forest conservation and the appointment of Indian-trained forest officers in the Cape and Natal. The mid-19th century Cape and Indian precedents and the legislation flowing from them led to the creation of forest reserves in Botswana, Malawi, Zambia and Zimbabwe.

According to Grove (1987), conservation thinking in the colonies, including that in South Africa, was ahead of the metropolitan powers in the mid-19th century. India probably led in this regard as Hooker (1872), the Director of Kew Gardens in London, considered that it alone had an adequate conservation policy. Two successive Cape botanists were largely instrumental in shaping the early Cape philosophy guiding nature conservation. Both used the government's fear of drought and water shortages to promote and publicize their concepts.

Pappe, appointed in 1858, focused his conservation thinking around maintaining forests for conserving water (Pappe, 1862). Brown, who took over from him in 1862, broadened this to include all natural vegetation and the way it was being managed, and added species conservation. It is interesting that G P Marsh, who 'fathered' the conservation and national park movement in the US, through his book *Man and Nature* (1864), knew of Brown's work and persuaded him to publish it, which he did in 1875 (Brown, 1875a; Brown 1875b). From an early stage there was a cross-pollination of conservation ideas, but a divergence in their application between Europe and North America on the one hand, and the British colonies around the Indian Ocean, including Australia, on the other. Conservation in Europe and North America tended to focus on large mammal species while the emphasis in South Africa, at least, was what we would now call ecosystem oriented.

Grove (1987) believes that the conservation ethic based on Indian and Cape colonial thinking evolved into a comprehensive policy in southern Africa because of the coincidence of three interests. These were: (a) an amalgam of scientific botanists, and aesthetic and amenity value protagonists; (b) white settler farmers; and (c) government's fear of the effects of drought on farming. Government commitment to conservation largely collapsed when white farmers' fear of droughts apparently diminished, until the interests of black peasant agriculture were threatened in the 1930s. Expert conservationists were able to again reassert their influence, thus illustrating their propensity for turning immediate political concerns to the advantage of conservation. A scenario in which scientific bureaucrats entrusted with conserving a nation's renewable resources worked loyally within prevailing political systems, but advanced their professional goals whenever opportunities arose, was repeated many times during the next 60–70 years.

TRADITIONAL CONSERVATION

The colonial conservation that grew up in southern Africa was devised mainly by white people of European stock. Little has been written about traditional measures to conserve and regulate the use of wild resources before white settlement. The following is gleaned largely from living, working and interviewing indigenous people, mostly in remote areas, over the better part of 60 years.

Not surprisingly, local knowledge about wild resources varies inversely with the extent to which the people used and depend on them. In the late 1950s the Tonga people in the tsetse-ridden Kariba Basin knew much more about grasses and rodents, which they used to augment their meagre crops, than did rural Ndebele on the nearby tsetse-free plateau, where they depended on livestock and crops. Whereas the Tonga ate fish and had a good knowledge of the local fish fauna and its habits, the Ndebele did not: they equated them with lizards, and had only a very rudimentary knowledge about them.

With harvesting technology limiting use, rather than resource scarcities, indigenous understanding concentrated on the biological knowledge needed to obtain and use species useful as food, medicine or for other purposes. At this level the knowledge was often extensive. For example, I gleaned the seasonal behaviour of eland before it was described scientifically, by questioning Masarwa Bushmen of Botswana, for whom eland are both a religious icon and highly desirable food. What was generally lacking in traditional cultures, however, was the socio-economic understanding to conserve and use the resources sustainably. They lacked the allocatory institutions to manage scarcities.

Two generalizations emerge regarding the traditional use of renewable resources from ongoing interest in the literature and personal curiosity on all occupied continents. They are usually sustainably only at low human densities where resources are plentiful, relative to the number of people and their ability to harvest them. Uses are then often wasteful. When human numbers rise leading to resource scarcities there is frequent abuse, ranging from shifting agriculture, through overgrazing, to unregulated harvesting of wild plants and animals. Where traditionally institutions limited wild resource use it was to people's needs and not to the biological capacity of the resources to sustain the harvest. Concern to maintain productivity requires more advanced institutions to regulate use; but these are not socially justified until the abuse commences. They then become an imperative. Conservation is the socio-economic process by which societies endeavour to manage resource scarcities and limit offtakes to within the biological capacity of the systems to sustain production.

Increasingly, it is being accepted that conservation is driven largely by proprietorship and price (see, for example, Child, B 2000a; Child, B 2000b; Child, G and Chitsike, 2000), acting within the biological parameters that limit a sustainable offtake. Many traditional systems for conserving a species in the savannas of southern Africa were weakly developed as stronger institutions were unnecessary at the low population densities prevailing when white people settled in the region. They acted through such devices as: taboos against killing species like hyaena, hammerkop or chameleon; prohibitions on people hunting or eating their totem animals like eland, zebra, monkeys, squirrels or crocodiles; forfeiture of scarce or valuable products to the ruler, in the case of ivory, pangolin meat, leopard pelts and the like; or the creation of areas whose use was limited to specific purposes. These areas were mostly small and were often set aside for various religious purposes and included sacred groves and hills in Zambia and Zimbabwe, and burial sites in southern Malawi. King Lobengula of the Ndebele proclaimed a large royal hunting preserve on the Shangani River north of Bulawayo, not too far from the present Hwange National Park.

The best example I know of traditional regulation of harvesting of animals or plant relates to beaver hunting by the Cree Indians south of Hudson Bay. It apparently represented sustainable indigenous use of animals in which the control mechanisms were unfortunately overrun by modern commercial hunters from the south. Beavers breed quite slowly and were relatively scarce, but were greatly valued by the Cree for their pelts and meat. The local communities were divided into groups which each hunted only in its own hunting area. Here the harvest was set annually by the elder in charge according to the level of the resident beaver populations. The criteria of both price (the value of the animals in the Cree economy) and proprietorship (limited access to hunting in a given area), necessary for ensuring sustainability were met.

The Islamic water law is an ancient institution regulating resource conservation and use that compares in scope with the conservation ethic that emerged in the British Colonies and US in the mid-19th century. Water was the first renewable resource essential to human survival to become scarce on a broad front. This goes back well over 1000 years before the law was codified about 1400 years ago, and applied across the deserts of Central Asia, the Middle East and North Africa. The law prescribes in detail how scarce water should be conserved, rationed and used in different ways, depending on its availability. If water and its flow are substituted for renewable biological resources and energy flows there is little in the World Conservation Strategy (IUCN et al, 1980) that is not covered by the ancient water law. Furthermore, the water law goes beyond the Strategy and prescribes how benefits from different levels of permissible use should be rationed to yield the greatest social good (Child and Grainger, 1990).

The interesting thing about the wisdom contained in this ancient law is its pragmatic survival value. It does not require an equal sharing of water by all who are thirsty, but ensures that those who looked after their source of water can satisfy their reasonable requirements first. For example, if there are a number of irrigators dependent on a source of water, the law requires that the first of these to develop his land gets enough to grow his crops. A similar amount of water is then allocated progressively to each of the next irrigators to arrive, until the supply is exhausted, with late arrivals missing out altogether if there is not enough water. This means that some crops will receive enough water to survive and bear fruit while those belonging to late arrivals are abandoned, optimizing the food produced with the water available. It encourages business risk by providing an incentive to people to open up new schemes where they will have a lasting advantage over those who follow. In economic terms it is more capitalistic than socialistic, which may carry important lessons for the conservation and use of other scarce renewable resources.

Wildlife was not a single resource in African cultures whose use could be regulated by uniform institutions. Ivory is a low bulk high value almost bullion-like commodity that influenced African politics for over 1000 years. It usually belonged to the ruling chief who represented the state and was traded to the east along with the slaves used to transport it. Anyone acquiring it was required, along with valuable and difficult to obtain wildlife commodities like pangolin meat and leopard pelts, to take it to the king. In some tribes hunting of dangerous animals was a means of demonstrating manhood and followed different rules from those applying during traditional social hunts (see, for example, Reilly and Reilly, 1994). Most hunting is less formalized, however, and benefits those participating, with traditional mores determining how the quarry was divided up. In the forests of central and west Africa (Asibey, 1974) and the Kalahari (von Richter, 1976; von Richter, 1979) this hunting of mainly small animals like cane rats, springhares and small forest duiker provides a regular source of food. Conversely, among people in the savannas of southern Africa hunting is generally opportunistic, except in poor agricultural seasons when wildlife and fish are viewed as resources of last resort. With the growth of national economies lagging behind burgeoning human populations, rural poverty has become widespread and 'every year is seen as a bad year', irrespective of rainfall.

Earlier we noted that indigenous institutions for conserving wild resources were generally weak prior to white settlement in southern Africa, mainly because they were not needed and would have been a burden on the societies. White governments then marginalized most citizens from wildlife for 100 years or more. The picture that emerges is that white domination commenced before indigenous institutions were necessary or had become generally effective. It continued and spanned the period when populations burgeoned, resource scarcities intensified, and these might have combined to induce effective local measures to safeguard the resources. Instead, the void was filled by Anglo-French protectionist game laws, which inhibited local institutions from developing, as they did in other spheres of life where customary law remained in force and could evolve under white rule (see, for example, Child, H, 1965).

We can only guess at the form that unrestrained indigenous black conservation legislation might have taken. What is apparent is that legislation, introduced by Namibia and Zimbabwe towards the end of white rule, giving land holders rights to use and trade in wildlife, was more acceptable to the pragmatic African cultures than centralized protectionism. Sustainable use of wildlife was promoted, imposition of the cost of conservation on poor rural dwellers was limited, benefits from conservation were apportioned more equitably, and artificial wastage from animals dying during drought or from similar habitat limitations was reduced. While not the only stimulus for the community-based natural resource management (CBNRM) that has emerged across the region, it facilitated it in Zimbabwe, at least (Child, 1996a).

THE POST WORLD WAR II SPURT IN NATURE CONSERVATION

Led by Public Servants

Following the tradition set by the early Cape Botanists the conservation of renewable resources throughout the region, from the soil through the vegetation to wild animals, was led by public servants. In the case of nature conservation, they enjoyed only sporadic professional support from particular individuals outside government. The domination of public servants was a progressive process, beginning in the 1930s and accelerating after World War II, as jurisdictions acquired the necessary skills and built up specialized professional agencies. Once in place government scientific resource managers maintained their pre-eminence for 20–30 years into the 1990s.

Many conservation leaders had a formal scientific training, although there were notable exceptions. Importantly, as a body, government-employed conservationists combined the best traditions of a professional civil servant with their scientific discipline, usually agriculture, forestry or a biological science. They were loyal to the government of the day which gave them credibility that allowed them to work towards achieving conservation goals, as then perceived. Land hunger was seen as a major threat to conservation as human populations grew exponentially, doubling every 20 years from the middle of the 20th century. Creating a network of ecological reserves to represent the ecotypes under their jurisdiction thus became a prime objective of nature conservations in southern Africa from the mid-1950s. It was seen as an urgent imperative for conserving biological diversity in the face of the combined challenge from burgeoning populations, and the rapid agriculture and technological expansion that followed World War II.

The period was also remarkable for the rapid evolution in nature conservation thinking that took place across southern Africa, led by conservation agencies with a strongly biological bias. Most academics stood aloof from this conceptual evolution, although a number of university-based biologists, notably Fritz Eloff, Waldo Meester, Rudi Bigalke, John Skinner and, especially, Brian Walker, did become involved and contributed significantly to purely scientific aspects of nature conservation. It is perhaps surprising that the leaders of these agencies in Botswana, Namibia, Zambia, and Zimbabwe, in particular, pioneered many of the socio-economic concepts now being applied to conservation across the region and beyond.

Opposition from the Livestock Industry

Progress in conservation was not achieved without hindrance and ill-considered pressures from within governments. Powerful veterinary authorities backed by draconian animal health laws and a strong livestock industry fearing competition from wildlife have often been in opposition to the conservation and use of wildlife. A Eurocentric view blamed livestock diseases on wildlife and were a pretext for its frequently unnecesary destruction throughout the region where, in any case, it was seen as valueless competition for livestock grazing. Examples of game destruction programmes in South Africa, Botswana, Mozambique, Swaziland, Zambia and Zimbabwe were to control tsetse fly (see, for example, Child et al, 1970; Child and Riney 1987), foot-and-mouth disease and other ailments common to livestock and game.

In the case of Zimbabwe, at least, the tsetse control hunting, miles of cordon fences, the use of persistent insecticides like dieldrex and DDT, and the habitat destruction that accompanied these actions proved to be an official scam that was perpetuated for more than 60 years. It was based on a false initial assumption that tsetse recessions around the turn of the 20th century were due to the rinderpest pandemic that swept though the region in the late 1890s (Summers, 1971). Tstse fly was eventually eliminated in South Africa and parts of Zimbabwe using fly traps, but where this was achieved by other means it led to significant lasting veldt deterioration and loss of ecological productivity (Riney, 1963).

Expensive cordon fences to control foot-and-mouth disease criss-crossed miles of country and cost the taxpayer millions of dollars in Botswana, Malawi, Namibia, South Africa, Swaziland, Zambia and Zimbabwe. This was to allow beef to be exported to

Europe, but most fences later proved to be unnecessary, ineffective or economically unjustified. There was little opposition to such measures while the livestock industry was paramount in much of the region and the colonial-type game laws rendered wildlife virtually valueless. With wildlife able to realize its comparative advantage over livestock and landholders able to capture this value, the situation is changing. This came about with the introduction of more enlightened institutions to guide and regulate the use and trade in wildlife, and it was accentuated by the deteriorating global terms of trade for red meat and other livestock products. Many farmers in ecologically marginal areas for livestock who had believed that they could not 'farm in a zoo', now realized that they could not farm profitably outside 'the zoo'.

Key Events

Two events, more than any others, contributed to the enlightened institutional transformation that has taken place throughout the region. Both took place in Zimbabwe. The first event was a two- to three-year-long visit by three outstanding Fulbright Scholars from the Aldo Leopold school of thinking in California. This was organized by Reay Smithers, Director of Museums, who recognized the potential but institutionally suppressed value of large game animals and the research opportunities they offered. Thane Riney, Ray Dasmann and Archie Mossman planted many innovative ideas and combined with local personnel like Archie Fraser to re-engineer the institutional framework guiding the wildlife industry in Zimbabwe. The Wild Life Conservation Act 1960, which was the test bed for the Parks and Wild Life Act 1975 (Taylor 1990, Child, 1995a; Child, 1996b; Child, G, in preparation); game ranching, linking wildlife conservation to the broad conservation movement that had been tried and tested in the agricultural sector, the emphasis on biological diversity; adaptive management; and research in the responsible agency, were among the initiatives they helped sponsor. Riney, in particular, stressed the critical links between ecological, economic and socio-political forces in successful conservation, as well as biological diversity and ecosystem conservation, as early as 1958.

The second event was the reorganization of the Southern African Commission for the Conservation and Utilization of the Soil (SARCCUS) which gave rise to a regional network of highly influential conservation leaders. The network encouraged free thinking and greatly facilitated the spread of the Fulbright-catalysed model that first emerged in Zimbabwe, but had extended to Botswana by late 1965. SARCCUS was one of three such bodies set up in Africa by the Technical Cooperation Commission for Africa South of the Sahara (CCTA) after World War II. Initially, as its title implies, SARCCUS was an international organization concerned with soil conservation, but it quickly expanded to cover all renewable resources. To start with it comprised senior government agriculturists, but it was reorganized into 11 standing committees, including Management and Use in Nature Conservation (MUNC), responsible for nature conservation wildlife management and use. It was served by a small secretariat of one person provided by the South African Ministry of Agriculture and this restructuring, to better reflect the organizations expanded functions, was done at a watershed meeting in September 1968.

Zimbabwe and Botswana played a prominent part in the setting up of MUNC, which met annually for the next 12 years at least. It comprised the heads of the nature conservation agencies in southern Africa and their most senior advisors, with the exception of South African Parks. By entrusting its representation to a deputy director, South African Parks became a follower instead of a leader and forewent an opportunity to strongly influence the direction of nature conservation in the region.

From the outset MUNC provided a formal and informal week-long gathering at which the heads of agencies (nature conservation being a provincial responsibility in South Africa (see Hay, 1977b)) could share policy ideas among peers. We were able to learn from the strengths and weaknesses of each other's experience. Namibia and Zimbabwe were at the forefront of debate concerning the devolution of authority to landholders to manage the wildlife on their land (see, for example, Joubert, 1974; de la Bat, 1977; Child, 1977; Child, 1995a; Child, 1995b). They championed the idea that unless wildlife had a tangible value from which private landholders could benefit it would disappear outside ecological reserves.

Zimbabwe and Botswana led discussion on what has become CBNRM from 1971 (Child, 1971; Child, 1996b), although we later learned that Zambia had independently conceived some of the same ideas. Natal led concerns relating to human population growth and park interpretation (Geddes Page, 1977) and most jurisdictions, perhaps led by Botswana and the Cape (Child, 1970; Campbell, 1973; Hay 1977a), stressed the importance of integrating wildlife and ecological reserve management into the local rural economy. The Transvaal perfected the use of bomas to capture game animals, using fixed fencing (Riney and Kettlitz, 1964). Zimbabwe made the process mobile by replacing the fencing with netting (Child, 1968a) and Natal enhanced the mobility and effectiveness of the technique by introducing plastic sheeting (Oelofse, 1970) and led in efficient game capture and the sale of game animals to private landholders. The rapid institutional and technical progress that these examples epitomize, and the list is by no means exhaustive, allowed southern Africa to pioneer paradigms for conserving wild resources. This was globally significant and has been described as the single most important breakthrough in nature conservation during the 20th century.

The spurt in conceptual evolution which applied mainly to wildlife outside ecological reserves was beginning to plateau and slow down by the late 1970s. This was at least partly because the members of MUNC, with their essentially biological backgrounds, had reached their intellectual ceiling with regard to innovative socio-economic advance. We lacked the jargon to conceptualize the ideas we were applying successfully on the ground and this inhibited building even more progressive thinking on that experience until we acquired the services of economists.

Zimbabwe was the first to do so, but even this was a saga in overcoming the difficulties in the bureaucratic environment in which we all had to work and with which we had to conform. In 1978 the Zimbabwean agency secured the funds from the Treasury to employ an economist, but the Public Services Board, which had to approve all appointments, ridiculed the need for such a post, especially at a time when tourism was in decline. An unimaginative Public Services Board Inspectorate thus delayed progress for about five years that, judging from subsequent events, would have benefited the whole region. In was not until 1983 that Zimbabwe 'worked the system' and employed the first two wild-resource economists in the region, but as ecologists. They worked on game ranching and the various national CBNRM programmes that gave rise to the second regional communication network among wildlife managers.

Rapid conceptual progress outside ecological reserves was not matched by similar innovative progress towards improved management in these reserves. There appear to have been several reasons for this. The region had some of the best-managed parks and reserves worldwide, judged against international standards (see, for example, MacKinnon, J and MacKinnon, K, 1986), which led to complacency: there were few threats to the areas, which reduced the challenge to improve. To compound the problem we did not appreciate the extent to which the international model we were following was flawed (see Hess, 1993; Kay, 1997; Child and Child, in preparation). Furthermore, whereas wildlife management outside reserves benefited from diversity, as jurisdictions sought innovative approaches to similar issues, subject to the discipline of differing local land use and commercial competition, this did not extend to the management of reserves. Here government park management agencies had a monopoly.

Adherence to a standardized management agenda by the jurisdictions in the region engendered confidence, was viewed as a strength and was taken to mean they were acting correctly. This was not always true. Although unity may bring political strength, diversity brings evolutionary progress. The region broke out of the strait-jacket of conventional nature conservation dogma outside ecological reserves only when the responsible agencies began to discuss at a high policy level their differing approaches to managing wildlife here. The resulting progress in management outside conservation areas, in fact, exacerbated the problem inside reserves. The conservation agencies' superficial efficiency and uniform approach inside reserves combined with the pragmatic handling and support for the growing wildlife industry to build government and public support. The general excellence of the service the agencies provided in the reserves masked any ineffectiveness or defects in their management agendas and further inhibited criticism of the way in which reserves were being managed.

Land set aside as parks and reserves increased considerably as the value of wildlife and the wildlife industry became apparent. A spurt in the creation of ecological reserves in southern African countries began in the 1930s and, apart from a lull during World War II, has continued to the present (IUCN and UNEP, 1987). Starting with some of the early colonial governors in the Cape and Natal in the mid-19th century, heads of state have often played a prominent role in acquiring land and fostering nature conservation. At the turn of the 20th century, Cecil John Rhodes bought land privately in Zimbabwe and bequeathed it to the nation as two parks, and President Paul Kruger of the Transvaal Republic was at least nominally instrumental in setting aside the Sabi Game Reserve. Matetsi was acquired for the Zimbabwean Parks and Wild Life Estate at the personal instigation of Prime Minister Ian Smith, and Hastings Banda and King Sobhuza II did the same in Malawi and Swaziland (Anstey and Hall-Martin, 1977; Reilly and Reilly, 1977; Reilly and Reilly, 1994). President Kenneth Kaunda was a strong supporter of parks in Zambia (Child, B, in preparation).

The management of these areas built on a tradition of modern parks and reserves going back to the beginning of the 20th century. It was clearly influenced by the American or Yellowstone model (Hess, 1993), although it diverged from it in the emphasis on large game rather than spectacular mountain scenery. Many of the reserves, including a number that later became well-known national parks like Kruger, Whange, Kafue and Chobe, started off as game reserves and continued to be viewed as such by the public into the 1970s and later. The public perceived national parks more in the light of scenic parks like Matobo and Nyanga in Zimbabwe's eastern mountains and Matobo hills, or the Royal National Park in the Drakensberg mountains in Kwazulu-Natal.

MANAGEMENT OF ECOLOGICAL RESERVES

Managing Biological Reserves

Parks and reserves have had a dual purpose almost from their inception and in southern Africa at least since the turn of the 20th century. They are areas reserved to conserve nature, especially Africa's spectacular megafauna, and for outdoor recreation. This is indicated clearly in the documents covering their creation, such as the provisions of Cecil Rhodes' will in 1902 and the legislation bringing many of the areas into existence and defining their purpose.

Development and management of the areas for outdoor recreation and tourism had run in parallel, but was often functionally separate from management to protect the areas and maintain their biological assets. Not surprisingly there was sometimes disagreement between the day-to-day management of tourists and biological resources, where separate specialist personnel were employed for the two functions. This was accentuated by the grant-dependent nature of most of the organizations. With no clear link between an area's capacity to earn revenue from tourism and its recurrent expenditure on conservation, friction was likely unless the objectives of the two branches were clearly defined and related to each other in overall management policy.

Attitudes towards managing ecological reserves went through several fairly clearly defined phases in southern Africa. The first is epitomized by the military mentality. During this phase park management authorities became smart, disciplined, uniformed paramilitary organizations. Their task was to explore and secure the new parks and reserves, which often extended over vast remote areas with poor communications (see, for example, Stevenson-Hamilton, 1937; Austen and Riney, 1961; Davison, 1967).

The second phase merged with the first and was characterized by the stock raisers' mentality, which was not questioned by the essentially agrarian public. Wardens of the time were concerned to build up animal numbers in their reserves to create a popular spectacle and justify retention of the areas for nature conservation. In the mistaken belief that predators control prey, rather than prey density regulating predator numbers, they set about eliminating predators from reserves like Kruger, Hwange and Victoria Falls. In Kruger the warden and his staff killed 18,440 mammal, bird and reptile predators of all types between 1903 and 1927 (Orford, 1996), and wild dogs were still being shot as late as 1960 in the dying throes of the predator control programme in Hwange.

The desire to provide a better spectacle of animals also led to manipulation of habitats. Burning to create a 'green bite' and artificial game water-holes were used to attract animals and make them more visible to visitors. Killing top predators may seem a drastic measure but, on balance, probably had little lasting impact on the reserves and their fauna as it acted at a high trophic level in the ecosystems. Not so the habitat manipulations. They acted at the primary production level in the systems, leaving a legacy of modified habitats, often characterized by bush encroachment at the expense of the perennial grasses on which soil stability usually depends in savannas.

The consequential effects on the fauna combined with reduced hunting and predation, and the increased isolation of parks and reserves, to promote a syndrome of events. These are often epitomized by a loss of some species like roan, sable and tsessebe, which are sensitive obligate grazers. The losses are accompanied by an increase in others like kudu and impala, which are mixed feeders favoured by low levels in the ecological seer, or elephant, buffalo and hippo, which are bulk roughage feeders. The imbalances created in the species composition of the fauna (see, for example, Cumming, 1982; Child and Child, 1986) act to further suppress ecological values and make the downgrading process more complicated and more permanent as it passes over successive thresholds (Child and Grainger, 1990).

Growing distortions in the ecosystems in parks and reserves gave rise to the era of ecologists which commenced in the 1950s and increased through to the 1970s. Research intensified and, even if much of it was poorly focused to meet management needs, it led to some good range ecology (for example, Riney, 1960; Riney, 1963; Riney, 1982; Walker et al, 1981; Walker, 1982; Walker and Goodman, 1983) an educated evaluation of the state of the veldt and an appreciation of the need to maintain soil–moisture–plant–animal relationships. It became obvious that even the largest parks and reserves are not self-regulating ecological units, and that carefully orchestrated intervention, based on objective monitoring of the integrated ecosystems, is necessary to maintain their sustainability. It was also obvious by the 1960s that managers would have to use the best understanding available and apply what has come to be called adaptive management (Martin, 1999; Martin, 2000), in order to devise and implement time and area specific solutions to complex local problems. It was also clear by then that ecosystems and the animal populations had to be maintained within the capacity of these systems to support them as precipitation fluctuated, if the systems were to be sustainable.

The ecologists' era brought a serious attempt to maintain the integrity of wild ecosystems. General predator control was abolished. Attempts to blanket parks with artificial waterholes to 'create' as many animals as possible were abandoned. Instead, efforts were made to rationalize the availability of water and forage and to keep animal numbers within the capacity of the range to support them (see, for example, Child 1968b; Pienaar, 1983). Expensive attempts were made to eliminate wildfire, and deliberate burning of the veldt was more circumspect and focused to achieve particular objectives. An appreciation of the role of micro-base levels and how their erosion affected ecosystem integrity was emerging in Mozambique by the early 1970s (Tinley, 1971; Tinley, 1977; Tinley, 1979).

Zimbabwe, for example, rationalized this programme by giving it clear goals. These were to cushion the effects on habitats caused by modern man, which commenced on a significant scale with the arrival of white settlers in 1890. The goal was to maintain the physiognomic structure of the vegetation as close as possible to that in 1900, before the forces unleashed by white settlement had accelerated the process. It also acknowledged that there was no such thing as a 'pristine' environment as all had been modified by man over millennia. This is one of the few examples of clearly defined objectives for habitat maintenance of which this author is aware and, with hindsight, even they were too broad.

Most management of the wild ecosystems attracted little public attention, but not so the culling of animals to curb overpopulation and consequent range degradation. Culling took place in most countries in east and southern Africa. It was strongly opposed by animal lovers, who did not believe that killing animals, to save the habitats on which they and other species depended, was justified. On the other hand, they applauded the capture and relocation of animals to achieve the same purpose. While it is obvious which causes the least anguish to these animal rightists, it is arguable whether killing, or capturing and moving an animal to a strange area, causes it more trauma. This open question illustrates the force that uninformed, subjective emotionalism is exerting on objective management. As with modern warfare during the recent Iraqi war, it is becoming more complex and more open to public scrutiny, armchair generals and media hyperbole, as societies become more democratic.

The ascendancy of ecologists did not diminish the requirement to protect parks and reserves from poachers and other outside threats. The need, in fact, increased as land hunger grew and poaching became more sophisticated. It also expanded to cover a whole range of 'new' challenges like controlling wildfire and the encroachment of human settlement, or cushioning the impacts of mining and up-river impoundment. Likewise, the need to justify ecological reserves and to ensure management is sustainable has also intensified and diversified, as they have increased in number and size to around 10 per cent of the global real estate, and as human demands on the biosphere have intensified.

The original objectives of park management have not disappeared, but have changed and broadened. The process continues with the realization that parks cannot be islands of conservation in a sea of often-degraded resources supporting a growing social demand (see, for example, Child and Heath, 1990; Child, 1994). Park management is big business, getting bigger and more complex every day, especially with the international expectation that it will be the prime mechanism for maintaining global biological diversity.

The last is an awesome responsibility, shrouded in imprecision and emotion, which in many cases is not being achieved. Too many parks, from the savannas of Africa to the Rocky Mountains in the US, exist only on paper or are overpopulated animal slums (see, for example, Hess, 1993; Kay, 1997). In 2002, Zimbabwe, which can support around 50,000 elephant, physically counted 86,000 head. This is not a conservation success to be proud of, but it epitomizes the sort of management failure that is widespread in ecological reserves in southern Africa and beyond.

Under present management regimes, biological diversity and other natural values are being eroded in the very areas set aside to conserve them, and the areas are neither sustainable nor demonstrations of sound land management. They represent an abrogation of responsibility by the responsible agencies, which lack clear vision and are not being held accountable for failure to deliver on their mandate. If ecological reserves are to survive, each must be an example of sustainable management and an integral part of the socio-economic environment in which it is embedded. They cannot continue as state-managed areas of poorly executed nature conservation, but should become bridgeheads for better land use. Instead of being black holes for scarce national resources they should be engines for rural development and the alleviation of poverty.

These objectives must be achieved without prejudicing the natural values that the areas were created to preserve and on which society is increasingly dependent. What is often overlooked is that the ethical attraction of preserving biodiversity is compounded many-fold by the socio-economic imperative of doing so. Biological diversity underpins future social well-being by allowing society to adapt to shifts in its environment. Without adequate biological diversity, society will be trapped in an evolutionary cul de sac and will be unable to adjust to the economic and ecological changes that face it continuously.

Management and Development for Tourism

It is difficult to pinpoint the commencement of public use of parks in southern Africa as it was an insidious process in a land where, historically, there has been a strong tradition of outdoor recreation. Tracing the appearance and growth of nature-based tourism and the use of parks for this purpose should reward research and would benefit from careful documentation. Not least because people began hunting and using the recreational opportunities in areas like Table Mountain, the Drakensberg, Nyanga and the Matobo hills from an early stage, often before their formal proclamation as reserves. Facilities grew up around this use which later came to be regulated to preserve the quality of the experience it was providing for more and more people. The pattern in game reserves in remote wilderness was a bit different because of their remoteness and because from the outset access was regulated. Ted Davison (1967) describes how early tourists to areas like Hwange were often little more than personal visitors to the Warden and his staff, who often provided them with rudimentary guiding and other services. They had to seek out the sparse animals on foot under the guidance of a scout.

It was not until after World War II that tourism to national parks and similar reserves developed rapidly, for example increasing in the Hwange National Park from 2771 visitors in 1949 to 25,351 in 1965 (Davison, 1967). This necessitated the building and maintenance of rest camps and tourist roads, which became a major consideration for most park management agencies, as they began to rival law enforcement in the proportion of the annual budget that it was necessary to spend on them.

Early park visitors were mainly self-drive family parties. The first roads were mostly rough dirt tracks, and tourist accommodation comprised simple huts for sleeping, outdoor cooking facilities and communal ablution blocks to serve the huts, camping grounds or caravan parks. Most accommodation and other visitor facilities were clustered in 'camps' catering for 400 or more guests. Considerable inter- and intra-agency competition developed among park wardens across the region to see who could provide the best tourist services and most luxurious tourist accommodation at the low costs that ruled in the camps. This competition and the importance of ensuring that park buildings were of natural materials like stone and thatch, or were painted in natural colours to harmonize with the natural setting and avoid unfortunate visual impacts, was well established by the late 1950s. It did much to enhance the standard of the services offered.

As their numbers increased, visitors were expected increasingly to conform with a strict code of behaviour, especially in areas with big game, in order to protect the park, its assets and the enjoyment of other visitors. They had to adhere to strict speed limits, activities such as driving off the road, alighting from their vehicles except at designated sites, using open vehicles, being out in the park after the prescribed closing time, disturbing game, or the like were prohibited. A tendency to over-regulate, coupled with a lack of public involvement in park planning, led to some visitor-unfriendly behaviour among over-officious staff, who were thin on the ground and not well trained in handling the public. This was an unfortunate irritation to the visiting public who often had to accept a 'take it or leave it' attitude by park authorities that provided the amenities and recreational opportunities that they considered appropriate to their area without consulting their customers. Nevertheless parks were greatly appreciated and the number of people wishing to visit them greatly exceeded those that could be accommodated.

The designation of parks and reserves was very confused throughout the region where the general trend had been towards 'upgrading' game reserves to national parks. It was not until the early 1970s that Zimbabwe led the way and rationalized the classification of the areas in the Parks and Wild Life Estate to denote their conservation status and the types of uses to be permitted in them in terms of the Parks and Wild Life Act, 1975. Each reserve was then divided into a number of zones of permissible use, in terms of the policy document defining how each reserve and the zones into which it was divided was to be managed. These zones usually included:

i) 'Special conservation areas' of limited size for scientific or conservation purposes where public and even staff access was strictly prescribed.
ii) 'Wilderness areas', large areas where development and numbers of visitors were strictly limited, but visitors enjoyed the maximum freedom of action commensurate with preserving the quality of an area.
iii) 'Wild areas', often large areas in which public use was facilitated for a greater number of visitors, through the provision of paths and roads, but where visitors had less freedom of action.
iv) 'Development areas', of limited size for permanent buildings for staff and management facilities and visitor amenities (Child, 1977).

As the number of people using parks and their internal roads increased and as modern family saloon cars became less robust and less suited to rough roads, so the quality of the roads had to be improved. From rudimentary tracks they became made-up gravel roads and eventually more and more were paved. Paving the roads in scenic parks like Cape Point and Matopos raised little adverse comment, but paving the roads in remote game reserves like Kruger and Hwange aroused considerable public opposition, apparently being perceived as an urban intrusion into the wilderness.

Private Sector Participation in Tourism to Parks

The grip of state-managed tourism in parks and reserves did not begin to weaken until the mid-1960s. Previously, private sector involvement had been through management of such places as the Rhodes Hotel in the Inyanga Park, but this was very much the exception. However, from the mid-1960s non-hunting safaris began to operate in reserves like the South Luangwa National Park in Zambia and the Chobe National Park and Moremi Wildlife Reserve in Botswana. The trend has gathered momentum since the early 1970s, with big hotels being built by the Southern Sun Group, in particular, to serve large game areas like Chobe and Hwange.

Growth and transformation of the relationship between public and private sector tourism to parks in countries like Zimbabwe has been interesting, but space does not permit it to be adequately explored here. Instead we limit ourselves to a broad brush description and evaluation of the changes that have taken place. Government-sponsored park tourism was first developed to cater for the domestic market, but soon began to attract foreign visitors, including those from overseas, especially as air travel grew after World War II. After Rhodesia unilaterally declared its independence from Britain and the United Nations applied mandatory economic sanctions to the country, the government paid special attention to developing tourism. This was motivated by the desire to earn essential foreign exchange and provided the country with favourable exposure in an influential market place. The tourism being managed by a government agency in parks and reserves, which had already earned an enviable reputation for its excellence, was an ideal vehicle and catalyst for the government's purpose.

It meant that government could offer a high quality tourism package at a low cost which made Zimbabwe highly competitive in international tourism markets, as nature-based tourism expanded rapidly. It also provided many of the standards and benchmarks that government used to encourage growth of an intrinsically competitive private sector, which was able to grow rapidly in the favourable climate created by government as it captured an increasing throughput of visitors. Combining forces and pooling resources under an influential and effective joint coordinating board, the two sectors were able to hone their particular strengths in friendly symbiotic competition and the greatly increased scales of operation. Arrivals in the country and visitors to the Parks and Wild life Estate peaked in 1972, in spite of the UN sanctions imposed seven years before.

Park authorities learned a great deal about tourism from the experience, while the private sector gained a deeper appreciation of the business opportunities from well-managed nature-based tourism. After Zimbabwe's independence in 1980, the private sector was better capitalized and remained more nimble and able to grasp the new opportunities that emerged, while the parks authority was increasingly starved of finances and became mired in political dogma and intrigue. As less competent and less confident park managers emerged, they resented the competition from the private sector and sought to use their regulatory clout to stifle it, thus making the country less competitive for investment and as an international tourist destination.

The sequence outlined was particularly stark in Zimbabwe but, with qualifications, has been or still is discernible in much of the region. Some governments have already heeded its inherent dangers and taken remedial steps while others have yet to do so. With nature tourism being such a highly competitive international industry, the success of the region will depend on how well each jurisdiction performs and how well they combine in a unified package to attract a significant proportion of the global market. The spectacular African megafauna supported by an adequate physical infrastructure gives the region a comparative advantage in nature-based tourism and outdoor recreation over much of the world, including the rest of Africa. Exploiting this potential means using the lessons of the past to grow an agile competitive industry that will enable the sub-region, as a cooperative entity, to secure its fair share of future markets.

DISCUSSION

Conceptual Lessons

The Comparative Advantage of Wildlife

Nature conservation in southern Africa is conveniently divided into that within ecological reserves and that on land outside, supporting conventional productive enterprises like farming. The institutions evolving outside parks and reserves are generally adequate to be socio-politically acceptable and to allow wildlife to achieve its comparative advantage over other forms of land use. This advantage is based on environmentally benign hunting and tourism services and is often considerable in dry savannas. These savannas cover three-quarters of Africa south of the Sahara where crop and livestock production, on a broad scale and without irrigation, are economically and ecologically hazardous and faltering (Child and Child, 1986).

Put bluntly, conventional agriculture is not sustainable in vast areas of these savannas under present or foreseeable international production and marketing conditions. The situation is compounded by the deteriorating global terms of trade for ubiquitous agricultural commodities like red meat or cereals. By contrast, the value of the spectacular African macrofauna, with its inherent global comparative advantage, is increasing as demand for wildlife-based activities escalates, allowing wildlife to out-compete other uses of the land. Unfortunately, there are still many examples where this potential continues to be subverted artificially by inappropriate institutions driven by outdated thinking in regard to both rural development and nature conservation.

With their high dependence on elastic service industries through tourism and recreational hunting, which add economic tiers to an animal production system, wildlife enterprises can be both sustainable and profitable. Profits from the finite ecological energy can be harvested from natural systems without stressing them and can be increased by growing either the volume or quality of the services. It does not require over grazing or greater extraction of energy from the natural ecosystems. Tourism and hunting markets also favour a diversity of healthy animals in well-maintained and varied habitats, with the result that wildlife ventures are environmentally friendly, socio-politically acceptable to most societies and favour nature conservation.

Institutions and Devolution of Authority

Southern Africa, having broken with much conservation propaganda and dogma, is reforming institutions and forging new paradigms for managing wildlife outside ecological reserves. Generally, the new institutions show promise, although over-regulation, driven by outdated centralized protectionism or a bureaucratic aversion to relinquishing ineffective power over landholders, still lingers and leads to unnecessarily high transaction costs. The paradigm that is emerging is providing an enabling environment for enhancing both conservation and human welfare, not only in Africa but in grassland habitats from tundra and dry desert, through steppe to savanna. Future progress will probably lie in defining the issues affecting nature conservation more precisely and devising more effective institutions to guide sustainable wild resource use.

Lack of Progress in Parks

While southern Africa is leading in aspects of nature conservation outside ecological reserves, the local picture is not all optimistic. Many regional national parks and equivalent nature reserves that have been held up as flagships of conservation are in a sad state. As we have noted, some are paper parks, others are animal slums. The determination, capacity and ability to manage these ecological reserves effectively, which has always been less than adequate, is declining still further. Several jurisdictions now accept habitat modification from wildfire and overgrazing as unavoidable, notwithstanding evidence that they are destroying ecological productivity and biodiversity.

These two primary indicators of the effectiveness of conservation are being disregarded just as the conservation community is championing biodiversity as the major justification for parks. By the same token, poaching is increasing. It has already eliminated black and white rhino from several parks, and elephant are in danger in many. The malady seems deeper than a lack of proficiency, among parks and wildlife agencies, to fulfilling their core obligation to preserve the sustainability and integrity of the areas for which they are responsible. It seems to lie more in a failure of the way in which parks and reserves around the world are being managed (Chapter 6).

Society has yet to come up with a more effective way for conserving natural values than one based on parks and reserves. Why then are these areas seldom managed well anywhere in the world? Nature conservation literature abounds with what should be done, but is largely silent on how to do it. Ineffectiveness is often blamed on inadequate finances, but applies in both rich and poor countries. It is seldom attributed to failure of a system that 'owns' 10 per cent of global real estate, but must be subsidized to survive. That the responsible agencies are having increasing difficulty attracting and holding intelligent young people, a sign that they are in decline (Drucker, 1973; Hamel and Prahalad, 1994), hardly warrants mention.

The contradiction, between growing nature tourism and shrinking assets to support this vast industry, is seldom raised. Neither do park managers question why private-sector neighbours with limited wildlife can prosper and reinvest in their resources while parks with abundant wildlife deteriorate and are cash strapped. The dichotomy between booming wildlife-based tourism and a declining resource base implies serious misalignments in the philosophy, resource allocations or institutions governing nature conservation.

Expanding Mandate and Discipline

Successful park management requires a much wider perspective than that provided by 'conservation biology' if it is to understand and manage the challenges it faces. Our work suggests that the solution lies in the way society sets about conserving and using parks and reserves. The key appears to lie not in making management more *efficient*, but in defining exactly what it aims to accomplish, so philosophies and institutions can be re-aligned to make it more *effective*. Help towards achieving this effectiveness is likely to come from disciplines that are largely foreign to conservationists. They will probably include branches of learning like economics, new institutional economics, politics, the study of institutional and organizational development, and the theory of modern business management.

With demand for wildlife and wild places outstripping supply, nature conservation carries the seeds of its own salvation. Progress depends on thinking 'outside the box'. It means replacing the dogma, entrenched propaganda and misleading jargon of a closed, inbred culture, with innovation and objectivity: hard fact must replace woolly thinking and soft emotionalism. Value judgements may still be important, but should be guided by what can be defended objectively in a multicultural society whose demography and perceptions are changing.

Success will depend on analysing the business of nature conservation, defining what it should be, and developing strategies of how to get there. It needs clear goals and objective milestones for measuring progress towards those goals. It will have to justify itself and determine how to add value to society, while remaining account-able for maintaining the natural values critical to the future quality and productivi-ty of the human environment. This requires new corporate cultures and institutions that are suited to local conditions. They should understand the dualism between generating benefits in the present while maintaining the unimpaired ability of the wild systems to do so in the long term.

CONCLUSION

Conservation thinking has been led by khaki-clad men who had a strongly biological bias, working in the field and with the public, especially landholders. The gulf evident in other countries emerged in southern Africa between these practitioners and academics and is proving difficult to bridge. It occurred between what was viewed as pragmatic conservation, with its many variables, and ivory tower academics endeav-ouring to write about it without the essential knowledge and credentials gained from practical experience in management.

Unfortunately this dichotomy appears to be growing. It seems that even university biologists are retreating behind their computers to model the real world, using untested assumptions, and a new order of social scientists is emerging that is critical of all that went before. Past conservation measures are viewed in the light of modern politics rather than in terms of the situation that prevailed when the action was taken. Conservation has also become highly urbanized and politicized, to the extent that 'polit-ical correctness' has usurped ecological and economic reality in guiding decisions. Non-governmental organizations have acquired increased power without assuming any more accountability and a growing number of government resource managers live in capital cities, removed from the problems on the ground.

Is conservation perhaps entering a phase characterized by medicine 300 years ago? Then, doctors would not perform operations as these caused pain and were thus against their Hippocratic oath. Instead they sat on 'ivory' high-chairs telling barbers, who actually did the operations, what to do, using Latin that the barbers did not understand. If the operation was a success the doctor took the credit, if it was a fail-ure the barber was to blame. Are experienced conservation practitioners becoming like the barbers of old and more or less irrelevant in the modern urban conservation culture? We hope not. To paraphrase a South Africa cricket commentator, 'there is much about conservation that can be learned only from experience in the field, it does not come with a university degree and cannot be purchased in a supermarket'.

REFERENCES

Anstey, D and Hall-Martin, A (1977) 'Present day status and future of nature conservation in Malawi', *Koedoe Supplement*: 106–15

Asibey, E O A (1974) 'Wildlife as a source of protein in Africa south of the Sahara', *Biodiversity Conservation* **6**(1): 32–9

Austen, B and Riney, T (1961) *'Poaching Control in Wankie National Park, Southern Rhodesia'*, Report Department, National Parks, Rhodesia and Nyasaland, Salisbury

Brown, J C (1875a) *The Hydrology of South Africa*, Henry King, Edinburgh

Brown, J C (1875b) *The Crown Forests of the Cape of Good Hope*, Oliver Boyd, Edinburgh

Brynard, A M (1977) 'Die Nasionale Parke van die Republiek van Suid-Afrika', *Koedoe Supplement*: 24–37

Campbell, A (1973) 'The national parks and reserve system in Botswana', *Biodiversity Conservation* **5**: 7–14

Child, B (2000a) 'Making wildlife pay: Converting wildlife's comparative advantage into real incentives for having wildlife in African savannas; Case studies from Zimbabwe and Zambia', in H T Prins, J G Grootenhuis and T T Dolan (eds) *Wildlife Conservation by Sustainable Use*, Kluwer Academic Publishers, London, pp333–87

Child, B (2000b) 'Application of the Southern African experience to wildlife utilization and conservation in Kenya and Tanzania', in H T Prins, J G Grootenhuis and T T Dolan (eds) *Wildlife Conservation by Sustainable Use*, Kluwer Academic Publishers, London, pp459–67

Child, B (in preparation) 'History of wildlife conservation in Zambia', in B Child (ed) *Parks in Transition: Biodiversity, Rural Development and the Bottom Line*, vol 2, SASUSG, Pretoria

Child, B and Child G (1986) 'Wildlife economic systems and sustainable human welfare in the semi-arid rangeland of southern Africa', in Report on the FAO/Finland Workshop on Watershed Management and in the Arid and Semi-arid Zones of SADCC Countries Maseru, pp81–91

Child, B and Child G (in preparation) *Managing National Parks to be Sustainable*

Child, G (1968a) *Behaviour of Large Mammals during the Formation of Lake Kariba*, Trustees National Museum, Rhodesia

Child, G (1968b) *Report to the Government of Botswana on an Ecological Survey of North-Eastern Botswana*, Food and Agriculture Organization, Rome, pp155

Child, G (1970) 'Wildlife utilization and management in Botswana', *Biodiversity Conservation* **3**(1): 18–22

Child, G F T (1977) 'Problems and progress in nature conservation in Rhodesia', *Koedoe Supplement*: 116–37

Child, G (1971) 'The future of rural land use in Botswana', in Proceedings of the SARCCUS Symposium, Gorongoza National Park, Mozambique Sept 1971, pp75–8

Child, G (1994) 'Strengthening protected area management: A focus for the 1990s, a platform for the future', *Biodiversity Conservation* **3**: 459–63

Child, G (1995a) *Wildlife and People: The Zimbabwean Success*, WISDOM Foundation, Harare, pp267

Child, G (1995b) 'Managing wildlife successfully in Zimbabwe', *Oryx* **29**(3): 171–7

Child, G (1996a) 'The role of community-based wild resource management in Zimbabwe', *Biodiversity Conservation* **5**: 355–67

Child, G (1996b) 'Realistic 'game laws', *Oryx* **30**(4): 228–9

Child, G (in preparation) 'The history of nature conservation in Zimbabwe', in B Child, (ed) *Parks in Transition: Biodiversity, Rural Development and the Bottom Line*, vol 2, SASUSG, Pretoria

Child, G and Chitsike, L (2000) 'Ownership of wildlife' in H T Prins, J G Grootenhuis and T T Dolan (eds) *Wildlife Conservation by Sustainable Use*, Kluwer Academic Publishers, London, pp247–66

Child, G and Grainger, J (1990) *A System Plan for Protected Areas for Wildlife conservation and Sustainable Development in Saudi Arabia*, vol I, NCWCD/IUCN Report, Riyadh, vol 1: pp335

Child, G and Heath, R (1990) 'Underselling national parks in Zimbabwe: The implications for rural sustainability', *Society and Natural Resources* **3**: 215–27

Child, G and Riney T (1987) 'Tsetse control hunting. I. Zimbabwe, 1919–1958', *Zambezia* **14**(1): 11–71

Child, G, Smith, P and Von Richter, W (1970) 'Tsetse control hunting as a measure of large mammal trends in the Okavango delta, Botswana', *Mammalia* **34**(1): 34–75

Child, H (1965) *The History and Extent of Recognition of Tribal Law in Rhodesia*, Ministry of Internal Affairs, Harare

Cumming, D H M (1982) 'The influence of large herbivores on savanna structure in Africa', in B J Huntley and B H Walker (eds) *Ecology of Tropical Savannas*, W Junk, The Hague (*Ecological Studies* no 42): pp217–45

Davison, T (1967) *Wankie – The Story of a Great Game Reserve*, Books of Africa, Cape Town: 211

de la Bat, B J G (1977) 'An evaluation of the conservation areas and their importance to the economy of south west Africa', *Koedoe Supplement*: 84–94

Drucker, P F (1973) *Management: Tasks, Responsibilities, Practices*, Harper Collins, New York

Geddes Page, J T (1977) 'Interpretation and education in nature conservation', *Koedoe Supplement*: 197–202

Grove, R (1987) 'Early themes in African conservation: The Cape in the nineteenth century', in D Anderson and R Grove (eds) *Conservation in Africa – People, Politics and Practice*, Cambridge University Press, Cambridge, UK, pp21–39

Hamel, G and Prahalad, C K (1994) *Competing for the Future*, Harvard Business School Press, Boston

Hay, D (1977a) 'Man, nature and conservation', *Koedoe Supplement*: 49–54

Hay, D (1977b) 'The history and status of nature conservation in South Africa', In A C Brown (ed) *A History of Scientific Endeavour in South Africa*, Royal Society of South Africa pp132–63

Hess, K Jr (1993) *Rocky Times in Rocky Mountain National Park*, University Press of Colorado, p167

Hooker, J D (1872) 'Forestry', *Journal of Applied Science* (August), 221–223

IUCN and UNEP (1987) *IUCN Directory of Afrotropical Protected Areas*, IUCN, Gland, Switzerland, pp1034

IUCN, UNEP and WWF (1980) *World Conservation Strategy: Living Resource Conservation for Sustainable Development*, IUCN Gland, Switzerland

Joubert, E (1974) 'The development of wildlife utilization in South West Africa', *Journal of the South African Wildlife Management Association* **4**(1): 35–42

Kay, C E (1997) *Yellowstone Ecological Malpractice*, Political Economy Research Center, Report No 15, Bozeman, Montana, USA

Marsh, G P (1864) *Man and Nature: Or Physical Geography as Modified by Human Action*, G Scribner, New York

MacKinnon, J and MacKinnon, K (1986) *Review of Protected Area System in the Afrotropical Realm*, IUCN, Gland, Switzerland

Martin, R B (1999) 'Adaptive management; the only tool for decentralised systems', in Proceedings of the Norway/UN Conference The Ecosystem Approach for Sustainable Use of Biological Diversity, Trondheim, Norway, pp1–14

Martin, R B (2000) 'Adaptive management the application of feedback', guest lecture at the Norwegian Environmental Institute, Trondheim, Norway, 17 February

Natal (1880) *Report of the Commission Enquiring into the Extent and Condition of the Forest Lands in the Colony*, Government Printer, Pietermaritzburg

Oelofse, J (1970) 'Plastic for game capture', *Oryx* **5**:306–8

Orford, J H L (1996) 'Why the cullers got it wrong', *African Environment and Wildlife* **4**(2): 81–2

Pappe, L (1862) *Silva Capensis, or a Description of South African Forestry Trees and Arborescent Shrubs*, de Villiers, Cape Town

Parker, I and Amin, M (1983) *Ivory Crisis*, Chatto and Windus, London

Pienaar, U de V (1983) 'Management by intervention: The pragmatic/economic option', in R N Owan-Smith (ed) *Management of Large Mammals in African Conservation Areas*, Haum, Pretoria, pp23–36

Reilly, T E and Reilly, E A (1977) 'The state of nature conservation in Swaziland: Past and present', *Koedoe Supplement*: 152–70

Reilly, T E and Reilly, E A (1994) *The Lion Roars Again: A Reflection on the History and Significance of Hlane Royal National Park and Other Conservation Achievements of the Monachy in the Kingdom of Swaziland*, Hlane Royal National Park, Swaziland

Riney, T (1960) A field technique for assessing physical condition of some ungulates, *Journal of Wildlife Management* **24** (1): 92-94.

Riney, T (1963) 'A rapid field technique and its application to describe conservation status and trends in semi-arid pastoral areas', *African Soils* **8**: 159–258

Riney, T (1982). *The Study and Management of Large Mammals*. John Wiley and Sons, New York

Riney, T and Kettlitz, W L (1964) 'Management of large mammals in the Transvaal', *Mammalia* **28**(2):189–248

Stevenson-Hamilton, J (1937) *South African Eden – from Sabi Game Reserve to Kruger National Park*, Hamilton and Co, London, pp320

Summers, R (1966) 'Archaeological distributions and a tentative history of tsetse infestation in Rhodesia and the northern Transvaal', *Arnoldia (Rhodesia)* **3**(13): 1 18

Taylor, R D (1990) 'Zimbabwe', in C W Allin (ed) *International Handbook of National Parks and Nature Reserves*, Greenwood Press, Connecticut, pp493–515

Tinley, K L (1971) 'Sketch of the Gorongoza National Park, Mocambique', in *Proceedings of the SARCCUS Symposium; Nature Conservation as a Form of Land Use Gorongoza National Park*, pp163–72

Tinley, K L (1977) 'Framework of the Gorongoza Ecosystem, Mozambique', DSc thesis, University of Pretoria

Tinley, K L (1979) 'The maintenance of wilderness diversity in Africa', in I Player (ed) *Voices of the Wilderness*, Jonathan Ball

von Richter, W (1976) 'Wildlife utilisation and management as a land use in Botswana', *Applied Science and Development* **13**: 145–55

von Richter, W (1979) 'The utilization and management of wild animals as a form of land use in marginal areas in Africa', *Animal Research and Development* **10**: 93–102

Walker, B (1982) *Management of Semi-Arid Ecosystems*. Elsevier, Amsterdam

Walker, B H and Goodman, P S (1983). Some implication of ecosystem properties for wildlife management, In R N Owan-Smith (ed) *Management of Large Mammals in African Conservation Areas*, Haum, Pretoria.

Walker, B H, Ludwick D, Holling, C S and Peterman, R M (1981), 'Stability of semi-arid savanna grazing systems', *Journal of Ecology* **69**: 157-188

Chapter 3

Private Land Contribution
to Conservation in South Africa

Ivan Bond

with

Brian Child
Derek de la Harpe
Brian Jones
Jon Barnes
Hilary Anderson

INTRODUCTION

Conventionally, the responsibility for conservation has been left to the state in the form of national parks. In southern Africa, approximately 17 per cent of land is formally protected (Cumming and Bond, 1991) (see Table 3.1). Over the past 15 years, however, most of the new conservation effort has been on land, both communal and private, outside the formally protected areas. Although it is the community conservation programmes that have grabbed the bulk of the resources, the headlines and much of the research effort, it was the emergence of conservation on private land that provided the confidence that conservation by landholders was an effective and powerful option. Private conservation is restricted largely to South Africa, Namibia and Zimbabwe because these are the only countries in southern Africa with extensive areas of private land outside arable plots and also where the policy and legislative environment was conducive to this land use. It was a reaction to the failure of coercive or legislated conservation measures on private land, where some wildlife was exterminated to make way for livestock, whereas much wildlife and ecosystem productivity was lost to livestock overgrazing, competition and neglect.

Table 3.1 *Percentage land apportionment by tenure for Botswana, Namibia, South Africa, Zambia and Zimbabwe*

	Botswana	Namibia	South Africa	Zambia[3]	Zimbabwe
State land	23	15	5	31	16
Communal land	71	41	13	8	49
Private land	6	44	73	23	35
Other	—	—	9	38	—
Totals	100	100	100	100	100

Source: Cumming and Bond (1991); land allocation in Zambia from B Child (personal communication)

In the early 1960s, a process began that returned the rights over wildlife to landholders, and which at the same time increased its commercial value. This chapter provides a description of the private conservation sector in southern Africa and its contributions to conservation and the economy.

Nationalizing the Wildlife Resource

Privately owned land in southern Africa was a product of colonization. Before colonization, land and natural resources were managed through traditional leaders although strongly modified by religious or traditional belief systems (Murphree and Cumming, 1991). Wildlife and natural resources were important in precolonial economies, but sustainability was not a significant issue because of the low human population densities and large areas of wildlife habitat. At the turn of the 19th century, however, colonial administrators were faced with severely depleted herds of wildlife and domestic stock. This was the result of epidemics of bovine pleuropneumonia (1850s) and rinderpest (1896–97), combined with the overexploitation by slave traders, hunter explorers, prospectors and adventurers (see Bond and Cumming, in preparation). Alarmed at the loss of wildlife, newly established colonial administrations introduced protectionist legislation. Its effect was to centralize control of the wildlife resource and to ban commercial and subsistence use; this served to alienate commercial and communal farmers from wildlife. For the indigenous peoples of southern Africa, this was the start of a process that effectively alienated them from land and wildlife, and in many cases resulted in weak state control degrading to open-access property regimes (Child, 2001). Unlike the legislation for other natural resources that allowed harvest for domestic purposes, the wildlife legislation did not allow any form of use at all. The legacy of this legislation is still being dealt with today. Despite the major significant political and economic changes that have occurred, many southern Africans still have a deep-seated belief that wildlife is the property of the state, is not theirs and is a threat to their agropastoral production systems.

Mixed Signals on Wildlife Conservation

The first Game Law Amendment Act (1891) and the Game Preservation Ordinance Act (1899) preceded the recovery of wild herds, and brought about the end of frontier exploitation by adventurers like ivory hunters. The formation of protected areas like Kruger, where wildlife was protected and managed, also contributed to the recovery of wildlife populations over time.

As wildlife populations recovered, however, so did the populations of tsetse fly, which posed a direct threat to the viability of emerging livestock production by commercial farmers. This led to the contradictory situation whereby land holders were alienated and prevented from using wildlife, supposedly as a conservation measure, but the state was simultaneously trying to eradicate large mammals to control the spread of tsetse fly. This continued, especially in Zimbabwe, as late as the 1970s and resulted in the eradication of nearly a million head of wildlife (Child and Riney, 1987).

By the 1960s it was clear that the legislation preventing the commercial exploitation of wildlife was ineffectual because it was nearly impossible to enforce and it did little to address the problem that there were no incentives to conserve wildlife. Many landholders actively eliminated wildlife to protect their crops and the grazing of livestock: the culling of large animals that were left to rot in the field is an infamous reminder of this period. Perhaps more importantly, however, was the benign neglect of wildlife, with fencing (including the fencing of water-points to assist livestock management) and overgrazing by livestock resulting in most wildlife being replaced by livestock.

By the 1960s and 1970s there was a growing appreciation across the region that the loss of habitat and competition with domestic stock were the primary causes for the continuing decline in wildlife populations outside the protected-area system.[1] Policy and legislation changes in Namibia (1967), Zimbabwe (1960, 1975) and in South Africa (where landholder wildlife is generally controlled by provincial rather than national legislation) granted various degrees of user rights to commercial farmers. These legislative changes, with improving terms of trade for wildlife, resulted in the development of a substantial wildlife-based economy on commercial farmland in Namibia, South Africa and Zimbabwe, and to a lesser extent in Botswana and Zambia.

The Purpose of this Chapter

This chapter analyses the performance of wildlife as a land use on commercial or private land in southern Africa. It starts by describing and defining the four primary wildlife production systems, with a detailed discussion of wildlife and land use in semi-arid rangelands, because this is where the economic and conservation impact is highest. It then looks at the legislative and economic reasons why private wildlife utilization has been so effective in southern Africa, before looking at its impact on ecosystem conservation and economic growth. The most frequently asked questions relate to the sustainability of commercial use, especially hunting, if private conservation is indeed to be a legitimate conservation mechanism, and we devote some discussion to this. Given the issues of land distribution and racial equity and its potential impact on private conservation, brought to the fore by recent events in Zimbabwe, we believe it important to look also at sustainability of property rights and the political legitimacy of white, private conservation. The chapter relies largely on the work of Child (1988), Jansen et al (1992), Bothma (2002a; 2002b), Anderson (2003) and Krug (2001). This indicates the paucity of research given the size of the private wildlife economy.

WILDLIFE PRODUCTION SYSTEMS AND PRIVATE CONSERVATION

Within southern Africa, there are four general wildlife production systems. The categories are based primarily on the intensity of the production systems (modified from Krug (2001) and Bond and Cumming (in preparation))[2]. They are as follows.

Intensive Single-species Production Systems

These are characterized by the industrial production of single species, usually crocodiles or ostriches. Production is land, capital and management intensive. Both species are produced primarily for their skins, but with meat being an increasingly important by-product. These systems do not directly contribute to the maintenance of wildlife habitat. However, they have been shown to be important for the protection of single species in their natural habitats, an example being the monitoring and protection of wild crocodiles in Zimbabwe.

Semi-intensive Multispecies Production Systems (Game Farms)

This describes wildlife properties that are relatively small (up to about 5000ha in size) and enclosed by wildlife fences. Commercial activities, usually managed by the landholder, are diverse including lodge accommodation, trophy or meat hunting, meat sales as well as live capture and sale. Production may be supplemented with external inputs such as pastures, crop residues, feeding and parasite control. The property may be devoted exclusively to wildlife, but wildlife is often part of a much wider enterprise mix that includes livestock and arable agriculture. Game farms often involve manipulation of wildlife species composition, as well as introduction of some locally alien species.

Extensive Multispecies Production Systems (Game Ranches)[4]

These are typically larger properties characterized by free-ranging populations of wildlife. Depending on their size, location, country and production objectives, these extensive systems may or may not be fenced.[5] As with semi-intensive systems, income is earned from a range of activities including international trophy hunting and tourism. However, effective protection inevitably results in expanding wildlife populations so a by-product on many properties is meat production as well as live capture and sale. Unlike livestock ranching, most biomass and enterprise effort is targeted towards recreational uses of wildlife (not meat production) because this is where most value is added.

Generally, the commercial activities on the property are still performed by the landowner, although there are increasing numbers of properties where the commercial functions, especially trophy hunting and tourism, are outsourced to commercial tenants. The land and wildlife management remains under the control of the landholders.

CONSERVANCIES

This is a term that has evolved to indicate the cooperation between landholders for the management of wildlife, and represents a scaling up of the previous two categories. There is a range of conservancy models in southern Africa. At its simplest, a conservancy can be a protocol governing wildlife management by landowners across their properties. More commonly, conservancies represent an integrated approach to wildlife management characterized by binding agreements to remove internal fencing, reduce or eliminate domestic stock, provide water and law enforcement, and follow similar management and offtake regimes. Two well-known conservancies are NamibRand In Namibia and the Save Valley in Zimbabwe (Krug, 2001). With the formation of the Save Valley Conservancy, 29 landholders pooled over 350,000ha of land, jointly funded an external fence and wildlife protection according to the size of their property, removed all internal fencing and developed a common wildlife management model. This included jointly agreed quotas, but with individuals being responsible for commercial activities. As with the semi-intensive and extensive production systems, landowners within a conservancy derive their revenue from a broad spectrum of wildlife-based activities at the scale of a property. The advantages of conservancies include large, unfragmented wildlife habitats at a scale that encourages a higher quality and diversity of consumptive and non-consumptive activities. For example, some conservancies are large enough to re-introduce elephant, lion and wild dog, which obviously has ecological and commercial advantages. An interesting observation is that as specialization increases there is a tendency within conservancies to sub-contract the management of enterprises.

The fact that highly individualist landholders are overcoming the transaction costs of working together reinforces the importance of scale, and points to the sub-optimal nature of fragmented and fenced wildlife properties. In Namibia and parts of South Africa, game fencing is a prerequisite for most consumptive use rights, a requirement related to the perceived need to control a fugitive resource like wildlife. Our observations are that legislation that forces landowners to invest in wildlife-proof fencing is generally undesirable. This is because fencing fragments habitats and prevents the natural movement of wildlife. Many wildlife species are relatively sedentary and territorial, so fencing is a largely unnecessary expense. Fencing allows game to be over-stocked where, in the absence of fencing, it would move to better habitats. Moreover, with enterprises in semi-arid rangelands being extensive, the high cost of building and maintaining fences can make the difference between a viable and non-viable business.

Conservancies are a response to these conclusions, but we highlight some exceptionally far-sighted and effective legislation for the management of natural resources. In the 1940s, Zimbabwe's McIlwaine Commission determined that resources such as soil, grazing and trees needed to be protected, that the state was an inefficient and inappropriate organ of primary control, but that communities of landholders might well be able to cheaply and effectively control the abuses of individual members. Thus the Natural Resources Act of 1941 provided the legal framework for neighbourhood land-holders' associations called intensive conservation areas (ICAs) (Child, 1995). The legal rights and responsibilities for controlling the abuse of natural resources was vested in these ICAs, although recourse was allowed to the state for appeal or arbitration, and the state maintained the right to intervene as a last resort. Thus, if an individual landholder did not build contour ridges, cleared too much land or overgrazed his range, the ICA (in other words his community) could place a legal banning order on him outlining the restrictions or corrective measures to be taken. This was so effective that when the Parks and Wild Life Act of 1975 devolved the authority for wildlife to land-holders, it used this same mechanism to control wildlife.

For this analysis, the conservation value and contribution to biodiversity of 'intensive single-species production systems' will not be considered. This is because, although they form important economic industries, they do not constitute a major and extensive use of land, and this chapter is largely concerned with the conservation of private land. This does not mean that these systems do not contribute to conservation. The empirical evidence suggests that the development and existence of intensive production of ostriches and crocodiles has directly led to the recovery of wild populations (Kievit, 2000; Child, 1995). Indeed, the lessons learned from the intensive market-based production of these species could well be applied to other species (particularly protected species), especially as these are species for which other traditional conservation tools such as law enforcement, 'specially protected' species status and trade restrictions (Convention on International Trade in Endangered Species of Wild Fauna and Flora; CITES) have largely failed (Child, 1995).

THEORETICAL AND EMPIRICAL FOUNDATIONS OF COMMERCIAL WILDLIFE PRODUCTION

A common logic in southern Africa is that the sustainable use of wildlife offers the solution to the conservation and economic agendas required in some parts of some developing countries. As we show below, the transfer of user rights over wildlife to the commercial sector has resulted in the allocation of land to wildlife production, and this contributed to the conservation of biodiversity. This experience has also provided major opportunities for learning about how conservation works, including commercialization and product development, the importance of institutions and legal use rights, the ecological and economic bases for any comparative advantage that wildlife may have, and the empirical testing of ecological, financial and economic assumptions. This section outlines this improved understanding of the theoretical and empirical opportunities of wildlife production in the semi-arid savannah.[6] Such innovation seldom occurs in poor rural communities, or indeed in the public sector. The conceptual foundations for wildlife production systems that have been developed, tested and proven by the commercial sector are directly relevant to the new paradigms sought for the management of community and protected areas across the region.

African rangelands evolved under indigenous multispecies systems typically carrying 15–25 ungulate species (Cumming, 1994). Although first exposed to domestic livestock 2000 years ago, wildlife has only been replaced by single-species livestock systems in the past 150 years. By the 1980s, well under 10 per cent of herbivore biomass on Africa's savannahs was in the form of wildlife (Cumming and Bond, 1991) indicating the extent of the domination of domestic production systems. In 100 years, the livestock industry had effectively squeezed out wildlife except in a few areas.

In the commercial sector the domination of livestock production systems was a function of institutional and technological variables. Clearly, the overriding institutional issue was that legislation prevented commercial farmers from legally exploiting the wildlife resources on their properties. Many wildlife species were considered direct competitors with domestic livestock for scarce grazing resources. Carnivores were also problematic. Hence the oft quoted 'you cannot farm in a zoo' and the loss of wildlife on private land. The absence of any rights to wildlife and therefore any incentive to conserve it were reinforced by other institutional factors.

In addition to the legislation, there were direct and indirect subsidies to cattle producers which limited any form of investment in wildlife management (Child, 1988). Direct measures included price support, price controls, cheap loans for restocking, provision of fodder in droughts, and policies that provided cheap labour. Indirect subsidies to livestock producers included massive state investments in the control of endemic livestock diseases, appropriate infrastructure (abattoirs, fencing), research and development. One of the more iniquitous policies in Zimbabwe was the compulsory de-stocking of the communal lands that allowed commercial producers to access communally produced livestock at below-market prices (Phiminster, 1978). Technologically, the growth in the livestock sector was supported by the development of supplementary nitrogen feeds, which spread cattle production into areas of higher agro-ecological potential that had previously been marginal for livestock because of the low quality of the winter forage (Child, 1988).

The extent and support of livestock producers that often defied very simple economic logic was made possible through the dominance of 'farmer lobbies' in the pre-independence governments of South Africa, Namibia and Zimbabwe. This was reinforced by international efforts to isolate pre-independence regimes, as farmer lobbies emphasized how well they served strategic goals such as those of 'food security'. In all three countries, independence has resulted in the removal of most of the direct and indirect support for the commercial farming sector (Child, 2001; Bothma, 2002; Krug, 2000). Cattle producers still managed, however, to find external mechanisms to support livestock production. For example, in Zimbabwe, cattle producers were able to co-opt, with the support of the government, international donors such as the European Union (EU) to maintain support for livestock production. The EU injected massive capital investment (abattoirs, veterinary fencing, disease control) to support a quota of 8100 tonnes of beef for European markets. Despite its high cost, this did little to reverse the declining fortunes of the beef industry. Yet it did considerable harm to the emerging wildlife sector. Fencing and movement restrictions hampered efforts to restock land with wildlife, as well as the marketing (and therefore price) of game meat and live animals.

At the farm level, the degree to which landowners have adopted wildlife production has largely been dictated by micro-level variables. These include the biophysical properties of the farm, its location, and other on-farm enterprises as well as the skills of the owner (Bond, 1993). Location and land use within the general area appear to be very important variables for farmers changing land use. For example, farms near urban centres have often introduced wildlife and tourism enterprises, thereby exploiting niche markets within the business and diplomatic communities. Similarly, properties near large national parks have tended to switch to high-end wildlife activities (eg Klaserie near Kruger, and Dete near Hwange National Park) to take advantage of the general increase in the levels of wildlife-based tourism.

The importance of this historical analysis does not lie in championing wildlife production systems over those for domestic livestock. Conservationists in southern Africa have always been more concerned with the quality of the land than with species conservation. This is why economic and ecological comparative advantage of alternative land uses (rather than conservation) has tended to dominate decision making (see Chapter 2). Thus, wildlife enterprises resulted from the search for the land use that created the most economic growth with the least environmental damage. It is important to note, however, that poorly managed animal production systems of either form can lead to severe environmental degradation and loss of habitat.

The critical issue for the long-term conservation of biodiversity in southern Africa is to understand why wildlife production systems are currently more viable to many landowners. We implicitly distinguish between rain-fed agricultural zones and rangelands, with a crossover point around 700mm rainfall. In the former, where crop production is possible (that is, primary production) it is invariably a more productive and profitable land use. However, even within these areas of high agricultural production, there still maybe opportunities where wildlife is a viable land use, for example using marginal land or where access to tourism markets are good. For this discussion, we focus on the ecological properties of the semi-arid savannahs, which constitute approximately 70 per cent of southern Africa.

Sustainable use of semi-arid rangelands depends primarily on converting grazing and forage into useful products through herbivores. The two central questions are whether it is better to use wild or domestic animals, and whether it is better to produce meat or services such as recreation. These water-limited ecosystems are characterized by variability, both in the patchiness of vegetation and in the episodic nature of rainfall, fire and frost. By definition, primary and therefore secondary production in semi-arid savannahs is governed by the amount of moisture available for plant growth (plant-available moisture). At landscape level, wildlife biomass (Coe et al, 1976), human population and livestock biomass (Cumming and Bond, 1991) are all determined by the amount of rainfall. At a micro-level these relationships will be modified by other variables including soil fertility, the management of the vegetation at the soil surface to retain water, diseases (especially trypanosomiasis), infrastructure and land tenure (Bell, 1982).

Fundamentally, the sustainable use of semi-arid savannahs needs to consider issues of productivity over extended periods. Their diversity, patchiness and stochastic characteristics can easily mask the nature of structural ecological changes, and changes in primary and therefore secondary productivity. This makes measuring real change difficult and is at least partly responsible for the vigorous debate about the nature and extent of rangeland degradation. Conventional wisdom argues that degradation and the loss of productivity is characterized by a transition from a grass-dominated ecosystem to one dominated by woody species. This is often accompanied by erosion, the loss of grass thus reducing the system's ability to retain rainfall. This reduces plant-available moisture, nutrient flows and ultimately the productivity and resilience of the ecosystem. Evidence to support this approach has been collated from macro- and micro-level studies (see, for example, Child, 1988). A competing hypothesis has emerged that argues that semi-arid savannahs are much more resilient and therefore less susceptible to losses in productivity than previously proposed (Sandford, 1983; Abel and Blaikie, 1990; Scoones, 1990). However, a review of the ecology of semi-arid rangelands has noted that there is little scientific evidence and long-term monitoring to support the latter hypothesis (Campbell et al, 2000).

Notwithstanding the resolution of the debate over rangeland degradation and losses of productivity, wildlife production systems appear to offer a solution to the apparent decline in productivity of conventional livestock production systems. Initially, wildlife production systems were considered as an alternative source of protein to livestock. However, the costs of harvesting and processing fugitive wildlife plus stringent hygiene and veterinary restrictions meant that it was not viable as an alternative source of protein. Moreover, the real advantage of wildlife is not duplicating livestock by the conversion of grazing resources into meat, but in an entirely new production system that converts grazing into services and where economic output is therefore much less directly linked to ecological input. Thus, the value of wildlife lies in recreation (eg trophy hunting), and in adding multiple tiers to the production system (eg photo-tourism + trophy hunting + meat production) rather than in using a different, albeit more diverse, set of animals to convert grass into meat. This is borne out by empirical research: wildlife became substantially more profitable than meat production systems. The development of wildlife as a land use in other countries may not have followed the common Zimbabwean model where trophy hunting was the point of entry. In the more arid environments of Botswana and Namibia, non-consumptive tourism has often been the main use of wildlife resources, albeit with other livestock production systems. The principle, however, that the value of wildlife lies in its recreational uses is important and consistent across southern Africa (Barnes and de Jager, 1996).

In the 1960s and 1970s there was a considerable literature on the relative productivity advantages of wildlife systems compared with cattle. This aimed to show that wildlife could produce more meat, of better quality, than livestock, while causing less environmental damage. Meanwhile, landholders had discovered that the best way to use wildlife was by selling trophy animals. With relatively depleted wildlife populations, the southern Africans began by selling 'mini safaris' against the much higher-profile and quality hunting in East Africa, the epicentre of the classic African safari popularized by Theodore Roosevelt and Ernest Hemingway. The decline of wildlife or hunting conditions in Kenya, Sudan, Central African Republic, etc, as well as the 1976 hunting ban in Kenya, created important opportunities for the growth of southern Africa's market (Bond and Cumming, in preparation). Consequently, South Africa, Namibia and Zimbabwe (and Botswana) moved from being minor players in the 1960s to controlling a market share approaching 70 per cent by the 1990s.

The market opportunities and the appreciation that the real value of wildlife lay in its recreational uses really provided the impetus for wildlife to emerge as a viable and alternative land use to domestic livestock production. Livestock production, or even protein-based wildlife production systems, were dependent on the direct relation between primary and secondary production. This often meant that to remain viable, landowners had to produce more meat; in doing so they often exceeded stocking rates and mined environmental capital, causing a cycle of degradation and loss of productivity. Shifting production to services, as with international trophy hunting, removed the direct link between profit and the conversion of primary biological production into protein. In sharp contrast, financial viability now depended on the diversity and quality of wildlife species (rather than bulk quantity), the limited offtake of males, and the provision of an African wilderness experience. The incentive was for landowners to maintain or rehabilitate rangelands and the quality and diversity of wildlife. The emergence of the global demand for tourism opportunities and the growing demand for trophy hunting in the mid-1980s merely served to reinforce the advantage of wildlife production systems over domestic livestock.

We have already mentioned the early economic research in Zimbabwe that suggested that wildlife was more viable than livestock and why (Child, 1988). This was followed by a much more detailed assessment of enterprise viability in the 1990s (Jansen et al, 1992), which confirmed that wildlife was generally more profitable than cattle production systems. Despite five decades of support only 5 per cent of the cattle enterprises were categorized as profitable (Figure 3.1). This research also showed that rangeland enterprises, and wildlife in particular, were prejudiced by government fiscal policies (Jansen et al, 1992).[7]

The implications of the private-sector experience over the past 40 years for the future management of protected areas in southern Africa are profound. First and foremost it can be argued that in the long term wildlife is the most appropriate form of land use in many semi-arid rangelands. Wildlife can make more money and create more jobs, with less pressure on the environment. Thus, maintenance of protected areas no longer has to be solely justified in terms of the conservation of biodiversity. Madikwe, for instance (see Chapter 7) is primarily justified as a social investment. Successful private conservation provides the evidence that more state-protected areas in semi-arid regions should be financially viable. The fact that they are not suggests ineffective management. It follows that if these parks were made

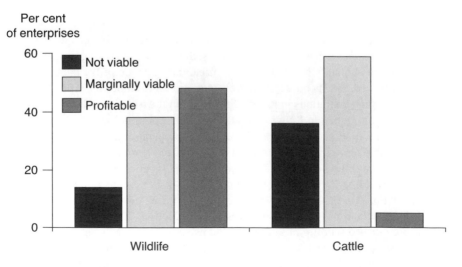

Figure 3.1 *Relative financial viability of wildlife and cattle enterprises*

viable, this would release money for conservation of biodiversity in areas where it is not financially sustainable. South African National Parks, for example, is considering increasing the commercialization of its current protected areas (eg sale of excess rhino; reduction in tourism subsidy) and using this money to buy more land for conservation. Making conservation pay is particularly important in countries where there is a high demand for land. Secondly, the economic success of wildlife production not only contributes to biodiversity but it legitimizes wildlife as a primary form of land use in that it provides things that are important to developing societies: economic growth and jobs. This is important because it makes conservation politically palatable. There remains, however, a residual feeling in some sections of southern Africa society that private wildlife conservation, despite its economic and ecological contribution, is not a legitimate enterprise and that land used for wildlife is in some sense under-used.

POLICY AND LEGISLATION FOR COMMERCIAL WILDLIFE PRODUCTION

The emergence of policies and legislation in South Africa, Namibia and Zimbabwe that devolved rights over wildlife to landowners was a necessary but not sufficient condition for the development of commercial wildlife production. For these three countries, the starting point for policy change was a general appreciation that wildlife and the area of wildlife habitat outside the state-protected areas was declining.

In Namibia, the first legislation that granted landowners user rights over certain species was promulgated in 1967 (Schoeman, 1996). This legislation was incorporated into the Nature Conservation Ordinance (No. 4 of 1975) and granted user rights to landholders over certain eclectic-mix species of wildlife designated as 'huntable game'. Upon application, the landholder could also apply for quotas over specially protected species. Permission to use the so-called specially protected species depended on the farmer erecting a wildlife-proof fence around the area or areas to be hunted and on having the populations surveyed by the state wildlife management agency. Upon further application, the farmer could also become a 'hunting farm', allowing international trophy hunting (Barnes and Jones, in preparation). Although the legislation proved to be very effective in stimulating the commercial wildlife sector in Namibia, it can be argued that the fencing requirements are both ecologically and economically undesirable. Ecologically, the legislation led to the fragmentation (at least in terms of wildlife production) of the landscape. This was undesirable given the general aridity of Namibia and the highly variable annual rainfall (Jones and Barnes, in preparation). Under these conditions, animal production systems need to be flexible and mobile to pursue opportunistic grazing strategies. It is estimated that there are currently 24 wildlife conservancies, covering 4 million hectares of land, with sizes ranging from 65,000ha to 387,000ha. Unfortunately, many of these conservancies still have significant amounts of internal fencing that restricts the movement of some species such as rhino and may well result in overgrazing and inbreeding problems.

The policy and legislative changes for the management of wildlife in Namibia were developed in close cooperation with the Zimbabwean authorities (Child, 1995). After the Wild Life Conservation Act (1960), Zimbabwe initiated a system whereby farmers wishing to use their wildlife could apply for a permit. Initially, the Department of Wildlife insisted on undertaking a survey, although the demand for permits and surveys soon exceeded their capacity to do them. User rights over nearly all species were transferred to all large-scale commercial farmers under the 1975 Parks and Wild Life Act (Child, 1995). The Act designated the landholder as the 'Appropriate Authority' for wildlife, with significant proprietorship and fewer conditions than in Namibia. In Zimbabwe, the government opted to manage wildlife through the existing farmers' organizations and institutions, rather than using fences as in Namibia. Thus, the spirit of the Act was that 'most species are best protected by landholders and landholders communities' (Child, 1995). As introduced above, the role of landholder communities was interesting and crucial. Compliance was achieved largely through ICA committees which, comprising local farmers, were mandated to monitor and discipline farmers that neglected or abused their land and natural resources. For wildlife, they were empowered to mediate in disputes between landholders, and if necessary to set quotas and impose restrictions on use (quotas were not mandatory, and were only imposed where this was deemed necessary). This co-management mechanism, essentially a precursor of the current conservancy approach, was highly successful and widely respected by the farmers and authorities alike (Child, 2001). There is no doubt that the strength of the 1975 Wildlife Act contributed to the success of wildlife as a land use in Zimbabwe. Crucially, and unlike Namibia, it did not require investments in fencing or surveys for a landholder to start managing and using wildlife. Consequently, many wildlife enterprises were initiated using rather depleted existing populations, building both the enterprise and the resource incrementally.[8]

There is very little published about the legislative background that allowed the emergence of the massive private wildlife sector in South Africa. In some areas, certainly, fencing was a requirement as in Namibia. Wildlife legislation for landholdings is set at a provincial level and is therefore variable, but we can find little evidence of proactive legislation. It may well be that the commercial impetus for wildlife set in place a sector that was well ahead of legislative mechanisms, which is not unusual in natural resource management (see Chapter 4).

We have already pointed to the importance of a combination of private land and wildlife use rights. However, what is less recognized is the presence of a regulatory environment that provides for both industry coordination and collective action without imposing burdensome requirements. Also vital is the presence of a large, viable and innovative commercial sector to drive change and product development. The cornerstone of this approach is the transfer of control of wildlife from a few techno-bureaucrats to many independent and experimenting landholders.

This implies a major shift in the role of government, which instead of actively managing all wildlife, is responsible for providing a regulatory and institutional framework. This framework should encourage and create incentives for wildlife enterprises but should also control abuse. A common objective must be to keep the transaction costs imposed by such a system as low as possible. In Zimbabwe, we have already mentioned the importance of ICAs and conservancies. However, the Zimbabwean wildlife authorities also set about giving the authority for sectors such as hunting, crocodile or ostrich farming to industry associations, thereby encouraging and empowering self-regulation wherever possible. In several cases, these associations also pooled resources for technological development and marketing

(Bond and Cumming, in preparation). Thus, the rapid growth in Zimbabwe's hunting and tourism sectors was in no small part due to the highly professional training and standards mechanisms established for guides and professional hunters.

The alternative model is for total control by government. Although the free market may be far from perfect, there are probably more dangers in centralizing control in under-funded bureaucracies where accountability and transparency can be problematic (see Chabal and Daloz, 1999). This is well illustrated by comparing hunting in southern Africa with that in Zambia, where the whole sector was tightly controlled by the political and bureaucratic leadership in collusion with a closed and uncompetitive private sector (Dalal-Clayton and Child, 2003). The conditions for successful wildlife enterprises are very similar to those for any other enterprise. First, government should restrict itself to providing a regulatory framework for companies and individuals. Where possible, standards and self-regulation should be encouraged by professional member organizations. Second, opportunities to use wildlife resources for consumptive and non-consumptive purposes should be allocated through free markets (Child, 2001). Bureaucratic methods of allocating wildlife opportunities lead to accusations of corruption and invariably mean that the land manager, whether commercial, communal or state, does not receive the free market price of the resource. They also drastically reduce the value of wildlife. This does not only apply to the landholder concerned, but to a country as a whole because the subsidization of tourism or hunting by the state sector, for example, undercuts the price of these resources. Thus, the conventional policy of providing cheap accommodation in national parks drives down the price of tourism generally and reduces the likelihood of landholders in the buffer zones around the parks switching to wildlife.

The importance of the policy and legislative framework created by the Namibian and the Zimbabwean governments for the management of wildlife on private land cannot be underestimated. In both countries, legislators appreciated that the decline of the wildlife numbers and area of wildlife habitat outside the protected areas was due to the absence of proprietorship and incentives for its management. In both countries there was considerable scepticism that the policy changes would indeed work. In effect, wildlife production was being liberalized in a social and economic environment that was characterized by a high degree of control by government.

RISK, AND THE STATUS OF MARKETS FOR WILDLIFE PRODUCTS

It is important to note that the policy and legislative changes discussed above were necessary but not sufficient for landholders to start investing and managing wildlife. For wildlife to become a viable land use it was essential that there were markets for the wildlife goods and services produced by private landholders. Thus, although less directly dependent on primary rangeland production than livestock, it has been that argued that wildlife producers are highly exposed to another exogenous variable, namely the vagaries of the market for wildlife products (Barrett and Arcese, 1995).[9] Wildlife-based tourism, which encompasses both international trophy hunting and photographic tourism, is a luxury product with a high-income elasticity. This means that a decline in real incomes in the consumer (mostly Organization for Economic Cooperation and Development; OECD) countries will result in a fall in demand. Conversely, rising incomes, as is the case, is likely to increase demand.

The status and the future of wildlife markets has always been a critical variable for private sector and communal wildlife producers with their need for profitability and incentives respectively (Bond, 2001). It will also become an increasingly important variable for the managers of state-protected areas as a result of commercialization (Chapter 8). Unlike their colleagues in state-protected areas, producers of private and communal wildlife also need to be aware of the market prices of products from competing land uses, and they will switch between uses according to the incentives they face.

At the global level, it has been argued that rangelands of southern and eastern Africa have an absolute comparative advantage in the production of unique, charismatic fauna. No other ecosystem in the world supports the diversity and numbers of mammals that are found here (Skinner and Smithers, 1990). Importantly, the nature and the structure of these ecosystems means that these animals are highly visible to tourists, unlike the spectacular but rarely seen fauna of the rainforests of central Africa, or Central and South America. Wildlife producers are also fortunate in the diversity of uses of wildlife. Although international trophy hunting and tourism are the primary products of wildlife producers, there are markets for meat, live animals and other animal products (Bothma, 2002a).

International trophy hunting has been the market entry point for many commercial wildlife producers in Namibia, South Africa and Zimbabwe. Counter-intuitively, this has proved to be an ideal use of depleted wildlife populations. First, this is because hunters focus on the quality of the individual trophy rather than the diversity, numbers or the photographic opportunities required by tourists, so relatively small populations can be used effectively (Child, 2001). Second, it allows populations to recover rapidly because only males are taken, and offtake rates average 2 per cent compared with population growth rates of about 10 per cent for the large species and more for animals like warthog and impala. Third, the capital costs required to develop and support a hunting enterprise are usually substantially lower than for tourism (Barnes, 1998). Fourth, based on the evidence from Zimbabwe, the market and price for trophy hunting are increasing steadily (Figure 3.2). Importantly, this market is robust even in the face of, for instance, Zimbabwe's civil strife, as trophy hunters are less risk averse than tourists (Muir and Bojo, 1994). The effect of the current political instability in Zimbabwe shows that the gross value of the industry declined by only 10 per cent in 2000 compared with the 75 per cent fall in gross revenue from tourism (Booth et al, in preparation).

At national levels, data for trophy hunting for private land are rarely disaggregated from other hunting, or from the wildlife sector, so the exact economic contribution of trophy hunting to the southern African economies is unclear. However, the overall impression of the market for international trophy hunting is one of increasing demand over time. The national market shares of the hunting market are interesting. South Africa commands the highest share of the market, with annual earnings in 2000 of over US$50 million. Unlike the other four countries in the region, this revenue is entirely earned from hunting on private land. In contrast, only between 20 and 30 per cent of the total revenue earned in Zimbabwe can be directly attributed to international trophy hunting on private land (Bond, 1992). The balance is derived from the communal and state sectors.

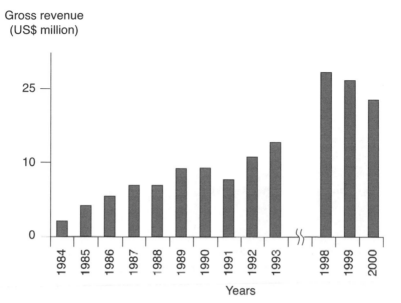

Figure 3.2 *Changes in gross hunting revenue, Zimbabwe 1985–2000*

Successful wildlife-based (non-consumptive) tourism requires, among other conditions, that the destination has either exotic or photographic appeal (Murphree, 2001). In addition, the entry of wildlife producers into this market required much higher levels of capital investment (Barnes, 1998). The analysis of this market is also severely constrained by limited information. Statistics on tourism entry are generally disaggregated by activity (namely business, visitor, health, education, other) and not spatially referenced. Of the countries covered by this analysis, South Africa receives the highest number of tourists annually followed by Zimbabwe (Table 3.3). More significantly, the data suggest that tourism numbers rose significantly between 1990 and 1998. Qualitative analysis of the tourism arrivals suggests that at least 70 per cent of international tourists[10] have been attracted by the region's unique and accessible wildlife (Krug, 2001). Private landholders across the region have proved to be extremely adept at providing innovative activities and products that meet and develop the diverse demand of the tourist market. Consequently, the range of tourist activities in southern Africa is far wider than exists in East Africa, where the wildlife sector is heavily dependent on access to state-protected areas, albeit having spectacular wildlife opportunities. This flexibility is a product of the entrepreneurship that is characteristic of the private sector and the absence or reduction in the regulation governing the tourists' interaction with wildlife.

The limited data available appear to indicate that there is strong and growing demand for wildlife-based tourism products at national and regional levels. Tourism in particular has a high income elasticity of demand. This means that it is sensitive to changes in income in the consumer countries. International tourists visiting the region are primarily from high-income OECD countries. These markets are also particularly risk averse, and are highly sensitive to insecurity. There are multiple

Table 3.2 *Changes in the gross value (US$ millions) of international trophy hunting in Botswana, South Africa, Nambia, Zambia and Zimbabwe*

Country	1985	1995	1996	1997	1998	1999	2000
Botswana	—	—	—	—	—	—	1.5
South Africa	—	—	25.4	33.0	28.8	38.4	53.0
Namibia	—	—	—	—	—	—	20.1
Zambia	—	—	—	—	—	4.0	—
Zimbabwe	—	—	—	—	22.0	21	18.5

— no data available

Sources: Botswana Wildlife Management Association (BWMA) (2001), Anderson (2003), Booth et al (2003), Humavindu and Barnes (2003)

sources and levels of risk. For example, the political insecurity at the country level (namely Zimbabwe or northern Namibia) can easily cause the complete collapse of the tourism sector in that country. Another source or level of risk results from the insecurity caused by the perceived threat of international terrorism or regional conflicts. A third level or source of risk, recently experienced, was the severe acute respiratory syndrome (SARS) virus, which substantially reduced international air travel and tourism.

The significance of the substantial and unique domestic tourist market in South Africa is important to wildlife producers. The domestic tourism market acts as a buffer and reduces the risk to the wildlife producer of changes in the external market due to international conflict or disease or both. In the other countries, the local demand for wildlife tourism on private land is generally limited to the wealthy elite and the expatriate community.

Commercial wildlife producers in South Africa and to a limited extent Namibia have the added advantage of domestic markets for meat, live animals and 'biltong hunting'. The expansion of the wildlife sector in South Africa has created a vibrant market for live animal sales. An indicator of the value of this market is the gross turnover of auctions of live animals. It has been estimated that these expanded from R17 million in 1991 to R81 million in 2001, an average annual increase of nearly 19 per cent (Amalgamated Banks of South Africa (ABSA), 2002), and that auctions only account for a third of the total live sales. Thus, the total gross value of this market to the wildlife producer is estimated to be roughly R180–R200 million annually (Anderson, 2003). These subsidiary and domestic markets are important, both for increasing revenues and particularly for improving the robustness of wildlife enterprises. They allow commercial wildlife producers to diversify farm income and lower the risk from focusing on a single market such as international trophy hunting.

Notwithstanding the limits on the available information, the markets for wildlife products appear to be strong and possibly strengthening. There will be short-term fluctuations in demand caused by perceptions of personal safety, macro-economic performance in the OECD countries that constitute most of the demand for wildlife, and the strength of the currencies, particularly the rand. As noted, wildlife producers in South Africa, and to a lesser extent in Namibia and (formerly) Zimbabwe, have the distinct advantage of a substantial domestic market for their products,

Table 3.3 *Numbers of tourists arriving in Botswana, Namibia, South Africa, Zambia and Zimbabwe between 1990 and 1998*

Country	1990	1991	1992	1993	1994	1995	1996	1997	1998
Botswana	543	592	590	607	625	644	707	734	740
Namibia	—	213	234	255	326	399	405	502	560
South Africa	1029	1710	2703	3093	3669	4488	4944	5653	5898
Zambia	141	171	159	157	141	163	264	341	362
Zimbabwe	605	667	738 951	1105	1529	1743	1495	2090	

— no data available

Source: modified from World Bank (2000)

which diversifies markets and reduces the risk of focusing on a single product or market. The highly developed infrastructure and communications network of these countries is also a significant advantage to wildlife producers. Analyses of the emerging commercial wildlife producers in Botswana and Zambia, for example, note that poor infrastructure and communications are one of many constraints (Hachileka, in preparation). So far, southern Africa has withstood the impact of instability in the Middle East, the 'war on terror' and the SARS outbreak, but not of domestic strife (namely Zimbabwe). Despite the strengthening of demand, wildlife producers nevertheless will face changes in the market for wildlife products, and the importance of having commercial producers and a large private sector is that they are invariably at the forefront of understanding and responding to these changes.

THE IMPACT OF PRIVATE WILDLIFE UTILIZATION

This section investigates the impact of the wildlife as a land use on private land. As previously noted, there is little information on the private land wildlife producers in all three countries. Even more significant is the absence of methodologically rigorous studies that examine the ecological and economic impacts of the massive changes in land use. Casual observation suggests that the adoption of wildlife as a land use has had substantial ecological advantages. Similarly, the limited evidence that exists shows that the overall economic benefits are substantive.

Impact on Biodiversity and the Ecological Status of Commercial Land

There are few comprehensive data measuring the impact of the switch from livestock to wildlife on ecological condition. One detailed study of Buffalo Range Ranch in Zimbabwe showed range conditions declining under cattle and improving under wildlife (Taylor, 1974; Child, 1988), a relation that personal observations suggest pertains widely (Krug, 2001). We therefore take as our starting point a positive relation between land used for wildlife and the conservation of biodiversity, while noting, however, that wildlife production systems do not guarantee the maintenance of ecological process. The mismanagement of wildlife populations can lead to very similar ecological consequences as the overstocking of domestic, single-species productions systems. This is particularly relevant where game fencing is used and landholding size is small. In some areas the introduction of exotic non-native species, such as blesbok and nyala to Namibia, may have detracted from the positive conservation value of wildlife ranching.

In general, the correlation between wildlife production and improving ecological status appears to be supported. An increase in the diversity of mammal species is associated with wildlife production systems in both Namibia and Zimbabwe (Child, 1988; Barnes and Jones, in preparation). In southern Zimbabwe, obligate grazers (in other words sensitive grazers that like longer grass) like sable, roan and hartebeeste were eliminated from large areas by cattle pressure, but are now common on conservancies. In Namibia it is estimated that:

- Approximately 18–24 per cent of the commercial land is used for wildlife production properties (Krug, 2001). There are over 400 registered commercial hunting properties (Barnes and Jones, in preparation).
- Between 1972 and 1992, the number of wild animals on commercial land increased from 700,000 to nearly 1.2 million (Jones and Barnes, in preparation).
- There are 24 conservancies covering close to 4 million hectares compared with approximately 12 conservancies covering 2 million hectares in 1998.

In South Africa it is estimated that:

- There are approximately 5 million hectares of land under commercial wildlife production, which represents 8.5 per cent of the country.
- The number of commercial wildlife producers has increased from 10 in the 1960s to approximately 5000 in 2000 (van Hoven and Zietsman, 1998, quoted in Anderson, 2003).
- Between 1993 and 2000 the number of wildlife producers increased at an annual rate of nearly 7 per cent (Anderson, 2003).
- The largest number of commercial wildlife ranchers is in Limpopo Province (2482), whereas the largest area of land under commercial wildlife production is in the northern Cape (4.8 million hectares) (Anderson, 2003).

In Zimbabwe, before the current intensive phase of the resettlement programme, it was estimated that:

- The area under wildlife production had risen from approximately 35,000ha in 1960 to 2.7 million hectares in 2000, representing nearly 7 per cent of the country.
- Of the approximately 4000 commercial farmers, 1200 were actively engaged in wildlife production.
- There were at least three large conservancies (Save Valley, 326,000ha; Chiredzi River, 80,000ha; Bubianna, 127,000ha) for the management of wildlife, which indicates its scale and importance.
- Hunting offtake data suggest that wildlife populations quadrupled between 1984 and 2000 (Booth et al, in preparation).

These points highlight the current status and assumed ecological contribution of commercial wildlife production. Importantly, the figures also convey the rapid growth in the of commercial wildlife production, especially over the past decade. In each of the countries commercial wildlife production adds significantly to the area of land under wildlife management

Economic Performance of Commercial Wildlife Production Systems

The same, if not worse, methodological problems apply to estimates of the value and contribution to the economy of commercial wildlife production across the region.

In Namibia it is estimated that:

- The total net value added because of wildlife between 1972 and 1992 rose from N$22 million–N$41 million (see Note 11).
- Commercial wildlife production contributes 24 per cent of the total net value added from all wildlife based activities (excluding marine resources).
- The market price of land with wildlife has increased at a greater rate in real terms than agricultural land without wildlife (Krug, 2000).

In South Africa it is estimated that:

- The total gross value added for the commercial wildlife sector, excluding non-financial values, is approximately SAR1.4 billion (see Note 12) per annum.
- The value of the commercial wildlife sector has doubled in the past few years, and is growing at about 7 per cent per annum, although some of this is an arte-fact of improved data and analysis.
- The total number of people employed by the commercial wildlife sector is approximately 45,000.

In Zimbabwe, before the current intensive phase of the resettlement programme, it was estimated that:

- Wildlife enterprises were more likely to be financially viable than livestock production systems, but there were profitable, marginally profitable and unprofitable examples of both (Bond, 1993).
- Wildlife populations, and the size of the wildlife-based tourism industry, approximately quadrupled between 1990 and 2000 (Booth et al, 2003).

These key points show the significance and growth of the economic contribution of the commercial wildlife sector to southern African economies. In Namibia, commercial wildlife production is an important and growing land use, especially with the current trend towards the formation of conservancies. Importantly, the data justify the contention that wildlife is more likely to be more profitable than livestock production. It should not, however, be interpreted that livestock production is never viable and that wildlife production is always the more viable option. At the level of the farm, there are many variables that affect viability of an enterprise: these include its location, size, the adjacent land uses as well as the skills of the owner (Bond, 1993). One of the major reasons that Namibian farmers were managing and using wildlife was that it was a means of diversification to reduce risk (Ashley and Barnes, 1997). Typically, risk-averse farmers will start to manage and use wildlife, often through international trophy hunting, in conjunction with livestock. As they become familiar with a new set of skills and activities, they devote more and more land to wildlife. From a perspective of cash flow, this incremental approach is very sound, as the switch from livestock to wildlife can reduce cash flow for up to a decade as wildlife populations recover. The contrast is provided by the owners of the properties in the Save Valley Conservancy who all had sources of income from other agricultural enterprises to buffer them during the lengthy transition from a domestic to a wildlife production system.

Contribution to Conservation by the Commercial Farming Sector

This section has sought to document the ecological and economic impact of wildlife production on private land in South Africa, Namibia and Zimbabwe. It has highlighted the ecological and economic performance of wildlife as a land use in the commercial farming sector. The absence of data often means that the sector's critical role in the process of conserving the region's biodiversity is not fully represented. First, it was through the experiment of devolving proprietorship over wildlife that moved conservation away from the protectionist paradigms derived from the post-frontier phase wildlife laws to concepts of devolved management and sustainable use. Second, without the positive example of commercial wildlife production, it is very unlikely that the second stage of the process would have been initiated, whereby some rights over wildlife and natural resources have been devolved to communal landholders in the region (see Hulme and Murphree, 2001). Third, commercial farmers are providing innovative solutions to the management of semi-arid rangelands through the formation of large-scale conservancies that require the cooperation of different landholders and stakeholders. These models are especially important given the recent moves towards the management of natural resources, especially wildlife, across boundaries, to form transfrontier conservation areas (TFCAs). Fourth, political and economic forces are making commercial farmers look outside their boundaries to actively engage with their neighbours. This is leading to creative solutions to problems of equity and economic development. An example is Save Valley Conservancy, which has proposed the formation of a trust that includes their immediate communal neighbours, such that they can own wildlife within the conservancy which yields an annual dividend (du Toit, 1999). These are vital models and experiments for the state-protected areas, which are much more conservative and introspective than the commercial sector. The freedom that commercial wildlife producers enjoy is a valuable asset in the exploration of new opportunities in wildlife-based tourism. Fifth, some private sector operations provide a benchmark for state-protected areas, thus challenging them to improve performance. Sixth, the success of southern Africa provides a global example in a sector in which experimentation is rare and could be well emulated elsewhere in the world: for example, in the US there are large tracts of private land with considerable wildlife potential.

The contribution of commercial wildlife producers to conservation in southern Africa is therefore much greater than the sum of the economic and ecological performance indicators. The commercial sector has been a powerful force in the process of managing and conserving wildlife and wildlife habitat in the region, and in developing and testing a new conservation paradigm based on the principles of proprietorship, commercialization and subsidiarity. This paradigm states that if wildlife is valuable (commercialization), if this value is captured by the landholder (proprietorship), and if control is not arrogated upwards except by choice (subsidiarity), then there is a high likelihood that wildlife will prosper. Thus, the spirit of the southern Africa conservation movement is that the primary beneficiary from wildlife should be the landholder. To maintain its role and leadership, however, the region will have to address its own weaknesses, particularly those arising from the highly skewed ownership of land in the context of a population facing extreme poverty and land shortages.

CHALLENGES FACING COMMERCIAL WILDLIFE PRODUCERS IN SOUTHERN AFRICA

The previous sections of this chapter have provided some background information on wildlife as a land use and have reviewed the impact or performance of commercial wildlife producers. As discussed, the sector makes a highly significant contribution to the process of wildlife management, the conservation of wildlife habitat, and biodiversity. We now turn to the threats to this success, the most important being the region-wide issue of skewed ownership of land and commerce by racial groups, although there are subsidiary issues of markets and management are discussed.

Land Distribution and Racial Equality

Reviews of commercial wildlife production typically focus on its ecological and economic performance (Hill, 1994) and only deal peripherally with the critical issue of racially equitable distribution of land (see Bothma, 2002). The commercial sector has undoubtedly made a substantial contribution to the conservation of wildlife and has the potential to do so in the future. In addition, it has clearly contributed to the growth of wildlife-based tourism in each of the countries by increasing the supply, diversifying the product and creating new and better employment opportunities. Racial equality in the distribution of land (and business), however, is a critical issue in the entire region. In Zimbabwe, the current land redistribution process is relatively advanced. The politics driving the process overshadow any economic and ecological considerations, which means that many of the opportunities for wildlife-based land reform have been lost. Like Zimbabwe, South Africa and Namibia are characterized by highly skewed land distribution patterns (see Table 3.1). The conservation communities and the commercial wildlife producers would be wise to analyse the lessons learned in Zimbabwe and apply proactive solutions. Failure to do so will mean that the valuable contribution of the sector will remain politically vulnerable.

An insightful analysis (Hill, 1994) of Zimbabwe's commercial wildlife sector posed three important questions, namely: what was the realized and potential economic role of wildlife; what were the political implications of wildlife ranching; and will economic efficiency or political considerations ultimately prevail in the future of the industry? Given the current changes that are taking place in Zimbabwean commercial farming sector,[13] this analysis and its results must be considered in the wider southern African context, where redistribution and restitution invariably eclipse arguments about economic efficiency and growth. In terms of its economic contribution, the analysis concludes that the commercial wildlife sector played an important role in the development of tourism as the third largest foreign currency earner. It also concludes that the sector had at a macro-level played a very important role in the maintenance and conservation of biodiversity.

In answering the second question, the analysis considers the political legitimacy of wildlife production. It notes that the liberation movements that form Zimbabwe's current government opposed the entire wildlife sector. It also charts the development of the relationship between the government and the Commercial Farmers Union (CFU).[14] For the political legitimacy, the analysis identifies the emerging conflicts between the economic rationale for wildlife production and the political imperatives for land redistribution. In its early stages the government policy signals were mostly couched as veiled threats to farmers that they should not jeopardize national food security. An ominous warning was sounded by Minister of Finance Herbert Murerwa in June 1993, who noted, '... And to put it bluntly, most of this income ends up in the bank accounts of whites. This is now a political problem. I am expected to alter the situation. I must shift the balance. But it is far from easy' (Hill, 1994). The reaction of the commercial landowners to these and other threats was interesting. There was a deep philosophical divide between those who felt that it was unwise to engage in wildlife production as it would expose them to a higher risk of designation for resettlement. The other, larger group felt that wildlife production would be a buffer against resettlement as they could demonstrate a substantial economic contribution. Implicitly, this group also felt that international pressure from global conservation organizations would also provide a safety net. Hill's analysis concluded that wildlife production was actually detrimental to farm security and raised the potential of resettlement. The scale of the current land reform makes it difficult to ascertain whether this has materialized or not. It is, however, interesting to note that the Save Valley Conservancy has been able to legitimately engage with the government with one voice. This, its innovative approach to its communal land neighbours, plus the presence of many black rhino, have apparently allowed the Conservancy up to this point to avoid large-scale resettlement. It remains one of the largest contiguous blocks of commercial farmland in the country.

In answer to the final question posed in the analysis, namely 'will economic efficiency or political considerations ultimately prevail in the future of the industry?', the response is unequivocal and eerily accurate. Hill proposed that the commercial farmers would 'be frozen out' and that despite their economic contribution and ecological gains, commercial wildlife production would succumb to the political imperative of land redistribution. In July 2000, the government of Zimbabwe started the second phase of its 'Fast Track Resettlement Scheme'. The aim of the programme was to resettle 160,000 families on 9 million hectares of land by December 2001. A further objective was introduced: the creation of 51,000 small- to medium-sized indigenous farms.[15] The severe social, political and economic disruption that has been created primarily by the resettlement programme means that there is little accurate analysis with which to assess its performance. There is, however, extensive anecdotal evidence to suggest that wildlife production systems have not been a buffer to resettlement. More importantly, however, is that the speed of the reform, the absence of technical advice and the general erosion of property rights have resulted in the extensive loss of wildlife and wildlife habitat. Wildlife did not suffer alone, as a highly viable commercial agricultural sector was all but destroyed.

Within southern Africa as a whole, 70 per cent of the population lives in the rural or communal areas. It is estimated that over 70 million people live in extreme poverty. Land and tenure reform is a region-wide issue and is not only confined to the three countries that form the focus of this study. Failure to address the issue of land redistribution and restitution in South Africa and Namibia is potentially a serious threat to regional stability. In other countries in the region such as Mozambique, Malawi, Zambia and to a limited extent Botswana, land tenure reform is essential for economic growth. In South Africa, the land reform programme has three elements: redistribution, restitution and tenure reform. The redistribution component comprises the transfer of white commercial farmland to black Africans, whereas the restitution encompasses settling claims for land lost under apartheid. Within the wildlife sector, the Makuleke Land Claim in the north of Kruger National Park is a good example, and shows that with innovation land can be returned to its former owners while simultaneously pursuing economically based conservation objectives (see Chapter 7). Finally, and equally important, is the element of land tenure reform within the former 'bantustans' or homelands. This is significant because across the region the politically and racially charged redistribution tends to overshadow the critical issue of land and natural resource management in the communal lands. Land redistribution and a racially equitable solution to the land problem do not solve the problems of land and natural resource management that exist in many of the communal lands in most southern African countries (Rukuni, 1994). These have their roots in the absence of clear property rights. CBNRM programmes are perceived as offering potential solutions; indeed, because they have been able to use wildlife to fiscally empower grass-roots communities, they offer one of the few real examples of devolved governance on the continent. In brief, there is evidence that with community proprietorship at village level, rural communities appear able to manage wildlife enterprises (often with private-sector partners), mimicking as a 'village company' the situation pertaining to private conservation areas. This solution favours areas where there is a relative abundance of natural resources (especially wildlife) and low human population densities (Bond, 2001). The breakdown of proprietorship and resource management within areas of high population pressure and relatively low levels of natural resource is characterized by appropriation or privatization of land and resources by wealthy or ruling elites. Failure to deal with tenure within communal lands will compromise the stability and the conditions necessary for economic development, and indeed for the management of wildlife in areas where it has a comparative advantage as sensible land use succumbs to an open-access scramble to extract resources.

The formal land redistribution programmes in Namibia, South Africa and Zimbabwe (1980–2000) have generally been characterized by very slow rates of implementation. The slow pace of implementation does not alleviate the problems but does provide opportunities for reflection and innovation. There are two sets of problems associated with the redistribution of commercial land that is currently under wildlife production. The first are purely practical and pertain to the general lack of expertise and resources that have been made available to support the redistribution of land. The experience gained from the implementation of CBNRM programmes highlights the need for, among others, substantial financial resources to support transaction costs, capacity building and organizational development, extended timescales to allow for process, as well as committed, skilled facilitators (see Chapter 4). In general, the major land redistribution programmes have not had sufficient resources for the supporting agro-pastoral production systems, let alone the complexity of implementing wildlife as a primary land use. If the substantial economic and ecological gains of the commercial sector are to be secured, the extended conservation community needs to be looking at investments similar to or greater than those that have been invested in the CBNRM programmes in the region. The second set of problems concerns the potential models that might be appropriate for testing and implementation. One of the key variables for these models is proprietorship. This can be represented in a continuum from models of partnership with the current land owners to models where the new land managers or owners of the land have total proprietorship.

Resettlement with wildlife as a primary land use requires governments to think seriously about tenure on resettled land. A critical limitation of early Zimbabwean resettlement models, which mitigated against land and natural resource management as well as settler investment, was the lack of proprietorship over land and natural resources: the tenurial conditions that allowed the deterioration of communal land were simply transferred to newly acquired private land. It has been argued that the first generation of CBNRM programmes in the region have been constrained by 'aborted devolution' (Chapter 4). This means that governments have been unwilling to devolve the necessary levels of proprietorship to wildlife producer communities to allow them to fully adopt wildlife as a primary landuse option. A necessary but insufficient condition for successful wildlife-based resettlement is that levels of proprietorship equal to or greater than those currently enjoyed by commercial farmers are granted to the new owners of the land.

Another challenge for the development of resettlement models based on wildlife is to deal with the issue of habitat fragmentation. Over the past 50–60 years, the commercial farming sector throughout the region has seen a consolidation or amalgamation of production units to achieve economies of scale. Latterly, this has been represented by the formation of conservancies in the wildlife sector. The long-term trends of consolidation are in direct conflict with the political aims that require as many people to be resettled as possible. Thus, a challenge to wildlife-based resettlement will be how to avoid the disruption of wildlife production and the loss of wilderness quality through habitat fragmentation. Theoretically, it is possible to scale up from many small landholders to achieve the same results, but the organizational challenges are large.

The development of innovative and creative models drawing on the experiences of other countries and the extensive lessons learned from the CBNRM experience is an urgent and necessary first step if resolution of the equity problem is not going to create a growing economic predicament. The approach needs to engage all the stakeholders, from landowners to international development agencies. Governments in particular need to clarify their positions with respect to wildlife as a primary landuse option and the levels of proprietorship that they are willing to consider. Defining the legitimacy of wildlife as a land use is important. Experience from the commercial and communal resettlement programmes in Zimbabwe has shown that many government officials still consider land allocated to wildlife to be under-used (Hill, 1994). Despite the progress achieved by devolving rights to wildlife, there remains a powerful legacy, at least among officials, that wildlife is somehow different from other natural resources and should be owned by the state. It can hardly be coincidental that centralized ownership gives officials, and the politicians they serve, power to control access to wildlife that is not always used for the greater good (Gibson, 2000).

It is also incumbent upon the international donor, and development and conservation communities, to be more proactive in their attitudes to commercial landholders. Too often it appears that these stakeholders shy away from engaging with the commercial farming sector for political reasons. The paucity of real data describing this remarkable conservation success story is but one consequence of this. The preceding analysis implies that the maintenance and potential expansion of the conservation gains of the past 20 years now require these agencies to engage immediately with the commercial sector on these issues. It is important for all stakeholders to experiment with shifting ownership from a single landholder to a community or multiple owners, while maintaining the fundamental property rights that facilitated wildlife as a land use. These experiments will provide tangible models for government policy makers and legislators to observe the performance of wildlife as a land use under resettlement. Proactive involvement and investment in economically efficient land reform, by the international donor, development and conservation communities, might help in reducing the destructive elements in land redistribution, which have been prevalent in Zimbabwe. This is a good place to test and develop the concept of private-community ownership (Rukuni, 1994). If this works, and given the power of demonstration pilots to influence policy, it has massive implications for land tenure reform in southern Africa's vast areas of communal land.

Markets

We have already noted that at the moment there is a strong and improving demand for wildlife activities, including international trophy hunting and tourism, despite short-term challenges caused by international conflicts, national political uncertainty, changes in exchange rates, and fluctuations in economic performance within the major consumer countries.

For wildlife producers in the commercial sector, markets are a critical long-term variable. The role of the market is also a primary source of concern to conservationists who oppose commercialization of natural resources. For commercial land managers in a free-market environment, the choice of production system will depend on the relative viability of alternative land uses. The area under wildlife management has increased because of the higher returns on investment compared with competing uses. Similarly, a change in relative prices may see other land-use systems becoming more attractive and possibly eroding the benefits to biodiversity. As noted, wildlife production systems provide the land manager with a choice of options, some of which may be less compatible than others. Of the options that a wildlife production system provides, the greatest uncertainty must pertain to the international trophy hunting,[16] at least in the long term.[17] As more people in the wealthier economies move away from the land and into highly urbanized, industrial societies, they become less tolerant of consumptive forms of wildlife use, especially when undertaken as a sport.

Social pressure may therefore, in the long term, reduce the demand for international trophy hunting, notwithstanding the powerful links between hunting and the maintenance and conservation of wildlife and wildlife habitat. It must be stressed that at the moment there is very little evidence to suggest that this might happen. Indeed, all the evidence suggests that markets for trophy hunting, particularly in the US and mainland Europe, are strengthening, and prices have been improving for at least four decades. However, we might speculate that part of the reason for southern Africa's increasing prices was the closure of hunting markets (eg Kenya), the loss of wildlife (eg much of West Africa), or the loss of hunting access (eg Sudan) to other African countries. Should these countries replicate the conditions of southern Africa, one argument is that prices would drop. Alternatively, African hunting represents a small proportion of the world hunting market. The impact of increased supply impact on prices would be negligible: at least 7 million people hunt regularly in the US compared with a total of some 2000 international clients to Zimbabwe, which at one time comprised almost a quarter of Africa's market.

Another possibility is that tastes in the consumer countries will change. Increasingly, there is a demand for adventure-based tourism activities, challenging wildlife businesses to diversify their product. So far, most wildlife-based tourism has been very sedentary, namely 'game viewing from a vehicle', especially in countries where the market is dominated by the less adaptable state sector (eg Kenya). As the numbers of tourists from the OECD countries visiting Zimbabwe increased, the average number of nights that they stayed in the country decreased. One of the responses from the tourism sector was to diversify the tourism product by introducing walking, night drives, better-quality guiding, improved cuisine, cultural products and adventure activities (such as canoeing, rafting, ballooning, bungee jumping). The greater flexibility that tourism operators have on commercial land compared with state-protected areas provides an opportunity to diversify and experiment with wildlife products to increase the tourists' level of 'activity' and thereby raise the average length of each visitor's stay.

Land and Wildlife Management in the Commercial Sector

The issue of management and management skills was highlighted as one of the key factors influencing the profitability of wildlife production units in Zimbabwe (Bond, 1993). As with the issue of land redistribution, the skills of private landholders are seldom discussed in the context of commercial wildlife production. Similarly, the price–proprietorship–subsidiarity paradigm that is central to this book implicitly assumes that the management skills exist at the lower level, to allow the landholder to exercise full proprietorship. The paradox is that the empirical performance and growth of the commercial wildlife sector, first in Zimbabwe and latterly in South Africa and Namibia, do not immediately imply that management is a key constraint. Historically, the success of southern Africa's commercial agricultural sector was built on the experience of decades of government-funded technological development, something that the recently emerging wildlife sector does not have. The skills that are required to manage wildlife and wildlife enterprises are quite different to the skills required to manage traditional agricultural activities. Some range management and animal husbandry skills are directly transferable from agriculture to wildlife. However, the critical skills for a commercial wildlife operation, such as hospitality, guiding, institutional development and negotiation (eg in dealing with politics or neighbours, or in scaling up towards conservancies), are highly specialized. It has been noted that wildlife ranching in South Africa 'is still being approached in a remarkably amateurish way...'. Moreover, this amateurism has not changed for 26 years (Bothma, 2002). Similar observations have been made for emerging commercial wildlife producers in Zambia (Hachileka, in preparation).

It is important that commercial wildlife producers become more professional, for at least two reasons. First, the commercial wildlife sectors of in Namibia and South Africa have been growing extremely rapidly, possibly as fast as 25 per cent per annum,[18] over the past 10 years, implying that the supply of wildlife recreation has increased at a similar rate. It is unlikely that either the international or domestic demand for wildlife-based recreation has increased at these rates given the global recession, international conflicts and the fear of SARS, the common figure stated being between 7 and 20 per cent. With supply increasing faster than demand, the increased competition in the market place is likely to cause some wildlife-based enterprises to fail.[19] Competition would select for improved management skills, particularly of the commercial elements of the enterprise, as they would increase the chances of survival and profitability in an increasingly challenging environment.[20]

The second rationale for improved management of wildlife enterprises relates to the primary issue that the sector needs to deal with: that of land redistribution. Land taxes, based on area, are likely to be used as an economic mechanism to release under-used land onto the market, allowing governments to purchase it for resettlement. As with the assumption of increasing market competition, it is assumed that through improved management it is possible to increase productivity, thereby allowing the owner to pay land taxes and still remain viable. More importantly, however, the development of new models for wildlife production in the commercial farming sector will require farmers to actively engage with a wide range of stakeholders. Their willingness and conduct in the process of developing, testing and ultimately implementing the collaborative models will have a direct bearing on their role and stake in a 'restructured sector'. Their long-term future stake in the sector requires that they become both more professional and more extrovert in the management of their enterprises, and to proactively engage in the political process.

One possibility to improve performance is specialization, with the landholder concentrating on producing good land and wildlife, and outsourcing the management of commercial activities to specialized operators. This has several advantages. It can reduce the direct risks to the landowners from short-term changes in the market; if properly constituted, it can also reduce their risk by reducing their direct capital investment in the commercial activities. Interestingly, the practice of separating commercial activities from land and wildlife management is a model that has been extensively used by CBNRM programmes on communal land. It has also been used, albeit to a lesser extent, by state wildlife management agencies in protected areas. Indications from these other sectors are that the landholder can expect between 30 and 40 per cent of gross revenue from international trophy hunting operations and between

10 and 15 per cent of gross revenue from tourism-based activities (see Chapter 8). Carefully applied, outsourcing can provide opportunities to reduce racial inequalities that are so characteristic of the wildlife sector across southern Africa.

CONCLUSIONS

This chapter has reviewed the evolution and impacts of wildlife production on private land in southern Africa. The narrative has focused on three countries, namely South Africa, Namibia and Zimbabwe, as these are the countries that have significant areas of private land. The results of the analysis are also applicable, however, to other countries in the region where there are small areas of private land (Botswana and Zambia) or where land tenure is in transition (Mozambique). The observed changes in land use that have occurred in the private sector have been entirely market driven, and farmers have received little or no support from the state, either technically or financially. Private landholders have demonstrated that under a range of ecological conditions (that is, from the Cape region to Zimbabwe and across to Namibia) and under different economic and political conditions, wildlife can be a financially and economically viable land use in semi-arid savannahs. Critically, and for many reasons, the success of wildlife producers on private land remains undocumented and in many respects unacknowledged. There is, however, little doubt that if it had not been for the initial success of devolved wildlife management to the private sector similar opportunities would not have been created for wildlife management in the communal lands. This would have had serious implications for the development of the entire CBNRM approach to wildlife and natural resource management that exists across all countries in the region.

Within this context, the success of wildlife as a land use in Zimbabwe is particularly instructive. The policy and legislative framework that was created by the Zimbabwean government was probably the best example of its kind. Not only did it devolve proprietorship to all private landholders, it also did so with very few conditions. Zimbabwean landholders, unlike their Namibian and some South African colleagues, were not required to submit their properties to inspection, nor were they legally obliged to invest in wildlife-proof fences. Fencing and other investments were entirely the landholders' prerogatives. Assuming that landholders are rational and well informed, it can be argued that those that did invest in fencing did so for sound financial reasons. In addition, the Zimbabwean authorities used existing farmers' organizations and their institutions to ensure that the rights that had been granted were not abused. The extensive conversion of semi-arid rangelands to wildlife production only started in the late 1980s. This change occurred some 15 years after the legislation had been passed because for wildlife to be a viable land use required two further changes. The first was the removal of the perverse direct and indirect subsidies to the cattle producers. The second was development of political and economic stability that allowed Zimbabwe to develop into a major African hunting and tourism destination.

Another innovation by private landholders in Namibia, South Africa and previously Zimbabwe was the formation of conservancies, which represents another important development initiated by private landholders. Although the nature and the extent of a conservancy vary considerably, all conservancies imply cooperation between landholders for the production and use of wildlife. Their formation is yet another innovation in a tradition of creativity from private wildlife producers in southern Africa. This culture of innovation and the lessons that can be learned from the collective nature of conservancies are important for the future of wildlife and conservation. In the more creative and enlightened conservancies, cooperation is not simply between landholders of the same race, class and background, but as in Save Valley it has begun to include small-scale landholders on the periphery.

The dual agricultural systems found in southern Africa are a legacy of colonial and apartheid policies. The redistribution of land within Namibia and South Africa is inevitable. It is imperative that the landholders and the conservation community learn the lessons from Zimbabwe where the political imperative has overridden both economic and ecological logic. The consequences for the country and in particular for wildlife as a land use have been extremely serious, with little or no formal wildlife-based resettlement being implemented. Within Zimbabwe, previous efforts to implement wildlife-based resettlement have failed because of insufficient financial and technical resources, and no political conviction that wildlife was a financially viable option for resettled farmers. If the substantive ecological and economic benefits that have been realized over the past 20 years in South Africa and Namibia are to be retained, then greater resources must be committed to developing and implementing models immediately. The development of these models must draw on the culture of innovation and creativity that has characterized many private wildlife producers so far.

Landholders also need to examine their current approaches to management. Although some wildlife ranchers are developing as 'centres of excellence', too many believe that they can maintain the 'gut instinct' approaches that have worked for the past 20 years. Changes in technology need to be evaluated for the management objectives of wildlife producers. Experimentation with creative approaches to wildlife, range management as well as innovative tourism products, is desperately needed not only for the future of private or resettlement wildlife producers but also for the state-managed sector where the capacity for innovation has stagnated.

A large proportion of southern Africa is semi-arid and arid. These areas are really only suitable for extensive systems based on animal production. The history of livestock development programmes and projects over much of Africa has been poor, with few if any tangible benefits (Dyson-Hudson, 1984; Hadley, 1985). Granting user rights to private wildlife producers was a massive gamble that has had direct and indirect benefits. Wildlife production is now a major land use, not only on private land but also on communal lands. The wildlife community has also challenged other natural resource managers to consider innovative options under the mantle of CBNRM. Substantial challenges remain across all land tenure systems. This chapter has outlined those facing the private sector and alluded to some of the problems on communal and state land. It is incumbent, however, upon a new generation of conservationists, resource managers and academics to address the future with the same, or a greater, degree of innovation.

NOTES

1   The important contribution made by three Fullbright Scholars (Dasman, Mossmann and Riney) to this change has been noted and documented by Child (1995). In addition, he notes the role of two families (Henderson and Style) in the southeast lowveldt of Zimbabwe, whose interest, understanding and willingness to experiment with wildlife production systems were critical factors influencing the policy and legal changes that occurred in Zimbabwe.

2   Within Botswana, Namibia and South Africa, a legal option for private landholders has been to declare properties as 'private game reserves'. This option has in the past been used by landowners, but typically this status restricts land and wildlife options such as trophy hunting. For example, properties that were proclaimed as private game reserves have frequently been de-proclaimed to give the owner more flexibility over resources (J Barnes, personal communication).

3   The allocation of land in Zambia is complicated by the large proportion of the country that are game management areas (GMAs). In GMAs, land and resources are managed by the state, traditional authorities and local government. In Table 4.1, the land within GMAs has been deemed state land.

4   Although commonly called 'game ranches' in southern Africa, this often gives the wrong connotation, suggesting a dominance by animal production whereas enterprises are primarily linked to recreational uses, and therefore to a demand for 'natural' environments. A more accurate definition would be to re-categorize such properties as private conservation areas, especially as many properties that we commonly call game ranches actually fulfil the requirements for a category II protected area as laid out by the International Union for the Conservation of Nature (IUCN). These properties easily fit the definition of: 'A Protected Area [*managed mainly for*] resulting in ecosystem protection and recreation', but note that we adjust the active clause from an intention to a result, namely replacing 'managed mainly for' to 'resulting in'.

5   In Namibia, fencing is required if the landowner wants to hunt certain species of wildlife.

6   Analyses of the performance of CBNRM programmes in southern Africa frequently refer to the desire of newly independent governments to extend similar rights to communal farmers as those enjoyed by commercial farmers. For those developing CBNRM policy and legislation, the performance of commercial farmers was proof of the need to give control over wildlife and wildlife habitat to communal land farmers (Chapter 4).

7   Land use in southern Africa and particularly in Botswana has been strongly influenced by agricultural subsidies from the EU. If Botswana loses preferential access to high-value markets for beef in Europe, then the viability of beef production will decline significantly (Metroeconomica Economic Consultants, 1996).

8   Many landholders did invest in some fencing, but this was by choice rather than through legislation.

9   Hutton et al (2001) also make the point that the greatest threat to the conservation gains made by the intensive production of crocodilians are from 'potential price fluctuations ... that ultimately threaten the conservation of the resource'.

10 This statistic needs to be carefully interpreted and taken to refer to tourists or visitors from outside the region. Within the region, visitor numbers have been dominated by cross-border shoppers and traders.

11 Average annual exchange rate for 1992, US$1.00 = SAR2.84 (South African rand) (source: www.oanda.com).

12 Average annual exchange rate for 2003, US$1.00 = SAR7.66 (South African rand) (source: www.oanda.com).

13 At independence in 1980, Zimbabwe inherited a dual agricultural sector in which most of the prime land was owned by landholders of European and South African descent. Before 2000, only marginal changes had been made to the status quo. In mid-2000, the government announced a fast-track resettlement policy that was characterized by often violent invasions of privately owned farms (see Chaumba et al, 2003).

14 The CFU is the body that represented nearly all the (white) commercial farmers in the country. Even after independence, it was obligatory to be a member of the CFU to get a farming licence (Hill, 1994).

15 It is commonly suggested that the real objective is for a small elite to retain power and extract much of the country's assets and savings. Furthermore, most land has been acquired by the elite, many poor black farm workers have been displaced and dumped elsewhere, while relatively little has been done to give land to poor communal farmers.

16 The potential medium- to long-term weakness of trophy hunting is also a concern for the communal sector that derives a substantial portion of its revenue from hunting across southern Africa (Bond, 2001).

17 We have already pointed out that safari hunting has proved far more robust than tourism to political instability.

18 It has been estimated that the wildlife ranching sector has been growing at approximately 25 per cent per annum during the past decade (Amalgamated Banks of South Africa (ABSA), 2002, quoted in Anderson, 2003).

19 Alternatively, the rate of growth of wildlife production may well slow as land becomes a limiting factor, whereas signs are that demand for tourism may well continue to increase at rapid rates.

20 A simple example is the issue of wildlife numbers. A large survey of commercial wildlife producers in Zimbabwe (Jansen et al, 1992) found that most farmers only had vague estimates of wildlife numbers on their land, based mainly on indices of abundance (such as trophy quality) and 'intuition'. Optimizing management with such crude estimates is difficult (it is equally likely that wildlife enterprises were either over-harvesting or under-using their resources), and although no long-term threat to viability is implied given the robustness of trophy hunting, improved knowledge of wildlife numbers would have contributed to greater long-term viability.

REFERENCES

Abel, N O J and Blaikie, P M (1990) 'Land degradation, stocking rates and conservation policies in the communal rangelands of Botswana and Zimbabwe', ODI Pastoral Development Network, Paper 29a, ODI, London

Amalgamated Banks of South Africa (ABSA) (2002) *Game Ranching Profitability in Southern Africa*, 2002 edition, The SA Financial Sector Forum

Anderson, H J (2003) 'An econometric analysis of the wildlife market in South Africa', Master's thesis, University of Cape Town

Ashley, C and Barnes, J (1997) 'Wildlife use of economic gain: The potential for wildlife to contribute to development in Namibia', Studies in Environmental Economics and Development, Environmental Economics Unit, Department of Economics, Gothenburg University

Barnes, J (1998) 'Wildlife economics: A study of direct use values in Botswana's wildlife sector', PhD thesis, University College London

Barnes, J I and de Jager, J L V (1996) 'Economic and financial incentives for wildlife use on private land in Namibia and the implications for policy', *South African Journal of Wildlife Research* 26(2): 37–46

Barnes, J I and Humavindu, M N (2003) 'Economic returns to land use options in Gondwana Cañon Park, Karas, Namibia', unpublished report, Nature Investments (Pty) Ltd, Windhoek, Namibia

Barnes, J and Jones B (in preparation) in B Child (ed) *Parks in Transition: Biodiversity, Rural Development and the Bottom Line*, vol 2, SASUSG, Pretoria

Barrett, C B and Arcese P (1995) 'Are integrated conservation-development projects (ICDPs) sustainable? On the conservation of large mammals in sub-Saharan Africa', *World Development* 23(7): 1073–84

Bell, R H V (1982) 'The effect of soil nutrient availability on community structure in African ecosystems', in B J Huntley and B H Walker (eds) *Ecology of Tropical Savannas*, Springer-Verlag, Berlin

Bond, I (1993) 'The economics of wildlife and landuse in Zimbabwe: An examination of current knowledge and issues', Project Paper No. 36, WWF Multispecies Animal Production Systems Project, Harare

Bond, I (2001) 'CAMPFIRE and the incentives for institutional change', in D Hulme and M Murphree (eds) *Community Conservation in Africa: Promises and Practice*, James Currey, Oxford, pp227–43

Booth, V R, Bond, I and Khumalo, M (in preparation) 'An analysis of trophy hunting in Zimbabwe', WWF Occasional Paper Series, WWF–SARPO, Harare

Bond, I and Cumming, D (in preparation) 'Wildlife research and development', in M Rukuni and C Eicher (eds) *Zimbabwe's Agricultural Revolution*, 2nd edition, Agricultural Research Council, Harare

Bothma, J Du P (2002a) 'Some economics of wildlife ranching', paper prepared for the Wildlife Group Symposium on Game Ranch Management, SA Veterinary Association, Onderstepoort, 1–2 November

Bothma, J du P (ed) (2002b) *Game Ranch Management*, 4th edition, Van Schaik, Pretoria

Botswana Wildlife Management Association (BWMA) (2001) 'Economic analysis of commercial consumptive use of wildlife in Botswana', final report, ULG, Northumbrian Ltd

Campbell B M, Dore, D, Luckert, M, Makamuri B and Gambiza J (2000) 'Economic comparisons of livestock production in communal grazing lands in Zimbabwe', *Ecological Economics* **33**(3) 413–38

Chabal, P and Daloz J (1999) *Africa Works. Disorder as Political Instrument*, James Currey, Oxford

Chaumba, J, Scoones, I and Wolmer, W (2003) 'From Jambanja to planning: The reassertion of technology in land reform in Southeastern Zimbabwe?', Sustainable Livelihoods in Southern Africa, Research Paper 2, Institute of Development Studies, Brighton, UK

Child B A (1988) 'The role of wildlife utilisation in the sustainable development of semi-arid rangelands in Zimbabwe', DPhil thesis, Oxford University

Child G F T (1995) 'Wildlife and people: The Zimbabwean success. How the conflict between animals and people became progress for both', WISDOM Foundation, Harare and New York

Child, B A (2001) 'Making wildlife pay: Converting wildlife's comparative advantage into real incentives for having wildlife in African savannas, case studies from Zimbabwe and Zambia', in H T Prins, J G Grootenhuis and T T Dolan (eds) *Wildlife Conservation by Sustainable Use*, Kluwer Academic Publishers, Boston, Massachusetts, pp335–88

Child, G F T. and Riney, T (1987) 'Tsetse control hunting in Zimbabwe, 1919–1958', *Zambezia* **14**(1): 11–71

Coe, M J, Cumming, D H M and Phillipson, J (1976) 'Biomass and production of large African herbivores in relation to rainfall and primary production', *Oecologia* **22**: 341–54

Cumming, D H M (1994) 'Are multispecies systems a viable landuse option for southern African savannas', Project Paper No. 46, WWF Multispecies Animal Production Systems Project, Harare

Cumming, D H M and Bond, I (1991) 'Animal production in Southern Africa: Present practice and opportunities for peasant farmers in arid lands', Report prepared for the IDRC Regional Office for Eastern and Southern Africa, WWF (MAPS), Harare

Dalal-Clayton, B and Child, B (2003) 'A synopsis of events and issues', in *Lessons from the Luangwa. The Story of the Luangwa Integrated Resource Development Project*, IIED, Zambia, pp1–38

du Toit R (1999) 'Save Valley Conservancy as a model for the conservation of biodiversity in the African semi-Arid Savanna', presented at the IFC–SMA Programme Conference, Washington, May

Dyson-Hudson, N (1984) 'Adaptive resource use strategies of African pastoralists', in F di Castri, F Baker and F W G Hadley (eds) *Ecology in Practice*, volume 1, *Ecosystem Management*, UNESCO, Dublin, pp262–73

Gibson, C C (2000) *Politicians and Poachers: The Political Economy of Wildlife Policy in Africa*, Cambridge University Press

Hachileka, E (in preparation) 'Development of game ranching in Zambia', in B Child (ed) *Parks in Transition: Biodiversity, Rural Development and the Bottom Line*, vol 2, SASUSG, Pretoria

Hadley M (1985) 'Comparative aspects of land use and resource management in savanna environments', in J C Tothill and J J Mott (eds) *Ecology and Management of the World's Savannas*, Australian Academy of Sciences, Canberra, pp142–58

Hill, K A (1994) 'Politicians farmers and ecologists: Commercial wildlife ranching and the politics of land in Zimbabwe', *Journal of Asian and African Studies* **29**(3–4): 226–47

Hulme D and Murphree, M W (2001) 'Community conservation and policy, promise and performance', in D Hulme and M Murphree (eds) *African Wildlife and Livelihoods. The Promise and Performance of Community Conservation*, James Currey, Oxford, pp280–97

Humavindu, M N and Barnes, J I (2003) 'Trophy hunting in the Namibian economy: An assessment', *South African Journal of Wildlife Research* **33**(2): 65–70

Hutton J, Ross P and Webb G (2001) 'Using the market to create incentives for the conservation of crocodilians. A review', report prepared for the IUCN Crocodile Specialist Group, Cambridge, UK

Jansen, D, Bond, I and Child, B (1992) 'Cattle, wildlife, both or neither: A summary of survey results for commercial ranches in Zimbabwe', WWF Project Paper No. 30, presented at the 3rd International Wildlife Ranching Symposium, CSIR, Pretoria, October 1992

Kievit, H (2000) 'Conservation of the Nile crocodile: has CITES helped or hindered?', in J Hutton and B Dickson (eds) *Endangered Species. Threatened Conventions. The Past, Present and Future of CITES*, Earthscan, London

Krug, W (2000) 'Nature tourism and protected area pricing: lessons learned from Africa', in The Design and Management of Forest Protected Areas – Papers presented at the Beyond the Trees Conference, 8–11 May 2000, Bangkok, Thailand, WWF/WCPA, Gland, pp159–73

Krug, W (2001) 'Maximising sustainable national benefits from nature tourism in Namibia', PhD thesis, University College London

Metroeconomica Economic Consultants (1996) 'Development cooperation objectives and the beef protocol: Economic analysis of the case of Botswana', draft interim report, European Commission, DGVIII

Muir, K and Bojo, J (1994) 'Economic policy, wildlife and landuse in Zimbabwe', World Bank Environment Department, Working Paper Number 68, World Bank, Washington, DC

Murphree M W (2001) 'Community, council and client. A case study of ecotourism development from Mahenye, Zimbabwe', in D Hulme and M Murphree (eds) *African Wildlife and Livelihoods. The Promise and Performance of Community Conservation*, James Currey, Oxford, pp177–194

Murphree, M W and Cumming D H M (1991) 'Savanna land use: Policy and practice in Zimbabwe', paper presented to IUBS/UNESCO Workshop on Economic Driving Forces and Constraints of Savanna Land Use, 21–25 January 1991, UNEP, Nairobi, Kenya. Also Joint CASS/WWF Working Paper Series No. 1. University of Zimbabwe, Harare

Phiminster, I R (1978) 'Meat and monopolics: Beef cattle in southern Rhodesia. 1890–1938', *Journal of African History* **19**(3): 391–414

Rukuni, M (1994) *Report of the Commission of Inquiry into Appropriate Agricultural Land Tenure Systems*, three volumes, Government of Zimbabwe, Harare

Sandford, S (1983) *Management of Pastoral Development in the Third World*, Wiley, Chichester, UK

Scoones, I (1990) 'Livestock populations and the household economy: A case study from southern Zimbabwe', PhD thesis, University of London

Schoeman, A (1996) 'Conservation in Namibia: Laying the foundation', in *Namibia Environment*, volume 1, Ministry of Environment, Government of Namibia, Windhoek

Skinner J D and Smithers R H N (1990) *The Mammals of the Southern African Subregion*, University of Pretoria

Taylor, R D (1974) 'A comparative study of landuse on a cattle and game ranch in the Rhodesian lowveld', MSc thesis, University of Rhodesia

Van Hoven, W and Zietsman, M (1998) 'Game: S.A.'s hidden asset', *Farmers Weekly,* November 1998

World Bank (2000) *World Development Indicators* [CD-ROM], World Bank, Washington, DC

Chapter 4

Community-Based Natural Resource Management as a Conservation Mechanism: Lessons and Directions

Brian T B Jones and Marshall W Murphree

INTRODUCTION

Community-based natural resource management (CBNRM) in southern Africa is a variant of what Adams and Hulme label 'community conservation', which they define as 'those principles and practices that argue that conservation goals should be pursued by strategies that emphasize the role of local residents in decision-making about natural resources' (Adams and Hulme, 2001, p13). They contrast this stance with an earlier conservation strategy ('fortress conservation'), which sought to reserve places for nature, and to separate humans and other species. While noting that both approaches share similar roots in ideas about nature and about the need to control the human use of nature, they suggest that fortress conservation is philosophically grounded in the intrinsic values of nature and is basically biocentric, whereas community conservation is basically utilitarian and anthropocentric. We can describe this conjunction and disjunction in terms of means–end sequencing: for 'fortress conservation' conservation is the end and the fulfilment of human needs serves as a means to this end; for community conservation the fulfilment of human needs is the end and conservation is a means to achieving and maintaining this end.

For a variety of reasons relating, among others, to dominant development discourses and limited state capacities for environmental management, community conservation has become a favoured stance in Africa over the past two decades, ubiquitous in national political rhetoric and prominent in donor strategies.[1] 'Community conservation' is, however, a rubric that spans a wide spectrum of conservation interventions, from cosmetic and co-optive 'participation',[2] parks outreach, revenue and resource sharing and co-management to self-mobilized and empowered communal systems of resource management. Analyses of community conservation must therefore carefully disaggregate the rubric in terms of content, objective, context and implementation (Barrow and Murphree, 2001).

Southern African CBNRM, generally speaking, represents the last of the variants mentioned above. With the exception of Malawi and South Africa,[3] parks/people relationships have not been a primary focus; the objective (in intent if not necessarily attainment) has been the creation of robust devolution in natural resource management to localized regimes of proprietorship, particularly in regard to wildlife. Zimbabwe and Namibia were in the forefront of this type of CBNRM policy development. This was no accident, because of the outstanding economic and ecological success that the two countries had achieved through the devolution of strong proprietorial rights over wildlife to the owners of ranch and farmland (see Chapter 2). It was also due to a political demand arising at the independence of the two countries for the transference of this economic success on (white) private lands to (black) communal lands, and the presence in the environmental establishments of both countries of professionals who were willing to move beyond conventional conservation approaches and incorporate the insights of social and organizational science, particularly in dealing with the complexities involved in transposing the benefits of private individual proprietorship to private collective or communal proprietorship.[4]

It was out of this combination of ecological and economic success through devolution to private landowners, political demand for the transposition of this success to communal contexts and a systemic, trans-disciplinary approach that the core profile of CBNRM policy in the two countries arose. Focused primarily on high-value wildlife resources, conceptually this policy contained four elements, as outlined below.[5]

(a) Sustainable use as a conservation paradigm. In its broadest philosophical context, the policy is strongly linked to theories of sustainable use of wild resources. In contrast to preservationist theories of conservation, sustainable use theory suggests that the main threat to wild habitats and resources in Africa is not overuse but the conversion of land for agriculture and livestock (SASUSG, 1996). This suggests that biodiversity conservation primarily depends not on technical and scientific interventions to prohibit or limit use, but in providing the right incentives for landholders to adopt sustainable land uses that do not lead to environment degradation and loss of biodiversity. This in turn implies that conservation is a social, economic and political issue. The solutions to conservation problems will be achieved through providing the appropriate economic and institutional framework within which landholders can exercise choice about how to use their land and its natural resources.

SASUSG (1996) suggests that sustainable use is the use of resources that allows the continued derivation of benefits, tangible or intangible. The primary concern is that use should be sustainable at the level of the ecosystem. Provided a species population is not reduced to the level that extinction is a real threat, then use can be regarded as sustainable. The most suitable technical approach to sustainable use of species is adaptive management based on a monitoring system that provides information needed to adapt the use regime as becomes necessary. The highest probability of use being sustainable is where the prime beneficiaries of such use are the people living with and using the resources, because these people have a vested interest in ensuring that they can continue to derive benefit from the resource.

(b) Economic instrumentalism. The incentive component, central to the sustainable use approach to conservation, involves both tangible and intangible perceived benefits. However, in the rural southern African context, it was economic benefit that was identified as the major driver for sustainable use. It was concluded that the future of wildlife could only be ensured in a policy context where wildlife could be made an economically competitive form of land use. The assumption behind this was that most critical decisions about the allocation of land, resources and management investments are based primarily on economics, at the levels of both state and landholder. Policy should therefore seek to confer high economic values on wildlife and wild land. Policy on its own cannot confer high economic value directly, but it can create enabling conditions for this. This includes the removal of subsidies or taxation structures that favour livestock or crop production, restrictions on the use and marketing of wildlife that do not apply to livestock, and the encouragement of a wildlife and tourism industry with the required infrastructure and pricing. Conventional conservation perspectives have contributed to macro-economic structures that act as a perverse incentive to conservation, and which need to be changed (Child, 2003).

Policy should also seek to provide a supportive investment climate through enduring entitlements that motivate the sustainable use of wildlife. By 'investment climate' was meant robust tenurial entitlements held by land and resource holders, which addressed a central component of conservation, the willingness to accept current costs (either direct or opportunity costs) for future benefit.

There are corollaries to such economic instrumentalism. First, it implies that where wildlife cannot be made economically competitive, its displacement by other forms of land use must be accepted. Second, it moves wildlife conservation objectives much closer to rural development objectives in a mosaic that accommodates both. This is made explicit, for instance, in Zimbabwe's policy statement on CAMPFIRE, where the ultimate objective of the programme is stated to be 'the realization of an agrarian system able to optimize land-use patterns and maximize group and individual investment and effort' (Martin, 1986, p19).

(c) Devolutionism. Two factors influenced the development of this component of CBNRM policy. The first was pragmatic. Both countries share the colonial legacy of a highly centralized state system. Equally they have shared the experience, in both colonial and post-colonial phases, of governments with resources that are inadequate to meet the responsibilities of this status. In the wildlife sector this has been manifestly clear, with state agencies being hard pressed to manage the national parks, let alone perform enforcement and extension functions. Legislation notwithstanding, land occupiers were in fact the actual determinants of wildlife status and were generally in an oppositional relationship with government wildlife agencies. At the same time, because of their in-place location and experience, these same people constituted a vast untapped potential for sharing the responsibilities of wildlife management.

The second factor was the adoption of insights from studies and experiences in organizational and institutional dynamics. To tap the managerial potential of land and resource users, delegation of responsibility was not enough; responsibility had to be linked with the authority and entitlements of full proprietorship if it was to provide the right incentive package for committed and effective management. This meant the empowerment of devolution: the right to manage, the right to benefit and the right to dispose or sell (Child et al, 2003; Child, 2003; Murphree, 1998). Such devolution[6] follows what has been termed the principle of subsidiarity: 'leaving power as close to the action as possible' (Child, 2003).[7]

(d) Collective proprietorship. The devolutionism and economic instrumentalism of Namibian and Zimbabwean thinking on wildlife policy resulted, as described in Chapter 2, in the enactment in the 1970s of legislation conferring strong proprietorial rights over wildlife to the owners of private land in the commercial agricultural sector. The influence of this successful model on further policy evolution has been profound. In both countries there were compelling reasons to transfer this successful model to communal areas. These constituted large proportions of total land surface and often held significant populations of wildlife. After independence, there were political imperatives for the extension of the policy beyond the commercial, and largely white, commercial farming sector.

However, the transfer of the model from private lands to communal lands posed important legal and institutional issues. First, the proprietorship units analogous to farms and ranches in communal lands were communities of collective interest. How could these communities be defined, and could they develop effective institutions of collective management? Drawing on the insights of common property theory,[8] the answer was sought through the concept of a communal property regime, that is, a regime in which a defined group collectively manages and exploits a common property resource within a defined jurisdiction. To be effective such a regime requires strong internal legitimacy. Ideally its membership and jurisdiction should be self-defined. To be effective such a regime also requires external legitimacy. This raised a second important issue. How could tenurially strong units of collective proprietorship be created under conditions of state tenure in communal lands? The answer was, in part, to embark on a strategic process leading to legislative change providing devolution to such localized units, and in part by the evolution of structures of localized management adapted to operating in modern market conditions.

As an institutional economist, Child has suggested that the four conceptual elements outlined above involve three entry points in southern African CBNRM: organizational management, pricing theory, and the political economics of government. On this basis he is able to distil the conceptual core of CBNRM as follows: 'CBNRM builds on the price–proprietorship–subsidiarity paradigm. If the resource is valuable (price), if this value is captured by landholders (proprietorship) and if the principle is followed that no management action, decision or benefit is arrogated to a higher level when it is better and more appropriately conducted at a lower level (subsidiarity), there is a high likelihood of successful resource conservation and management' (Child, in preparation, b).

Outside Namibia and Zimbabwe, CBNRM in the other countries of southern Africa exhibits considerable differences in policy perspectives and programme emphases, which will be brought out in the case studies in volume 2 of this book. Generally speaking, however, they can in their conceptual roots be considered variants of the profile we have outlined above. In this synoptic chapter, having briefly touched on the historical, ecological and politico-institutional differences that CBNRM exhibits in the different countries of the region, we examine CBNRM performance so far, the issues that have influenced this performance and the challenges that CBNRM faces in a new generation of endeavour. The chapter concludes with a brief section that links CBNRM, initiated in southern Africa largely outside state park areas, with new configurations of protected-area policy.

ECOLOGY AND POLITICO-ECONOMIC BACKGROUND

The southern African region exhibits considerable diversity in ecological and politico-economic characteristics. Ecologically this diversity ranges from the deserts of Namibia, the most arid country south of the Sahara, to high-rainfall montane conditions in parts of Malawi, Mozambique, Zimbabwe and South Africa. Average rainfall in the Namib Desert in Namibia is less than 25mm annually, whereas Namibia's wettest region in the northeast has an average of 650mm, which is only marginal for rain-fed agriculture. Large parts of Botswana are classified as semi-arid as are parts of Zimbabwe (the Zambezi Valley and the southeastern lowveldt) and western South Africa, particularly the extensive Karoo.

In these semi-arid to arid regions, the dominant form of land use has been extensive livestock farming (either cattle where rainfall is higher or small-stock in drier areas). However, uncertain climatic conditions make livestock farming marginal in many of these areas without heavy government subsidies. Rainfall is not only low, but often varies considerably temporally and spatially. Many of the arid and semi-arid regions are also characterized by poor soils (Kalahari sand over much of Namibia, Botswana and parts of Zambia and South Africa), so irrigated agriculture is difficult, even where water is available for this. In higher rainfall areas of South Africa, Zimbabwe, Zambia, Mozambique and particularly Malawi, cultivation becomes the more dominant form of land use. In areas of the most intensive cultivation, habitat for wildlife has been lost and, because of high human population densities, will not be recovered. However, where extensive livestock farming is the dominant form of land use, habitat suitable for wildlife is usually retained as vegetation, is not cleared for planting and human population densities remain relatively low.

In Namibia, South Africa and Zimbabwe large areas of the most productive land remain under freehold tenure established by white settlers. Until recently most of this land in all three countries has remained under white ownership. All three countries are struggling to devise approaches to land reform that satisfy demands for land by the landless as well as groups who were dispossessed in colonial times or under apartheid in South Africa. In Zimbabwe, government-backed land seizures have led to the redistribution of white-owned land to a mixture of the landless and the political elite.

Communal land throughout the region is mostly owned by the state, and communal area residents enjoy only usufruct rights over the land and resources. In most countries the state centralized ownership of communal land at independence. This legal situation often clashes with the actual one of a continued perspective by local residents that land rights are vested in traditional leaders who are custodians of the land for a particular tribal grouping. Despite often being co-opted by colonial governments and having their powers reduced by law, traditional authorities are still respected by many rural residents and still play a strong role in land allocation in many parts of the region. The centralization of control by the state over resources such as wildlife and forests had begun during colonial times and was generally maintained by newly independent governments until the changes mentioned in this chapter were introduced. Generally, poverty is common in the communal areas of the region, and infrastructure such as good roads, clinics and schools is poor.

Politically, the transition from colonial rule to majority rule has been the dominant theme in southern Africa for the past 40 years. This transition has often been brought about through liberation wars that have taken their toll on the region, psychologically as well as economically. The politics of 'reconciliation' and 'transformation' have dominated those countries that have seen a shift from white rule through wars of liberation. Mozambique and Angola have suffered post-independence civil wars that led to the deaths of thousands and devastated their economies. Zimbabwe's radical approach to land reform and redistribution has exacerbated the economic decline experienced by Zimbabwe over the past five years and contributed to internal political instability. Botswana by contrast has remained stable politically and economically since its transition from a British Protectorate. Zambia and Malawi are still emerging from years of one-party rule and are struggling to define their own forms of democratic government. Namibia has enjoyed 13 years of peace and stability and moderate economic growth since its independence in 1990. Internal political stability in South Africa since democratic elections has ensured that it remains the economic powerhouse within the southern African region.

GENESIS, INCEPTION AND PROGRAMMATIC DEVELOPMENT

Although CBNRM in southern Africa is based largely on a common conceptual foundation, the details of its genesis, inception and programmatic development have differed within the region. These differences have been shaped by the politico-economic, institutional and social contexts of each country described briefly in the previous section. The introductory section has shown how some common factors helped drive the conceptualization of CBNRM in Namibia and Zimbabwe. Both countries also demonstrate some similarities in their programmatic development of CBNRM. In both cases, CBNRM developed as a national programme, with a spread across different regions of the countries and the involvement of various stakeholders encompassing government, non-governmental organizations (NGOs) and the private sector, showing elements of strong coordination at national level between the different stakeholders. Each country also received core funding from one main donor for a considerable period of time, providing stability in funding for key activities. The emergence of a national programme with stakeholders working towards a common goal in a structured manner helped to provide the necessary coordination and cooperation between institutional actors with different agendas and interests. In Zimbabwe the main mechanism for this cooperation and coordination was a 'collaborative group' of stakeholders that met regularly to discuss programme direction and policy. Originally chaired by the Department of National Parks and Wild Life Management (DNPWLM), leadership was later taken by the CAMPFIRE Association (Child, 2003), which represented the rural district councils to which authority over wildlife management had been devolved by central government. In Namibia, coordination was provided through the steering committee established to oversee the USAID-funded Living in a Finite Environment (LIFE) Project, the main vehicle for funding and technical support to CBNRM in Namibia. CBNRM in Namibia is now coordinated through an association of CBNRM organizations that provide services to local communities. Both conceptual and programmatic development benefited in Namibia and Zimbabwe from the diversity of individuals and organizations collaborating in the national programmes. In particular, the interaction between academics in applied social sciences, economists, development workers, ecologists and wildlife managers contributed to robust debate and internal monitoring and evaluation that led to innovation and adaptive management.

In Botswana, CBNRM has been strongly influenced by the establishment of a national land-use planning system. This identified in the remotest parts of the country wildlife management areas (WMAs) in which wildlife and tourism were expected to be the dominant land uses. The system also divided the whole country into controlled hunting areas (CHAs), some of which were designated for community management. The Wildlife Conservation Policy of 1986 established the principle of sustainable use of wildlife for the benefit of rural populations, particularly in the WMAs. It also established the principle that citizens should actively participate in wildlife utilization and management (Government of Botswana, 1986). Based on this policy, a joint directive by the government ministries responsible for wildlife, tourism and land affairs set out the mechanism by which local communities would be able to gain rights over wildlife in community-designated CHAs. Whereas most other countries in the region have used legislation to give communities rights over wildlife and tourism, the Botswana CBRM approach rests on policy and administrative directives.

The implementation of CBNRM in Botswana was driven initially by the USAID-funded Natural Resources Management Programme (NRMP), which helped to develop some of the policy approaches and CBNRM guidelines, was instrumental in developing management plans for the community-managed WMAs, and piloted CBNRM activities with local communities (Rozemeijer, in preparation). The NRMP (1989–1999), which was housed in the wildlife department, dominated CBNRM in Botswana for most of its tenure, partly because there were few local NGOs with the resources and capacity to assist local communities. In more recent years the number of organizations involved in CBNRM has grown, and coordination and direction are provided by the National CBNRM Forum. However, at the same time, donor support for Botswana has decreased considerably, local NGOs do not have their own funding bases and face severe financial problems, and government has not filled the gap left by donors (Rozemeijer, in preparation). As a result, the institutional support base for CBNRM is relatively weak, yet field experience in Botswana has shown that for communities to develop strong and effective resource management institutions, they need considerable support and facilitation over an extended period of time (Rozemeijer and van der Jagt, 2001).

The evolution of CBNRM in Zambia has been heavily influenced by political developments since independence in 1964, when the ruling UNIP party centralized natural resource management along with the nationalization of most enterprises (Child, in preparation, a). In the mid-1980s, in response to heavy poaching of rhino and elephant, conservationists developed programmes that aimed at more involvement of local people in wildlife conservation. The Luangwa Integrated Rural Development Project (LIRDP) brought poaching under control through law enforcement, and developed a community benefit programme through local chiefs. The Administrative Management Design (ADMADE) Project was established to direct a share of government revenue to local chiefs and their communities and hire village scouts to work with the conservation authorities to stop poaching. Building on the experience of these programmes, the National Parks and Wildlife Act (1991) made provision for formal community participation and benefit. The introduction of economic structural adjustment and increasing international acceptance of community management and sustainable development contributed to the recognition in Zambia's 1994 National Environmental Action Plan of the need for greater devolution of natural resource management to local authorities and communities (Child, in preparation, a). Legislation enacted in 1998 makes provision for community resource boards to manage natural resources. Throughout these changes, Zambia has retained an approach of revenue sharing between government and community, in contrast to Botswana and Namibia where income from wildlife goes direct to communities. The exception is the LIRDP, which returned 100 per cent of revenue to communities.

The development of CBNRM in Mozambique has followed a considerably different trajectory to the rest of the region. CBNRM has developed against the background of a country emerging from two decades of war and the effects of centrally planned economic and political strategies. According to Anstey (2001), the country's colonial and subsequent revolutionary heritage and the current transformation to a market economy have not provided Mozambique with a strong state or administration at either central or local levels. He suggests that the paradox of CBNRM in Mozambique is that elsewhere in Africa 'a strong state has proved to be a critical prerequisite for the decentralization and devolution required to empower local community institutions to manage and benefit from natural resources' (Anstey, 2001, p76).

A rapid transition towards community conservation in Mozambique took place in the mid-1990s. Anstey (2001) suggests that this shift took place not because of changes in policy or legislation, but partly because key staff in government departments saw the limitations of state–private sector partnerships when the state had little capacity to monitor and regulate and there was increased conflict with local people. Furthermore, specific NGOs and donors were promoting new ideas based on regional experience and signing up to the idea of community conservation, providing access to donor funding and technical support when government funding for natural resource management was declining.

Subsequently, the necessary policy and legislation has followed. CBNRM is a strategy adopted in the Forestry and Wildlife Policy of 1999, and securing rights over land under national legislation has been another entry point for the implementation of CBNRM (Nhantumbo et al, in preparation). NGOs have assisted local communities to gain group tenure over their land so as to protect people against existing or potential conflicts with the private sector, which has gained large tracts of communal land under lease from government. The process for obtaining land rights is relatively transparent with low transaction costs, but obtaining rights over forestry and wildlife carries high transaction costs for communities because of the bureaucracy involved and the need to have technical information for a resource inventory and to design a management plan (Nhantumbo et al, in preparation).

Contrary to the experience elsewhere in southern Africa, CBNRM in Mozambique is based more on forestry resources than on wildlife. This tends to limit the financial benefits that can accrue to local residents unless they can gain access to licences for commercial timber concessions.

The development of community conservation approaches in South Africa and Malawi has focused on linking local residents with protected areas, rather than on the management of natural resources on communal lands themselves. This is mainly because wildlife has largely disappeared from the communal lands of these two countries and large human populations live adjacent to many of the protected areas. The proximity of large numbers of people to national parks and game reserves has significant negative impacts on these state-controlled areas. In some instances people have been removed from their land so as to establish a protected area, and they wish to regain that land. In other cases there is pressure from poaching and encroachment into protected areas.

In Malawi some of these pressures led to the development of a community outreach and co-management approach to improve relationships between protected areas and neighbouring communities, give neighbours a greater economic stake in protected areas, and reduce the level of illegal use of resources in protected areas (Jones, M, in preparation). The co-management approach focuses on villages neighbouring protected areas, but stakeholders include tour and safari operators, government agencies and NGOs. Activities include allowing neighbours to use resources inside the protected area, revenue-sharing schemes for villagers and border-zone development projects.

In South Africa, protected-area conservation bodies have had to respond to processes initiated by the transition from a white minority government to a democratic system (Grossman and Holden, in preparation). The National Parks Board was restructured to reflect the demographics of South African society. The new organization, South African National Parks (SANParks), established a unit to specifically deal with park–people issues. This unit has five core functions: (a) community facilitation; (b) economic empowerment; (c) environmental education; (d) cultural heritage management; and (e) research and monitoring. Pollard et al (in preparation) note that currently the unit is not involved in CBNRM and that most of its effort is directed at outreach.

However, the National Parks Board, and latterly the new SANParks, have been involved in the establishment of new relationships with local communities through the establishment of 'contractual' parks (Grossman and Holden, in preparation). The South African land restitution policy allows communities to have land restored that was forcibly appropriated under apartheid. The Makuleke community bordering the Kruger National Park successfully launched a claim to regain land they were removed from to form the park. Under the settlement they will not re-occupy the land, but title has been restored to them. They will gain the income from all wildlife use and tourism on the restored land. A similar settlement has been made with the !Khomani San and Mier communities in the former Kalahari Gemsbok Park (now part of the Kgalagadi Transfrontier Park). They have been given 25,000ha within the park which will be run on a contractual basis by the park authorities. In 1991, before the transition to democracy in South Africa, the National Parks Board tried to establish a national park on communal land in the Richtersveld in the arid Namaqualand region. The proclamation of the park was resisted by local inhabitants who took the

Board to court. A settlement was reached by agreement on the establishment of a contractual park which would be co-managed by the people and the Board, which would pay a lease to the residents. Although forced by legal action by local people, the South African national park authorities have led the way in the region in developing co-management approaches to protected areas.

This brief summary clearly shows how colonial history, economic imperatives, donor agendas, politics, and war and reconstruction have shaped the development of CBNRM programmes across southern Africa as much as conservation or rural development goals. This diversity in genesis, inception and programmatic development provides a rich field of implementational experience from which to draw lessons about the performance of CBNRM, key issues and challenges.

PERFORMANCE

Programmatic Spread

CBNRM in southern Africa has, for the historical reasons outlined in the introduction to this chapter, focused mainly on wildlife and tourism, although several countries that focused primarily on these resources in their early stages of development have attempted to diversify into forest and veldt products. Mozambique has focused far more on community forestry management than any other country in the region. However, by far the greatest experience in implementation has been developed within the wildlife sector and there are data available to enable an evaluation of performance so far.

CBNRM activities across the region have typically focused on the following aspects:

- developing enabling policy and legislation;
- institutional development;
- capacity building;
- resource monitoring and management.

Ecological Impacts

The results of CBNRM in terms of ecological impacts have been considerable (Stuart-Hill and Taylor, in preparation; Rozemeijer, in preparation). They include the following, drawn from examples around the region.

CBNRM has made Conservation a Legitimate and Attractive Form of Land Use

By placing a value on wildlife and increasing the benefits to landholders, wildlife is able to compete more favourably with other forms of land use such as livestock. Wildlife has become more attractive to residents of communal areas in semi-arid and arid regions. According to Rozemeijer (in preparation), in Botswana: 'the actual and perceived value of wildlife has increased tremendously' over the years that CBNRM has been operating. Fourteen community-based organizations in Botswana have signed agreements with the private sector (for consumptive and non-consumptive tourism activities) worth a total of more than US$1.6 million (Rozemeijer, in preparation). In Botswana, Namibia and Zimbabwe, the shift from state-controlled wildlife pricing to free-market pricing has considerably increased the value of wildlife to land holders (Arntzen, 2003, Barnes and Jones, in preparation; Taylor, in preparation).

Additional Habitat for Conservation

As a result of placing a value on wildlife, CBNRM has secured additional habitat for conservation. Over the past 20 years the private sector and CBNRM have added significantly more habitat for conservation than has the expansion of state-owned protected areas (Stuart-Hill and Taylor, in preparation). CBNRM in Namibia, for example, has added almost 5 million hectares through the establishment of communal area conservancies (Jones and Weaver, in preparation) and the trend is on the rise. In Zimbabwe, Taylor (in preparation) found that in 1999 wild land in the main wildlife areas was being maintained in an intact state. For the 12 primary wildlife districts in Zimbabwe, the amount of wild land varied from less than 500km^2 to over 5000km^2, with an average size of 3300km^2. Of these, three districts had wild land in excess of 90 per cent of the district area, six had 50–70 per cent wild land, and in three districts only, less than 35 per cent of the district constituted wild land.

In Mozambique, CBNRM projects (mostly for forest resources) cover nearly 3.9 million hectares. In Namibia and Zimbabwe local communities are setting aside land exclusively for wildlife and tourism, which supports broad-based biodiversity conservation. In Kanyurira Ward in Zimbabwe, the village of Masoka has allocated land for crop growing and a residential area, leaving the bulk of its land as habitat for wildlife (Murphree, 1997). Their wildlife area adjoins a state-run hunting area, which itself links to a national park, providing contiguous wildlife areas under different forms of management and tenure. Communal lands under wildlife management in Namibia, Botswana, Zimbabwe and Mozambique form important migration corridors for wildlife seeking seasonal water or grazing and important resources such as rivers and core habitats. Wet and dry season movements of wildlife take place, for example, through communal land between the escarpment in Zimbabwe and the Zambezi River and Cahora Bassa Dam in Mozambique (Jones, B, 2002). Seasonal movements of various species of wildlife are an important part of the northern Kalahari ecosystem in Botswana. The community-managed CHAs and WMAs are crucial for many of these movements, and 46 Community-based Organizations (CBOs) are using natural resources in a controlled way in these areas.

CBNRM Has Helped Rural Communities to Tolerate the Negative Impacts of Wild Animals

Enabling residents of communal areas to realize the value of wildlife has led to changes in attitude towards wildlife that negatively impacts people's livelihoods. Residents are more willing to tolerate herbivores that eat crops or predators that kill livestock because they either gain benefit from wildlife or perceive the potential for gaining benefit. (These benefits are financial but also intangible, such as empowerment, new skills, community institutions, etc.) In Namibia, communal area conservancies employ their own game guards who, among other things, are responsible for dealing with problem animals. In northwest Namibia and Caprivi in the northeast, elephants are moving into new areas (probably re-colonizing former range) and are tolerated by local people. Despite the presence of an estimated 120,000 elephants in northern Botswana, incidents of problem animals being shot by villagers are few, despite crop growing being the main agricultural activity of many residents.

CBNRM Has Reduced Poaching and Unsustainable Harvesting

In many areas, poaching has been reduced because of community support for wildlife. In northwest Namibia, among other species,[9] black rhino are increasing on communal land[10] largely because of an absence of poaching, and elephant are expanding their range (Jones and Weaver, in preparation). In parts of Zimbabwe, Botswana and Mozambique, the numbers of several species have increased, partly because of reduced poaching. For example, in areas where the Tchuma Tchato project operates in Mozambique, previously high levels of poaching have been brought under control and anecdotal evidence from project staff and data from aerial surveys indicate that, overall, wildlife in the project area is increasing (Jones, B, 2002). Child (in preparation, a) suggests that from similar evidence from the Luangwa Valley in Zambia 'we can speculate that there is a causative link between participation and benefit in communities and increasing wildlife populations'.[11] In Botswana, unsustainable harvesting through the system of citizen hunting has been replaced in community-controlled CHAs by safari hunting and community-own-use quotas (Rozemeijer, in preparation). In 8 of the 12 primary wildlife-producing districts in Zimbabwe (those for which counts have been done consistently) total elephant numbers ranged from a minimum of 4181 in 1989 to a maximum of 12,707 elephants in 2001 (Taylor, in preparation).

CBNRM Has Led to Game Re-introductions

In some countries founder populations of wildlife have been re-introduced to certain areas. This has been made possible because of commitment by local people to conserve the re-introduced animals, and because institutions have been developed for taking local management decisions. In Namibia, for example, since 1999, more than 2500 mixed plains game animals have been re-introduced into six communal area conservancies (Jones and Weaver, in preparation). As a consequence of the safe environment created by the conservancies, the Namibian Ministry of Environment and Tourism is considering the possibility of experimental re-introductions of white rhino into some of the conservancies.

Mechanisms Have Been Created for Communities to Enjoy the Existence Value of Wildlife

Removing absolute state control over wildlife, placing decision making closer to the local level, and improved problem-animal management have enabled people to rekindle an aesthetic appreciation of wildlife. Financial incentives for conservation are often emphasized as being an important driving force for conservation in CBNRM. However, this emphasis can easily lead to underestimating the extent to which rural people value wildlife for aesthetic and cultural reasons. Two communal area conservancies in Namibia, Uukwaluudhi and Salambala, were established largely because community leaders placed a high value on the continued existence of wildlife in their areas for future generations (Jones, B, 1999).

CBNRM Provides Opportunities for Supporting Existing State-run Protected Areas

Protected areas can benefit from CBNRM approaches on their borders that aim to establish strong community level institutions with proprietorship and jurisdiction over their land and resources. Such units can provide the basis for negotiation and mutual support between state and community institutions on an equal level. Such opportunities have, with a few exceptions, been little explored within the region (see the last section of this chapter for a more detailed discussion).

Figure 4.1 provides a simplified conceptual model showing how CBNRM activities can provide conservation benefits based on actual examples from around the region.

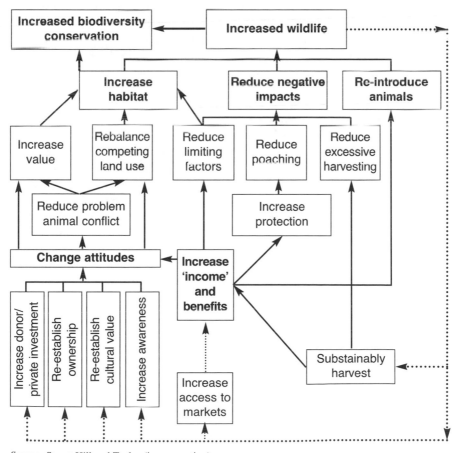

Source: Stuart-Hill and Taylor (in preparation)

Figure 4.1 *The links between CBNRM activities and conservation benefits*

Economic Performance

The economic performance of CBNRM has been mixed and patchy. Some communities in some countries of the region have been able to generate considerable income from wildlife and tourism. However, the income has rarely reached households in significant amounts. The results of CBNRM in terms of economic performance are as follows.

CBNRM Has Generated Income for Communities with High-value Wildlife and Tourism Assets

Communities with high-value wildlife and other high-value tourism assets are able to generate significant amounts of income at the collective level. In the Chobe Enclave in Botswana, the sale of consumptive and non-consumptive tourism concessions in 2002 brought the local community close to US$200,000 (Arntzen, 2003). The enclave is able to realize high values for its concessions because of a high annual elephant trophy hunting quota and proximity to the Chobe National Park.

One of the highest-earning conservancies in Namibia is the Torra Conservancy in the arid northwest. Economic benefits generated by the conservancy in 2002 are shown in Table 4.1. The overall value of economic benefits generated was US$102,000 and direct income to the conservancy was US$61,500 (see Note 12). Operating costs were around US$18,000, giving the conservancy a profit of US$43,500 which could be used for community projects or household dividends. Table 4.1 indicates the different ways in which wildlife and tourism can generate income for communities, an important aspect of CBNRM.

Annual income at the start of the CAMPFIRE programme in Zimbabwe in 1989 was US$350,000 (ZW$750,000) when only two Appropriate Authority Rural District Councils (RDCs) were in place and operational. This had increased to over US$2 million (ZW$128 million) in 2001, by which time there were 14 wildlife-producing RDCs with 'appropriate authority' (Taylor, in preparation). About half this income is allocated to communities, and 25 per cent for district wildlife management.

CBNRM Has Rarely Generated High Household Benefits

Although CBNRM has been able to generate income at the collective level, there have been problems in distributing income to household level. In Namibia and Botswana few community management bodies have opted for direct household dividends, finding it difficult to decide how to use their wildlife and tourism income (Arntzen, 2003; Jones and Weaver, in preparation; Rozemeijer, in preparation). Where household dividends have been distributed, such as in Zimbabwe, the financial benefit per household is often low. Bond (2001) found that in real terms the median benefit per household declined from US$19.40 in 1989 to US$4.9 in 1996 (see Note 13). He concluded that in most areas wildlife was not financially significant at the household level. In some cases, the sheer size of local populations relative to community wildlife income reduces the likely impact of household cash dividends.

However, where wildlife income is high compared with population numbers, the household income can be significant. Bond (2001) cites two examples within CAMPFIRE: Kanyurira Ward in the Zambezi Valley and Mahenye Ward in the

Table 4.1 *Economic benefits generated by Torra Conservancy,*
northwest Namibia, 2002

Activity	Income (US$)
Rental and percentage of turnover from up-market lodge	30,000
Trophy hunting concession	18,000
Live sale of game	13,230
Wages from lodge and trophy hunting	31,600
Value of meat distributed from hunting	5,383
Value of game hunted for own use	4,187
Total	102,400

Source: Jones and Weaver (in preparation)

southeast lowveldt. In these wards the average benefit per household from wildlife revenue exceeded the index of gross agricultural production in four out of the five years between 1989 and 1993. Bond concluded that there had been significant institutional change within these wards towards the management of wildlife and wildlife habitat. In 2002 the Torra conservancy in Namibia, with only 120 households, distributed its first cash dividend of US$63 per household to individual members.

Whereas income to households might be low in absolute terms, its significance becomes clear when one considers the economic circumstances of the beneficiaries. In Namibia the average income of subsistence farming households is estimated at US$700 a year and for the poorest 20 per cent of households around US$200 a year (Ashley and Barnes, 1996). In areas of the remote northwest of Botswana, average household income is estimated at around US$52 a month and the poverty datum line (PDL) for a family of seven at US$202 (Arntzen, 2003). In one CBNRM area in northwest Botswana, the wildlife income from trophy hunting divided per household per month amounts to around 87 per cent of the estimated average household income or 23 per cent of the estimated PDL. Arntzen (2003, p26) concludes that such revenue is 'highly significant in proportion to local incomes and needs'. There is also evidence from the region that the timing of cash income can also be highly significant for households if, for example, received in January after Christmas or when school hostel fees are needed (Ashley, 1998; WILD, 2003).

Further, different types of income from wildlife and tourism affect households in different ways. The income from a tourism lodge, trophy hunting and live sale of game indicated in Table 4.1 accrued to the conservancy at the collective level. However, the value of wages (the highest) and the value of meat and game that was hunted accrued at household level.

Organizational/Institutional Development

The implementation of CBNRM within the region has given rise to several different institutions for natural resource management. The shape and character of these institutions have been influenced by the policy and institutional contexts of each country.

In Zimbabwe, legislation assigns 'appropriate authority' over wildlife to RDCs. According to policy guidelines, the RDCs were expected to devolve authority to local wards, a lower level of administrative jurisdiction. However, few have actually done this and the RDCs themselves remain the main institutional beneficiaries of CBNRM. In Botswana and Namibia, management rights are vested in CBOs (a Community Trust in Botswana and a Conservancy in Namibia). The characteristics of these CBOs are similar. The CBO must have a constitution, a representative committee, defined membership and a defined area. In Botswana, the area and membership are defined by the boundaries of designated CHAs, whereas in Namibia, communities are able to define themselves and their own boundaries. In both countries the CBOs often cover relatively large areas of land, and the elected committees often represent relatively many people. In Zambia, policy and legislation provide for the establishment of Community Resource Boards which usually represent several villages. However, in the Luangwa Valley, authority and responsibility for wildlife management have been devolved to individual villages through village action groups (VAGs). Child (in preparation, a) demonstrates the institutional impact of devolution to the lowest appropriate level within a 'community'. He notes the following changes that occurred when income and decision making were devolved from the relatively large local-area level to the VAGs:

- At village level only 0.8 per cent of income was misused compared with 40 per cent at area level.
- In four years VAGs constructed over 150 community projects, compared with 10 in the earlier area-based phase.
- After four years, community appreciation of wildlife led to the employment of 76 scouts and a reduction in poaching, with the proportion of village income allocated to wildlife management increasing annually.

Throughout the region the tendency is to devolve rights over natural resources to some form of elected representative committee, which is then responsible for decision making on behalf of the local residents. Most of these committees have formal constitutions which define who may be beneficiaries, provide operating rules for decision making, re-election of office bearers and benefit distribution.

In most countries these new institutions are filling a vacuum in natural resources governance at the local level (eg Child, in preparation, a; Jones and Weaver, in preparation; Nhantumbo et al, in preparation). They provide a means for collective decision making over common property resources where governance regimes established by the state have failed, or previous governance regimes through traditional authorities have been eroded or have broken down.

The committees established to run these institutions have received considerable capacity-building support from NGOs and other service providers. This support includes financial management, running committee meetings and annual meetings, developing business plans, land use and other forms of natural resource planning and resource monitoring.

Field experience in the region suggests that the development of effective local-level resource management institutions requires time and a consistent level of support. These institutions gain external legitimacy from central governments through the provision of devolved rights and authority by policy and legislation. However, time is required for these institutions to gain internal legitimacy. Such legitimacy can be built through the direct participation by local residents in decision making, and through the delivery of benefits that are valued by residents. Time is needed for these institutions to develop appropriate forms of transparent and accountable decision making and for a flow of different benefits to begin at a level that impacts households. Time is needed for community-based organizations to develop the necessary skills in dealing with private sector operators and to develop an understanding of the tourism and safari-hunting sectors.

Rozemeijer (in preparation), while referring to Botswana, sums up regional experience with capacity building succinctly: 'Ten years of CBNRM implementation has shown that this capacity-building process takes much longer than expected. This has to do with the complexity of the approach (multiple sectors and multiple actors), the complexity of making decisions over natural resources you do not have full control over and the complexity of the community social fabric.'

ISSUES IN SOUTHERN AFRICAN CBNRM

Devolution

Although CBNRM in southern Africa has promoted the devolution of authority over wildlife to local rural communities, several constraints to achieving effective devolution can be identified. Government has shown a tendency to try to regain direct control over wildlife and/or wildlife income and reimpose the restrictions on use by landholders that earlier policy and legislation had removed (Jones and Weaver, in preparation; Jones and Butterfield, 2001; Martin, 2003).

Where governments have changed policy and legislation to assign rights to lower levels, this devolved authority has usually been limited. The tendency is to insist on quotas, permits and management plans and to assume that officials sitting in the capital have a better knowledge of the local situation than the locals themselves. In most CBNRM areas of Botswana and Zambia, communities tend to be passive recipients of income from wildlife, without engaging in active management, partly because the state retains considerable management authority itself (Gujadhur, 2001; Gibson, 1999).

In Zimbabwe, legislation provides for 'appropriate authority' over wildlife to be given to RDCs, but the original intention of the CAMPFIRE policy planners was that this authority should be devolved by councils further to the ward level (Jones and Murphree, 2001). Councils were encouraged by implementation guidelines to carry out this further devolution, but few have done this, or where it occurred, authority has been recentralized by councils.

In some cases, the reluctance of government to devolve rights and authority to lower levels can be explained by reluctance of political and economic elites to give up the benefits that accrue from controlling the wildlife resources. Gibson (1999) demonstrates how the dominance of the politico-economic elite affected wildlife policy and legislation in Zambia. According to Bond (2001), wildlife is an important and significant source of revenue to some RDCs, which partly explains the reluctance of such RDCs to devolve to lower levels. He found that in the absence of legislation giving wards proprietorship over wildlife and wildlife revenues, administrative guidelines have failed to create strong institutions with sanctioned use rights at the local level.

Murphree (1991a) framed the bureaucratic tendency to hold onto power in terms of a struggle over authority between different levels in a bureaucratic hierarchy. It is also important to recognize the need for institutional change and reform within the wildlife and tourism agencies, which are expected to implement new policies and legislation that promote devolution and participation of local resource users in management decisions. Often a failure to re-orient bureaucracies leads to a gap between the ideologies of the policy and legislation and those implementing the new approaches.

Policy and Legislation

Policy and legislation that devolve authority over wildlife to local resource users have in most countries been developed in isolation from policy and legislation in other sectors and from macro-economic policy. The results are inconsistencies and overlaps that hinder successful implementation of CBNRM.

In Namibia and Zimbabwe, the enabling legislation for use and control of most natural resources is fragmented and resource-specific (Bond, 2001; Jones and Weaver, in preparation). This gives rise to an arena of overlapping authorities and competing institutions in which new resource management institutions find it difficult to make decisions that they can enforce without being undermined by some competing institution.

Agricultural policy in Namibia and Zimbabwe has artificially supported livestock through subsidies and incentives (Barnes and Jones, in preparation; Child, in preparation). In Botswana, European Union (EU) subsidies for beef production have also artificially supported the livestock industry (Arntzen, 2003). Similar subsidies have not been provided by government for wildlife, creating barriers for wildlife to compete equitably with livestock as a land use. In the cases of Zambia and Zimbabwe, where government retains a considerable portion of income from wildlife, this represents a tax on wildlife as a land use, providing a disincentive for communal area residents to invest in wildlife.

CBNRM policy and legislation throughout most of the southern African region has provided communal area residents with resource rights, but has not dealt with the crucial issue of land rights. In most southern African countries, communal land is owned by the state, and local residents have certain user rights only. In CAMP-FIRE areas of the Zambezi Valley, local people have been unable to prevent the influx of outsiders onto their wildlife land. In Namibia, local communities are finding it difficult to stop outsider livestock owners from moving onto their land that is zoned for wildlife and tourism. In Botswana, the community trusts are able to gain resource use leases from the land boards, but they do not gain a lease over the land itself. In Zimbabwe and Namibia, proposals for giving communities secure land tenure have been blocked by politicians

The lack of exclusive group rights over land remains a crucial constraint to the promotion of the sustainable use of natural resources within CBNRM. If communities cannot prevent other people from using the land they wish to set aside for wildlife and tourism, then there remains little incentive to maintain wild habitats. There is little likelihood that management inputs and investments will be rewarded, and the land might as well be converted to grazing for livestock, or crop lands.

Further, a lack of secure land tenure means that communities cannot easily raise capital loans themselves based on their land as security. It is also difficult for communities to attract investors as partners in tourism joint ventures where rights to the land are not secure and the investment risk is therefore higher.

Within the region, Mozambique has gone the furthest in enabling local communities to gain secure tenure over their land. Under recent legislation they are able to gain long-term leases if they identify the boundaries and develop a management plan. However, government is not promoting the implementation of its own legislation and is still allocating leases to the private sector that cut across community claims on land (Nhantumbo et al, in preparation).

Although policy and legislative changes have been introduced in the region, they do not go far enough in removing the bureaucratic hurdles that increase transaction costs; they have not gone far enough in giving full management authority to resource users; they have not gone far enough in treating wildlife as a competitive form of land use; and they have not gone far enough in providing local residents with secure and exclusive rights over their land.

Communal Institutions

CBNRM implies that a 'community' of people 'has an adequate institutional base for management, and this in turn implies that it has a sanctioned authority that implements its responsibilities' (Murphree, 1994, p405). We have seen above how policy and legislation have provided for the establishment of such 'sanctioned authorities' and have devolved some form of rights and authority, or proprietorship, over wildlife to these institutions. These policy and legislative provisions provide a form of external legitimacy, but if these institutions are to function effectively, they also need to be legitimized from within. For this internal legitimization to take place, the community represented by the sanctioned authority needs to be defined. Much recent social science scholarship has highlighted the fact that 'communities' are highly differentiated in terms of socio-economic status and power and that different interest groups within communities are engaged in a 'struggle' for power and influence over the allocation of various resources (eg Leach et al, 1997). As a result, it is argued, there are difficulties in defining a 'community'. CBNRM assumes that despite often high levels of differentiation within groups of people, social units can be identified where people interact directly and have a collective identity. It is further assumed that the ongoing dynamic conflicts within such social units can be contained by collective agreement and compliance facilitated by a 'coalescent authority structure' (Murphree 1994).

Within the region, the 'community' is often pre-defined by government political or administrative units such as the wards in Zimbabwe and the CHAs in Botswana. These units can throw together groups of people who might not usually identify themselves as having a collective identity or who would cooperate in resource management. In other areas (such as some conservancies in Namibia) the 'community' consists of several thousand people. In both these sets of circumstances it is often difficult for a 'coalescent authority' that can contain internal conflicts to emerge. Where policy and legislation allow communities to define themselves (Namibia, Mozambique) the potential for developing a coalescent authority is likely to improve.[14]

The institutional form of the sanctioned authorities that has emerged under CBNRM in the region is largely based on formal mechanisms such as committees, constitutions and written plans, and they largely conform to the way that external support agencies themselves structure their own governance. In part, this approach has been driven by the need for communities to form legal entities that can enter into formal contracts with the private sector and other entities. However, as Bell (2000) has suggested, these mechanisms run contrary to the customary or 'informal constitutions' that operate in communities, and they conflict with the systems of decision making in communities that are based on negotiation and consensus-building. Murombedzi (2001) suggests this has been a problem in Zimbabwe, where a focus on creating new 'formal' institutions has tended to ignore important pre-existing 'traditional' institutions, resulting in an alienation of communities from the CAMPFIRE programme.

The 'hard' boundaries created by formal, written land-use plans, zoning and fencing are very different to the 'soft' boundaries that communities use to enable overlapping and easily negotiable rights of access. Certainly in Namibia the introduction of hard boundaries such as borders of conservancies, fences for core wildlife areas and wildlife use zones has led to the revitalizing and hardening of existing inter- and intra-community conflicts that had been largely dormant previously. Internal legitimacy is more likely to be built if the new resource management institutions can be more consistent with existing local forms of governance.

New institutions for resource management do not operate in a vacuum, and they need to interact and develop relationships with existing institutions. Traditional authorities are important in this regard because in many countries they are 'owners' of the land in the minds of many residents: they allocate land, have authority over natural resources, and they play an important role in local dispute resolution and the administration of justice (Jones and Weaver, in preparation).

Incentives

CBNRM is largely an incentive-based programme. The incentives that are provided through policy and legislation operate at different levels. So far, CBNRM in the region has been successful in creating financial benefits at a collective 'community' level rather than at the individual level. In many cases, it might be argued that the financial benefits of wildlife management are not outweighing the cost to households in terms of damage to crops and livestock losses, nor are they significant when compared with the contribution of other livelihood activities. However, CBNRM is delivering several benefits that need to be viewed in terms of an incentives package, of which financial benefit forms a part. Another benefit is the creation of new institutions that provide management regimes for common property and take on other local-level institutional functions, including interaction with external institutional actors such as government. In Namibia, some communities view CBNRM as an opportunity to strengthen their hold over their land in the absence of strong group land rights. Aesthetic and cultural incentives are also important, but often ignored.

In Namibia, there is evidence for suggesting that the relative importance of different types of incentive shifts over time and between generations. Thus, in northwest Namibia CBNRM was founded on giving responsibility and authority over wildlife to traditional leadership and local elders before the possibility of financial benefit was a reality. Now a younger generation of leaders is often more dominant on conservancy committees, and the need for jobs and household income is a much higher priority (Jones, B, 2001).

Scale

Scale is an important factor in CBNRM in several arenas. In the discussion of community institutions above, reference was made to problems associated with a community made up of many people. Apart from differences in resource endowment among local communities, there are strong variations in size of these communities and the land they occupy. In Mozambique, the size of individual CBNRM areas varies from 10,000ha to 4,612,400ha, whereas the number of households in these areas varies from 759 to 10,360 (Nhantumbo et al, in preparation). Some practical approaches are required to deal with the institutional and organizational problems presented by large numbers of people often spread over a large geographical area.

Small social units provide the opportunity for direct interaction between residents, particularly in terms of collective decision making. Such 'participatory democracy' (Child, 2003; Child, in preparation, a, b) facilitates accountability and transparency and is likely to ensure that local household needs will be met when decisions are taken about the use of collective wildlife income. Peer pressure can play a role in the monitoring of compliance with local resource use rules. Community normative values are more likely to play a role in compliance and determining collective interest at a small social scale (Murphree, 1994).

At the same time that local units of jurisdiction need to be small, these units do not operate in isolation. Such units will need to interact with each other and cooperate in aspects of resource management (wildlife is a mobile 'fugitive' resource that, particularly in open systems in more arid regions, moves over large distances). Such units will also need to find ways of interacting and 'nesting' with state hierarchies from which they need to derive legitimacy and sometimes arbitration in disputes (Ostrom 1990; Murphree, 2000). Once boundaries have been closed by creating local units of jurisdiction they need to be transcended for these units to articulate with other jurisdictions at different scales. Murphree (2000) suggests this can be done through first applying the principle of 'jurisdictional parsimony', by which the management requirements of specific resources are matched to jurisdictions no larger than necessary. The next component is for local jurisdictions to scale up through aggregation based on delegation of aspects of their responsibility and authority to units of collective governance of greater scope. Importantly in this hierarchy, accountability remains downwards, ie the larger level units of governance are accountable to the constituent smaller units. Policy and legislation need to allow space for local residents to experiment in finding appropriate size-localized units of jurisdiction as well as to find appropriate institutional arrangements for scaling up.

Business Relationships

CBNRM relies heavily on links between local communities and the private sector for the generation of financial benefits. Typically, community management bodies lease photographic and safari concessions or quotas to a private company. Depending on the country context, the income or a share of income from the tourism and hunting activities is returned to local communities. Two key issues emerge from analysing the relationships between the private sector and the community wildlife management institutions. One of these issues is the extent to which communities themselves have control over the land and resources that are the subject of the contractual arrangement with the private sector. Ashley and Jones (2001) suggest that communities are better able to secure favourable deals with the private sector where there are strong community institutions with legal rights over the land and/or resources. If the community has control over a desirable asset then the private sector is forced to negotiate with the 'proprietor', despite the higher transaction costs often associated with such negotiations.[15] At the same time, a community's market power also depends upon the market value of its assets. This leads to the next important issue. In negotiations between communities and the private sector there is often an imbalance of power. The private sector has the capital, knowledge of the industry and implementational expertise. Often, communities do not understand the value of their resource. They need to be able to value their resource and they need an understanding of the tourism industry and the various benefits and costs that safari hunting or photographic tourism might bring. Facilitation by outsiders can help redress this power imbalance.

Experience from Namibia (Ashley and Jones, 2001) and Zimbabwe (Murphree, 2001) also indicates that successful partnerships between communities and the private sector can be based on a coincidence of interests as well as enlightened private sector motives. Various synergies exist. A long-term investment horizon coincides with community interests in long-term management of the resource and sustainable benefit. A successful partnership with the community can be an important selling point in the ecotourism market.

Process

CBNRM in southern Africa can be viewed as a set of activities that support the promotion of sustainable management of natural resources, or it can more usefully be viewed as an ongoing process characterized by experimentation and adaptive management (of the wildlife resources as well as of the process itself). As part of the process, CBNRM has gone through various stages of evolution. Initial activities were focused on the establishment of appropriate enabling policy and legislative environments, with experience in the freehold sector and some limited field implementation in communal areas helping to inform the development of policy and legislation (Jones and Murphree, 2001).

The focus then shifted to supporting the development of local community bodies that could function as effective organizations, holding meetings, running committees, hiring staff, interacting with other organizations and institutions, and negotiating contracts with the private sector. During this phase there was considerable emphasis on developing appropriate methods for resource monitoring by local communities. Through internal programme monitoring and evaluation and critical analysis, the focus is shifting much more towards addressing key institutional and governance issues. Regionally, the programme is exploring options for devolution to smaller social units that can promote participatory decision making, and greater accountability and transparency. Individual countries have learned from the experience of others with regard to key issues for policy development and implementation. Although isolated geographically from other countries that have implemented CBNRM, and by language barriers, Mozambique has leapfrogged most other countries in the region with its land policy and legislation. In this, Mozambique points the way to the next phase of CBNRM evolution, which must be to address the issue of communal land rights and tenure.

An important part of the process of CBNRM has been the style of facilitation adopted by many practitioners in the region. This has been called consistent and persistent 'light touch' community empowerment and facilitation (Hitchcock and Murphree, 1995). This approach involves working directly with communities and not only through local government institutions or traditional leaders. It includes regular visits to the communities concerned, staying in touch with community power shifts and internal dynamics, assisting communities to identify key issues and potential problems, helping them to work through these issues, and then developing appropriate decisions, solutions and actions.

The idea of CBNRM as a process has implications for implementational time frames. Time is needed for the new community resource management institutions to gain internal legitimacy, develop accountable and transparent governance systems, realize the full potential of income generating opportunities, develop into sufficiently strong political constituencies that can demand services from government, and advocate for stronger proprietorship over land and resources. Time is also required in some areas for wildlife numbers to recover such that significant benefits can be derived from various forms of use. The time horizons required for CBNRM to mature do not usually match the three- or four-year funding periods on which most donor-funded projects are based. Further, the idea of CBNRM as a process needs to incorporate the trajectories of change within individual communities or country programmes, which do not necessarily follow simple upward or downward curves. Over time, there is likely to be considerable fluctuation in progress, depending upon both internal and external factors. In many ways progress needs to be measured by the degree of resilience over time that programmes and local institutions show to internal and external factors, rather than the benefits and outputs that result at any given point in time.

DIRECTIONS FOR A SECOND-GENERATION CBNRM

The previous section has outlined the range of issues that have confronted CBNRM as it has attempted to translate concept into practice during what can be considered its 'first generation' era, roughly the period from the mid-1980s to the early 2000s. Many of these issues are implementational, anticipated in early conceptualization but without a full grasp on the intricacies involved. Others (for example scale) had not received adequate attention in early planning. And still others involve fundamental assumptions about the nature of social interaction that remain open to debate.

The interplay between these issues and unfolding results has produced a profile of mixed performance in CBNRM. The earlier section on performance delineates aspects of this, instancing evidence (substantiated or inferential) of success. But it also shows failure or retarded progress. It is fair to say that performance has rarely approximated promise, and in some cases has been abysmal. This mixed performance has fuelled a contemporary chorus of criticism of CBNRM, stemming from several quarters. For those philosophically opposed to conjoining conservation and livelihood concerns, it has provided the opportunity to renew their attacks on the sustainable use paradigm of conservation (Hoyt, 1994; Oates, 1999).[16] Donors, impatient with the slow pace of progress in realizing the goals of CBNRM, have begun to question their investment in the approach and to seek 'new' initiatives in conservation and development. Most substantially serious scholarship has questions about some of the core assumptions on which CBNRM has been based (Rozemeijer, in preparation).[17]

If CBNRM in southern Africa is to retain the vitality of its initial stages into a second generation of incremental growth, it must candidly deal with these critiques, learn from its mistakes and misdirections, revisit its assumptions, build on its successes and adapt to the changing circumstances of the times. In doing so we suggest that the following three directions in conceptual and programmatic development are of prime importance.

Dealing with Devolution

Devolution, as discussed in the introductory section to this chapter, is one of the conceptual pillars of CBNRM policy in southern Africa. There was an assumption behind this aspect of the policy: that governments would be willing, either through professional suasion or political demand, to carry forward the rhetoric of its rationale to actualization in the legal conferment of the necessary level of rights and responsibilities required to achieve efficient localized regimes that enhanced sustainability.

It is difficult, however, to find a single case in the region where this bundle of necessary entitlements has been conferred on local regimes in communal conditions (in contrast to alienated land). There are instances of effective, in-place devolution, where through local assertiveness or administrative dispensation, communities hold these rights as exceptional cases.

In general, however, devolution under CBNRM policies has been partial, fragmented, discretionary and aborted. Partial and fragmented, in that communities have been granted rights to benefit flows from natural resources but not to the land on which they exist (Botswana: Rozemeijer, in preparation; Namibia: Jones and Weaver, in preparation; Zimbabwe: Taylor, in preparation) or to land but not the natural resources on it (Mozambique: Nhantumbu et al, in preparation), but not to both. Discretionary, in that the rights conferred have been made conditional on compliance to detailed regulatory lists, judgements on this compliance being administrative rather than legal. This has resulted in bureaucracies often blocking the devolutionary intent of policy and indeed legislation where it exists.[18] Aborted, in the case of

Zimbabwe, where devolution reaches down only to the level of rural district councils and not further to the communities that produce the revenue and provide on-the-ground management.

Paradoxically, one of the other conceptual pillars of CBNRM, the emphasis on realizing true market values for natural resources, inhibits the actualizing of devolution. If these values are realized, the hegemonic interests of the state to retain their benefits are reinforced, and it is less disposed to surrender them. This is illustrated in Zimbabwe's CAMPFIRE Programme, where devolution to rural district councils has led to significant increases in council revenues and where in some cases wildlife is now the main source of council revenues (Bond, 2001). This is of great value to central government, which is relieved of the necessity of providing administrative and development subsidies to such councils. Neither councils nor government are thus inclined to loosen their grip on these benefits and the power they represent by further devolution to producer communities. 'In such cases', Murombedzi notes, 'the top-down preferences of central governments on communities have merely been replaced by the top-down preferences of local governments on communities' (Murombedzi, 2001, p255). In effect, in Zimbabwe's CBNRM programme devolution has been emasculated to mean decentralization.

We should see this resistance to devolution against the backdrop of larger and more enduring debates on the political philosophy of governance and democracy generally, and on the political history of post-colonial Africa in particular. At a generic level we can note that devolution and democratization are inextricably linked. Devolution in tenure, in responsibility, in rights and access to benefit streams is a fundamental issue of politics and allocation. Power structures at the political and economic centre are not disposed to surrender their privileges and will use their power, including their abilities to shape policy and law, to maintain the monopolies of their position.[19] This disposition was characteristic of colonial Africa and has endured in its post-colonial phase. 'In dealing with the problem of controlling popular demand for an overhaul of colonial property rights, while at the same time extending some land and resource control to indigenous citizens, the post-liberation state has not sought to change the colonial dispensation. Rather, it has maintained, in some cases even perfected, colonial practices of resource control. Despite the discourses of 'communal tenure' and devolution to local communities, the state has also retained rights to and control over the so-called 'communal lands' of the region.' (Murombedzi, 2003, p136). Ake reaches a similar conclusion: 'An interesting commentary on the status of democratization in Africa is that the political class, both those in power and those out of power and demanding democratization, seem to have no interest even now in transforming the autocratic postcolonial state' (Ake, 2000, p160).

It is therefore evident that the expectation that governments would actualize robust devolution as part of their more generalized espousal of CBNRM has been more of an aspiration than a verified assumption. It is, however, a critically important aspiration for several reasons:

- It is a pivotal fulcrum in dynamizing innovation, entrepreneurship and organizational development at local levels. This is abundantly evident in the experience of devolution to individual proprietors (see Chapter 2), and in the instances of effective devolution to collective proprietors in CBNRM.

- Even when achieved in a piecemeal manner, devolution provides a powerful incremental lever in raising wider aspirations for self-actualized livelihoods and resource sustainability in rural localities.
- It enables CBNRM to avoid the isolation of being merely a 'conservation mechanism' and aligns it with the broader dynamic of pressures to move African politics to a more participatory democratic mode. In its fusion of devolution and economic instrumentalism, southern African CBNRM follows Ake's prescription of 'making economic development itself a process of democratization' (Ake, 2000, p173).

How can a second generation of CBNRM in southern Africa sustain the centrality of devolution in the face of the apparent intractability that its realization faces?[20] We suggest that the following should be on the strategic agenda that deals with this issue.

Persistence

Pressure should be maintained on the consciousness of establishment actors about the political imperatives of devolution, particularly in the long term. Politicians may be prone to the enchantments of acquiring power, but some are astute enough to recognize that maintaining power involves flexibility and compromise. Supporting devolution may well involve the immediate divestment of elements of power but also may reap future political dividends in terms of maintaining constituency support. Advocates and practitioners of CBNRM should be persistent in proclaiming this message: devolution relates to complex and evolving bio-social systems, with the promise of rewards to those perceived to be enhancing their resilience.

Contextual Opportunism

CBNRM history in southern Africa (see Chapter 2 and Child, in preparation, b) has shown that the convergence of given circumstances (political, economic, ecological or organizational) at a single point in time can create the space for radical policy change. Frequently, such convergences are seen in terms of 'crisis,' the incapacity of institutions to fulfil their former mandates. They may, however, be viewed positively, as opportunities for novelty and innovation.

As it has done in the past, southern Africa currently continues to provide such episodic convergences of circumstance that provide the societal context for institutional redundancy and reformulation. Perhaps the clearest examples are to be found in Zimbabwe and South Africa where several factors (see Chapter 9) have led to the imperative of land reform, including land restitution and land redistribution. In South Africa the process continues; in Zimbabwe, the government has recently declared that the land reform exercise has been 'completed'. If, however, we examine the structures under which the bulk of the farmers in the region operate through the linkages between tenure, sustainable use and devolution, we can see how redundant they are, and how the most fundamental land reform of all has scarcely begun. Devolution is a critical aspect of this reform and current context, with its upheavals and fluidity, provides the opportunity for its promotion. The exploitation of this opportunity by CBNRM should be high on its strategic agenda.

Constituency Building

By its nature CBNRM concentrates on moving power and initiative to local levels. The danger is that this may fragment successful CBNRM experience, which needs to coalesce at national levels into a powerful political constituency that has an effective voice in advocating devolution. National associations to represent CBNRM communities and to lobby for their interests at the national centre have been formed in Namibia, Zimbabwe and Botswana. These associations have raised the profile of CBNRM in their respective countries and played a role in resisting attempts by governments to recentralize some of the power that has been dispersed through CBNRM programmes (Child et al, 2003). However, there has been a tendency for these associations to become another layer of inflated bureaucracy on the CBNRM scene and, in the case of Zimbabwe, to represent rural district councils rather than their communal constituents. CBNRM strategy should be to encourage the formation of such associations throughout the region, while carefully tailoring their structure and role to be genuinely representative of their constituencies' devolutionary interest.

Incrementalism

Although CBNRM in southern Africa has so far exhibited only partial or 'aborted' devolution, strategy should not discount the impact of instances of effective, in-place devolution that have been achieved. These instances have a powerful lateral demonstration effect, raising the horizons of aspiration in other communities that have as yet not reached this level of empowerment.[21] Strategy should incorporate efforts to enhance this demonstration effect through various techniques of communication and exchange.

Step-wise progress towards full devolution can also be effected when, in CBNRM projects, small shifts towards local initiation and control produce new configurations of actor-networks that open up policy spaces 'with new forms of bureaucratic practice emerging. This has often started at the local level through the discretionary actions of 'street-level bureaucrats', but sometimes has permeated upwards and outwards into structural organization reform' (Keeley and Scoones, 2000, p26). Although no substitute for a robust devolution conferred by the state, this form of bottom-up empowerment has incremental salience in infiltrating state policy.

Dealing with 'Community'

The issue of 'community' has already been introduced in the section on communal institutions. As noted there, this conceptual pillar of CBNRM thinking involves (like devolution) an assumption: that in certain circumstances collectivities of land and resource users interacting at local levels can create viable regimes of communal property use and management maintained by relatively stable normative consensus. In other words, in certain circumstances collective good can institutionally supercede individual or sectional instrumentality.

This was the assumption propounded by common property theory in its inceptive stages as a counter-argument to assertions like those of Hardin (1968) that the sustainable use of common-pool resources could be achieved only by state or individual proprietorship. Indeed, it was a verified assumption, built on a wide range of enduring, self-governing common-pool resource institutions.[22] Localized collective management can work in certain circumstances. Since its inceptive stages, common property theory has effloresced into a vast body of scholarship concerned with what these circumstances are, and are not.[23]

One stream in this scholarship has pointed out major deficiencies in any simplistic programmatic application of this assumption. It isolates the local from larger societal structures; it assumes local homogeneity in the face of manifest differentiation; it is ahistorical; it ignores power relationships; and it tends to be overly determinative. In the light of these critiques a social constructionist stance is presented and adopted, using the theoretic frameworks used by Long and Long (1992), Berry (1993), Leach et al (1997), Peters (1994) and others. In essence, this stance regards normative patterns (institutions) as being highly dynamic and flexible, subject to constant manipulation by individuals or interest groups for their own instrumental purposes. Normative positions are subject to continuous reconstruction stemming from the socio-political location of the wide spectrum of social actors concerned, and this in turn affects behaviours and outcomes. Recent scholarship on southern African CBNRM reinforces these conclusions (eg Madzudzo, 2002; Sithole, 1999; Venter, 1998; Malasha, 2003).

In its second-generation stage, southern African CBNRM must take on board these insights. They do not invalidate the basic assumption that communal regimes of resource management can be viable, but they serve to warn against naïve assumptions of local homogeneity and detachment. They also serve to dispel any notion that the creation of viable and effective localized regimes is simply a matter of good extension work and training in organization and fiscal management. They tip interventions away from formulaic and determinative approaches to a more systemic and process-oriented mode.

This shift implies several intervention stances that should be adopted in 'dealing with communities' by CBNRM in its next phase. We list these in a propositional form, to emphasize that the list is not a formulaic blueprint that provides answers to all the obstacles to local natural-resource regime development.

(a) Effective Collective Action Emerges, It Is Not Imposed

Such action and the structures it evolves are the result of choice, and this choice requires the presence (latent or actual) of collective will and the social capital to implement it. This cannot be provided by third parties.[24] Communities of resource users are not 'developmentees'; they may, however, be groups with sufficient endogenous incentive and cohesion to collectively participate in the governance of their own lives and the resources on which they depend. From this fundamental proposition several corollaries arise which should guide CBNRM interventions.

(b) Accept Negative Signals

When the preconditions for emergence mentioned above do not exist, CBNRM should accept this and direct its energies elsewhere. Certainly it should avoid falling into an impositional mode in pursuit of inclusiveness. CBNRM was conceptualized as a programme of voluntary incorporation, and should maintain this stance.

(c) Protect the Conditions for Emergence

When the preconditions for emergence exist, protect and enhance them. Protecting these conditions primarily involves the insurance that local social capital remains intact, ie that local collective aspirations and normative institutions are allowed to grow and evolve free from threats of disempowerment. Such threats usually arise from imposition: the imposition of regime scope and boundaries (characteristic in Zimbabwe, avoided in Namibia; see Taylor, in preparation; Jones and Weaver, in preparation), the imposition of unrealistic implementational time frames and the imposition of externally designed patterns of output or input distribution. Withdrawal from CBNRM programmes in response to such impositions must always be an open option rather than a covert tactic. The option of open withdrawal is, in fact, an important component of empowerment. Enhancing the conditions of emergence involves the encouragement of experimentation, the freedom to make mistakes and learn from them, and the facilitation of copying and variability.

(d) Assume Differentiation and Conflict

Internal competition and conflict are characteristic of small-scale organizations, currently exacerbated by the impacts of commoditization and differential accumulation. This assumption should be the norm rather than the premise of homogeneity that is so often fostered by superficial 'rapid rural appraisal' research techniques. Facilitation can only be effective when it goes deeper than this and offers a suite of informed options for compromise and conflict resolution.[25] But the solutions must come from within the community members themselves; it is they who have the prerogative and responsibility to seek centripetal consensus to counter the centrifugal tendencies of sectional interest.

(e) Anticipate Change and Evolution

All structures of social organization are subject to change, and this is true of local regimes as they experiment, innovate and surmount or succumb to challenge. CBNRM experience demonstrates this: a good example is the way some conservancies in Namibia have split into separate entities as experience has dictated smaller regimes for reasons of organizational efficiency and social cohesion (Jones and Weaver, in preparation). Anticipating change and evolution has its implications for CBNRM evaluations. These must be diachronic or longitudinal, not based on synchronic 'one-off' static profiles from one point in time. There is no inexorable unilinear trajectory of 'success' or 'failure' in such local endeavours. A regime judged at one moment in its history as floundering may at another exhibit a renewed vigour. The reverse is also true. Only iterative evaluations over significant periods can give a reliable indication of trend.

(f) Refine Adaptive Management

As already indicated, adaptive management has been an in-built component of CBNRM since its inception. To work, however, adaptive management requires specified goals, techniques of performance measurement, and analyses leading to adaptation. Without these the approach drifts into mere trial-and-error (Lee, 1993, p9).

In CBNRM this learning and adaptation must be at community levels, by local managers themselves. In the region, considerable progress has been made in developing local competence in measuring sustainable wildlife offtakes, Zimbabwe being the outstanding example in its training programme facilitated by the World Wide Fund for Nature (WWF) (see Taylor, in preparation). This example should be replicated in the other countries of the region. Far less has been done on the organizational and institutional aspects of adaptive management, and this is a glaring weakness in current CBNRM. A new phase of the programme should make this a high priority.

(g) Promote Extended Timescales in Local Planning and Perspectives

Temporal scale features prominently in the analysis of systemic ecologists, who are concerned with scale mismatches between short-term practice and long-term ecological processes. Sustainability is a concept inherently related to temporal scale and the relationships between the present and the future. Temporal scale also features in debates on inter-generational equity.

The time frames used in dealing with temporal scale vary. Typically, however, time frames used in planning and action are short, dictated by immediate economic and political considerations. Caricatures exist: the politician's time frame is determined by the length of time between elections; that of the subsistence farmer by annual or biannual seasons of crop production. These are exaggerations, but have some substance in terms of actual investments in the future. They are also over-generalizations, masking the fact that different time frames are applied by different people to different things. The investment by poor households in rural Africa in their children's education is a striking example; here the time frame is multigenerational.

The fact remains that planning for the use of nature is generally done in short time frames at national and local levels. In their survey of case studies in Africa, Bernstein and Woodhouse conclude that 'Indigenous communal institutions do not appear to act on matters of (long-term) resource management as distinct from (current) allocation ...' (Bernstein and Woodhouse, 2000, p207). Imposed planning and implementation does little better, and marches to the 2–5-year time horizons of donor-funded projects. At local levels, dealing with significant timescales is also defective, because communities rarely have the entitlements necessary for them to experiment.

The emphasis of CBNRM on the emergence and empowerment of effective local regimes implies that the locus in 'visioning' the future must be the local. The value of local experience, knowledge and perspectives is now generally accepted in development discourse, but too often this value is co-opted for other, externally generated, agendas (Long and Villareal, 1994). CBNRM programmes must avoid this tendency. The role of researchers and facilitators requires a different kind of involvement with the local: invited rather than imposed, directed rather than directive, facilitative rather than manipulative. It should represent professional science in the service of local civic science. To quote Emery Roe: 'The obvious challenge is to come up with varieties of inside-out planning for ecosystem management, where local leaders and residents are themselves the experts and where the planning process is itself initiated and guided from within the local ecosystem.' (Roe, 1998, p130).

One of the most promising approaches to such 'inside-out' planning is scenario modelling, in which communities collectively construct their preferred vision of the future of their localities for specified time frames, based, among other things, on their projected needs (both material and cultural), their resources, their modes of production, their institutions and their extra-local relationships. Scenario modelling must, however, include not only 'visioning' and aspirations: it must incorporate a consideration of constraints and alternatives and it must include an agenda for action. Finally, it must include iterative evaluations and corrective adjustment. This takes us back to adaptive management, and scenario modelling may well be one of the best techniques for its application to the organizational and institutional aspects of CBNRM.

(h) Be Cautious with Intervention

If we accept that robust localized regimes of land and resource management emerge endogenously under the right conditions, we must also accept that CBNRM cannot be a pre-packaged strategy delivered or imposed at local level. Professional CBNRM practitioners (researchers and government or NGO agents) thus have a facilitative rather than directive role, and their interventions must be carefully calibrated. Whether and when to intervene (or not) is not a trivial question and it is often better to let the local system generate its own course.

There may, however, be appropriate conditions for intervention. Ruitenbeek and Cartier have suggested what these might be, posed in a series of questions (Ruitenbeek and Cartier, 2001, p30). In slightly amended form we replicate them here:

1   Will the intervention itself generate a learning experience? Minimally, this requires monitoring the effect of the intervention, but it also requires introducing opportunities to change or withdraw the intervention.
2   Do I as a designer know more about the system than the agents in introducing this intervention? This is a common presumption but is not always true. External agents may well have access to information on larger contexts not locally available; on the other hand, local system dynamics are usually better understood by those who operate within them.
3   If I as designer do know more than the agents, am I better off implementing the intervention or simply giving the information to the agents? In general, implementation is better left to local agents.
4   Is the timing right? One needs to consider the timing of an intervention in the context of the system. Given that a complex system goes through various adaptive stages, it follows that there may be good times and bad times to introduce interventions.

CBNRM facilitation needs to take these questions seriously. To this we can add that intervention must be demand responsive. No demand is indicative of system inertia, or poor facilitation–community relationships. When these relationships are good, and when perceptions of empowerment are high, requests for facilitation are likely to be open and constant. Facilitation properly done is vital to CBNRM progress but is in short supply. Its provision in the modes we have suggested opens up new roles for government extension agents and is a central function for supporting NGOs. The agencies involved, in the second phase of CBNRM, are thus presented with heavy responsibilities and demanding challenges.

Dealing with Diversity

CBNRM strategy in southern Africa was not conceptualized as a competing, mutually exclusive conservation paradigm to conventional state-managed protected-area policies.[26] Rather, it was a complementary strategy to deal with conservation through sustainable use on land outside national parks where governments could not provide the necessary levels of effective conservation management. Even on this land (where the bulk of national biodiversity lies) CBNRM has not claimed to be a panacea for all conservation problems, particularly those that are industrially induced. Critiques of CBNRM that claim that it has not fulfilled the 'promise of panacea' are thus misdirected.

It is true, however, that proponents of CBNRM have sometimes carelessly encouraged the notion of CBNRM polyvalency in rural communal contexts, sometimes in response to donor aspirations for comprehensive solutions to the problems of rural livelihoods and development. This has raised unrealistic expectations and resultant disillusionment, with particularly negative results when the notion has been propounded indiscriminately at local levels. In part, this is because effective CBNRM hinges critically on devolution, which as this chapter shows has rarely been present at operationally viable levels. As Child comments, 'The bad name increasingly given to CBNRM arises because the logo is attached to programmes that purport to be CBNRM programmes, but in fact do not follow the rigour of [its] principles' (Child, in preparation).

In part, however, this is also due to the fact that another of it principles, economic instrumentalism, rests on conditions that are not evenly distributed across the rural landscape. In its first phase, CBNRM has largely proceeded on the assumption of the presence at local levels of natural species (primarily wildlife but also forest products) of sufficient economic value to make them a competitive form of land use. (Or, in some cases, the presence of habitat into which they can be introduced.) The fact of the matter is that such resources are not evenly distributed, and in many localities resource/demand ratios are such that the presence of these species can only be of symbolic or ecological value. In such contexts a CBNRM initiative promising the delivery of direct economic value is doomed to fail; its configuration of benefit must be based on other values.

In its next phase CBNRM will have to deal with this diversity more systematically, recognizing that it cannot grow in one form only; there are, in fact, several forms of CBNRM. In this disaggregation we provide below a notional contextual profile, the aim not being to impose any rigid typology but to provide a framework in which circumstance, objective, implementation and expectation can be more closely matched.

(a) Local Regimes with High (Present or Potential) Market Value Natural Resources

Where these circumstances apply, current CBNRM approaches, with their emphasis on economic instrumentality, should be pursued with vigour. Such contexts have provided most of the successes of CBNRM so far when the enabling principles have been present. Where these principles have not been applied this should be addressed, in ways already discussed in this chapter. Where tenure fragmentation has occurred (for instance through resettlement) and appear to preclude collective management, consideration should be given to the voluntary re-aggregation of management in various configurations of selective collaboration already pioneered in private-sector game ranching.

(b) Local Regimes with Low/Medium Market Value Natural Resources

In these circumstances, the emphasis should shift away from direct natural-resource market values towards other institutional and ecosystem values. Sustainable agro-biodiversity should be the generalized goal, with the more diffuse but powerful incentives of collective empowerment providing the dynamic. This has an important corollary: CBNRM in this mode needs to avoid being 'locked in' to its current alliances with environmental and conservation establishments and form new alliances with those connected with agricultural development and extension. The structures of government bureaucracies, donor interest and NGO foci have tended to separate agricultural and natural resource issues. This is largely a conceptually imposed distinction and not the way rural peoples tend to think. For them, both are components in one livelihood system derived from a common biophysical resource: 'agriculture' in a broad sense of the word. CBNRM has a lot in common with this perspective and has great potential to contribute to the region's agricultural development. The development of this potential should be a major focus in the future of CBNRM.

(c) Local Regimes Adjacent to State-Protected Areas

As noted earlier in this chapter, people–parks relationships have not been a focus of southern African CBNRM, with the notable exceptions of Malawi and South Africa. However, demographic and tenure changes, coupled with the creation and expansion of large transboundary protected areas, are likely to give this kind of context more prominence throughout the region in the future, calling for new forms of relationship and collaboration. Owing to their location, the CBNRM regimes involved are likely to fall into the category of those with high market value natural resources, but we categorize them separately because of the special state–community relationships involved. More will be said on this set of relationships in the concluding section of this chapter.

(d) Local Regimes for Aquatic Resources

CBNRM in southern Africa has so far been largely focused on terrestrial resources. Some initiatives to deal with aquatic resources and their associated regimes in marine environments and large inland freshwater bodies have developed,[27] but these experiences have not been closely integrated into larger regional CBNRM networking and analysis. In dealing with diversity, CBNRM needs to give attention to the particular attributes of this category. The necessary cohesion for fisher regimes presents particular organizational issues, and the mobile and dispersed nature of the resources involved presents problems for regimes based primarily on spatial delimitations (Degnbol, 2002). Terrestrial and aquatic contexts may therefore require different approaches, although many of the basic issues remain the same in both cases.

A Next Phase in CBNRM: Concluding Remarks

We have in this section discussed directions for a second-generation CBNRM in southern Africa under three headings: dealing with devolution, dealing with community and dealing with diversity. These we consider to contain the core issues that CBNRM must address if it is to maintain the momentum it has generated in its first phase. The three headings do not, however, provide a comprehensive coverage of all the issues with which CBNRM must grapple. There is, for instance, the matter of more effectively integrating bureaucratic and technical establishments into CBNRM activities and processes. Even when policies and legislation change in accordance with CBNRM principles, the ethos of these establishments and their personnel tends to lag behind, developed and trained as they are in obsolete 'command-and-control' perspectives. These establishments are a critical fulcrum in CBNRM implementation and without their committed engagement this implementation will be obstructed at many junctures. CBNRM must therefore give more attention to 'mainstreaming' its perspectives in these establishments (see Jones and Weaver, in preparation). Another issue is donor–CBNRM engagement. The record so far on this engagement is mixed. Some of the most successful 'best practice' case-study examples show little or no direct donor involvement, and indeed CBNRM should now be strong enough to develop without donor support. There is, however, no doubt that judicious donor support, if it is properly targeted and cast in appropriate time frames, can enhance the conceptual and programmatic development of CBNRM. This issue thus needs further consideration as CBNRM moves into its next phase.

These are but two of the many items for a fuller agenda for the future of CBNRM. The scope of the agenda is challenging but we can take confidence in this future when we consider the competence and commitment of the new generation of professionals and practitioners who now carry the responsibility of translating this agenda into success.

CBNRM AND PROTECTED AREAS

We conclude this chapter with a brief section on the relationship between CBNRM approaches and 'protected areas', conventionally exemplified by areas set aside and managed by the state for a range of conservation objectives. More recently, this perspective has been questioned and it has been suggested that protected areas may well exist outside state systems, managed by private individual or non-state collective proprietors.[28]

CBNRM philosophy in southern Africa is consistent with this view. It suggests that a well-managed local regime of sustainable natural resource use is a form of protected area, in that controls are in place to conserve and protect against abuse. Furthermore, such regimes may well designate areas within their jurisdiction for specific forms of protection for wildlife habitat, forest zones, areas of special scenic beauty, or sites of particular cultural or religious significance. In other words, such regimes act as 'the state writ small', zoning and managing for particular purposes. In this way CBNRM, properly instituted, expands a nation's protected-area landscape far beyond what the state's capacity to establish and maintain such area would allow. CBNRM and state park systems are not antithetical; rather, they are complementary approaches to the same general objective. Which approach is more appropriate in given contexts depends critically on the nature and constituency of the commonage to be protected (see Chapter 9).

Here, however, we focus particularly on the relationships between state managed parks and their close neighbours. This has long been a concern for parks policy, which has recently turned from a 'fences-and-fines' approach to a 'fences-

and-friends' approach. In its more advanced forms the 'fences-and-friends' tactic has developed into a 'no-fences-and-mutual-benefit' model in which the state management authority enters into agreement with its neighbours to 'co-manage' contiguous areas for natural benefit in exchange for cooperation and compliance with given conditions. South Africa's current 'contract parks' initiative is an example.

This certainly raises the level of mutual participation, but even co-management arrangements can act as a fig-leaf for continued state hegemony, particularly if they represent agreements between partners of different legal status. This is typically the case in southern Africa, where state parks abut on land under communal tenure. Thus, for instance, Magome and Murombedzi observe that 'the co-management agreements of the Richtersveld and Kruger National Parks are the result of unequal negotiation between relatively disadvantaged community representatives and sophisticated and advantaged officials of SANParks' (Magome and Murombedzi, 2003, p119). The result is a sense of manipulated compliance and continued expropriation on the part of the park's communal neighbours.

Co-management by unequal status partners is therefore not enough. To unleash the potentials for sound management and entrepreneurial success that effective collaboration holds, what the parks need and what their neighbours need are negotiated contractual agreements between parties with legal persona, holding rights to veto or withdrawal. The ecological and economic benefits of such agreements are manifest in the flourishing private conservancies that border Kruger National Park, but such agreements will not be possible for its communal neighbours until their status is changed to that of being legally recognized private collective entities.

In their survey of South African contract parks, Grossman and Holden (in preparation) reach similar conclusions on the impediments raised by limited community empowerment. They also emphasize the importance of consensus at community levels. We are thus back full circle to the two pillars of CBNRM that have been emphasized in this chapter: robust devolution and communal institutional cohesion. State parks systems and CBNRM have common cause on these issues, and this congruence of interest should provide a new entry point for processes leading to their attainment.

NOTES

1   For an elaboration of the appeal of community conservation see Adams and Hulme (2001, pp15–18).

2   On cosmetic participation, Adams and Hulme comment that such approaches might be regarded as 'conventional conservation projects "retrofitted" with a participatory or community conservation approach' (Adams and Hulme, 2001, p14). For typologies of participation, see Oakley (1991), Pimbert and Pretty (1994) and Barrow and Murphree (2001).

3   South Africa presents a mixed picture. Before independence in 1994, almost all community conservation initiatives were directed at parks–people interactions. Many continue to be so, but more recently 'stand-alone' communal regimes have been initiated, such as spin-offs from the Greater St Lucia Wetland Park (Venter, 2003) and Richtersveld (Magome and Murombedzi, 2003). A variant that has emerged under South Africa's current land restitution initiative has been the development of 'contract parks' containing elements of co-management and devolving a range of rights to communities adjacent to national parks (Grossman and Holden, in preparation; Pollard et al, in preparation).

4   Child (2003) comments: 'By the 1990s, key wildlife officials were just as passionate about the potential to use wildlife as a tool for rural democratization and governance as the necessity for wildlife to ensure its own economic survival. In some places, even these conservationists recognized that demography might preclude wildlife as a long-term economic option, but in the meantime it could serve as a tool for improvements in governance.'

5   For a more extended discussion of the conceptual roots of CBNRM in Namibia, see Jones and Murphree (2001), from which much of this material is drawn.

6   We distinguish between deconcentration and devolution. Deconcentration is a structural dispersal of state control to sub-units of the state in a bureaucratic hierarchy. Devolution involves the surrender of elements of authority and responsibility to units with non-state constituencies.

7   The argument for placing 'power as close to the action as possible' in natural resource management is put by Murphree as follows: 'The further down the hierarchy of scale we go the closer we get to hands-on management and use. And it is here that the determinative decisions on use are made. At these levels decisions are personal rather than abstract, they are operational rather than propositional, they emphasize positive effort rather than passive compliance and their implementation is direct, carried out by those who make them. Because they are generally made in contexts distanced from any effective instruments of international or state coercion they are relatively autonomous, responsive to private or local agendas rather than those set by the abstractions of the international conservation discourse' (Murphree, 1998: pp4–5).

8   Various sets of principles incorporating sustainability, economic instrumentalism, subsidiarity and collective action were developed (eg Murphree, 1991b), re-examined and refined in regional debates (eg Rihoy and Steiner, 1995). The classic statement on 'design principles' for common property resource institutions is found in Ostrom (1990). Martin had anticipated several of the components involved: 'The key institutional change is the reorganization of communities to operate as land and asset management associations. This involves the transfer of management rights to a community level, the right of communities to earn income directly from natural resources, and the territorial control of communal land by resident communities' (Martin, 1986, p18).

9   In northwest Namibia, where community-based conservation has been established since the mid-1980s, between 1986 and 2002 springbok have increased from an estimated 2000 to an estimated 94,000, Hartmann's mountain zebra from an estimated 900 to 14,000 and oryx from an estimated 800 to 27,000 (Durbin et al 1997; Stuart-Hill and Taylor, in preparation).

10 The only communal land in Africa where this is happening.

11 Definite causative links are often difficult to prove because of external factors, such as drought or periods of high rainfall, affecting reproduction rates.

12 At 2002 exchange rates.

13 Although this is largely because of an increase of non-wildlife-producing districts becoming part of the programme.

14 Interestingly, in Namibia, a proposed conservancy that covered a large area of land and contained several different ethnic groups and factions within ethnic groups, split into three separate entities, each consisting of people who defined themselves as having some form of collective identity and willingness to cooperate.

15 Such transaction costs can include the length of time that negotiations may take and associated financial costs or opportunity costs in terms of capital investment (Ashley and Jones, 2001) or might include the costs of having to deal with sometimes complex bureaucratic hurdles or institutional arrangements (see the Mahenye case discussed by Murphree (2001).

16 Little attention is given here to this particular form of critique because it is prescriptively sterile, offering very little other than a return to unproductive previous policies.

17 Much of the critical evaluation of southern African CBNRM comes from scholar-practitioners in the region, a factor that constitutes one of its most valuable assets.

18 See Corbett and Jones (2000), particularly Table 2, p23.

19 See Murphree (1999) for an elaboration.

20 Ake, in his advocacy of participatory democracy, analyses these apparent intractabilities by commenting that the changes involved 'entail bringing ordinary people to the center, privileging them and removing their vulnerabilities. In addition, they entail a radical redistribution of power and resources away from the small elite which currently monopolizes them to the masses. Unfortunately, those who have the power to effect the changes which democratization requires have a strong interest in resisting these changes, and those who have an objective interest in the changes do not have the power resources to effect them. Power and desirable change are pulling in diametrically opposite directions' (Ake, 2000, p190).

21 Ian Parker wrote in 1993 a brief essay on why CAMPFIRE would fail. He found its fatal flaw to be in its aborted devolution, concluding 'Hopefully the dichotomy in policy is transient: a stepping stone to conceding the benefits of full ownership. Yet if it sticks halfway – as at present – the CAMPFIRE programmes will stress to the owners what they are missing – not what they are getting. And for this reason the project will fail' (Parker, 1993, p3). While agreeing with much of this analysis, we suggest that to the farmers of communal lands, the delineation of what they are missing is a critical step in the escalation of their assertiveness. The role of CBNRM in raising this assertiveness and channelling its voice is strategically one of its most important directions.

22 Ostrom's classic 'design principles' were based on four empirical examples, the youngest of which is more than 100 years old and the oldest of which exceeds 1000 years (Ostrom, 1990, pp58–102).

23 For a contemporary, state-of-the-art summation, see National Research Council (2002).

24 Kaplan provides the following acerbic comment: 'If development interventions are designed by third parties, and not through the free interaction between development worker and client, then it must categorically be stated that the result is not development work; it becomes at best a patronizing collusion, at worst a cynical manipulation' (Kaplan, 1999, p16).

25 CBNRM experience, regionally and internationally, offers several such options, eg the 'tradable assets' approach (Tietenberg, 2002; Scura, 2002).

26 The establishment professionals who initiated CBNRM were strongly committed to the maintenance of parks estates. In Zimbabwe, for instance, Martin was the primary author of the following official policy statement: 'The Department of National Parks and Wild Life Management is an ecological land use agency with special responsibility for the conservation and proper use of the nation's parks and wildlife resources. Its objectives are to protect these resources, which will include representative samples of the country's biological diversity, and to permit their controlled use for the benefit of people, according to the status of the land where they occur.' (Government of Zimbabwe, 1989, p3).

27 Inland water bodies in Malawi, Zambia and Zimbabwe have received particular attention (see Njaya, 2002; Hara et al, 2002; Nyikahadzoi, 2002; Malasha, 2002).

28 This issue is one of the important agenda items that was debated at the World Parks Congress in Durban in September 2003.

REFERENCES

Adams, W and Hulme, D (2001) 'Conservation and community: changing narratives, policies and practices in African conservation', in D Hulme and M W Murphree (eds) *African Wildlife and Livelihoods: The Promise and Performance of Community Conservation*, James Currey, Oxford, pp9–23

Ake, C (2000) *The Feasibility of Democracy in Africa*, Dakar, CODESRIA

Anstey, S (2001) 'Necessarily vague: The political economy of community conservation in Mozambique', in D Hulme and M W Murphree (eds) *African Wildlife and African Livelihoods: The Promise and Performance of Community Conservation*, James Currey, Oxford, pp74–87

Arntzen, J (2003) 'An economic view on wildlife management areas in Botswana', CBNRM Support Programme Occasional Paper no. 10, IUCN/SNV CBNRM Support Programme, Gaborone

Ashley, C (1998) *Intangibles Matter: Non-financial Dividends of Community Based Natural Resource Management in Namibia*, WWF LIFE Program, Windhoek

Ashley C and Barnes J (1996) 'Wildlife use for economic gain: The potential for wildlife to contribute to development in Namibia', in F Smith (ed) *Environmental Sustainability: Practical Global Implications*, St Lucie Press, Delray Beach, Florida, USA

Ashley, C and Jones B (2001) 'Joint ventures between communities and tourism investors: Experience in Southern Africa', *International Journal of Tourism Research* 3: 407–23

Barnes, J I and Jones, B T B (in preparation) 'Game ranching in Namibia', in B Child (ed) *Parks in Transition: Biodiversity, Rural Development and the Bottom Line*, vol 2, SASUSG, Pretoria

Barrow, E and Murphree, M (2001) 'Community conservation: From concept to practice', in D Hulme, and M W Murphree (eds) *African Wildlife and Livelihoods: The Promise and Performance of Community Conservation*, James Currey, Oxford, pp24–37

Bell, R H V (2000) 'Building constitutions for community based organisations', *CBNRM Newsletter*, Programme for Land and Agrarian Studies (PLAAS), University of the Western Cape, Cape Town

Bernstein, H and Woodhouse, P (2000) 'Whose environment? Whose livelihoods?', in P Woodhouse, H Bernstein and D Hulme (eds) *The Social Dynamics of Wetlands in Drylands*, James Currey, Oxford, pp195–213

Berry, S (1993) *No Condition is Permanent: The Social Dynamics of Agrarian Change in Sub-Saharan Africa*, University of Wisconsin Press, Madison

Bond, I (2001) 'CAMPFIRE and the Incentives for Institutional Change', in D Hulme and M W Murphree (eds) *African Wildlife and African Livelihoods: The Promise And Performance Of Community Conservation*, James Currey, Oxford, pp227–43

Child, B (2003) 'Origins and efficacy of modern community based natural resources management (CBNRM) practices in the southern African region', Paper presented at a workshop Local Communities, Equity and Protected Areas, Centurion, South Africa, 26–28 February

Child, B (in preparation, a) 'CBNRM in Zambia', in B Child (ed) *Parks in Transition: Biodiversity, Rural Development and the Bottom Line*, vol 2, SASUSG, Pretoria

Child, B (in preparation, b) 'The economic history of the use and conservation of wildlife and rangelands in southern Africa', in B Child (ed) *Parks in Transition: Biodiversity, Rural Development and the Bottom Line*, vol 2, SASUSG, Pretoria

Child, B, Child, G, Jones, B, Watts, S and Cooper, J (2003) 'Key policy bottlenecks and challenges to sustainable use of natural resources in southern Africa', in B Won wa Musiti (ed) *2nd Pan-African Symposium on the Sustainable Use of Natural Resources in Africa*, IUCN, Gland, Switzerland, and Cambridge, UK, pp243–70

Corbett, A and Jones, B (2000) 'The legal aspects of governance in CBNRM in Namibia', Research discussion paper no. 41, Directorate of Environmental Affairs, Windhoek, Ministry of Environment and Tourism

Degnbol, P (2002) 'Protected areas and the commons — the fisheries case', *Common Property Resource Digest*, no. 60, pp6–7

Durbin, J, Jones, B T B and Murphree, M (1997) 'Namibian community-based natural resource management programme: Project evaluation, final report', Integrated Rural Development and Nature Conservation and World Wide Fund for Nature, Windhoek

Gibson, C C (1999) *Politicians and Poachers. The Political Economy of Wildlife Policy in Africa*, Cambridge University Press, Cambridge

Government of Botswana (1986) *Wildlife Conservation Policy*, Government Printer, Gaborone

Government of Zimbabwe (1989) *Policy for Wildlife*, Department of National Parks and Wildlife Management, Harare

Grossman, D and Holden, P (in preparation) 'Contract parks in South Africa', in B Child (ed) *Parks in Transition: Biodiversity, Rural Development and the Bottom Line*, vol 2, SASUSG, Pretoria

Gujadhur, T (2001) 'Joint venture options for communities and safari operators in Botswana', IUCN/SNV CBNRM Support Programme, Gaborone

Hara, M, Donda, S, Njaya, F (2002) 'Lessons from Malawi's experience with fisheries co-management initiatives', in K Gehab and M Sarch (eds) *Africa's Inland Fisheries. The Management Challenge*, Kampala, Fountain Press, pp31–48

Hardin, G (1968) 'The tragedy of the commons', *Science* **162**: 1243–48

Hitchcock R K and Murphree, M W (1995) 'Report of the field assessment team. Phase III of the mid-term assessment of the LIFE Project'. USAID, Windhoek

Hoyt, J A (1994) *Animals in Peril. How 'Sustainable Use' is Wiping Out the World's Wildlife*, Avery Publishing Group, Garden City Park, New York

Jones, B (1999) 'Rights, revenues and resources: The problems and potential of conservancies as community wildlife management institutions in Namibia', Evaluating Eden Series, Discussion Paper no. 2, International Institute for Environment and Development, London

Jones, B (2001) 'The evolution of a community-based approach to wildlife management at Kunene, Namibia', in D Hulme and M W Murphree (eds) *African Wildlife and African Livelihoods: The Promise and Performance Of Community Conservation*, James Currey, Oxford, pp160–76

Jones, B (2002) 'Evaluation report. Tchuma Tchato Programme, Tete Province, Mozambique', Provincial Directorate of Agriculture and Rural Development, Tete

Jones, B and Butterfield, R (2001) 'Draft report on institutional aspects of renewable natural resources governance and management through special districts: Namibia case studies', ARD, Inc, Vermont

Jones, B and Murphree, M (2001) 'The evolution of policy on community conservation in Namibia and Zimbabwe', in D Hulme and M W Murphree (eds) *African Wildlife and African Livelihoods: The Promise And Performance Of Community Conservation*, James Currey, Oxford, pp38–58

Jones, B and Weaver, L (in preparation) 'CBNRM in Namibia: Growth, trends, lessons and constraints', in B Child (ed) *Parks in Transition: Biodiversity, Rural Development and the Bottom Line*, vol 2, SASUSG, Pretoria

Jones, M. (in preparation) 'Community outreach in Malawi's protected areas: The example of Nyika National Park and Vwaza Marsh Wildlife Reserve', in B Child (ed) *Parks in Transition: Biodiversity, Rural Development and the Bottom Line*, vol 2, SASUSG, Pretoria

Kaplan, A (1999) 'The development of capacity', Geneva, UN Non-Governmental Liaison Service, Development Dossier no. 10

Keeley, J and Scoones, I (2000) 'Environmental policy making in Zimbabwe: Discourses, science and politics', University of Sussex, Institute of Development Studies, IDS working paper 116

Leach, M, Mearns, R and Scoones, I (1997) 'Challenges to community based sustainable development: Dynamics, entitlements, institutions', *IDS Bulletin* **28**(4), Institute for Development Studies, Sussex, pp 4–14

Lee, K N (1993) *Compass and Gyroscope. Integrating Science and Politics for the Environment*, Island Press, Washington, DC

Long, N and Long, A (eds) (1992) *Battlefields of Knowledge. The Interlocking of Theory and Practice in Social Research and Development*, Routledge, London

Long, N and Villareal, M (1994) 'The interweaving of knowledge and power in development interfaces', in I Scoones and J Thompson (eds) *Beyond Farmer First*, Intermediate Technology Publications, London, pp41–52

Madzudzo, E (2002) 'Outcomes of community based natural resources management programmes. A case study of the communal areas management programme for indigenous resources in Bulilimamangwe district of Zimbabwe', PhD thesis, Roskilde University, Roskilde

Magome, H and Murombedzi, J (2003) 'Sharing South African national parks: Community, land and conservation in a democratic South Africa', in W Adams and M Mulligan (eds) *Decolonising Nature: Strategies for Conservation in a Post-colonial Era*, Earthscan, London, pp108–34

Malasha, I (2002) 'The outcome of a co-managerial arrangement in an inland fishery: The case of Lake Kariba (Zambia)', in K Gehab and M Sarch (eds) *Africa's Inland Fisheries. The Management Challenge*, Fountain Press, Kampala, pp89–106

Malasha, I (2003) 'Fisheries co-management. A comparative analysis of the Zambian and Zimbabwean inshore fisheries of Lake Kariba', DPhil thesis, Centre for Applied Social Sciences, University of Zimbabwe, Harare

Martin, R B (1986) *Communal Areas Management Programme for Indigenous Resources (CAMPFIRE)*, revised version, Branch of Terrestrial Ecology, Department of National Parks and Wild Life Management, Harare

Martin, R B (2003) 'Conditions for effective, stable and equitable conservation at the national level in southern Africa', Paper presented at a workshop Local Communities, Equity and Protected Areas, Centurion, South Africa, 26–28 February

Murombedzi, J (2001) 'Committees, rights, costs and benefits', in D Hulme and M W Murphree (eds) *African Wildlife and African Livelihoods: The Promise And Performance Of Community Conservation*, James Currey, Oxford, pp244–55

Murombedzi, J (2003) 'Devolving the expropriation of nature: The 'devolution' of wildlife management in southern Africa', in W Adams and M Mulligan (eds) *Decolonising Nature: Strategies for Conservation in a Post-colonial Era*, Earthscan, London

Murphree, M W (1991a) 'Research on the institutional contexts of wildlife utilisation in communal areas of eastern and southern Africa', in J G Grootenhuis, S G Njuguna and P W Kat (eds) *Wildlife Research for Sustainable Development*, National Museums of Kenya, Nairobi, pp137–45

Murphree, M W (1991b) *Communities as Institutions for Resource Management*, University of Zimbabwe, Centre for Applied Social Sciences (C.A.S.S.), University of Zimbabwe, Harare (reprinted 1993 as '*Communities as Resource Management Institutions*', International Institute for Environment and Development Gatekeeper Series no. 36, London)

Murphree, M W (1994) 'The role of institutions in community-based conservation', in D Western, R M Wright and S C Strum (eds) *Natural Connections. Perspectives in Community-based Conservation*, Island Press, Washington, DC, pp403–27

Murphree, M W (1997) 'Congruent objectives, competing interests and strategic compromise: Concepts and process in the evolution of Zimbabwe's CAMPFIRE Programme', Community Conservation in Africa working paper no. 2, Institute for Development Policy and Management (IDPM), University of Manchester

Murphree, M W (1998) 'Enhancing sustainable use. Incentives, politics and science', Working paper no. 2, Berkeley Workshop on Environmental Politics, Institute of International Studies, University of California, Berkeley

Murphree, M W (2000) 'Boundaries and borders: The question of scale in the theory and practice of common property management', Paper presented at the Eighth Biennial Conference of the International Association for the Study of Common Property (IASCP), 31 May – 4 June, Bloomington, Indiana

Murphree, M (2001) 'Community, council and client: A case study in ecotourism development from Mahenye, Zimbabwe', in D Hulme and M W Murphree (eds) *African Wildlife and African Livelihoods: The Promise And Performance Of Community Conservation*, James Currey, Oxford, pp177–94

National Research Council (2002) *The Drama of the Commons*, National Academy Press, Washington, DC

Nhantumbo, I, Chonguica, E and Anstey, S (in preparation) 'Community-based natural resources management in Mozambique: The challenges of sustainability', in B Child (ed) *Parks in Transition: Biodiversity, Rural Development and the Bottom Line*, vol 2, SASUSG, Pretoria

Njaya, F (2002) 'Fisheries co-management in Malawi: Implementation arrangements for Lakes Malombe, Chilwa and Chiuta', in K Gehab and M Sarch (eds) *Africa's Inland Fisheries. The Management Challenge*, Fountain Press, Kampala, pp9–30

Nyikahadzoi, K (2002) 'Contesting inequalities in access rights to Lake Kariba's Kapenta fisheries: An analysis of the politics of natural resource management', in K Gehab and M Sarch (eds) *Africa's Inland Fisheries. The Management Challenge*, Fountain Press, Kampala, pp74–88

Oakley, P (1991) *Projects with People*, Blackwell, Cambridge

Oates, J F (1999) *Myth and Reality in the Rain Forest. How Conservation Strategies Are Failing in West Africa*, University of California Press, Berkeley

Ostrom E (1990) *Governing the Commons. The Evolution of Institutions for Collective Action*, Cambridge University Press, Cambridge

Parker, I (1993) 'Natural justice, ownership and the CAMPFIRE Programme'. Unpublished essay

Peters, P (1994) *Dividing the Commons: Politics, Policy and Culture in Botswana*, University Press of Virginia, Charlottesville

Pimbert, M P and Pretty, J N (1994) 'Participation, people and the management of national parks and protected areas: Past failures and future promise', Mimeo, United Nations Research Institute for Social Development, International Institute for Environment and Development and WWF, London

Pollard, S, Shackleton, C and J. Carruthers, J (in preparation), 'Beyond the Fence: People and the Lowveld Landscape', in B Child (ed) *Parks in Transition: Biodiversity, Rural Development and the Bottom Line*, vol 2, SASUSG, Pretoria

Rihoy, E and Steiner, A (eds) (1995) 'The commons without the tragedy? Strategies for community based natural resources management in southern Africa', Report of the Annual Regional Conference of the Natural Resources Management Programme, SADC Wildlife Technical Coordination Unit, Lilongwe

Roe, E (1998) *Taking Complexity Seriously. Policy Analysis, Triangulation and Sustainable Development*, Kluwer Academic Publishers, Boston

Rose, C (2002) 'Common property, regulatory property, and environmental protection: Comparing community-based management to tradable environmental allowances', in *The Drama of the Commons*. Academy Press, National Research Council, Washington, DC, pp233–57

Rozemeijer, N (in preparation) 'CBNRM in Botswana', in B Child (ed) *Parks in Transition: Biodiversity, Rural Development and the Bottom Line*, vol 2, SASUSG, Pretoria

Rozemeijer N and van der Jagt, C (2001) 'Community based natural resource management (CBNRM) in Botswana: How community based is CBNRM in Botswana?', Paper prepared for the research project Community-based natural resource management: where does the power really lie?, Institute for Environmental Studies, University of Zimbabwe and the Natural Resources and Rural Development Programme of the Council for Industrial and Scientific Research (CSIR) of South Africa

Ruitenbeek, J and Cartier, C (2001) *The Invisible Wand: Adaptive Co-management as an Emergent Strategy in Complex Bio-economic Systems*, Center for International Forestry Research (CIFOR), Bogor, Indonesia

SASUSG (1996) *Sustainable Use Issues and Principles*, SASUSG, Harare

Sithole, B (1999) 'Use and access to dambos in communal lands in Zimbabwe', unpublished DPhil thesis, Centre for Applied Social Sciences, University of Zimbabwe, Harare

Stuart-Hill, G and Taylor, R (in preparation) 'Conservation benefits delivered through CBNRM', in B Child (ed) *Parks in Transition: Biodiversity, Rural Development and the Bottom Line*, vol 2, SASUSG, Pretoria

Tietenberg, T (2002) 'The tradable permits approach to protecting the commons: What have we learned?', in *The Drama of the Commons*, Academy Press, National Research Council, Washingon, DC, pp197–232

Taylor, R (in preparation) 'The performance of CAMPFIRE in Zimbabwe 1989–2001', in B Child (ed) *Parks in Transition: Biodiversity, Rural Development and the Bottom Line*, vol 2, SASUSG, Pretoria

Venter, A K (1998) 'Protected area outreach programmes: A case study and critical evaluation', PhD thesis, Institute of Natural Resources, University of Natal, Pietermaritzburg

Venter, A (2003) 'Community-based natural resource management in South Africa: Experience from the greater St Lucia wetlands area', in B Won wa Musiti (ed) *2nd Pan-African Symposium on the Sustainable Use of Natural Resources in Africa*, IUCN, Gland, Switzerland and Cambridge, UK

WILD (2003) *Preliminary Findings from the Wildlife Integration for Livelihood Diversification Project*, MET/DFID, Windhoek

Chapter 5

Performance of Parks in a Century of Change

David Cumming

INTRODUCTION

Parks exist within a matrix of evolving biophysical, social and economic landscapes. For this reason their performance must be assessed within the context of a shifting and increasingly complex set of objectives that have developed over the past century. On the one hand their relevance to society in southern Africa is under scrutiny. On the other hand a rapidly expanding tourism industry and the increasing competitiveness of wildlife as a productive land use have resulted in a rapid increase within southern Africa of wildlife-based enterprises and in the area of land devoted to wildlife conservation. This is not altogether surprising given that a very high proportion of southern Africa comprises arid and semi-arid rangelands and that the region's advantage lies in its unique and spectacular wildlife resources rather than in livestock production on its extensive rangelands. Current interest in wildlife-based land use is now more firmly supported by economic incentives than it was even 25 years ago.

The first reserves were created about 100 years ago primarily as areas in which large mammals were protected. These game reserves were a response to rapid declines in game populations from overhunting and, during the 1890s, the effects of the rinderpest pandemic that swept through southern Africa decimating wildlife and livestock populations alike. The early reserves were established mostly in remote areas, on land that was sparsely populated, still had some game, and was considered unsuitable for agricultural development. The 1933 Convention for the Protection of the Fauna and Flora of Africa (hereafter the '1933 Convention') heralded a change in the roles and objectives of parks in sub-Saharan Africa. Progress was inhibited by World War II but this was followed by a particularly rapid increase in the number and area of parks between 1945 and 1975. Most of the large parks in the region were created during the period of colonial rule, but the parks and wildlife estate continued to be maintained and expanded by independent governments. The rapid growth and evolution of parks as a recognized form of land use that should occupy at least 10 per cent of a country has carried with it increasing responsibilities as conservation values have evolved over the past 100 years. The system has been remarkably resilient but in many countries of the region major reconfiguration and renewal will be required if they are to survive other than as paper parks.

Answering the question, 'How are southern African parks performing?' in any definitive way has proved to be unexpectedly difficult for the simple reason that the data sets required are not available, or park agencies are reluctant to disclose them, or both. It seems very likely that for the most part they do not exist, itself a serious indictment of existing park management. This chapter, then, is an idiosyncratic, broad brush attempt to assess performance at a regional scale against a background of evolving objectives and park responsibilities over the past century. Freshwater and marine conservation issues have been badly neglected in the region and are not covered here.

How Do We Measure Park Performance?

Park objectives in southern Africa have evolved and been added to over time, and four main phases are evident. The first was the establishment of preserves to protect 'game', that is large wild mammals. The second phase embodied the ideas of protecting 'fauna and flora', spectacular landscapes, and sites of cultural and scientific importance for the 'benefit, enjoyment and education of the public' – a phase that developed in the wake of the 1933 Convention. The third phase emerged with the development of conservation biology as a discipline during the 1980s and, reinforced by the Convention on Biodiversity, it is characterized by an increasing focus on conserving the full range of biological diversity, from genes to ecosystems, functional landscapes and evolutionary processes. The fourth and most recent phase places increasing emphasis on social and economic benefits, 'parks for people', and the potential role of parks in rural development.

These evolving and superimposed roles for parks and protected areas (Figure 5.1) raise the question, 'By what criteria should one assess performance?' There have been several attempts to assess park performance at global levels (see, for example, Machlis and Tichnell 1985; Bruner et al, 2001). A comprehensive review of the Afro-tropical realm protected-area system, which would bear repeating, was completed by McKinnon and McKinnon in 1986. There has been considerable recent interest in developing evaluation systems for parks (see, for example, Hockings et al, 2000), and some parks in South Africa are adopting the ISO 14001 Environmental Management Systems approaches to park planning and management that incorporate ongoing evaluation at the park scale. These systems have not yet been applied at national or regional levels within Africa. All require considerable amounts of detailed and comparable data that are seldom readily available at park or national levels, let alone regional levels. Elegant and workable systems are simple and there is a danger that current approaches to performance monitoring and assessment may founder. Given these difficulties, I have chosen to focus attention on a few indicators and the results that parks have, or have not, achieved at regional scales in the following areas of endeavour:

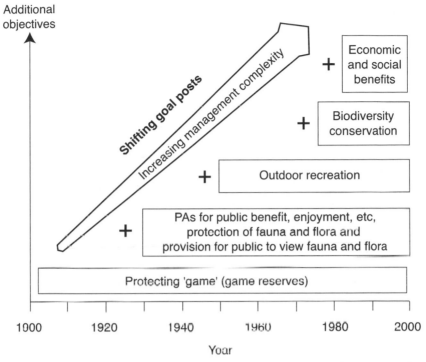

Figure 5.1 *Conceptual diagram reflecting the changing objectives and responsibilities of parks and protected areas in southern Africa during the past century*

- conservation of biological diversity;
- providing benefits to the public;
- contributing to economic development; and,
- parks management – meeting the varied responsibilities now placed on parks and parks systems.

CONSERVATION OF BIOLOGICAL DIVERSITY

The effectiveness of game reserves in meeting the initial objectives of 'protecting the game' is reflected in species extinctions and the status and trends of large mammal populations at regional and national levels. The success of subsequent objectives, such as to protect all fauna and flora (eg the 1933 Convention), can be gauged by the status and trends of plant and vertebrate taxa in protected areas at regional, national and local levels. The area of representative habitats protected and the status of those habitats provide a basis on which to assess the more recent objective of protecting at least 10 per cent of the area of representative biomes or major habitat types that occur within a country (IUCN, 1987). The extent to which national and regional protected-area systems can conserve threatened species and endemics, let alone the full range of biodiversity, is currently a central area of concern and research. Park objectives in this sphere are vague and performance is not easy to assess because of the enormous gaps in information on the distribution and status of most taxa within the region. Similar considerations apply to the conservation of ecological processes and ecosystem integrity.

Conserving Large Mammals ('Protecting the Game')

The earliest park objective was to 'protect the game'. Only three large mammals (blue antelope, Cape warthog and quagga) have been driven to extinction in the region in the past 300 years, but these extinctions took place before the establishment of game reserves. Over the past 100 years white rhino were lost from Botswana, Mozambique, Namibia and Zimbabwe, and later re-introduced during the 1960s from the only surviving population of the species in Natal. Black rhino were lost from Botswana and Zambia during the 1980s. Tsessebe and giraffe appear to have been lost more recently from Mozambique (East, 1998) and Lichtenstein's hartebeest was lost from South Africa where the species was on the fringe of its range. On the other hand, the recovery of white rhino and elephant populations has been spectacular and several other species (eg bontebok, black wildebeest, mountain zebra in South Africa) on the brink of extinction in southern Africa were saved by the creation of parks (Pienaar, 1978). At a regional level no large mammal species (and so far as is known, no small mammal species) has become extinct over the past century – a result largely attributable to the early establishment and subsequent maintenance of 'game reserves'. Neglect of marine protected areas has, however, resulted in dangerously low numbers of dugong along the Mozambique coast, where they are threatened with extinction.

Without active metapopulation management, however, species losses of small populations can be expected from isolated protected areas (Soule et al, 1979; East

Table 5.1 *Summary of the status of larger herbivore species in seven southern African countries*

| Species status | Country | | | | | | |
	Bw	Mw	Mz	Na	SA	Zm	Zw*
Declining	7	6	12	3	3	16	4
Stable	14	6	1	5	8	6	11
Increasing	3	1	0	18	15	2	8
Uncertain	3	5	9	4	4	1	2
Number of species	27	18	22	30	30	25	23
Species declining (%)	26	33	55	10	10	64	16

* The status of large mammals in Zimbabwe has declined since 1998 and the percentage of species declining in 2003 is estimated to be 44 per cent

Notes: Bw, Botswana; Mw, Malawi; Mz, Mozambique; Na, Namibia; SA, South Africa; Zm, Zambia; Zw, Zimbabwe

Source: Summarized from a more detailed listing in Cumming (1999) and based on data compiled by the IUCN Antelope Specialist Group (East, 1997; East, 1998)

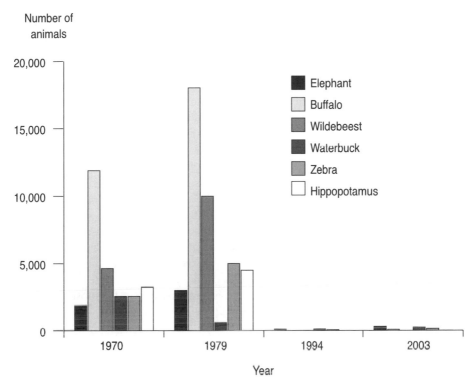

Source: Data for 1970–1994 from Cumming et al (1994); for 2003 from R Zohlo, personal communication

Figure 5.2 *Changes in large mammal populations in Gorongosa National Park between 1970 and 2003*

1981; Burkey, 1995). Active management, as opposed to benign neglect, is often required to maintain demographically and genetically viable populations of rarer species or of smaller isolated populations. Trends in species number and distribution thus become a key indicator of their status and the extent to which conservation is succeeding. A broad assessment of recent national trends in a range of large mammal species reveals an alarming level of population declines within the region (Table 5.1). Detailed data, at park level, are not readily available so it not easy to separate out the contribution to trends from populations within specific protected areas from those in unprotected areas. The impacts of subtle changes in climatic cycles on rare or less abundant species on the fringes of their range have only recently been elucidated. Dunham et al (2003; 2004), for example, recently found that a prolonged series of dry years and declining dry season rainfall was a major factor in the decline of tsessebe on ranches in the midlands of Zimbabwe and in Kruger National Park. Owen-Smith and Ogutu (2003) extended this analysis to explain the decline of sable and roan antelope and tsessebe in Kruger National Park – declines that had previously been ascribed mainly to predation.

In some countries and parks the causes of decline are more direct. Civil wars and political instability have affected the status of many large mammal species in

Angola, Mozambique (see, for example, Figure 5.2) and more recently in Zimbabwe. Yet the endangered giant sable has survived in the Luando Reserve through 25 years of civil war in Angola (Estes, 2002). Major declines in wildlife populations in Botswana followed the erection of veterinary fences to control foot-and-mouth disease and secure export markets for beef to Europe. Although populations of many species in Botswana have increased over the past two decades their numbers are unlikely to return to the levels that existed before the introduction of fences. Declining numbers of browsing antelope in Hwange National Park are likely to be a result of an ever-increasing elephant population (Valeix, 2002).

The figures on declining large mammal populations (Table 5.1) also reflect an association between macro-economic factors, governance and commercial opportunities for wildlife-based land use. Countries with strong economies and commercialized wildlife sectors, such as South Africa and Namibia, show the highest proportion of increasing species populations. A large increase over the past five years in the proportion of declining species in Zimbabwe reinforces this relationship. However, a key issue for most of the region is that the capacity to monitor, explain (through targeted research) and take appropriate conservation action hardly exists for large mammals and is certainly absent for most other taxa (see the section on park management below).

Conservation of 'Fauna and Flora' and Endemic and Threatened Species

After the early successful establishment of game reserves and the recovery of game populations, park objectives were extended to protect 'fauna and flora', and suitable wording was included in enabling legislation after the 1930s. However, in practice this did not include all species or necessarily the full range of biodiversity as currently understood. The elimination of predators that might affect the recovery of game populations was a common practice, and wild dogs in particular were singled out. Most countries in the region had scheduled lists of vermin, most of which included wild dogs, and for which governments paid bounties. These practices survived through to the 1960s and early 1970s and although bounties may no longer be paid, baboon, wild dog, hyaena and jackal were still on a 1996 schedule of problem animals under Zimbabwe's Parks and Wild Life Act.

With the advent of goals to protect the full range of biodiversity, increasing attention has been paid to the distribution of endemic, rare and threatened species and the extent to which they are represented in the protected-area system. In those countries and areas where the relationships between the distribution of endemic species richness and protected areas have been examined, the overlap has generally been poor. Furthermore, the distribution of areas of high species richness and endemicity for plants and vertebrates, or for mammals, birds, reptiles and amphibians, seldom match. In Namibia, for example, the areas of greatest species richness and endemicity for all groups differ but none are covered by the protected-area system of the country (Barnard, 1998). In KwaZulu-Natal, where the most thorough analysis in the region has been conducted, 45 per cent of 85 threatened plant species, 10 per cent of threatened birds, 20 per cent of endemic reptiles, and only two out of four endemic amphibians, occurred in protected areas (Goodman, 2000). Essentially similar problems in the mismatch between

Table 5.2 *Biodiversity ranking (species richness and endemicity) and the proportion protected for each of seven southern African countries*

Country	Biodiversity ranking	Proportion of country protected (%)
South Africa	1	5.5
Mozambique	2	6.7
Zimbabwe	3	12.8
Malawi	4	10.7
Zambia	5	8.4
Namibia	6	8.3
Botswana	7	17.3
Region		ca. 11.7

Source: Biodiversity rankings from Cumming, 1999; area protected from Table 5.3

the distribution of species richness and endemicity, between various taxa, and between these and protected areas, occur across the region (Lombard, 1995) as they do elsewhere in the world (Nott and Pimm, 1997). Analytical procedures to assist in the optimal design of protected-area systems are now well developed (Pressey et al, 1993; Pressey and Cowling, 1999). However, other than in South Africa (Lombard 1995; Cowling et al, 1999; Reyers et al, 2001), they do not appear to have been used elsewhere in the region at a country level to assess the coverage of existing protected-area systems in relation to species and wider biodiversity conservation issues.

At a regional level it is worth noting that the countries with the greatest number of species and the highest levels of endemicity of plants and vertebrates are those with proportionally the lowest areas under protection (Table 5.2). It is also clear that with expanding rural populations and associated land cover change in large parts of the region there is an urgent need to repeat the type of assessment done in KwaZulu-Natal (Goodman, 2000) at national and regional scales.

Conservation of Representative Habitats and Ecosystems

A fundamental benchmark for conservation is the area of land, freshwater or sea that is protected. The number and area of terrestrial parks has shown impressive growth in southern Africa over the past century (Figure 5.3). There was an initial period of slow growth, followed by rapid growth during the middle of the 20th century, and declining growth of state-owned protected areas during the last 20 years. Although estimates of the overall area of land under wildlife are available (Table 5.3), growth in the area of protected wildlife land under private and communal tenure has not yet been reliably captured because appropriate recent surveys have not been done. In some countries, such as Namibia, recent growth has been rapid, with the area under conservancies in both freehold and communal land increasing by 40 per cent or more over 5 years (WWF–SARPO, unpublished data). In others, such as Zimbabwe, land reform has resulted in a marked decline in wildlife and wildlife land during the period 1998–2003.

As the area and number of parks in the region has grown, the mean size of parks has steadily declined – a factor that has implications for the long-term conservation

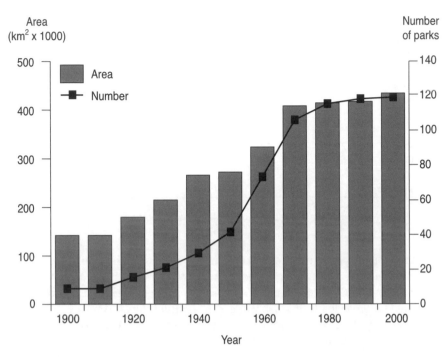

Figure 5.3 *Growth in the area and number of parks in seven southern African countries (as in Table 5.3) between 1900 and 2000; for South Africa only national parks and larger game reserves are included*

of species populations within what may already be isolated ecological islands. Average park size also varies greatly between countries in the region, with the greatest average park area occurring in arid and less densely populated countries such as Botswana and Namibia (Table 5.3). Measured in terms of area and extent of its parks and wildlife estate, the region has performed remarkably well and compares favourably with other regions of the world (Groombridge, 1992). The current interest in the development of transfrontier conservation areas (Griffin et al, 1999) is serving to extend the area of land under wildlife, even if these extensions are not necessarily state-protected areas.

The first game reserves were established on a largely opportunistic basis in areas where there was little settlement or development and consequently still some wildlife to protect. Some smaller reserves, such as the Bontebok National Park and the Mountain Zebra National Park, both in South Africa, were established in the 1930s to protect particular species (Pienaar, 1978). The need to protect representative examples of a full range of habitats developed later and with it the objective of placing at least 10 per cent of a country or region under protected-area status. Most countries in southern Africa are close to, or have surpassed, the '10 per cent rule' (Table 5.3) but not for all biomes and habitats.

MacKinnon and MacKinnon (1986) reported the extent to which major vegetation types occur within protected areas at national levels. They used White's (1983) vegetation map of Africa as the basis for their habitat classification. National

Table 5.3 *State-protected areas, communal land (game management areas, wildlife management areas), and freehold land available to wildlife in southern African countries*

	Botswana	Malawi	Mozambique	Namibia	South Africa	Zambia	Zimbabwe	Total
State land (protected areas):								
Total area (km²)	103,953.0	12,622.0	52,250.0	114,079.4	66,418.0	63,585.0	49,418.0	462,375.2
Per cent of country	17.3	10.7	6.7	13.8	5.4	8.4	12.7	11.66
Number of protected areas	9.0	9.0	10.0	21.0	404.0	19.0	30.0	519.0
Mean size (km²)	11,550.3	1,402.0	5,225.0	5,432.4	164.4	3,346.6	1,647.3	890.9
Communal land:								
Game area (km²)	120,074.4	0.0	1.0	25,237.0	0.0	160,488.0	8,000.0	313,800.4
Per cent of communal land	28.2	0.0	0.0	7.7	0.0	24.0	4.2	11.50
Freehold (and long lease) land								
Game area (km²)	1,000.0	0.0	0.0	38,076.0	160,000.0	2,197.0	12,000.0	213318.5
Per cent private land	2.8	0.0	0.0	10.3	17.9	9.4	8.7	15.84
Number of freehold farms	200.0	0.0	0.0	5,500.0	120,000.0	4,000.0	4,500.0	134,200.00
Number of game farms	5.0	0.0	0.0	450.0	8,500.0	15.0	40.0	9,011.0
Per cent of farms	2.5	0.0	0.0	8.2	7.1	0.4	1.0	6.71
Total area under wildlife	225,027.4	12,622.0	52,251.0	177,392.4	226,418.0	226,270.0	69,418.0	989,494.1
Per cent of country	37.5	13.4	6.7	21.5	18.5	30.1	17.8	25.28

Source: updated from Cumming (1999)

Table 5.4 *Proportion of major habitats* (vegetation types) protected in seven southern African countries (those listed in Table 5.3)*

< 2.5%	2.5–7.5%	7.5–15%	> 15%
Coastal forest	Lowland forest	Wooded edaphic grassland	Baikiaea woodland
Montane scrub/ forest/grassland	Miombo	Kalahari-Namib transition	Mopane woodland
Mopane/Namib transition	Undifferentiated Woodland	Flooded grassland	Fynbos
Bushland thicket	Namib-Karoo	Namib Desert	Lowland fynbos < 1%
Karoo/Highveldt transition	Afro-montane	Swamps and salinas	
Highveldt grassland			

Note: *Habitat types are from Cumming (1999) and represent a simplified version of White's (1983) vegetation map of Africa. Proportions of each habitat type in protected areas are from MacKinnon and MacKinnon (1986)

coverage using country biome, vegetation or habitat maps are available for Malawi (Clarke and Bell, 1986), South Africa (Low and Rebelo, 1996), Namibia (Barnard, 1998), and Zimbabwe (Taylor, 1990; Child and Heath, 1992). However, because vegetation classifications and mapping scales differ from country to country, comparisons at a regional scale are difficult. MacKinnon and MacKinnon's (1986) findings for the region were reworked using a simplified version of White's vegetation map (Cumming, 1999) in which 19 as opposed to 47 vegetation types were used. The status of these major vegetation types in terms of areas under protection in 1986 (Table 5.4) revealed that habitats with the greatest plant species richness and endemism (eg lowland fynbos, Afro-montane grassland and forests, lowland forest and the Karoo) were the least protected. However, this analysis is based on mapping that used traced overlays at a scale of 1:5,000,000. Although the overall picture is unlikely to have changed greatly since 1986 the exercise needs to be repeated using current maps and geographic information systems that can be updated readily and so provide an ongoing basis for monitoring and evaluation. Despite these shortcomings, it is clear that the savannah and desert biomes are well represented in protected areas, but species rich biomes such as lowland fynbos, Karoo, forests and montane grasslands are not.

Again, the example of KwaZulu-Natal (Goodman, 2000) is instructive. Seventy-six per cent of 115 landscape types was under-protected, that is less than 10 per cent of the area they covered in the Province occurred within protected areas, and 30 per cent of landscapes had been transformed to the extent that ecological processes were likely to be compromised. Only 2 of 16 grassland types were adequately protected. Seven of the 23 plant communities found in the Province are considered endemic and all were under-protected – most with less than 3 per cent in protected areas. The assumption that landscapes, ecosystems and habitats occurring within parks are adequately protected is not always true. More than 80 per cent of the miombo woodland within protected areas in Zimbabwe has been severely impacted by elephants and fire (Cumming et al, 1997). The extent of elephant impacts on the conservation of biodiversity remains a contentious issue in a region where there are now more than ten times as many elephants as there were 100 years ago (Spinage, 1990; Cumming, 1993).

Conserving Ecological and Evolutionary Processes

With the exception of a few protected catchments in the region, the boundaries of most parks were delineated with little if any consideration being given to ecological processes, even such obvious processes as large mammal migrations and seasonal habitat movements. Many of these phenomena had, of course, been disrupted by the population crashes that occurred during the 19th century, and information on ecological processes was not available when the reserves were established. Nevertheless, the result is that the ecological processes in many parks are compromised by contrasting land uses on their boundaries or even further afield in the case of river systems. Park size becomes a primary consideration in dealing with the conservation of ecological processes and few, if any, parks systems in the region have dealt with the issues or started to monitor and evaluate their performance against explicit ecological process goals. At the level of individual parks, Kruger National Park has been working on these issues for some years, particularly for its rivers (Rogers and Biggs, 1999; Rogers and O'Keefe, 2003). Criteria have been developed, using thresholds of concern, to monitor system performance and to guide management action and research (du Toit et al, 2003).

A key issue for parks in the region is the development of appropriate indicators and monitoring tools. As Brian Child (Chapter 6 in this volume) and others (Gunderson and Holling, 2002) have pointed out, the rates at which components of ecosystems or biodiversity change and recover in response to disturbances vary greatly. Populations of small mammals and ephemeral herbs, for example, crash and recover over small spatial and temporal scales, but large, long-lived animals and trees take far longer, whereas damage to soils and landscapes can take centuries to recover, if they recover at all. These issues are not yet part of the annual audit of parks systems in the region and clearly need to become so – it is too easy to be distracted by the short-term issues while deeper, long-term and large-scale changes, such as nutrient loss, go unnoticed.

PROVIDING BENEFITS TO THE PUBLIC AND SOCIETY

Social, cultural and educational responsibilities for national parks were explicitly specified in one of the clauses to the 1933 Convention, which stipulated that a national park is an area that is:

set aside for the propagation, protection and preservation of objects of aesthetic, geological, prehistoric, historical, archaeological, or other scientific interest for the benefit, advantage or enjoyment of the general public.

and, in a related clause:

... facilities shall, so far as possible, be given to the general public for observing the fauna and flora in national parks

The enabling legislation for national parks in most countries includes similar sentiments about the function of parks over and above those concerned with conservation. The Zimbabwe National Parks and Wild Life Act of 1975, for example, states that natural landscape and scenery, wildlife and plants and the natural stability of wildlife and plant communities are to be preserved and protected

for the enjoyment, education and inspiration of the public, and so far as is reasonable, practicable and compatible with such purposes, to provide facilities for visitors thereto.

Many indicators could be used to assess the extent to which parks have met their responsibilities to the public. One avenue is to measure public perceptions of parks services and benefits through questionnaire surveys and polls at national, local and visitor levels. An alternative is to measure investment in providing facilities for public use and enjoyment of parks, and the extent to which the parks and their facilities are used. Statistics that would provide an appropriate basis for comparative assessments between parks and countries are:

- number of local (national), regional (SADC) and overseas visitors per year;
- the facilities and infrastructure (lodges, restaurants, shops, self-catering chalets, caravan sites, camping sites, hides, types and state of roads) available for visitors;
- diversity of activities offered (game viewing, hiking, canoeing, horse riding, etc);
- the area of the park available to visitors and types of access (length of roads and types of access road – sedan, 4 × 4, all-weather);
- cultural sites, their preservation and associated interpretive displays and information;
- scientific and educational services (number of visiting scientists, papers published, agreements with universities, etc);
- interpretive services and range of information available to visitors and the public (maps, information sheets, books, scientific reports, annual reports and performance statistics);
- public involvement in park policy, planning and decisions (formal structures and social institutions, legal and customary instruments and rules that facilitate public participation and accountability).

More is not necessarily better, and clearly many of these indicators need to be related to carrying capacity or planned levels of service delivery to the public.

It has, however, proved remarkably difficult to access these data for countries, let alone regionally, so that an assessment of current and past performance of parks for their social responsibilities has not been possible. Some of the required statistics appeared in the past in park annual reports, but even these are no longer published in many countries in the region. The Department of National Parks and Wild Life

Management in Zimbabwe, for example, has not published an annual report since 1977 – a period of 25 years. This worrying trend signals a lack of accountability on the part of government conservation agencies within the region. It is, however, heartening to note that South Africa is currently introducing legal provisions for the monitoring, reporting and auditing of performance that should set an example for the level of transparency and public accountability required in the region.

CONTRIBUTING TO ECONOMIC DEVELOPMENT

Parks in southern Africa are widely considered a central component of regional and national tourist industries. Statistics on international arrivals are generally available but the numbers of these visitors that then go on to visit parks are not. Similarly, information on the numbers of visitors, their origins and spending patterns in relation to parks once within the country are not available, except perhaps as occasional studies. The general absence of trend data for park and wildlife-based revenues from tourism makes it difficult to quantify the extent to which parks are contributing to national and regional economies. An exception to this dearth of information is the rich data set available for the Communal Areas Management Programme for Indigenous Resources (CAMPFIRE) programme in Zimbabwe (see Chapter 4).

For the most part, parks in the region can be described as extractive rural economies in the sense that revenue earned is spent either in them or, more frequently, returned to central or provincial governments. Little hard information is available on this topic, and the flow of direct and indirect benefits from parks to their neighbours urgently needs to be examined and quantified.

In some cases, parks act as a centre for the development of wildlife-based tourism industries operating on their borders. Clear examples of where this has led to the viable and productive use of land for wildlife conservation include the conservancies neighbouring the Kruger National Park in South Africa, the Hwange Safari Lodge and other enterprises neighbouring Hwange National Park in Zimbabwe. Communal land hunting concessions under CAMPFIRE in Zimbabwe draw on the larger populations in adjacent parks and wildlife land, and similar considerations may apply to Game Management Areas (GMAs) in Zambia and Wildlife Management Areas in Botswana. At the level of local resource extraction, some parks have made provision for neighbouring communities to harvest thatching grass or honey or caterpillars, as in Kasungu National Park in Malawi. However, grossly exaggerated claims (see, for example, McNeely (1993) of US$198 per hectare for caterpillars and US$230 from beekeeping) have been made for the returns to micro-enterprises from these harvesting projects.

More pertinent indicators of park support to local economies would be statistics on the following, with information on the revenues and employment that they generate:

- number of contracts awarded to local (that is on park borders or park neighbours) companies or bodies to provide services to the park (eg fence repairs, game drives, number of people employed, jobs created);
- the area and extent of compatible land uses developed on land surrounding the park and into which animals from the park can disperse;
- number of commercial lodges and other tourist facilities, which depend on the park for game viewing opportunities;

- the extent to which institutions are developed with local partners to involve them in wildlife conservation-based economic development, planning and resource management;
- number of jobs created and value added to local and national economies.

Primary research will almost certainly be required to assemble an initial data set on indicators such as these. Once an appropriate appraisal and analysis of these data is completed it should be possible to establish indicators and routine protocols to monitor park performance in economic development.

The KwaZulu-Natal Parks and Wildlife Service has statistics that reflect some of these indicators and the returns are substantial. However, the data on trends are not readily available and do not appear to have been published in reports. Results for 1995–1996 from the former Natal Parks Board (S McKean, personal communication, 2003) indicate that resources worth US$728,000 were gathered from parks and that the income earned by neighbouring people from employment in parks amounted to US$1.61 million. Furthermore, a community levy is paid by all guests entering parks in KwaZulu-Natal and the project funding increased from US$38,000 in 2000 to an impressive US$740,000 in 2002.

PARK MANAGEMENT

As Martin (1996) has so clearly argued, certain minimum levels of funding and staffing are required to protect and manage parks. If these thresholds are not met the park will fail. Once budget and staffing levels are above the required threshold other factors such as policies, knowledge and management capacity become important determinants of effectiveness. Park budgets can also reflect the willingness of society to invest in conservation either through public funding or direct revenues earned by parks from fee-paying visitors. More detailed analysis of park budgets can reveal the levels of investment in various park management activities such as protection, training and capacity building, development of tourist facilities and amenities, research, interpretive services and public education. Attempts to get trend data, even for recent years, for national park budgets in the region failed. However, old, but still relevant, information plus fragmentary recent data from two countries, Zambia and Zimbabwe, support the following analysis.

As part of a study of resources available for the conservation of elephants and rhinos in Africa, the African Elephant and Rhino Specialist Group conducted a questionnaire survey of park budgets, staffing levels and equipment across Africa (Cumming et al, 1984). The results showed a very wide range in resources available to government agencies to manage protected areas. In a subsequent survey in 1987, the pattern of gross underfunding had not changed (Cumming et al, 1990).

The only countries for which some long-term trend data on national budgets and staffing levels could be obtained were Zimbabwe and Zambia (Figure 5.4a). Three data points were available for the Hluhluwe-Imfolosi Game Reserve in KwaZulu-Natal, and one current estimate for Gorongosa National Park in Mozambique (Figure 5.4b). For Zimbabwe, these data reflect declining budgets, increasing numbers of employees and therefore marked declines in operational budgets and capac-

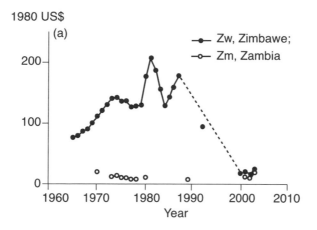

Source: Data for Zambia during the 1970s from Pullan (1983) with more recent data from ZAWA
(V. Nyirenda, personal communication, 2003). Zimbabwe data for 1965–1987 (D Cumming,
unpublished data); 1992–1993 from Martin (1994); figures for 2000–2003 are approximate revenue
and expenditure figures (M Townsend personal communication, 2003)

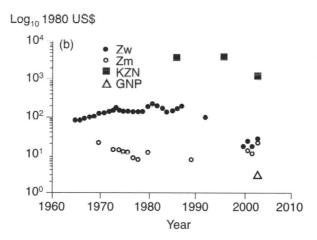

Source: Zambia and Zimbabwe data as for Figure 5.4a. Kwa-Zulu Natal data from Cumming et al
(1990) and S MacKean (personal communication, 2003)
Data for Gorongosa National Park from R Zolho (personal communication, 2003)

Figure 5.4 *(a) Annual government allocations in 1980 US dollars to the parks and
wildlife agencies of Zambia and Zimbabwe. An inflation rate of 3% has been
assumed for the period before and after 1980. A National Parks and Wildlife
Authority has replaced the Zimbabwe Department of National Parks and Wild Life
Management. A similar change has occurred in Zambia where the Zambia Wildlife
Authority has assumed the responsibilities of a former government department
(b) Annual government allocations per square kilometre in 1980 US dollars (note
log scale on y-axis) to the parks and wildlife agencies of Zambia (Zm) and
Zimbabwe (Zw), with limited data points for KwaZulu-Natal (KZN) and
Gorongosa National Park (GNP)*

ity. For Zambia, the budgets have changed little over 30 years but show a decline once inflation is considered (Figure 5.4a). When translated into expenditure per square kilometre, the budgets for Zambia and Zimbabwe differ by an order of magnitude during the 1970s and 1980s (Figure 5.4b). A striking discrepancy in financial resources between two prime national parks within the region is revealed in the budgets available to Gorongosa National Park and Hluhluwe-Imfolosi Game Reserve, with budgets of less than US$5 and greater than US$3000 per square kilometre, respectively (Figure 5.4b). A similar comparison between several southern African countries, and between them and the US, as an example of a developed country, further reveals disparities as great as three orders of magnitude between countries within southern Africa and between them and the developed world (Figure 5.5a). Similar considerations apply to staffing levels (Figure 5.5b). These data, although 20 years old, almost certainly reflect the current state of affairs in most countries in southern Africa, with the possible exceptions of South Africa and Namibia. Budgets and staffing levels in South Africa approach those of the US, and James et al (1996), in a global review of funding levels for conservation, give an average expenditure density figure of US$1770 per square kilometre for North America and US$143 per square kilometre for sub-Saharan Africa during the early 1990s. Staffing levels for North America and sub-Saharan Africa were very similar: between 24 and 25 staff per 1000km^2 – or one member of staff to 40km^2.

The impacts of underfunding in the region are perhaps most clearly reflected in the region's inability to stem the tide of rhino poaching outside of South Africa. Leader-Williams and Albon (1988), in their analysis of black rhino extinction in Zambia, provide strong arguments to support Parker's earlier estimate (1984) that an expenditure of at least US$200 per square kilometre was required to protect elephant and rhino populations from poaching threats. Martin (1996) has modified this rule by linking the expenditure to the size of the area being protected, with larger areas requiring less per unit area than smaller areas. Even with this modification it is clear that most of southern Africa is spending far less than is required on conservation and park management — a conclusion that is well supported by the inability of the region to monitor its performance and, consequently, to take appropriate corrective action.

CONCLUDING COMMENT

Parks are complex ecological and social systems (or eco-social systems), and their performance is influenced by factors operating at many scales. Global factors such as wars, disease and economic downturns affect tourist arrivals. Climate change and the El Niño southern oscillation affect rainfall patterns and the severity of droughts and floods. National factors such as macro-economic policies and economic performance affect national parks systems as a whole and may have differential effects on parks within countries. At a local level, adjacent land-use practices and socio-economic factors influence pressures on natural resources both within the park and in adjacent areas. Human resources and capacity within the park itself will greatly influence performance in relation to multiple, and sometimes conflicting, park objectives. The multiple levels and key drivers influencing park performance merit further exploration and analysis.

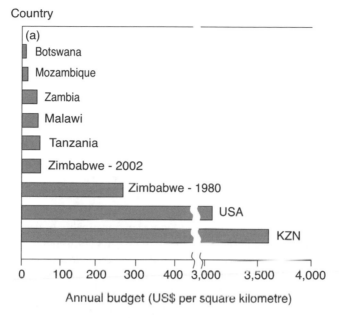

Source: Initial data from Cumming et al (1984) and Cumming et al (1990)

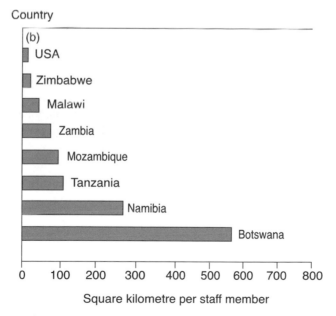

Source: Data from Cumming et al (1984) and S MacKean (personal communication, 2003)

Figure 5.5 *(a) Expenditure density for selected countries in southern Africa compared with that in the US in 1980 and KwaZulu-Natal (KZN) in 1986. Note the updated figure for Zimbabwe in 2002. (b) Area of parks and wildlife estate per staff-person in selected countries in southern Africa compared with the US*

Differences in park performance within the region are, not surprisingly, influenced by national economic performance. Disparities within the region are great with per capita gross domestic product (GDP) varying between about US$165 in Malawi and US$1800 in South Africa. Differences in environment-related expenditure and park management resources are correspondingly great. Because of these disparities, which do not necessarily translate into equivalent differences in conservation performance, it is essential that lean, efficient and sustainable management and performance monitoring systems are developed. This will not be an easy task, but one well worth pursuing if parks are to continue to play a meaningful conservation role while contributing to rural development.

The continuing focus on ever more elaborate, and mostly impracticable, rigid 'park plans' needs to change (Holling and Meffe, 1996). We need to understand why so many park plans either remain unimplemented, or after a year or two of enthusiastic adoption are quietly shelved and forgotten. I suggest that this pattern reflects, in large measure, a conflict between a blueprint management model and the reality of dealing with complex systems. Those in head offices and ivory towers are comfortable with blueprints and rigid project management cycles, whereas those in the field are faced with the realities of dealing with the inevitable shocks and surprises of complex system behaviour – and the despair of attempting the impossible. The despair is heightened in management cultures where the principle of subsidiarity[1] is replaced by highly centralized control. As Ludwig (2001) has so cogently argued, 'The era of management is over' and we need a paradigm shift that will provide parks with the policy frameworks and tools to cope more effectively with complex adaptive systems.

ACKNOWLEDGEMENTS

I thank Brian Child, Meg Cumming and Russell Taylor for critically reading earlier versions of this chapter and for their constructive contributions to improving it. My thanks are also due to Mike Jones, Steve Johnson, Steve McKean, Vincent Nyirenda, Mick Townsend and Roberto Zolho, who generously provided me with much-needed background material and unpublished information.

NOTES

1   First enunciated by Pope Leo X, the principal of subsidiarity holds that '*it is an injustice, a grave evil and a disturbance of right order for a larger and higher organization to arrogate to itself functions which can be performed efficiently by smaller and lower bodies*'. As Handy (1990) says, 'To steal people's decisions is wrong.'

REFERENCES

Barnard, P (1998) *Biological Diversity in Namibia: A Country Study*, Namibian National Biodiversity Task Force, Windhoek

Bruner, A S G, Gullison, R E, Rice, R E and da Fonseca, G A B (2001) 'Effectiveness of parks in protecting tropical biodiversity', *Science* **291**: 125–8

Burkey, T V (1995) 'Faunal collapse in East African game reserves revisited', *Biological Conservation* **71**: 107–10

Child, G and Heath, R A (1992) 'Are Zimbabwe's major vegetation types adequately protected?', *Geographical Journal of Zimbabwe* **23**: 20–37

Clarke, J E and Bell, R H V (1986) 'Representation of biotic communities in protected areas: A Malawian case study', *Biological Conservation* **35**: 293–311

Cowling, R M, Pressey, R L, Lombard, A T, Desmet, P G and Ellis, A G (1999) 'From representation to persistence: Requirements for a sustainable system of conservation areas in the species rich Mediterranean desert of southern Africa', *Diversity and Distributions* **5**: 51–71

Cumming, D H M (1993) 'Wildlife products and the market place: A view from southern Africa', in L A Renecker and R J Hudson (eds) *Wildlife Production: Conservation and Sustainable Development*, University of Alaska, Fairbanks, Alaska, pp11–30

Cumming, D H M (1999) *Study on the Development of Transboundary Natural Resource Management Areas in Southern Africa, Environmental Context: Natural Resources, Land Use, and Conservation*, Biodiversity Support Program, Washington DC

Cumming, D H M, du Toit, R F and Stewart, S N (1990) *African Elephants and Rhinos: Status Survey and Conservation Action Plan*, Gland, Switzerland, IUCN

Cumming, D H M, Fenton, M B, Rautenbach, I L, Taylor, R D, Cumming, G S, Cumming, M S, Dunlop, J M, Ford, A G, Hovorka, M D, Johnston, D S, Kalcounis, M, Mahlangu and Zand Portfors, VR (1997) 'Elephants, woodlands and biodiversity in southern Africa', *South African Journal of Science* **93**: 231–6

Cumming, D H M, Mackie, C, Megane, S and Taylor, R D (1994) 'Aerial census of large herbivores in the Gorongosa National Park and the Marromeu area of the Zambezi Delta in Mozambique: June 1994', IUCN Regional Office for Southern Africa, Harare

Cumming, D H M, Martin, R B and Taylor, R D (1984) 'Questionnaire survey on the management and conservation of elephant and rhino', in D H M Cumming and P Jackson (eds) *The Status and Conservation of Africa's Elephants and Rhinos*, IUCN, Gland, Switzerland, pp46–62

du Toit, J, Biggs, H and Rogers, K (2003) *The Kruger Experience: Ecology and Management of Savanna Heterogeneity*, Island Press, Washington DC

Dunham, K M, Robertson, E F and Swanepoel, C M (2003) 'Population decline of tsessebe antelope (*Damaliscus lunatus lunatus*) on a mixed cattle and wildlife ranch in Zimbabwe', *Biological Conservation* **113**: 111–24

Dunham, K M, Robertson, E F and Grant, R. (2004) 'Trends in rainfall explain the rise and fall of tsessebe in Kruger National Park', *Biological Conservation*

East, R (1981) 'Species–area curves and populations of large mammals in African savanna reserves', *Biological Conservation* **21**: 111–26

East, R (compiler) (1997) 'Current Status of Burchell's Zebra in Africa with Additional Information on Grevy's Zebra and Cape Mountain Zebra', report to IUCN/SSC Equid Specialist Group

East, R (1998) 'African Antelope Database 1998', IUCN/SSC African Antelope Specialist Group Report

Estes, R D (2002) 'Giant sable survey – at last', *Gnusletter* **21**: 18–20

Goodman, P (2000) *Determining the Conservation Value of Land in KwaZulu-Natal*, final report KwaZulu-Natal Nature Conservation Service, Cascades, KwaZulu-Natal

Griffin, J, Cumming, D H M, Metcalfe, S, t'Sas-Rolfes, M, Singh, J, Chonguica, E, Rowen, M and Oglethorpe, J (1999) *Study on the Development of Transboundary Natural Resource Management Areas in Southern Africa*, Biodiversity Support Program, Washington DC

Groombridge, B (1992) *Global Biodiversity: Status of the Earth's Living Resources*, Chapman and Hall, London

Gunderson, L H and Holling, C S (eds) (2002) *Panarchy: Understanding Transformations in Human and Natural Systems*, Island Press, Washington DC

Handy, C (1990) *The Age of Unreason*, Arrow Books, London

Hockings, M, Stolton, S, and Dudley, N (2000) *Evaluating effectiveness: A framework for assessing management of protected areas*, IUCN, World Commission on Protected Areas, Gland, Switzerland

Holling, C S and Meffe, G K (1996) 'Command and control and the pathology of natural resource management', *Conservation Biology* **10**: 328–37

IUCN (1987) *Action Strategy for Protected Areas in the Afrotropical Realm*, IUCN, Gland, Switzerland, and Cambridge, UK

James, A N, Green, M J B, and Paine, J R (1996) 'Financial indicators for biodiversity assessment: In situ conservation investments', in *Workshop on Investing in Biodiversity*, Paper presented at a Workshop on Investing in Biodiversity, Buenos Aires, Argentina, 1–3 November, http//:biodiversityeconomics.org/pdf/961101-01.pdf

Leader-Williams, N and Albon, S D (1988) 'Allocation of resources for conservation', *Nature* **336**: 533–5

Lombard, A T (1995) 'The problems with multispecies conservation: Do hotspots, ideal reserves and existing nature reserves coincide?', *South African Journal of Zoology* **30**: 145–63

Low, A B and Rebelo, A G (1996) *Vegetation Map of South Africa, Lesotho and Swaziland*, Department of Environmental Affairs, Pretoria, South Africa

Ludwig, D (2001) 'The era of management is over', *Ecosystems* **4**: 758–64

Machlis, G E and Tichnell, D L (1985) *The State of the World's Parks: An International Assessment for Resource Management, Policy and Research*, Westview Press, Boulder, CO

MacKinnon, J and MacKinnon, K (1986) *Review of the Protected Areas System in the Afrotropical Realm*, IUCN/UNEP, Gland, Switzerland

Martin, R B (1994) 'Should wildlife pay its way?', Keith Roby Address, Perth, Australia, 8 December 1993, Department of National Parks and Wild Life Management, Zimbabwe, Harare

Martin R B (1996) *Costs of Conserving State Protected Areas in Southern Africa*, Fact Sheet no. 6, Africa Resources Trust, Harare, Zimbabwe

McNeely, J A (1993) 'Economic incentives for conserving biodiversity: Lessons from Africa', *Ambio* **22**: 144–50

Nott, P M and Pimm, S L (1997) 'The evaluation of biodiversity as a target for conservation', in S T A Pickett, R S Ostfeld, M Shachak and G E Likens (eds) *The Ecological Basis of Conservation: Heterogeneity, Ecosystems and Biodiversity*, Chapman and Hall, New York, pp125–35

Owen-Smith, R N and Ogutu, J (2003) 'Rainfall influences on ungulate population dynamics in the Kruger National Park', in J du Toit, H Biggs and K Rogers (eds) *The Kruger Experience: Ecology and Management of Savanna Heterogeneity*, Island Press, Washington DC

Parker, I S C (1984) 'Conservation of the African elephant', in D H M Cumming and P Jackson (eds) *The Status and Conservation of Africa's Elephants and Rhinos*, IUCN, Gland, Switzerland, pp69–77

Pienaar, U de V (1978) 'Nature conservation in Rhodesia and South Africa: Yesterday, today and tomorrow', Wankie National Park 50th Anniversary, typescript

Pressey, R L and Cowling, R M (1999) 'Reserve selection algorithms and the real world', *Conservation Biology* **15**: 275–7

Pressey, R L, Humphries, C J, Margules, C R, Vane-Wright, R I and Williams, PH (1993) 'Beyond opportunism; Key principles for systematic reserve selection', *Trends in Ecology and Evolution* **8**: 124–8

Pullan, R A (1983) 'The use of wildlife in the development of Zambia', in Ooi Jim Bee (ed) *Natural Resources in Tropical Countries*, Singapore, University of Singapore Press, pp267–325

Reyers, B, Fairbanks, D H K, Van Jaarsveld, A S and Thompson, M (2001) 'Priority areas for the conservation of South African vegetation: A coarse filter approach', *Diversity and Distributions* **7**: 79–95

Rogers, K H and Biggs, H (1999) 'Integrating indicators, end points and value systems in the strategic management of Kruger National Park', *Freshwater Biology* **41**: 439–51

Rogers, K H and O'Keefe, J (2003) 'River heterogeneity: ecosystem structure, function and management', in J du Toit, H Biggs and K Rogers (eds) *The Kruger Experience: Ecology and Management of Savanna Heterogeneity*, Island Press, Washington DC

Soule, M E, Wilcox, B A and Holtby, C (1979) 'Benign neglect: A model of faunal collapse in the game reserves of East Africa', *Biological Conservation* **15**: 259–72

Spinage, C A (1990) 'Botswana's problem elephants', *Pachyderm* **13**: 14–9

Taylor, R D (1990) 'Zimbabwe – A history of nature conservation in Zimbabwe', in C W Allin (ed) *International Handbook of National Parks and Nature Reserves*, Greenwood Press, Connecticut, pp493–515

Valeix, M (2002) 'Structure of ungulate communities: A test for the role of megaherbivores in interspecific competition', MSc thesis, Universite Pierre and Marie Curie de Science a Paris, Paris

White, F (1983) *The Vegetation of Africa: A Descriptive Memoir*, UNESCO, Paris

Chapter 6

Park Agencies, Performance and Society in Southern Africa

Brian Child

with

Steve McKean (KwaZulu-Natal),
Agnes Kiss (Uganda),
Simon Munthali (Mozambique and Malawi),
Brian Jones (Namibia),
Morris Mtsambiwa (Swaziland),
Guy Castley, Chris Patton and Hector Magome (South Africa)
George Pangeti (Zimbabwe)
Peter Fearnhead and Steve Johnson (South Africa and Provinces)
Gersham Chilikusha (Zambia)

BACKGROUND

The commercial potential of wildlife has been increasingly demonstrated by the private and community sector, yet wildlife in the state sector is characterized by decline. As a response to this park agencies in southern Africa are undergoing considerable change, and this chapter looks at its political, managerial and performance implications.

Structurally, these responses can be seen in a general trend towards converting wildlife agencies into parastatals more independent from the political centre; in increased commercialization involving both revenue generation and the installation of more efficient managerial practices; and in the development of partnerships with communities, the private sector and non-governmental organizations (NGOs).

The means–end relationship governing parks is also changing. Greater emphasis on economic potentials and social responsibility is increasingly providing the justification and mechanism for maintaining parks and almost as a by-product the more conventional objectives of national biodiversity preservation. Subsidized biodiversity conservation is also being questioned in favour of broader social responsiveness, including employment and economic growth. Whereas park management remains highly centralized, this model is also being questioned in favour of the localization of management and benefit, and the use of parks as economic bridgeheads to promote wildlife-based economic development and landscape consolidation. This challenge to conventional park management is a response to the possibilities of a triple-win situation. Capturing the full economic potential of wildlife provides economic growth and social benefit, it has relatively few biodiversity opportunity costs, and it also addresses the underfunding of parks both directly and indirectly. Our central argument is that the decline of parks is a symptom of a serious misalignment between parks and the society they serve, and that park sustainability is best served through a changed means–end relationship, built around the commercialization and localization of park management.

As centralized state agencies, a major determinant of the performance of park authorities is the general status of the political and administrative environment. Therefore, to provide a situation analysis, we draw on Grindle and Thomas's (1991) excellent generalized description of the policy environment in developing countries. They note that governance in developing countries tends to be over-centralized and over-politicized, with individuals having considerable power yet insufficient and unreliable technical or economic information on which to base decisions. Consequently, political power becomes the central determinant of policy outcomes, which tend to be politically rather than economically oriented. Centralized, non-representative governance has structural roots in colonial rule, but is exacerbated by the fear that decentralization will lead to political dissolution and conflict in states cobbled together from different ethnic groups. Additionally, donors have buttressed the growth and domination of the state by channelling aid to governments that, in an era of central planning, were seen to be 'engines of development'. This created government agencies with the power to control and allocate critical resources, including jobs. In the absence of mechanisms of accountability, this has lead to political control, privilege, patronage and ultimately corruption. The size of the civil service has increased, lowering standards of service, and admission has acquired important political objectives. Officials are directed through powerful hierarchical controls, and the system is subject to relatively little scrutiny. The state has replaced the market as the allocator of scarce resources, and there is often a strong ideological predisposition against profit-seeking entrepreneurs, with government seeing itself responsible for ensuring local equity and control of the economy by nationals. There is a serious suspicion of private business and the profit motive, which are seen as self-serving and anti-egalitarian.

Park agencies are no exception, and have been used to allocate state resources with, until recently, considerable suspicion of the private sector. However, in the examples provided in this chapter, we document a critically important change in the political economy of parks, demonstrating a shift from using them as political tools to managing them as economic implements. The emergence of the park parastatal is the most obvious indicator of the increasing independence of parks from political control. Most countries are in the process of replacing highly centralized and politicized planning and control systems, and the administrative allocation of resources, with systems based more on the principles of free-market mechanics and devolved, technically and economically based, governance. Within organizations, this massive change in corporate culture is driven by a decline of government financing and a drive towards financial self-sustainability, whereas at the macro-economic level there is a realization that the parks and wildlife sector has considerable potential to generate sustainable economic growth in rural areas (Figure 6.1).

The History of Conservation Agencies

Much of southern and eastern Africa was colonized by the British. Somewhere between 1940 and 1960, countries established a government department responsible for parks, wildlife or both. These were usually highly professional technical agencies with a small staff, and were responsible for setting up a system of parks across the country. Initially this was a simple, if technical, task. Human populations were low, and parks were usually established where there were few people. In Zambia and Zimbabwe, for instance, and much against the grain of current sympathy, almost nobody needed to be re-located from parks, and those few that were invariably found land of an equivalent quality. These park managers were not mired in the social complexity of today, but were practical men, building roads and accommodation for themselves and tourists, and undertaking basic law enforcement, again with far fewer pressures than today. Although the control of problem animals was a major function, and often the seed from which these conservation organizations grew, these agencies were predominantly technical and interacted relatively little with people and politics. Even when they did, their constituency was usually a small, white minority, with a strong interest in conservation and a willingness to prioritize public funds for conservation.

The situation is now very different. In most countries, the population has increased 20-fold since 1900, land is no longer abundant, government budgets have collapsed and the polity is responsive to a majority that is often mired in poverty. Whereas pressures have built up on parks, budgets have withered and staffing structures have bloated, leaving little money for implementation. In several countries, wildlife agencies have become an instrument of political patronage. At one level they provide a source of employment and security. At another, they are used for political or personal gain (Gibson, 1999), most notably in the allocation of tourism or hunting concessions, permits, permissions and other use rights. In the first decades after independence, technical skills have been sacrificed to political or even personal priorities,[1] with the collapse of management systems and technical competence. If one believes the thesis of Chabal and Daloz (1999), this has been a deliberate effort by those in power to muddy the waters of control and accountability to facilitate predation.

In parallel to the politicization of park governance, the management of wildlife and parks has ignored and alienated constituent societies to the extent that societal disinterest becomes the ultimate cause of underfunding and neglect, simultaneously opening more space for elite predation. As a consequent of this misalignment of values and incentives, many wildlife agencies have deteriorated since the glory years of the 1960s, in marked contrast to the dynamic tourism industry that feeds off them.

The positive news is that most governments in southern and eastern Africa have recognized these problems and potentials, and have begun to distance park management from political influence. Consequently, park managers are struggling with governance and managerial issues related to the de-nationalization of the wildlife resource, and with shifting allocatory decisions from the political to the economic

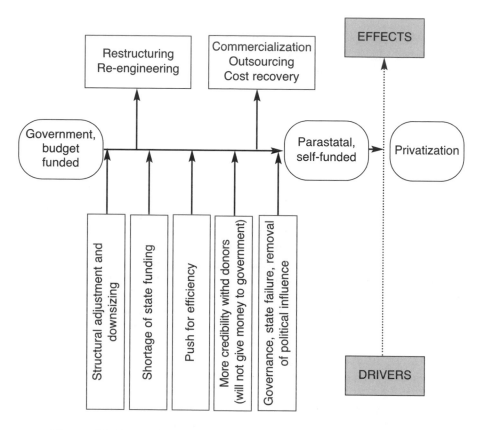

Figure 6.1 *Forces driving the de-nationalization of wildlife resources, the formation of parastatals and commercialization*[2]

market place. Several forces are driving this process (Figure 6.1). In re-engineering park agencies around functions, cutting costs, increasing efficiency and generating more revenue (that is, commercialization) the common model is the potentially self-funding quasi-government parastatal.[3] Wildlife and parks have within them the potential to perpetuate themselves, and many park agencies are experimenting with ways to realize this potential. This requires major innovations in the economic relationship between parks and society, in the political relationship between park agencies and national leadership, in the psychological mindset of control versus liberalization and in the way parks are funded, managed and their goals prioritized.

ANALYTICAL FRAMEWORK

This chapter analyses the lessons to be gleaned from the changes occurring in park management across the region. At the centre of this analysis is the question of accountability: first, what parks deliver to whom; and second, how well they deliver.

In other words, are they doing the right thing, and are they doing it right? We begin from first principles, with the starting point that parks are common pool resources set aside for society to provide collective goods and services where market forces have failed. The conventional response to imperfect markets, which is also the underlying philosophical rationale for national park authorities, is that the state is a better judge of what is good for society. At the centre of the paradigm shift occurring in southern Africa is a questioning of the assumption that the centrally planned, command-and-control model is any more perfect than imperfect markets. This opens up several questions about how best to provide and monitor the provision of conservation outputs.

That protected areas are common property regimes set aside to provide collective goods and services for society introduces the central question and challenge of constituency accountability. Is the state accountable for using protected areas to provide appropriate value to society? Are systems of national parks providing the collective goods and services that societies want? And are they doing this well?

Conventionally, parks are supposed to conserve biodiversity. In Chapter 5 we have already ascertained that although this is the main claim for the existence of state funding, and they may well contribute to this, the monitoring and management of biodiversity is seldom systematic and is often not even prioritized. We speculate that the reasons for this are both technical complexity and its low social or managerial priority, and we provide preliminary suggestions for how to improve this aspect of park management in Chapter 10. In transitional economies like those of southern Africa, moreover, jobs and economic growth are undoubtedly more important than wilderness values or outdoor recreation in themselves. If parks were accountable to society we would expect a shift in this direction, especially given the positive correlation between the commercialization of wildlife and conservation outcome (Chapter 7). To what extent is this happening? And how does this shift towards locally derived priorities affect the global priority of biodiversity conservation?

We term the second set of issues that we address, value accountability, or the ability of parks to focus on activities that add value. Value accountability is built into businesses. The flow of revenues is related directly to the value a business provides to customers, and revenues flow upwards through the organization. Businesses will not survive if they lose focus on creating value. Less obvious is the importance of the direction of revenue flows. The upward flow of revenues through businesses, and the linkage between people working at the customer face and value added, is the central insight of modern business practice, and the plethora of terms like subsidiarity, self-managed teams, flattened hierarchies and the like. It is also the central insight of community-based natural resource management (CBNRM) (see Chapter 4).

Park agencies are budget-funded public institutions, and this is perhaps the most fundamental challenge to accountability. Unlike businesses, park agencies lack the direct linkage between the amount of value they add and incentives. Money is usually dumped centrally on the organization with the optimistic expectancy that, in the absence of bottom-line discipline, it will trickle downwards to the place where it adds most value. A common symptom of central financing and planning is an ever-widening mandate (as we illustrate in Chapter 5), the growing importance of image and publicity, and little accountability for delivery of real results. Public agencies are guided by bureaucratic or political priorities, and in responding to an ever wider set of stakeholders are unable to concentrate on core competency: they must placate everyone.[4] Managing this challenge is the central and most difficult challenge of public service agencies (Drucker, 1973).

There are generally two solutions. Accountability is sought by placing the agency directly under political control, usually a minister. However, as noted in the description of the general policy environment provided in the introduction, direct political accountability has been problematic across the region, in terms of setting and controlling mandates and performance and, less benignly, where the lack of accountability provides space for political patronage and even predation. As recent scandals like Enron in the US show, this is not a problem unique to park parastatals. Company boards work best where board members are direct owners, and costs and benefits are internalized. However, company boards that represent a multitude of stakeholders also face the challenges of constituency accountability and the personal interests of executives and board members. We use the regional experience to determine where and how distancing park agencies from political control has advantages.

The second solution to the accountability problem is leadership and goal setting. In the absence of market tests, service institutions have performed best where leaders have given priority to defining the institution's mission and purpose, and to setting and concentrating on a few priorities, in short performance accountability. For service institutions to perform in the absence of the discipline of markets and the bottom line, they need to impose discipline upon themselves by: (1) defining their mission ('what is our business and what should it be'); (2) setting clear objectives and goals; (3) prioritizing outputs with clear targets and standards; (4) defining measurements of performance; (5) instituting feedback and control systems; and (6) formally auditing objectives and results to enable adaptation and especially the sloughing off of redundant functions (see Drucker, 1973). Even in the provision of public services, measured competition yields vastly superior results. Wherever a market test is truly possible, it will result in improved performance and results, but equally clearly the market is not capable of organizing all institutions.

We use our case studies to assess whether political systems want, or are allowing, park agencies to set clear goals. This concerns issues of power, and political and institutional economics. At another level, it concerns the economics of public goods and natural resources and the philosophical challenge of determining exactly what parks and park agencies are for, what they should provide and who best to do so. Finally, we need to draw on business management principles, and how to achieve these goals effectively and efficiently. Before embarking on improving park performance, we need to be clear about objectives. This involves complex and value-laden choices, made especially difficult because, in placating all the stakeholders, choices have tended to be fudged.

For example, one important choice is political and economic: do we aim to provide jobs and economic opportunities, or do we provide wilderness values? How much recreation and education do we provide? And is this a business or a social service? Because of the domination of the protected-area movement by developed countries, the trend has been towards wilderness and social services, but this is less appropriate in transitional economies.

A second decision to be made is how to prioritize among a range of competing stakeholders. The important decision made in southern Africa has been the primacy of the landholder (be this a park agency, private landholder or community) over the stakeholder.

Ecological choices are no easier. For instance a common dilemma is whether to emphasize the maintenance of ecological productivity and processes, or the numbers and diversity of large mammals. An important example is the trade-off between elephants on the one hand, and the loss of trees, avian and other biodiversity on the other.

Even once the importance of goal-based performance management is recognized, the examples given illustrate the challenges and progress of defining goals in a field as complex as park management. The failure to clearly define the goals of park agencies has been exacerbated by the tendency to lump them with the responsibility of providing both public and private goods.[5] Although this is a complex issue, there is nevertheless a tendency for park agencies to provide goods that are better left to private mechanisms (eg tourism facilities) rather than true public goods, which are often less tangible. It will be interesting to follow how the increasing autonomy of park agencies coupled with commercialization, which tends to replace administrative allocation and control with performance or market mechanisms, affects the provision of public goods including biodiversity conservation.

In the absence of bottom-line discipline, strong leadership is required to set clear or visionary goals in a public agency. An important aspect of the shift towards parastatals, therefore, is the effect on leadership quality. Also important is the development of management systems, especially given the contention that charismatic leadership can be counter-productive and that the revitalization of park agencies does not generally need better people, but people who know exactly what is expected of them, who do the management job systematically and who focus themselves and their institution purposefully on performance and results (Drucker, 1973).

Park agencies have conventionally been managed as command-and-control structures, with what Hersey and Blanchard (1988) describe as an X-mentality: because people are basically unreliable and lazy, top managers have to work through strong hierarchies to ensure that the agency performs, and discipline and sanctions are key ingredients of management. The opposite theory (theory-Y) is that because people are self-motivated, performance improves if individuals are given authority within a clear set of goals. This is the belief that lies behind the modern management practices of flat business structures and self-managed teams. With top-down funding, park agencies are predisposed towards hierarchy, whereas loosened management systems allow the potential of individual park staff to be unlocked. Thus, the degree to which park agencies have moved along this spectrum has implications for the effectiveness of management.

REGIONAL EXPERIENCES

Challenges to Emerging Park Parastatals

The emergence of park parastatals in southern and eastern Africa can be seen as a generally positive development, although we are still learning how to make them work effectively. Several issues are important. Accepting that parks must serve society will define the nature of the business, and given the priorities of southern African countries is likely to shift park goals towards economic growth and employment creation, with biodiversity conservation providing the limits within which this can occur rather then being the only or primary goals. Once this is decided, come the more mechanical managerial issues of how to structure work so that it gets done.

Ensuring that parks deliver what society needs is difficult, as the starting point is a significant philosophical shift in the perception of the roles of parks. Linked to this is the need to define what are legitimate public functions, and which are best done by the private sector, which leads to the task of allocating these roles to the type of agency best suited to perform them: for instance, regulation and monitoring to government agencies, and customer services to private firms.

Governance and accountability are also central issues. This includes the mechanism for linking the park agencies to the political system (eg through a board) without excessive or personalized political influence, and the mechanisms for holding the agency accountability for delivering appropriate value to society.

Improved performance accountability will be related to increasing use of market tests and, where these are not possible, to the clarification of performance expectations through the setting and monitoring of goals. Achieving the latter will require considerable innovation in the design of performance management systems and agency structure, and a key issue will be the decentralization of management to cost/profit centres. Too little emphasis has been placed on this aspect of commercialization (ie how to deliver more with less) and there is almost no analysis of management systems (Reed (2002) and the authors quoted by him are rare exceptions). Although commercialization includes structural and performance issues, it is more commonly perceived as increasing income by commoditizing park resources, and is sometimes associated with outsourcing.

Managing the tension between the institution's own financial survival and societal benefits will be the main challenge here, because the gap between the financial and the economic viability of parks is huge (see Chapter 7), and is complicated to manage. Financial viability is related to the circumstances of an individual organization, where economic viability measures costs and benefits at a societal level. As we discuss below, a park may be financially marginal even where it creates very significant economic benefits. In a few cases, governments are sophisticated enough to make economic investments by subsidizing park finances; unfortunately, this brings with it all the problems and challenges of dumping finances centrally and managing budget-driven organizations (eg Natal, Namibia). However, many governments do not recognize the net worth of investing in parks, hence the widespread decline (eg Zambia, Malawi, Zimbabwe).

In the remainder of this section we describe the experience of park agencies in the region, to support these arguments and as a prelude to an analysis of their accountability for performance. We aim to introduce important issues such as accountability, institutional design and managerial effectiveness, and to use these as our analytical framework, but are forced to rely on personal experience as these concepts are relatively new and the data to measure them are not available (see Chapter 5).

Zimbabwe Parks: What Made a Government Department Excellent and Why It Declined

Zimbabwe's Department of National Parks and Wildlife Management was renowned as an excellent organization. Nevertheless, it was a government department and all revenues were centralized through treasury, disbursed through the annual government budget process and staff were civil servants. It worked primarily for two reasons: in contrast to the findings of Grindle and Thomas (1991), the then Rhodesian government was small, professional, effective and highly responsive to its (albeit narrow) constituency; and for cultural reasons the department itself attracted quality staff and was well managed.

After independence, linkages to increasingly politicized central governance, and the replacement of meritocracy with patronage in the management of staff, steadily reduced performance. By the late 1990s, performance had declined so far that the agency was de-linked from government as a statutory authority (in 2003). The major causes of decline were politicized and non-meritocratic staff management, and the financial and staffing inflexibility of government.

However, it is informative to ask what were the factors that had enabled the organization to perform so well in the past even as a government department. This cannot be completely separated from ethnicity and culture. Zimbabwean whites received advantageous education, and despite the low pay, joining the department was a high-status position in a society that favoured the rugged outdoors. There were hundreds of applications for each ranger post, and of those recruited fewer than half remained after a year's experience. There was powerful selective pressure on staff.

Central to the organization are what Peters and Waterman (1982) call 'loose–tight' properties. Clear goals and standards were set for the organization, with well-articulated policies and performance expectations, with the latter being both documented and part of the organizational culture. All parks had a policy document, which also laid out management goals and development plans, and departmental policy covered many issues ranging from uniform and vehicle management, position descriptions and promotion criteria, to support of the private sector, crocodile management, visitor management, etc. Although far from perfect, and a little primitive by today's standards, this framework encouraged managers to be individualistic and innovative, and stories of how much was achieved with how little were part of departmental myth. Internal competition and performance rivalry was intense, communication was rich and informal, and peer review was regular, positive and powerful.

Yet behind this informality were criteria and systems for promotion, reporting and performance evaluation, containing both objective and subjective criteria. In short, performance emanated from quality staff, a highly competitive but informal culture that worked to clear goals, and a strong moral imperative to conserve parks, backed up by simple but essential financial and administrative systems. The department also displayed strong non-charismatic team leadership, largely independent of political pressures, and much of the department's success can be traced back to this (eg game ranching, Communal Areas Management Programme for Indigenous Resources (CAMPFIRE), kapenta fishing, crocodile and ostrich industries, elephant management, etc; see Child, G (1995) for a detailed description). A board comprising well-known figures in conservation and the tourism sector also served the department, but no member was a serving civil servant.

Perhaps the major problem was the centralization of income (to treasury), centralized budgets and centralized staffing systems, although these impacts were mitigated by effective administration and the adjustment of budgets or promotions to reflect performance. Despite this, and considerable innovation in the way individual managers used their limited expenditure, it took considerable effort to avoid the problems of bureaucratic budgeting, with budgets still tending to be based on the year before and managers rushing to spend end-of-year surpluses. Less was done to promote tourism than would have occurred had park budgets gained directly from tourism-related services or investments, and tourists were often seen as a nuisance. Tied into the Public Service Commission, creating new posts or eliminating old ones in response to changing demands was exceedingly slow and difficult. It took almost a decade for the department to recruit its first economists. The links between ecological research and park management were largely informal, and opportunities for synergy and the systematic management of biodiversity were lost.

Nonetheless, performance was generally impressive: parks were protected, tourism infrastructure provided, quality ecological research laid the foundation for management decisions (although monitoring tended to be neglected), and the department facilitated others to develop the game ranching, crocodiles and ostrich sectors as well as CAMPFIRE.

The strength of the system was also its ultimate weakness. Like Drucker's examples of the few high-performing service institutions, it depended on the ability of dedicated and enlightened leadership to articulate clear goals and values, focus on these, and improve performance through rich peer pressure, while resisting political pressures and intrusions. In an increasingly politicized and centralized environment, in many ways similar to Grindle and Thomas's generalization, a small, professional technical agency was unlikely to survive. Indeed, the department was centralized and politicized, and with increasing difficulties in attracting and rewarding staff, and non-meritocratic criteria dominating staffing decisions, performance quickly dissipated. Cooperation with the private sector and civil society declined, following the paradox that weaker leaders are threatened by transparency and tend to centralize activities, and the department lost its leadership position in the region.

Kenya Wildlife Service

By the 1980s, Kenya's rich wildlife biodiversity and valuable tourism sector was seriously threatened by organizational failure, with heavy elephant and rhino poaching, deteriorating infrastructure and plant, sinking morale, staff inactivity and corruption. In the early 1990s, and with significant World Bank and other funding, the Wildlife Conservation and Management Department was transformed into the semi-autonomous Kenya Wildlife Service (KWS). While this was a bold shift, some people in power were reluctant to make too aggressive a change. A board (15 members) provided formal oversight, but tended to be weak, was dominated by government officials (7) or Ministerial appointees (6), and was subject to cronyism, nepotism and political patronage (Reed, 2002).

Although the KWS supposedly had freedom to retain revenue and more flexibility over staff management, the degree of true autonomy over staffing and contracting was limited. Authority was not explicitly stated in enabling legislation, senior staff were regularly changed by political action, budget ceilings were imposed by the ministry, a government official in the ministry (not the CEO) remained the accounting officer, and bureaucratic procedures hampered contracts and payments. Thus the KWS is not a true test of autonomy in the management of parks agencies, although these problems are symptomatic of many parastatals. Other problems were the breadth of the organization's mandate, and that it was given too much money too fast, without the legal, institutional or managerial capacity to absorb it (Reed, 2002).

The overall impact of massive funding and institutional reform was positive. Management systems and morale improved, workplans were re-introduced, staffing was improved by reducing the establishment and removing non-performers, and training and equipment were provided. Capacity improved immediately, and better security reduced poaching and improved tourism. However, wildlife populations continued to fall outside parks (Ottichilo et al, 2000) owing to poaching and habitat loss and, ultimately, because landholders were given few use rights and the most valued uses (eg safari hunting) were banned. This is an example of the negative power of state agencies.

Considering the massive donor commitment, and the potential for tourism (US$350 million tourism turnover directly related to wildlife and parks), KWS underperformed and remained far from reaching goals of financial sustainability. It shows typical symptoms of a budget-driven organization, with a review concluding that: 'terms were too vague ... and donor- and fund-driven rather than guided by priorities' (TAESCO, 1998). As Drucker would predict for a budget-funded agency, expenditure was not related to added value and many redundant components were retained; while the parks earned 99 per cent of KWS income, less than 25 per cent of expenditure was on parks, with 80 per cent being spent on headquarters and outside activities. It is quite possible that, in response to the demands of the political system and the possibilities provided by central financing, KWS directors were building constituency support rather than cost efficiency or conservation effectiveness. Although some preliminary work was done, systematic ecosystem monitoring never occurred.

KWS also failed on both ends of the financial sustainability equation. Costs grew from US$11.5 million to US$30.3 million in seven years (42 per cent annually), and were seldom related to revenue-generating activities. Revenues increased from US$5.9 million to US$18.3 million, but this was well below expectations and some 10–30 per cent was not collected (that is, it 'leaked'). According to Read (2002), there was much cross-subsidization of non-core activities so that the expenditure deficit doubled from US$5.6 million to US$12 million in a situation where park conservation should have cost no more than US$6 million to US$10 million (Martin, 2003).

Poor performance was exacerbated by centralizing management in the hands of staff who were inexperienced with management systems (mainly biologically trained) and prone, as centralized staff often are, to political manipulation. Key management practices were never introduced; the centralization of emoluments encouraged overstaffing; the perennial problem of procurement slowed action; and staff were not held accountable for carefully described performance outcomes. The corollary is that these very same people might have coped adequately with a decentralized organization and well-defined and incentivized objectives.

South African National Parks

South Africa's National Parks Board was created in 1926, the first statutory board in South Africa. With a strong political imperative it was well funded (Carruthers, in preparation). Kruger in particular suffered the worst excesses of budget-funded institutions, building substantial infrastructure in the form of tourism accommodation, roads and offices, employing many staff, and internalizing the management of everything from hospitality, construction and sports clubs to the normal core functions of research and law enforcement. This strong aversion to outsourcing reflected a highly inefficient organization ('t Sas-Rolfes, undated), which was subsidized and managed for the sole benefit of white South Africans. Within the region, the organization was regarded as retrogressive, and was commonly said to use a steamroller to crack a nut.

After democratic majority rule in 1994, the agency was modernized and re-branded as 'SANParks'. It developed a mission statement and strategic plan aimed largely at cultural change and the inculcation of more business-like practice. Although the board remained lightweight, and more politically correct than technically skilled, the key strength of SANParks was its operating flexibility, large asset base and, particularly, an effective CEO who, in turn, was able to recruit strong executive managers and protect the organization from political intrusions. Despite the heavy investment in infrastructure and strong tourism markets, SANParks covered only 80 per cent of costs as late as 1997 (US$50 million). Amazingly, given its asset base, Kruger made a small operating loss (R20 million), whereas its tourism pricing policies neither maximized revenues nor satisfied social objectives; indeed they tended to subsidize richer, whiter tourism (Child, B, 2002a).

However, the situation is improving rapidly, with an internally driven change to reduce the government subsidy, to improve corporate culture and to remove old-fashioned attitudes. Reflecting the differences between old and new management, there was a major internal battle over the acceptability of outsourcing. Once done, this worked well. The revenue from shops increased from R8 million to R23 million within two years, whereas the revenue from a few private concessions reached R5 million in the same period, with a rapid trajectory to R20 million. Seen as well managed, SANParks has been entrusted with some R440 million to use for poverty alleviation (used largely as a social fund in the removal of exotic vegetation), perhaps a harbinger of a new role for well-managed park agencies that extend their reach deep into deprived rural areas.

Nevertheless, the agency is still building tourism lodges, reflecting just how difficult it is to shift from a budget-driven to a value-adding culture. At the practical level, managers still view budgets as a pot of money to be milked, so that cost control remains problematic, and non-value-adding functions are retained out of precedent (eg a large culling unit despite an eight-year break in elephant culling). As SANParks illustrates, park agencies still have a lot to learn about the dangers of unthinking cross-subsidization; the use of cost centres and activity-based budgeting to link expenditure to value-adding activities and to create financial understanding and discipline; and the use of benchmarking and internal comparisons to create performance competition (Child, B, 2002a).

Even in this relatively well-managed and successful organization there is substantial scope to improve performance, with staff often working at cross-purposes and without clear goals.

Only three of the twenty parks have reasonably defined management goals. No parks have implemented systems for controlling performance against these objectives. Parks are seldom audited on their performance in relation to their stated objectives. The weakness of the management system is emphasized by that fact that budget cuts are usually proportional and not linked to a careful assessment of priority activities. In short, the system lacks performance accountability and is likely to be inefficient as a consequence (Child, B, 2002a).

Such managerial weaknesses, so often associated with conservation and public organizations, can also have cultural or political roots. Reflecting global paradoxes and dilemmas, Child, B, (2002a) suggests that the failure to set clear, measurable priorities is costing conservation dearly:

Mirroring South Africa's dilemma between the philosophical position of rich urban societies, and the utilizationist philosophies of land-based communities, Kruger has had great difficult managing the contradiction between the Euro-centric hands-off conservation ideals with the strong, utilizationist South African outdoor culture. It is also transitioning from the earlier 'stockman' period when fire, water and predators were manipulated to increase game and game-viewing opportunities, to a more holistic ecosystems approach. Given these philosophical cross-currents (no less severe in many other countries and a general problem faced by 'conservation') Kruger has been somewhat schizophrenic in the application of resource use policy, allowing staff to pursue their cultural norms of fishing, shooting, gardening and cooking on wood fires, while insisting that visitors adhere closely to Euro-centric ideals (which, in several documents, have a certain purity about them). Similarly, there is a tension between a desire to leave the park in an untouched state, and an understandable discomfort with allowing any resources to go to waste (eg mopane worms, locusts, thatching grass). Deciding generally on the latter approach, management has mollified itself by ensuring that money did not 'soil' this decision by insisting only on personal or subsistence uses. However, at bottom, this is still an economic decision, but is an inefficient one. The overall result is the creation of a highly distorted market place, with plenty of ad-hoc use occurring, but without the benefit of the invisible hand to make these choices effective. Moreover, seldom have the costs and benefit of alternatives been compared, for example between gravel collection inside and outside the park. Use has also occurred in an atmosphere of denial and personal (staff) interest, resulting in inconsistency of purpose and the application of law. Thus, fee-paying hunting was prohibited, yet culling occurred, as did other higher-impact uses, including those prohibited in schedule 1 parks. This illustrates the difficult position in which park managers are placed by the absence of a clear, socially relevant and legitimate conservation philosophy.

SANParks is currently tackling these challenges, and an important general lesson from its experience is that financially driven organizations do better conservation than state organizations, partly because they have more money, but primarily because they can recruit quality staff with a value-adding mentality who drive progressive change from within the organization.

Kwa-Zulu Natal Conservation Organization[6]

Natal Parks Board (NPB) was formed in 1947 to manage 76 protected areas (6875km^2) constituting 7.2 per cent of KwaZulu-Natal (KZN) Province. By 2002, it managed 110 parks. This agency has a good reputation for conservation and for providing recreational opportunities (see Chapter 8). With just under half of its budget derived from own income, and having managed consistently to obtain a good government grant, KZN has a budget of US$5091/km^2. This is three times the estimated threshold operating budget of US$1524/km^2 (necessary to manage parks of this size using Martin's (2003) model and assuming an average park size of 90km^2), albeit noting that this expenditure includes commercial operations and conservation outside 'parks' which absorbs a substantial budget.

Operational freedom has resulted in good conservation, including the re-introduction and recovery of endangered species. These investments have generated economic growth, especially as NPB actively promoted private sector conservation with over 200 conservancies in the Province (Reed, 2002).

The success of NPB stemmed from its provision of affordable (subsidized) wildlife experiences to the white elite (certainly the case 15–20 years ago) and its rapid ability to adjust politically, with KZN Wildlife now focusing on rural communities surrounding parks, and actively promoting its facilities to all sectors of the population. With the removal of direct subsidization of recreational opportunities, there have been large price increases for accommodation in KZN parks. Initially, the agency managed all tourism activities itself, with mixed results. It was good at providing traditional park-based accommodation and services, but was weaker in other aspects. For example, a major investment in facilities at the Midmar Dam failed as the agency was too inflexible to manage seasonal, fashionable business and services. Consequently, there are now numerous outsourcing initiatives and, finally, the message is getting through that parks need much better marketing and tariff flexibility according to season, time, etc.

Assessed from the perspective of institutional economics and politics, government grants were strongly related politically to the provision of affordable accommodation to the ruling elite, and latterly to a good record in community support. However, that such a well-placed park agency, with strong asset base and ready market, is only 50 per cent viable, suggests that it suffers many of the ills of grant-funded organizations, especially the taking on of too many functions. For example, environmental education, research, extension, etc, will never pay for themselves and will probably always require government input.

KZN is certainly an agency with an ability to survive, and to adjust its mandate to the politics and funding priorities of the times. Assuming it does park conservation efficiently, these non-core activities consume two-thirds of the budget, and satisfy political constituencies in a way that is typical of a budget-funded organization. With the data available, we cannot judge if it is a well-managed efficient agency with sound financial structures and tasks well done, or if it is also effective in achieving clearly laid-out goals, unless we also know its performance against clearly defined and measurable conservation and social goals. Fifty-six years after it was formed, 'these goals are in the late stages of development,[7] with government insisting that each cent put into conservation is accounted for and allocated to achieving measurable conservation and social goals'. Although KZN is a characteristic budget-funded organization that is efficient, it also suffers the symptoms of such organizations. It would be extremely interesting to carefully evaluate it for effectiveness against clearly defined biodiversity and socio-economic goals.

Uganda Wildlife Authority[8]

The Uganda Game Department (UGD) was created in 1926. In 1952 national parks were established, beginning with Murchison Falls National Park and Queen Elizabeth National Park later that year, and placed under the jurisdiction of a newly created parastatal entity, the Uganda National Parks (UNP). The two organizations co-existed for over 40 years, with UNP responsible for gazetted national parks and the UGD responsible for game reserves, sanctuaries and controlled hunting areas, as well as the management and utilization of wildlife outside national parks and protection of people and their crops and livestock from wildlife depredation.

As a parastatal the UNP enjoyed some freedom from government control, including the ability to retain revenues, most of which came from park entry fees and 'gorilla trekking' fees. Although there is little information available about its revenues and costs, as a whole the UNP was relatively well resourced and managed to remain operational even during the years of civil conflict (1972–1985). Although wildlife populations within national parks suffered enormously as a result of hunting by local people and soldiers on both sides,[9] the parks themselves remained largely intact and unencroached. By contrast, as a government department, the UGD was completely dependent on very inadequate allocations from treasury and was unable to maintain an effective presence on the ground, even after hostilities abated and the new government took charge in 1985.

The idea of merging the UNP and UGD arose in the early 1990s, partly in recognition of the general ineffectiveness of the UGD. Initially, the idea was to absorb the UGD into the UNP. This corresponded to a general policy of the Uganda government at the time to 'spin off' agencies and departments as parastatals, which were intended to be largely, if not entirely, self-financing. There was, however, some resistance to the idea. One important issue was that the game reserves and other areas managed by the UGD earned no significant revenues, in part because a total ban on hunting had been put in place in 1985. Thus, it was feared that taking on the UGD liabilities could bankrupt the relatively successful UNP. However, because many of the game reserves were adjacent to the national parks, it was in UNP's interests that it became better managed, and to many it seemed to make sense to bring the areas under the control of a single organization. Both within government and internationally, there was a strong desire to rehabilitate the wildlife sector and revitalize the once lucrative nature-based tourism industry. Throughout the 1960s, an estimated 3000 foreign tourists per week passed through Entebbe airport. Tourism virtually disappeared during the war years, but had begun a slow recovery and had reached about 3000–5000 people per year by the mid-1990s.

The result was a long process of debate, supported by numerous donor-financed studies and workshops. By 1994 the idea of simply merging the UNP and UGD had been rejected in favour of creating an entirely new parastatal entity, to be called the Uganda Wildlife Authority (UWA). The process was finally completed in 1996 with new legislation that established UWA and designated it as primarily responsible for legally gazetted national parks and game reserves (wildlife protected areas), and as one of several agencies with powers to control land and resource use in wildlife management areas, which included wildlife sanctuaries and community wildlife areas. To ensure that the new parastatal, with its relative managerial and financial freedom, conformed to government policies and interests, a small Wildlife Department with a mainly policy-making role was established at the same time. The UGD and UNP were both abolished and their staff pensioned off with the option of applying for employment with UWA.

There were high expectations that the UWA would soon earn substantial revenues from tourism. However, unlike some others (eg Kenya, Zambia), the government of Uganda recognized from the beginning that, despite its revenue-earning potential, the UWA would continue to perform non-revenue-generating activities in the public interest and would therefore need a government subvention. The national budget continued to provide modest allocations to the UWA for payment of salaries and other basic recurrent costs. The combined resources from revenues and government subvention were far from adequate by themselves, but the UWA also benefited from substantial assistance from several donors, including US$10.6 million over three years from the World Bank and the Global Environment Facility.

The start-up of the UWA was fraught with difficulties due in part to the very long gestation period. There were power struggles, job insecurity and 'culture clashes' as the management and staff of the UNP and UGD struggled to find places in the new organization. Demoralized, unpaid field staff turned to poaching out of financial necessity and protest. It also soon became evident that the UWA had been launched without sufficient attention to the need to build basic management capacity and systems: the relatively informal and unplanned systems that had served the smaller UNP were not adequate for UWA with its much larger staff and responsibilities.

In 1998 the World Bank concluded that it could not approve the approximately US$60 million investment project that the Uganda government was seeking to revitalize its wildlife and tourism sector, because of the lack of implementation capacity within the main sectoral institutions, particularly the 'flagship' UWA. Instead, the government and the Bank agreed on a three-year, US$14 million 'institutional capacity building' project (of which US$10.6 million went to the UWA), which set specific targets for achieving the institutional 'maturity' needed to justify and manage a large-scale investment project. The project initially supported the recruitment of a highly experienced expatriate executive director for UWA, the contracting of a private firm to develop financial management systems, development of human-resource management systems, and preparation of strategic and operational plans and training. The project was soon revised to finance the bulk of UWA's recurrent operating costs, because of the virtual collapse of its revenues after the killing of tourists in 1999 by Rwandan rebels in the Bwindi Impenetrable National Park, and other security problems, which led to the closure of the Rwenzori National Park and restricted travel to Murchison Falls and Queen Elizabeth National Parks.[10] Although the parks have since re-opened, tourism numbers remain low and the UWA remains highly dependent on donor support for both its recurrent and capital budgets.

Despite these and other difficulties (such as repeated dissolution and appointment of new boards), the UWA made significant progress between 1998 and 2001. By the end of the World Bank/Global Environmental Fund (GEF) project, it had made a smooth transition to a national executive director, put in place transparent financial and human-resource management systems, adopted a procedures manual for its board, and developed a five-year overall strategic plan as well as general management plans for six of the protected areas. An area-based model had been adopted in which national parks and adjacent game reserves were managed as single units, and policies were developed for community relations and revenue sharing. Most importantly, staff morale had improved greatly as a result of receiving salaries and operating budgets on a regular basis and a substantial decentralization of decision making to wardens. Based on these achievements and the judgement that the UWA now had the necessary implementation capacity, the World Bank and GEF approved a US$28 million second phase investment project in 2002.

Zambia Wildlife Authority

The National Parks and Wildlife Service (NPWS), responsible for managing National Parks in Zambia, was transformed into the Zambia Wildlife Authority (ZAWA) between 1998 and 2002. In their assessment of existing capacities, Deloitte and Touche (2000) concluded that the NPWS was poorly organized and funded, and failed to achieve most core objectives including community conservation and park management. This stemmed from its highly centralized character, and because political interference permeated the organization and sector. As Gibson (1999) points out, it did not have reliable or audited accounts, and the allocation of safari-hunting concessions and other hunting licences was steeped in patronage and intrigue. There were certainly no workplans, budgets, policies or indeed plans to guide activities.

With wildlife being such an important patronage resource in Zambia (Gibson, 1999), the transformation was filled with intrigue. Junior staff levels were halved to 1000, but it took nearly three years to recruit senior staff. Donors, wary about governance in the sector, held back funding, and for months at a time staff were not paid, the opportunity to translate the excitement of newly recruited staff (released from oppressive conditions) into results being lost.

Unlike the Kenya Wildlife Service, ZAWA is far from being flooded with money. The agency has been able to obtain limited funding where they have convinced donors of their capacity to convert funding into results and, with an overstretched and underexperienced staff, this has often been in cooperative arrangements with consultants (eg resource protection in Kafue National Park; see Chapter 7) or with a clear link between performances and funding. In a marked contrast with the NPWS, which mistrusted and obstructed the private sector and NGOs, ZAWA is actively seeking partnerships at many levels, ranging from lodge operations to the complete outsourcing of parks. Although management systems remain rudimentary, financial systems are now sound and accountable, and there is a desire to introduce performance monitoring systems, if not yet the capacity to do so. Although the quality of management is definitely improving, it is still too early to report on tangible results. Perhaps the strongest indicator of progress in improved governance is that, for the first time in at least a decade, the allocation of hunting concessions has not been associated with intrigue, disputes have mostly been settled in court, and contracts are clear and transparent. Cleaning up the industry is a critical step towards improving performance.

With many of the same staff in place, these improvements stem from stronger leadership, a more commercial outlook that includes financial pressure and the ability (not usually present in government agencies) to raise money from donors or commercial partnerships, and a marked reduction in political interference. With no political party dominating government since the 2001 elections, and with politicians battling with each other over corruption charges, one can speculate that powerful individuals are less able to control the wildlife sector, and that this has left the techno-bureaucrats with more space to perform.

Like Namibia, the separation of park and tourism activities under different government agencies in Zambia proved disastrous to the quality of tourism facilities and the funding of parks. All tourism activities in Zambia have since been privatized, resulting in a significant improvement in quality and rapidly increasing park revenues, as the example of South Luangwa in Chapter 7 illustrates.

Malawi, Namibia, Mozambique, Swaziland

In Malawi, national parks are managed by a government department. This is not viable, and in a situation of scarce resources its performance has declined, with significant losses of wildlife in several of the parks. To combat this, all tourism has been outsourced, and although income has improved, the tourism sector is too small to fund the parks. There are also negotiations to privatize some parks.

In Mozambique, a combination of war, lack of clarity over the administration of parks and wildlife, and inadequate capacity to implement wildlife policy and legislation (Carruthers, in preparation) has left a highly variable but wildlife-depleted environment in which considerable experimentation is occurring, although most effort is still in offices and consultancy reports rather than in the field. Major initiatives, still in the very early stages of development, are the Great Limpopo Transfrontier Park, which is supported by a plethora of donors and NGOs, and the Niassa Game Reserve, which is managed through a business contract that includes government and the private sector, with provision for later community inclusion. With too little wildlife to generate revenues, except for Niassa where the skills and legislation are not in place to use a resource that could fund this 42,000km^2 reserve, the positive news is that partnerships are investing in rehabilitating the wildlife resource.

Namibia has extensive national parks, but a critical weakness is that the agency managing them has no revenue base and is entirely dependent on government grants and bureaucratic procedure. The tourism activities in parks are managed by an entirely separate parastatal, which lacks commercial imagination. The result is that Namibia's state wildlife and tourism sector underperforms, with most innovation occurring on private and community land. Subsidized tourism in parks undercuts the private and community landholders. The expansion of park tourism is discouraged by the park agency because this imposes costs but does not increase revenues (retained by tourism parastatal). With so little private sector involvement, imaginative tourism activities are also extremely slow to develop. The overall impact is of reduced tourism flows to the country. With government agencies having no incentives to coordinate and build a national industry, opportunities to build synergies in the sector are being lost. For example, by maintaining tourism to Etosha National

Park at much lower levels than are possible, the number of tourists to Namibia, and therefore the amount of money being spent on tourism on private and communal areas, remains well below potential.

Summary of Park Agency Performance

In April 2003, several agency directors and other professionals closely associated with park management in the region drew up the following table (Table 6.1), which summarizes the structure and performance of many of the park agencies in the region.

DISCUSSION AND CONCLUSIONS

Constituent Accountability

In this concluding section we focus on accountability. Whether parks are providing to society what is required of them and the choices this involves (constituent accountability). How park agencies, in the absence of a commercial bottom line, are held accountable for performance (political accountability). And finally, the factors that affect managerial effectiveness and efficiency (value and performance accountability). This is a rather new way of evaluating protected areas, so the intention is to introduce concepts that may well require further work.

At a general level, the neglect of protected areas in government budgets suggests that many southern African societies are neither investing in, nor showing much concern for, protected areas. In Zambia, for example, contributions to parks as a proportion of the national budget (which is shrinking) have halved in the past 20 years (Zambia Wildlife Authority, 2003). This introduces the question of whether parks would be valued more by society if, instead of focusing on intangible environmental outputs more aligned with the values of developed economies, they emphasized economic growth and the provision of jobs, albeit with a conditionality of biological sustainability. Within the region, we are seeing a strong trend in this direction. Whereas the up-front objective has been to improve park finances and management, commercialization and increased autonomy from political control are improving performance in terms of national job creation, economic growth and conservation. Although the net impact on biodiversity is positive, worryingly there is no systematic monitoring of what should be a core function (see Chapter 5). Perhaps the best example of this link between financial and biological performance is South Africa, where a relatively well-informed market demands good biological management and, in the case of Pilanesburg National Park, wildlife is included as an auditable component of the financial accounts.

Although aspects of motivation are difficult to assess, there is a correlation between the commercialization of park agencies, the perception that they are relevant to society and achieving national economic priorities, and park management budgets. Zimbabwe, Natal and South Africa all report that government subventions increased as they increased their own tourism incomes. An increased focus on economic factors, may ultimately and counter-intuitively result in a cultural shift in favour of wildlife conservation.

Table 6.1 *Summary of the structure and performance of*
'Protected Area Agencies' in the region

Country/Formal accountability	Reality/impact on performance
Malawi Government department	• Not viable, and no plans to become a parastatal • Negotiating to privatize some parks (eg Majete) • Declining performance because of serious financial problems, including loss of wildlife • Have privatized all tourism activities, with some improvement in income • Money goes to treasury and then back to department (not too bad). Nyika/Vwaza National Park retains revenue through a trust and disburses some (35 per cent) to communities
Swaziland Parastatal since early 1990s Board appointed by minister, but CEO a civil servant (no performance contract) Dual oversight from board and ministry	• Dominated by government, which still provides 85 per cent of funds • Retains revenue, but earnings still low (15 per cent of expenditure) • Financial pressure is forcing restructuring • With support form government and donors, agency is investing in tourism infrastructure, with government intending to run lodges and do product development.Probably sub-optimal • Has partly recognized value of outsourcing, but needs a wider and more commercial mandate to operate well
South Africa SANParks. National Organization, 18 on board, 9 appointed by minister and 9 provincial representatives CEO able to recruit good staff, with freedom in selection and good remuneration	• Board ineffective and lightweight; is politically correct but insufficiently skilled • Major strength is executive managers, with a strong CEO able to reduce political intrusion and recruit and allow professionals to focus on technical issues • Improving performance includes better financial and commercial management (eg outsourcing shops, etc, increased revenue from R8 million to R23 million; concessions R5 million ➡ R12 million ➡ R20 million) • Challenges with cost control, and sloughing off redundant functions • Internally driven determination to reduce subsidy, improve corporate culture and remove old-fashioned commercial attitudes • Strengths include good parks and infrastructure, tourism revenue base, internal market. • Quality of staff is mixed, and probably the major threat to sustainability

continues

Table 6.1 *continued*

Country/Formal accountability	Reality/impact on performance
South Africa *continued*	• The more viable the agency, the more financing is provided by government • Good planning, proposal and management capacity enabled SANParks to capture poverty relief (R240 million) and Working for Water (R200 million) funding • Developing as a regulatory agency with clear objectives; no activity has not been outsourced
South Africa Nine provincial wildlife/park agencies, 4 boards, 5 government departments. Diverse/mixed performance generally reflects the vision and capability of the leadership	• Boards outperforming departments, largely because of better staff • Boards have more infrastructure, are more commercially and private sector oriented, and invariably more viable • NW Parks set trends of modernization in South Africa. Champion driven, visionary, very modern and robust, with performance ensured through tight contracts with private sector • Natal, old-fashioned park agency, but effective, albeit highly dependent on grants and is therefore much more susceptible to political influence
Namibia Government department, with tourism activities split away from parks	• Tourism parastatal unionized, inflexible. Its underperformance threatens entire national tourism industry as it holds (but does not use) the cherries • Parks are state run with no income from tourism • No incentives for parks to encourage tourism, which is underdeveloped with major economic costs to the tourism sector • Strong conflicts between parks and tourism. • Neither is able to retain quality staff • The general comment was that management could hardly be worse
Uganda Uganda Wildlife Authority answers to a board (with terms of reference) and appointed by minister	• Significant improvements in performance under expatriate CEO and with World Bank financing • Board changed often by minister and procedures. are ignored • Not financially viable in short term because of civil unrest in the region

continues

Table 6.1 *continued*

Country/Formal accountability	Reality/impact on performance
Kenya Kenya Wildlife Service answers to a board selected by minister, with government officials in the minority	• Board non-functional and changed without criteria • KWS performs significantly better than its predecessor. Is this mainly attributable to because of heavy (excessive) donor funding (US$100 million+) or new structure and discipline?
Zambia Zambia Wildlife Authority answers to a board, 4/9 private sector. Formed in 2000	• Much less political interference than before Some in senior staff appointments. Hunting, sector previously dominated and seriously damaged by patronage linkages, has been radically cleaned up. How much of this is a result of space provided by high-level political uncertainty and in-fighting, a related anti-corruption drive and donor pressure on good governance? • Generally better senior staff • Performance improving, outsourcing slowly accepted, commercial improvements, but still a long way from viability given decades of deteriorating infrastructure and staff capacity
Zimbabwe Board of 10, good quality, often representing membership organizations	• Better staff and recruitment procedures (done by independent company) • Too new for any results (CEO appointed from 1 April 2003)
Mozambique Highly variable, and in the midst of change	• Limpopo National Park has a steering committee (government, donors, community, individuals) established through donor agreements • Niassa Game Reserve is outsourced, retains revenue but tax and use-right issues remain problematic and unresolved • No 'before' situation. Discussing a parastatal option for national wildlife agency

Shift towards Provision of Jobs and Economic Growth

After several decades of declining park agency capacity, the growing wildlife tourism sector is allowing park agencies to commercialize and distance themselves from political dependency and, across the region, the performance of park agencies is generally improving, although it is still generally weak. The older parastatals in South Africa are becoming increasingly sustainable financially, and are initiating modern business practices. In both Zambia and Zimbabwe, park departments are being transformed into parastatals, with a strong motivation being reduced government spending and payroll and hoped-for improvements in performance. KWS was planned to become self-sustaining, as was UWA although it was accepted that Ugandan circumstances made this a long-term strategy that required considerable subsidization. Thus, more by default than by design, parks are responding to the basic needs of society and providing economic growth and jobs.

Biodiversity Conservation

Although seldom explicitly stated, except by the groundbreaking efforts of North West Parks in South Africa (see Chapter 7; Davies, 2000), the overall effect has been to flip the relative priority of economic and conservation goals. Contrary to fears about the subversion of biodiversity to financial priorities, the record suggests that this is a positive development for biodiversity conservation, since empirically there is a positive correlation between financial performance and biodiversity conservation. At a crude level, there is a positive correlation between the size of the wildlife tourism economy and the status of parks, with Kenya, Zimbabwe (at least until recently), Namibia and South Africa maintaining or even expanding protected areas in the face of considerable land pressure. Poaching and encroachment are associated with countries that have failed to boost their tourism sectors or commercialize their park agencies (eg Malawi and Zambia, Kenya in the past), or with social conflict (Mozambique, Angola). Thus, commercializing wildlife, and booming wildlife tourism sectors, are good for conservation at a macro scale.

At a micro level, profitable conservation areas, whether managed by the state, private or communal people, tend to conserve wildlife best. The challenges are to capture a sufficient share of this economic growth to fund parks, and to prevent powerful park agencies from monopolizing sectors and excluding other actors, including the private sector and civil society, which are critical for sector growth. There is also the question of whether a conservation agency with scarce resources should focus on the most important parks, or should spread these resources thinly but equitably across all the parks, the problem with the latter approach being that all parks may decline.

Unlike the stork, which, in times of hardship, feeds one chick first, conservation agencies tend to cross-subsidize and dissipate gains widely thereby threatening the overall survival of park systems. One effect is that viable parks are taxed to subsidize non-viable parks to the extent that they are themselves threatened, a situation invariably exacerbated by excessive head office staffing and overheads. Another is that by spreading the gains from parks widely, instead of, for example, concentrating them in the communities around a park, the impact and support for parks is widespread but weak. Zambia faces this problem, and a potential solution is to manage the major parks to fund themselves, and to outsource the management of other parks to NGOs and the private sector with strict performance criteria.

However, despite being the much-vaunted goal of park agencies, we have not found a single example of methodical and comprehensive biodiversity monitoring and audit. Biodiversity monitoring appears to be unsystematic, and related to historical precedent or the interests of individual researchers. There is considerable monitoring of large mammals, but examples of monitoring of nutrient and water cycles, soil and long-term vegetation health are rare. What we find troubling is that the primary role of parks is neither clearly defined nor systematically audited.

Economic Value and Financial Sustainability

Economic analyses suggest that there is a strong economic justification for parks and conservation areas.[11] This is critical for political support and sustainability. However, as the example of South Luangwa shows (Chapter 7), capturing a sufficient share of the tourism economy to fund parks (eg as park fees) can be difficult, hence the paradox of declining parks in a booming sector that is based on them. The fact that the private sector turns a profit from lesser resources demonstrates that, in the main, this is troubling when associated with the relative commercial inefficiencies of the state sector.

Given the magnitude of economic benefits, however, there is often justification for the subsidization on purely economic grounds even of inefficiently managed parks provided they support a reasonable level of tourism activity (although first prize is obviously to enable parks to finance themselves, which most should be able to do if managed well: see management issues discussed below). Only in South Africa, however, is the understanding of the difference between financial viability and economic impact sophisticated enough to translate directly into the funding of protected areas. The subsidies given to SANParks, KZN Conservation and the capitalization of Madikwe and Pilanesburg (see Chapter 7) are examples. Even here, subsidization is done on historical precedent, rather than on specifically argued economic criteria. Indeed, analyses of the link between park tourism, what happens to tourism dollars, and their economic impacts, are rare, and this is an important gap in our understanding of the relationship between protected areas and society.

However, the general subsidization of parks can cause more problems than it solves if not handled carefully[12]. Subsidies are usually based on historical precedent or an overly general and seldom substantiated economic argument. It would be better to provide payments that are related far more specifically to carefully defined value-adding activities, for instance payments for the delivery of environmental audits, law enforcement success, education impact or tourism turnover. Moreover, the top-down and unspecific subsidization of park agencies should be avoided because it is often the root cause of ineffective management. Thus, we need to justify more clearly the subsidization of parks than we do at present, and to be more innovative in the way these payments are linked to the provision of services.

The Negative Power of State Conservation Agencies

A second consequence of the search for financial sustainability can be an inward-looking agency that, in the interests of the survival of the organization, ignores national priorities (in other words it gives precedence to the financial rather than the economic).[13] Given the potential of state agencies to dominate a sector, the negative power of state conservation agencies is probably the biggest danger associated with commercializing park agencies. Business monopolies are dangerous, but the power of institutions like park agencies goes well beyond what even the most monopolistic of businesses enjoys. Such is the power of wildlife agencies that they can disrupt entire sectors. They are backed by the coercive power of the state. They are both regulatory agencies and the main player in the sector. They can charge use fees unrelated to service, as with several licences. And, finally, they are still struggling to give up the notion that wildlife is best treated as a nationalized resource and to accept that the market can play a legitimate role in making choices. The logical extension of the liberalization argument is that one of the primary roles of government is to protect property rights rather than directly protecting the resource at issue.

Although seemingly benign, the subsidization of access to wildlife recreation by park agencies causes serious and economic perversities. By lowering the price of wildlife, this undercuts the private provision of these services and can prevent the spread of wildlife enterprises across the landscape. Devolved proprietorship was critical for the spread of wildlife on private and communal land in Zimbabwe, but so was a deliberate policy to introduce market pricing in parks (eg for safari hunting) and to allow neighbours to add value to wildlife enterprises through access to parks. The commercialization of parks is a positive development. By reducing subsidized access to outdoor recreation and increasing the price of wildlife opportunities, it improves the incentives for wildlife production outside parks, and therefore the amount of land conserved (see Chapters 3 and 4).

The state's negative power can be used for political or personal reasons that are economically unsound, and can impose large costs with little accountability, often unthinkingly. In Kenya, for example, consumptive use of wildlife is summarily banned, and it can hardly be a coincidence that while wildlife populations in southern Africa have doubled or even quadrupled,[14] those outside parks in Kenya have halved (Ottichilo et al, 2000) although, if Kenya's exceptional wildlife resources were free to compete unfettered, they would be highly competitive and able to reverse this trend (Child, B, 2002b).

Expecting park agencies to become self-funding, while also managing national assets and regulatory functions, has within it a serious conflict of interest that needs to be carefully managed. For example, the government of Zambia has withdrawn funding to the new ZAWA well before it is ready to fund itself. To survive, it is intending to use its power to charge landholders (both private and communal) as much as two-thirds of the net value of hunting fees. This is obviously a tremendous disincentive to investment in wildlife, and is economically disastrous. We use the example of the Mumbwa community programme alongside Zambia's Kafue National Park to illustrate this. Mumbwa game management area (GMA) is expected to earn US$120,000 from hunting. The community needs US$40,000 to employ and support 31 village scouts to protect this resource (excluding capital expenditure). If ZAWA carries through its intention to extract US$80,000 from this community, all money received by the community is absorbed by direct management costs, providing no incentive to the community to conserve wildlife. The US$80,000 will ensure the short-term survival of ZAWA including the management of 19 national parks, but this cross-subsidization is ultimately unsustainable, and has large economic costs to Zambia. Alternatively, ensuring that significant incentives reach the community, is likely to protect nearly 3000km^2 with wildlife, and provide at least 50 direct jobs and US$500,000 in turnover annually, amounts that will increase as protection continues.

Local or National?

The final question to discuss in terms of constituency accountability is whether the park constituency should be local or national. Unfortunately, there are few examples of locally centred systems, so we can draw evidence only from a few partial experiments, although these suggest an important role for parks as local engines of growth and development. For instance, managing South Luangwa to provide local jobs in tourism and to support safari hunting outside the park for household and community benefits[15] creates a local constituency for the park, and also assures national benefits: tourism currency, aircraft hire, etc. The fact that Pilanesburg established local business to provide inputs (eg bricks for construction) and provided specifically tailored tourism opportunities to local people has also made the park valuable to local people. This laid the economic and political foundation to create an entirely new park — Madikwe.

The same is not always true in reverse. Hwange National Park, for instance, generates considerable national benefit, but all revenues are collected or spent centrally while elephants and other animals raid local fields; at the locality level, Hwange is a negative asset, but is maintained because the state is strong enough to hold local threats (eg encroachment) at bay.

There is considerable merit in, at the very least, experimenting with the localization of park management. At this scale, benefits are internalized and therefore more tangible, so the perception of value among those most directly affecting the park is higher. There is considerable potential to use parks to create economic growth and jobs, without abrogating ecological or national responsibilities, and also to serve as a mechanism for consolidating wildlife conservation as a land use in park buffer zones.

Political Accountability

The colonial powers effectively nationalized the wildlife resource, and placed it under the control of central political agencies, so most park and wildlife agencies started as government departments and were answerably directly to a minister. The modern trend is towards parastatals that are answerable to a board, largely in an attempt to separate them from weaknesses in the political system.

This relationship between a technical agency and the political system has always been difficult to manage. The challenges are exacerbated where national governance is poor, or where the political system is used as an extractive tool by the elite; Chabal and Daloz (1999) provide a political analysis of this problem. Whereas political control is healthy in terms of democratic theory, politicians have often used nationalized assets such as wildlife and parks to their personal or political advantage where democratic checks-and-balances are weak. Moreover, because of their budget-funded nature and weak accountability for real results (see next section), park agencies have been particularly vulnerable to political 'interference'. Thus, where state failure is problematic (see Grindle and Thomas, 1991), harnessing wildlife agencies too closely to the state is similarly problematic.

In pre-independent Zimbabwe and South Africa, parks served their constituencies well, perhaps because these were minority societies that held government to account. There is considerable potential to use parks to create economic growth and jobs locally, which only strengthens the likelihood that they will provide national and global biodiversity and economic benefits. Moreover, this locality focus will go some way towards consolidating wildlife conservation as a land use in park buffer zones

The best-documented case of this is Zambia (see Gibson's (1999) detailed account of politics and patronage in the Zambian wildlife sector) although similar practices were widespread. A credible park agency under colonial administration, the parks department was weakened and over-centralized during one-party rule. The department was used to create employment, but was prevented from properly controlling poaching, which was politically risky to a government that had promised to give back wildlife to the people. Employment favoured relatives, and little is as harmful to agency performance as favouritism (Leonard, 1991). Systems of central control and authority were also used to extort payments for various permissions, to access cash or vehicles (often donor funded), or to allocate animals or hunting concessions within a system of patronage and kickbacks. Rural communities watching their leaders plundering natural resources have little incentive to conserve themselves. Moreover, this example supports Chabal and Doloz's theory of a polity deliberately breaking down systems of accountability to personalize control and make predation easier. Until recently, several park agencies did not even have audited accounts (eg Zambia and Uganda before they were transformed).

In an implicit recognition of accountability weaknesses within the political system, most park agencies in Africa have been converted into parastatals, often with a specific objective of increasing their autonomy from the political system. The pressure to perform financially, and the reduction in grant funding, has the added effect of partly converting them from budget-based to commercial organizations,[16] the effects of which are described in the next section.

Park Boards

In much of southern Africa, boards have replaced senior civil services and elected ministers as the controlling mechanism for the new wildlife authorities or parastatals. Created by an act of parliament, these are still public agencies but have more autonomy over financial, commercial and staffing arrangements. Legislatively, accountability and oversight is provided by a board, but the degree to which this board is, in turn, controlled by the political system varies. The minister usually appoints board members, and retains the power of oversight but not formally the power to override decisions.[16]

The institutional structure and autonomy of parastatals does theoretically offer advantages, but these are easily subverted by the political system. Far more important are behavioural changes in national governance, and there are signs that park parastatals are a symptom of improving governance and commercial attitudes. This is important to bear in mind, and the long battles to force through autonomous park agencies in Kenya, Uganda and Zambia, for instance, reflect a political reluctance to accept this model, and are inevitably associated with years of wrangling and compromise. Wildlife parastatals have tended to emerge where governments have proactively decided that they will improve performance (eg South Africa, Zimbabwe) or where donor funding has been linked to improved governance and performance (eg Uganda, Kenya, Zambia).

Reduced Corruption

In most cases, but not all, wildlife parastatals have been associated with reduced corruption. For the first time in over a decade, hunting in Zambia has been allocated transparently according to technical rather than political criteria. UWA has public accounts, and the KWS has been able to remove non-performing staff. As we have just discussed, it is less likely that this is a structural result from recruiting better managers, and more likely that better managers are a cultural consequence of a maturing political system that demands less corruption and better performance.

The Challenge of Board Performance

In transforming government departments into parastatals, the greatest challenge is to define the linkages to political systems because this is the underlying cause of many problems. Common among these is the appointment of technically weak board members or senior staff to serve political roles or masters. There is often a reluctance to devolve sufficient managerial authority (eg Kenya) and to clarify managerial authority, and even where roles and responsibilities are defined in writing these may be ignored (eg Uganda). This failure to allocate responsibility and accountability weakens managerial systems and cultures. However, despite these problems, boards have on the whole reduced political 'interference' and improved technical performance.

Board Membership and Roles

Without exception, boards are weaker than they should be. Generally, appointments include some government officials and representatives of major stakeholder groups. This often leaves boards weak in important technical skills (eg legal, financial, business). With civic and private-sector members often representing associations, there is also role confusion, with board representatives unsure whether to represent their interest groups when the primary responsibility of a board member must be to the park agency. The most important of these responsibilities are to agree strategic direction and major decisions, to hold the agency accountable for performance, to provide additional capacity (eg finance, legal, human resource) and to motivate the agency and provide linkages to useful partners.

Perhaps the most important challenge is for boards to hold the agency responsible for performance, although this is difficult because the imprecise roles of parks make accountability difficult (see below). Apart from a few strong personalities, there is little evidence across the region of boards being proactive or visionary. Theoretically, boards represent the owners, but like boards of large public corporations this is obviously not the reality, which means that boards are often simply management committees and ineffectual (Drucker, 1973).

Conceptually, a board is a review organ, with people of sufficient experience and stature to support agency staff and ensure that the agency has clear goals and achieves these. There is some evidence that boards help in this regard though, for political reasons, more members tend to be selected for their political affiliation than because they are technically strong. Second, boards appoint top management and remove them if they fail to perform. There is evidence that boards have improved recruitment of managers, and have protected them from political interference (eg Zambia), although again progress has been partial and they are prone to be overridden by political appointments. Third, boards provide access to influential people and to constituents. The same conclusion – of some improvements but significant potential for more – applies.

Therefore board performance, so critical to conservation, is an important area for monitoring and learning, including the incorporation of similar institutional experiences from outside the parks sector. This knowledge will become increasingly valuable as financial pressures encourage park institutions to be well governed. Moreover, donors are beginning to link funding to outcomes, while 'governance' issues are an important consideration to financing packages. In Zambia, for example, a minister attempted to fire the director general, despite strong endorsement of his performance by the board. Had the minister succeeded this would have been a signal for the donors to turn off the financial taps.

Board Selection

Selection of board members is widely problematic,[17] with political appointments, weak technical skills, excessive representation of the public sector and over-sized boards being the most common problems. The general consensus is that boards should have about nine people, at least half from the private sector. Domination by the public sector usually retards progress, made worse because representatives from public institutions seldom provide continuity or commitment. Conversely, the appointment of persons from representative institutions (eg tourism associations) seems to find stronger individuals. However, this requires a clear definition of responsibility, and the primacy of the interests of the agency (rather than the stakeholder group he represents) must be made clear.

There is a general consensus that board selection needs to pick stronger individuals (the use of a skills ratification system was even suggested), and to aim for an appropriate set of skills rather than turning boards into stakeholder meetings. To avoid patronage, selection should be less dependent on an individual politician (that is, the minister), and more people should be involved (eg a parliamentary committee) to create checks and balances. There is a suggestion that making board selection and accountability to a group (eg a parliamentary select committee) is preferable to the more common situation where a single individual, usually the minister, is responsible, and that this will work especially well where the political system is not dominated by a single party (eg Zambia). This can reduce political patronage, because accountability to groups incorporates more checks and balances, and is strengthened where the group includes opposition members of parliament.

Value and Performance Accountability

A profound difference between a park agency and a normal business is the way money and value flows. A business is paid directly for adding value and receives money when a customer purchases its goods and services. Another fundamental difference is that this money flows upwards from the customer through the organization. This creates tremendous competitive discipline within businesses, forcing continual innovation and the casting off non-productive functions. Flattened hierarchies and the demise of middle management and bureaucracy are a consequence of these pressures.

There is an elemental difference between firms that are paid because they provide value to customers and agencies that respond to budget allocations and the political systems that provide these budgets. The transition from department to parastatals reflects a transition in agency responsiveness from one form of incentive structure to another: namely, from the politics of budget allocation to the linkages between finance and value added. In southern Africa, we have an opportunity to test how increased commercial responsiveness is affecting agency performance.

The Problem of Expanding Mandates and Undefined Goals

Drucker (1973) predicts that public agencies will have ever-expanding mandates, lack the discipline to kill off unproductive activities and, needing to placate a wide constituency, cannot focus on core competency or make controversial choices. They are safer if goals are defined in only the broadest sense as feel-good mother statements. This is why they can simultaneously promote mutually exclusive objectives such as excessive wildlife populations and biodiversity conservation. The lack of accountability to clear goals leads to all manner of poor management, with excessive and unproductive meetings being a common example.

Chapter 5 provides a general description of these ever-widening mandates. The great difficulties that Cumming had in finding data to describe conservation success, and the anecdotal nature of these data, suggest that park agencies have never defined the parameters on which performance can be judged. To our knowledge, no park agency has clearly defined ecological goals, and certainly no agency consistently measures its contribution against these goals.

In a field as complex as park conservation, setting goals is not an easy task. However, park agencies, ostensibly established to provide collective goods and services where markets fail, have consistently failed to do so and, against their public mandate, have tended to provide functions with a strong private component. Explicitly, they have failed to define and systematically provide biodiversity conservation, and have used a disproportionate amount of their public resources providing private goods such as tourism. This is not to say that parks have not conserved biodiversity. They usually have, either simply by protecting areas from development, or because of the zeal of some plant and animal specialists. However, managerially, the point is that this effort is neither consistent nor measurable, suggesting considerable scope for improved performance.

The question is whether the transformation of agencies into parastatals, and associated commercialization, has helped park agencies to fulfil their obligations to society. This answer has several components. Yes, park parastatals have generally commercialized tourism with some success despite problems relating to their lack of commercial skills, resistance to change and, as in Zambia, high fees that curtail growth of the tourism sector. This has reduced the subsidization of private benefits,[18] and according to economic theory the removal of such distortions always affects society in a positive manner. It has also created greater financial surpluses, providing agencies with the wherewithal to improve.

The next question is whether additional income has been used well. In most agencies throughout the region, staff quality, incentives and conditions have improved, albeit from an extremely low base. This is leading to better leadership and management. In Uganda, for instance, the fact that staff are paid regularly and that each park has a monthly operational budget has had a significant effect on staff morale. In South Africa, several park agencies have been able to recruit quality leadership, resulting in some truly innovative approaches such as the expansion of parks to improve biodiversity coverage, the use of partnerships to achieve these aims, and even the use of parks as development instruments (see examples in Chapter 7).

Goal Setting and Performance Management

More generally, the distancing of park agencies from budget funding and political influence is leading towards improved systems of management. Park agencies are learning to clarify goals and define them in terms of measurable objectives, which is the basis of performance management systems. Although the conceptual development of park performance systems is still rudimentary, requirements for performance management have recently been legislated in South Africa, and SANParks and provincial agencies are beginning to experiment with management information systems. Most parastatal agencies have implemented basic management systems that were not present in government agencies, such as regular payment of salaries and operational costs, financial controls and regular auditing (eg Uganda, Kenya). As the examples of Zimbabwe's wildlife department and South Luangwa (Chapter 7) show, the introduction of peer-based performance evaluation has a major impact on performance. This supports the claim that poor performance is generally related to disincentivizing systems rather than the natural ability of the staff.

In a field so prone to a multiplicity of conflicting mandates, the clarification of objectives is the first step in enabling parks staff to know what is required of them. This provides the tight parameters within which responsibility can be devolved, and this combination of tight goals and loose structures in the key to dynamic organizations (Peters and Waterman, 1982). The evidence is beginning to emerge (eg the South Luangwa and Kafue examples in Chapter 7) that decentralizing control and budgets provides the empowerment on which rapid progress can be built.

The process of setting clear goals and performance indicators is an intellectually rigorous and highly philosophical exercise. It forces park agencies to define core activities and trade-offs, where before these were often fudged. In South Luangwa, for example, core park activities were defined as: (1) law enforcement; (2) ecological monitoring and audit; (3) commerce and tourism; (4) infrastructure development and maintenance; and (5) supporting community wildlife management outside the park. Feel-good but non-essential activities like ecological research and generalized environmental education were dropped, as were a multiplicity of conventional activities that added little value. This enabled more money to be targeted at core activities. Moreover, the rigour of defining desirable outputs forced clarity where none had existed before, and institutionalized a performance control and feedback system (that is, it operationalized adaptive management). For example, instead of talking generally about habitat conservation, this had to be defined by using indicators that quantified the limits of acceptable change of soil erosion and tree loss. This rigour has the knock-on effect that when ecosystem productivity is threatened, in this case by excess number of hippo or elephant, an explicit decision has to be taken either to cull animals or to sacrifice ecosystem sustainability. The manager can no longer hide behind ambiguity.

As Drucker (1973) concludes, the performance of public sector agencies is related to market tests, and where these are not possible, to clearly defined and measurable objectives. In southern Africa, we are seeing a positive trend in both regards, although there is much still to be learned. A system of performance comparison across the region that uses common indicators has much to recommend itself.

Funding Mechanisms: Shifting from Budget-driven to Market-driven Approaches

Related to goal clarification is the problem of funding mechanisms: dumping money at the top of an agency tends to exacerbate the problem of fudged goals and expanding mandates, whereas there are indications that emulating the market by paying directly for specific functions may be a powerful tool. Without doubt, KZN Conservation is an effective organization. In line with shifting political priorities, it has deftly shifted from the provision of outdoor recreation to facilitating rural development, and has marketed its successes well. This is a good example of a well-managed budget-driven agency, which has managed to respond to political imperatives and to maintain and even increases its public subsidy. However, the fact that it spends US$5091/km^2 of protected area, approximately three times the estimated optimal conservation operating budget of US$1524/km^2, is strongly suggestive of an excessive mandate.

KWS is probably the most extreme example of a budget-funded agency responding to political imperative at the expense of conservation and operational effectiveness, with some 80 per cent of a burgeoning expenditure being spent on non-park activities.

Before restructuring, the Luangwa Integrated Resource Development Project was guilty of the same (Dalal-Clayton and Child, B, 2003): a combination of excessive centralized funding and the need to survive politically led this project to support as many as 38 different activities, many of which were technically unproductive but built constituencies of beneficiaries among public agencies. This support to a wide range of agencies and functions, often in the form of meeting allowances, was a strategy that purchased political support and allowed the project to survive with some positive impacts (especially the control of elephant poaching), but it also resulted in high costs and non-performance in the delivery of a range of services.

Heavy, top-down funding of park agencies creates problems, especially where park goals are not precisely defined and funding is not performance linked. Top-down funding aggravates the weakness of public agencies in prioritizing and managing value-adding activities. It also increases the responsiveness of managers to the political market place where elites, techno-bureaucrats and lobby groups dominate.

Theoretically, performance would be improved if park agencies were funded according to the output of public goods. Whereas the commercialization of tourism, for instance, has been important in shifting services from the public to the private realm and therefore for linking incentives to the amount of value added, to our knowledge we have only one example of direct payment of a public service. In Kafue National Park (see Chapter 7), NORAD pays the Zambia Wildlife Authority US$17 for every person–day of anti-poaching effort, US$10 of which goes directly to the patrol scout, US$5 to the park warden to provide support services such as transport and administration, and US$2 for general headquarters overheads. So powerful are the incentive structures that scouts patrol three times as much as their counterparts elsewhere, and poaching has been rapidly brought under control at a cost of US$20/km^2, about half the cost of other areas. This suggests that there is considerable merit in clearly defining and auditing outputs, and then paying according to how much is provided. If the region's park agencies were paid for reporting the results of monitoring of ecosystem health and biodiversity, would not Chapter 5 have easily been able to summarize these results?

Improved Finances

James et al (1999) suggest that revenue retention makes an enormous contribution to conservation budgets, and that parastatals have higher funding intensity (three times) than departments and spend 2–15 times as much on conservation. In some cases, such as Kenya and Uganda, initial improvements in funding are donor derived. However, most parastatal agencies quickly try to improve revenues, typically with some success, and usually through improvements in fee collection and concessionairing, and the control of staff numbers, costs and performance.

Anecdotally, there appears to be a positive correlation between commercialization, the recruitment of better staff, and the provision of public services including biodiversity conservation. Private sector conservation is the most powerful example of this, as is the example of the environmental recovery and management by the highly commercial North West Parks, but this correlation between financial viability and ecological performance appears to be general. Indeed, there is little evidence of the much-feared trade-off that commercialization will have large environmental costs. The more viable a park agency the better is the ecological status of its estate, at least where this viability is internally generated rather than grant or donor funded. Even at a local scale, environmental management, and certainly wildlife numbers, are often better near lodges than away from them (although the problem of excessive herbivory is an increasingly serious consequence). The linkages between tourism, a healthy environment, and a financially sustainable management regime tend to promote, rather than negate, sound environmental management.

Improvements in Agency Culture and Leadership

The relationship between commercialization and the quality of agency culture and leadership is also positive. Weak managers and park agencies tend to over-centralize functions, with a strong reluctance to outsource activities even where the agency has little competence. Thus, we have biologists and wildlife police officers struggling with issues like marketing, hospitality management, contracting, road construction and other non-core activities. Although a function analysis suggests that park agencies should focus on activities critical to a regulatory authority (eg policy, regulation and monitoring) and perhaps also on policing, they still tend to dilute their effectiveness by taking on too many non-core functions. SANParks is privatizing tourism, but with some reluctance. KWS spends a lot of time and money on community development. ZAWA is sometimes more concerned with the hunting and social issues outside parks than on the parks themselves, and so on. Nevertheless, there is a positive trend towards working with core competency and outsourcing. Zambia, for example, is forming partnerships with NGOs and the private sector to manage aspects of park management (eg CBNRM, logistical support, performance auditing, project design). South Africa is increasingly outsourcing tourism activities, and using consultants for policy and project development.

Decentralization

The one aspect that is receiving less attention than it deserves is decentralization and, more specifically, the designation of parks as cost centres that internalize costs and income streams and have clear performance criteria. Although rather primitive in its application, the performance of Zimbabwe's wildlife department is suggestive of the power of such loose–tight arrangements. So too are the examples from South

Luangwa and Kafue National Parks in Zambia, and from North West Parks, where performance improved markedly by using relatively inexperienced staff through the application of devolved, but clearly defined, responsibility for finances and performance. The correlation between success and devolution in the CBNRM movement also supports the argument for devolution.

One aspect that is surprising is how little the business experience, in which decentralization is key, has been applied to conservation. As in conservation, devolution is one of the key insights of modern management theory and literature (Micklethwaite and Wooldridge, 1997), where structures are re-engineered around functions, and devolved implementation provides the impetus for innovation and performance (Peters and Waterman, 1982). Complex systems are better managed from the bottom, with the top setting broad goals and ensuring that performance is monitored. Too often, devolution and liberalization are treated as a rather indisciplined and anarchic process of the centre simply letting go. However, devolution is actually a highly disciplined and demanding process, whereby people are given the freedom to innovate but within the bounds of tough performance criteria. Skynner and Cleese (1993) emphasize that discipline is the ingredient of democratic devolution that separates order from chaos, whereas Handy's (1995) excellent chapter on subsidiarity and Peters and Waterman (1982) also underline the rigour of devolution, in what they term 'tough love'.

Park systems are particularly complex, whether this is related to ecological functions or the relationships with a multiplicity of stakeholders. The managers at park level have a far better chance of understanding this complexity than people in head office who are dealing with broader issues. This is why it is important that parks are managed by high-level individuals, and not simply by task managers. The situation where technicians in head office are more senior than park wardens is invariably a mistake.

Moreover, if we follow the logic that parks can be powerful tools for rural integration, the case for decentralization strengthens. The justification for managing parks as decentralized cost centres is strong. Furthermore, at this level there are often significant synergies that can be built with local landholders. An empowered park manager who is managing a park as a cost centre and therefore internalizing the full range of financial and social costs and benefits will have a strong incentive to work with his neighbours to bring out these synergies. Indeed, there may even be a case for parks to act as rural development agencies, as they often provide the most experienced personnel and the most vibrant economic forces in remote regions. By spending 5 per cent of the income from South Luangwa National Park, for example, the park manager is able to ensure that a community of 50,000 people is organized into some 45 village action groups. Organizationally, this community is able to manage and benefit from the wildlife outside the park, but in doing so significantly reduces the poaching threat to the park, including employing its own scouts at a fraction of the cost of the formal system. On purely financial criteria, it is much cheaper to spend 5 per cent of park revenues supporting and monitoring community organizations, than to employ many patrol scouts to prevent poaching.

Given the magnitude of potential gains from decentralization, both in improved park management and an increasing synergy between a park and the surrounding landscape and communities, the real surprise is how little decentralization has actually occurred. There is considerable room for experimentation in the region.

Staff Management

The early days of many wildlife agencies were characterized by zealous and idiosyncratic individuals. More robust and reliable control systems are needed as agencies mature, allowing ordinary people to do a good job without being dominated or dependent on a charismatic CEO. As the attractiveness of conservation positions and the ability to hold quality staff declines, Maslow's theory predicts that incentive mechanisms need to become more tangible (Hersey and Blanchard, 1988). This suggests the need for management systems with measurable performance criteria and the flexibility to link incentives to performance. These are unlikely to develop spontaneously in an underpaid, budget-driven, bureaucratic organization. Our examples suggest that commercialization shifts business culture towards a value-adding mentality, and imposes more discipline and meritocracy. Although this opens the organizational mind to performance management systems, few examples are actually in place, although several agencies are struggling with the problem. This suggests that investment in designing and experimenting with such systems should be a high priority for experiential learning and research.

Profit and Biodiversity

With the increasing importance of finance, there is a strong likelihood that the provision of income-generating services will improve. There are two views on how this will impact of biodiversity conservation. The first is that the organization will focus entirely on commercial activities, to the detriment of biodiversity. The second is that shifting towards a value-adding and performance business culture will have a positive impact on biodiversity through a general improvement in managerial capacity and motivation, and because the wildlife tourism business is ultimately linked to a healthy ecosystem. The greatest danger here is that park managers respond to the loudest signals, not the most important ones. They respond to the demand for animals to see, and the social aversion to killing animals, rather than to subtle shifts in ecological function. Overstocking and damage to long-term ecological process can be a result, which is why in Chapter 10 we are so adamant about improving ecological monitoring systems. Therefore, although we strongly support the increasing autonomy and commercialization of parks, we equally emphasize the importance of simple but rigorous biodiversity monitoring systems. To those detractors of this approach, we point out that non-commercial parks have often failed to conserve or monitor biodiversity.

CONCLUSIONS

In the past, the implicit rationale for parks has been biodiversity conservation; economic factors have been secondary. Although usually not stated explicitly, this balance is changing throughout the sub-region. In the context of poverty and transitional economies, this is a good thing because it makes parks more relevant to people. However, rather than an implicit drift in this direction, the region should have the courage to make this paradigm shift explicit and to manage it proactively, including a defined process of experimentation and peer and experiential learning.

The first step would be to define clearly the goals of parks as contributing to well-being appropriate to southern African society, which in the region's socio-economic context is likely to include economic growth, employment and park self-sustainability, with an important proviso that biodiversity is both monitored and maintained. The process of clearly specifying these goals should be extended to the design of appropriate performance management systems, and our prediction is that orienting parks around clearly defined and measurable objectives is likely to radically alter the functions, culture and structure of park management agencies. Important in this regard are the mechanisms for holding park agencies accountable to society, and replacing a culture of control with one of service and value. Indeed, the issue of value creation should be at the centre of these changes, and incentives should be linked directly to value, either directly to the market or through clearly specified targets. In addition to redefining motherhood goals, and appropriate performance indicators to reflect these goals, the decentralization of park management within this framework will be of great significance.

Regional park agencies are entering a period of considerable transition, where sustainability, biodiversity conservation and development objectives are crucial. Yet, there is little precedent to emulate, and park agencies are often venturing into unknown territory. Although this is essential for their long-term social acceptability and survival, robust mechanisms to measure performance and for learning from each other need to be put in place. In parallel with the transition of park agencies that we are witnessing and that are described in this and the next chapter, developing these adaptive learning processes and defining the biological and socio-economic criteria by which to judge the effectiveness of protected-area management should be the priority of the next decade.

NOTES

1   See Duffy (2000) for a sub-plot describing the intrigue and battle for control between Zimbabwe's wildlife technocrats and the political hierarchy, and Leakey and Morell (2001) who describe this battle in Kenya.

2   Although, as has happened with other denationalized resources, this is often a first step towards further privatization, with government taking a regulatory role and the delivery of goods and services left in the hands of private entrepreneurs.

3   A service institution is paid for good intentions, and for not alienating important constituents rather than satisfying any one group well (Drucker, 1973).

4   The economic nature of the goods determines whether or not collective intervention is needed to procure the goods in satisfactory quantity or quality. True public goods are non-excludable and non-divisible (eg ozone, watershed protection, gene banks, carbon sequestration), private goods are excludable and divisible, whereas many goods have components of both.

5   KwaZulu Department of Nature Conservation was added to the old Natal Parks Board to form an amalgamated organization called Ezemvelo KZN Wildlife (www.KZNWildlife.com).

6   Goals are contained in a draft 'business plan', a large document, set for all levels from corporate to park to individual staff. Park management plans are now a legal requirement in South African (new Protected Areas Management Bill) and are being structured to use funds against measurable objectives (S McKean, personal communication).

7   This section is based largely on notes provided by Agnes Kiss.

8   According to some estimates, 90–95 per cent of large mammals disappeared from the parks.

9   These four parks are by far the main sources of UWA's tourism earnings.

10 For example, Moinuddin et al (2002) show the impact of South Luangwa on the national economy, Davies (2000) demonstrates the economic impact of Madikwe, Castley et al (in preparation) does the same for Addo Elephant National Park, and there is ample evidence that wildlife production systems have significant economic impact and multipliers (see Chapter 4).

11 We use the term 'subsidization' loosely, as this actually represents a payment for socio-economic (as opposed to financial) value added, rather than a subsidy.

12 A financial analysis is done from the perspective of the individual or firm, whereas an economic analysis is done from the perspective of society, removes distortions and perversions from prices and, confusingly and somewhat contrary to the word itself, includes intangible and non-monetary values.

13 Booth (2002) shows a quadrupling of wildlife populations and quotas in Zimbabwe between 1985 and 2000.

14 Child and Dalal-Clayton (in preparation) give a detailed account on the impact of tourism jobs and carefully structured hunting benefits on community attitudes and conservation practice in the community neighbouring this park.

15 Drucker's (1973) chapters on Performance in the Service Institution are a 'must read' for anyone interested in how public institutions work. Porter (2000) confirms Drucker's supposition that prosperity depends on a culture of productivity rather than control of resources, a pathology he suggests afflicts many developing countries. Thus, economic culture (social capital) are key determinants of prosperity, and decentralization contributes to this cultural shift because it promotes democratization, trust and moderation (Harrison, 2000).

16 Parastatals have a mixed, but generally negative, record having dominated African agriculture and, in a few cases, led successful sectors (eg tea in Kenya; cotton in Zimbabwe). They are generally established to begin the process of commercializing nationalized industries where there is some social responsibility (eg food security, or conservation). They are sometimes the first step towards privatizing (eg telephones; airlines) in which case the business of providing services is usually privatized, but within a legislative framework set and monitored by a regulating agency. Moving from departments to parastatals and eventually to full privatization reflects greater internalization of costs and benefits (improving the efficiency and net value of resource allocation), and more personal and legal accountability for performance by board members and managers.

17 These conclusions represent the outcome of the SASUSG Workshop, Kruger, April 2003, by a group that included five park directors, board member, and persons (chiefs, consultants, development agency professionals) with wide experience of park agencies. This group combined collective experiences covering South Africa, Swaziland, Zimbabwe, Mozambique, Namibia, Zambia, Malawi, Kenya and Uganda.

18 McKinsey (see Child, B, 2002a) showed that SANParks was actually subsidizing tourists who could afford to go to Kruger, and not the poorer groups it was ostensibly targeting, who could not afford the transport to get there.

REFERENCES

Barzetti, V (1993) (ed) *Parks and Progress: Protected Areas and Economic Development in Latin American and the Caribbean*, IUCN/IDB, Washington, DC

Booth, V (2002) 'Analysis of wildlife markets (sport hunting and tourism)', WWF–SARPO, Harare

Borrini-Feyerbend, G (1996) 'Collaborative Management of Protected Areas: Tailoring the Approach to the Context', Issues in Social Policy, IUCN, Gland, Switzerland

Carruthers, J (in preparation) 'National Parks in South Africa' in B Child (ed) *Parks in Transition: Biodiversity, Rural Development and the Bottom Line*, vol 2, SASUSG, Pretoria

Castley, J G and Knight, M H, Gordon, J (in preparation) 'Making conservation work: innovative approaches to meeting conservation and socio-economic objectives, an example from the Addo Elephant National Park, South Africa', in B Child (ed) *Parks in Transition: Biodiversity, Rural Development and the Bottom Line*, vol 2, SASUSG, Pretoria

Chabal, P and Daloz, J (1999) *Africa Works. Disorder as Political Instrument*, African Issues, James Curry, Oxford

Child, B (2002a) 'The use of resources by South African National Parks', Policy Consultancy, South African National Parks

Child, B (2002b) 'Application of the southern African experience to wildlife utilization and conservation in Kenya and Tanzania', in H Prins, J Grootenhuis and T Dolan (eds) *Wildlife Conservation by Sustainable Use*, Kluwer Academic Publishers, Massachusetts, pp459–68

Child, B (2003) 'Review: Biodiversity, sustainability and human communities: protecting beyond the protected', *Nature* **421**: 123

Child, B and Dalal-Clayton, B (in preparation) 'Transforming approaches to CBNRM: Learning from the Luangwa experience in Zambia', in T O McShane and M P Wells (eds) *Getting Biodiversity Projects to Work: Towards More Effective Conservation and Development*, Columbia University Press, New York

Child, G (1995) *Wildlife and People. The Zimbabwean Success*, WISDOM Foundation

Clague, C (ed) (1997) *Institutions and Economic Development. Growth and Governance in Less-Developed and Post-Socialist Countries*, Johns Hopkins University Press, Baltimore

Dalal-Clayton, B and Child, B (2003) *Lessons from Luangwa. The Story of the Luangwa Integrated Resource Development Project, Zambia*, IIED Wildlife Development Series no. 13

Davies, R (2000) 'Madikwe Game Reserve: A partnership in conservation', in H Prins, J Grootenhuis and T Dolan (eds) *Wildlife Conservation by Sustainable Use*, Kluwer Academic Publishers, Massachusetts, pp439–58

De la Harpe, D (2000) 'Attaining financial self-sufficiency of national parks and other protected areas: A viewpoint from southern and eastern Africa', ICUN website, http://economics.iucn.org

Deloitte and Touche (2000) 'Zambia Wildlife Authority. Proposed ZAWA establishment', 4th Board Meeting, 17–18 April

De Soto, H (2000) *The Mystery of Capital. Why Capitalism Triumphs in the West and Fails Everywhere Else*, Basic Books, New York

Dixon, J and Sherman, P (1990) *Economics of Protected Areas – A New Look at Benefits and Costs*, Island Press, Washington, DC

Drucker, P F (1973) *Management: Tasks, Responsibilities, Practices*, HarperCollins, New York

Duffy, R (2000) *Killing for Conservation. Wildlife Policy in Zimbabwe*, African Issues, James Curry, Oxford

Gibson, C (1999) *Politicians and Poachers. The Political Economy of Wildlife Policy in Africa*, Cambridge University Press, Cambridge

Griffiths and Robin (1997), *Ecology and Empire: Environmental History of Settler Societies*, Edinburgh, Keele University Press, pp125–38

Grindle, M and Thomas, J (1991) *Public Choices and Policy Change. The Political Economy of Reform in Developing Countries*, Johns Hopkins University Press, Baltimore

Handy, C (1995) *The Empty Raincoat. Making Sense of the Future*, Arrow Books, London

Hamel, G and Prahlad, C (1994) *Competing for the Future*, Harvard Business School Press

Harrison, L E (2000) 'Introduction', in L E Harrison and S P Huntington (eds) *Culture Matters. How Values Shape Human Progress*, Basic Books

Hersey, P and Blanchard, K (1988) *Management of Organizational Behavior. Utilizing Human Resources*, 5th edition, Prentice-Hall International, London

IUCN (1994) *Guidelines for Protected Area Management Categories*, IUCN, Gland, Switzerland

IUCN (2000) *Financing Protected Areas: Guidelines for Protected Area Managers*, World Commission on Protected Areas of the IUCN, IUCN, Gland, Switzerland

James, A, Green, M and Paine, J (1999) *A Global Review of Protected Area Budgets and Staffing*, World Conservation and Monitoring Centre, Cambridge, England

Krug, W (2001) 'Private Supply of Protected Land in Southern Africa: A review of Markets, Approaches, Barriers and Issues', presented at World Bank/OECD International Workshop on Market Creation for Biodiversity Products and Services, 25–26 January, Paris

Landes, D (1998) *The Wealth and Poverty of Nations. Why Some Are So Rich and Some So Poor*, Abacus, London

Leakey, R and Morell V (2001) *Wildlife Wars. My Battle to Save Kenya's Elephants*, London, Pan Macmillan

Leonard, D (1991) *African Successes: Four Public Managers of Kenyan Rural Development*, University of California Press, Berkeley

Martin, R (2003) 'Conditions for effective, stable and equitable conservation at the national level in southern Africa', presented at Workshop on Local Communities, Equity and Protected Areas, TILCEP/PLASS/ART, Pretoria, 25–28 February

McNeely, J (1988) *Economics and Biological Diversity: Developing and Using Economic Incentives to Conserve Biological Resources*, IUCN, Gland, Switzerland

Micklethwaite, J and Wooldridge, A (1997) *The Witch Doctors. What the Management Gurus are Saying, Why It Matters, and How to Make Sense of It*, Mandarin Paperbacks, London

Moinuddin, H, Child, B, Jones, M, Dunham, K, Pope, C, Kemp, I, Sichilonga, C, Simukanzye, A and Mushinge, R (2002) *Project Document for Continuing Norwegian Support to SLAMU Phase V*, Zambia Wildlife Authority

North, D C (1995) 'The new institutional economics and Third World development', in J Harriss, J Hunter and C M Lewis (eds) *The New Institutional Economics and Third World Development*, Routledge, London, pp17–26

Olson, M (2002) *Power and Prosperity. Outgrowing Communist and Capitalist Dictatorships*, Basic Books, New York

Ottichilo, W, Grunblatt, J, Said, M and Wargute, P (2000) 'Wildlife and livestock population trends in the Kenya rangeland', in H Prins, J Grootenhuis and T Dolan (eds) *Wildlife Conservation by Sustainable Use*, Kluwer Academic Publishers, Massachusetts, pp203–18

O'Riordan, T and Stoll-Kleeman, S 2002 (eds) *Biodiversity, Sustainability and Human Communities. Protecting Beyond the Protected*, Cambridge University Press, Cambridge

Peters, T and Waterman, R (1982) *In Search of Excellence. Lessons from America's Best-run Companies*, HarperCollins Business, London

Porter, M E (2000) 'Attitudes, values, beliefs and the microeconomics of prosperity', in L E Harrison and S P Huntington (eds) *Culture Matters. How Values Shape Human Progress*, Basic Books

Reed, T (2002) 'The functions and structures of protected area authorities. Considerations for financial and organizational management', World Bank Internship Program

Ross, R (1988) *Government and the Private Sector: Who Should Do What?*, RAND Corporation Research Study, Craen Russak and Company, New York

Skynner, R and Cleese, J (1993) *Life and How to Survive It*, Vermilion, London

Soto, B (in preparation) 'Protected areas management in Moçambique', in B Child (ed) *Parks in Transition: Biodiversity, Rural Development and the Bottom Line*, vol 2, SASUSG, Pretoria

't Sas-Rolfes, M (undated) *The Kruger National Park. South African Heritage or Wasted Asset?*, unpublished report

TAESCO (1998) 'Review of the conservation impacts of the PAWS Project – final document', unpublished report prepared on behalf of the World Bank, TAESCO Consultants, Friedland, Germany

Zambia Wildlife Authority (2003) *Five-Year Strategic Plan 2003–2007*, Lusaka, Zambia Wildlife Authority

Chapter 7

Innovations in Park Management

Brian Child

with

Guy Castley, Michael Knight,
Jill Gordon (Addo Elephant),
David Daitz (Cape Peninsular),
Steve Johnson, Willie Boonzaaier, Rodger Collinson and
Richard Davies (North West Parks),
David Grossman and Phillipa Holden
(Contract Parks in South Africa),
Agnes Kiss (Masai Mara),
Peter Fearnhead (Marakele)

INTRODUCTION

In this chapter we describe and discuss some of the innovations that are being tested in southern Africa. As the mandate of park agencies grows, outsourcing is a logical step, and we look at this in terms of tourism enterprises, the support of non-governmental organizations (NGOs), and even the contracting of entire parks to the private sector. Second, we look at the contractual inclusion of other landholders into national parks. Third, although there has been surprisingly little experimentation or documentation of the development of management systems used to improve the performance of protected areas, we use two examples from Zambia to show how devolution and paying for services improve effectiveness. Fourth, we look at the potential role for parks as bridgeheads for better land use and engines for rural development. Instead of putting up the barricades, proactive and outward-looking parks can play a powerful role in changing economic and even governance systems in marginal rural areas. There are questions of whether rural development is a step too far beyond the park manager's core business, but this is countermanded by the argument that parks cannot survive as economic black holes disconnected from rural economies. The efforts by several countries to convert wildlife into a sustainable form of land use (see Chapters 3 and 4) have enabled the viability of this sector to be used to expand parks and their buffer zones. Parks are surprisingly well placed to take on this role, and we discuss its implications, as well as the emerging questions of whether parks should be locality focused, should promote a rural developmental role or even, and here we become sacrilegious, become primarily a development tool.

OUTSOURCING

Regional wildlife agencies have traditionally provided tourism accommodation themselves, including the management of restaurants and shops. This is not core business, and putting commercial and conservation functions together in the same budget also confounds financial management and analysis.

Outsourcing Tourism Facilities

Much of the methodology for outsourcing, especially open and competitive marketing, was developed in the hunting sector in the early 1990s (Child, 1995; WWF, 1997), primarily by community programmes. When Zimbabwe's Communal Areas Management Programme for Indigenous Resources (CAMPFIRE) adopted open, competitive marketing of hunting concessions by the community, for instance, it earned half again as much as government hunting concessions. A rule of thumb is that the landholder (that is, the 'producer community') should capture 33–40 per cent of the outfitter's turnover from safari hunting clients. The methodology soon spread to the marketing of tourism lodges in community areas, and later to the sale of hunting and tourism concessions by state wildlife agencies, with the large state wildlife agencies tending to lag a decade or so behind. This demonstrates an important advantage of a sector that is not dominated by a single state agency.

From the late 1980s, park agencies began to outsource tourism. In Zimbabwe, for instance, the department continued to provide medium-cost facilities, but the private sector developed the high-end market with quality tented and bush camps. Zambia had nationalized most tourism accommodation, but in the mid-1990s it outsourced all operations through competitive tenders. In South Luangwa, for instance, all bush camps (6–12 beds) and lodges (12–36 beds) are now operated by the private sector with 5–20-year leases. Guests pay approximately US$33 per night in the park, so in the short five-month tourism season, each bed earns the park roughly US$1500. Thus, the park retains approximately 10–15 per cent of turnover. Interestingly, medium-cost facilities outsourced by North West Parks also earn US$1500 annually. Tourism concessions tend to pay the park between 5 and 10 per cent of turnover.[1]

Merchandising in southern African parks tends to be poor, and shops have been traditionally managed by the park agency following the argument that remote locations increase prices, and that tourists can be exploited because of the lack of competition. In the one example where data are available, the outsourcing of shops in Kruger National Park increased revenues by R8 million and R23 million in the first two years of operation, respectively; earlier figures were too confounded with park finances to produce a profitability analysis.

Outsourcing Park Management

Having traditionally done everything in national parks, it is a difficult mental shift for park agencies to now provide services by coordinating policy, contractors and partners to 'produce' these services. As with outsourcing in general, it is the smaller, commercially nimble agencies, or the desperate ones, that have experimented with the outsourcing of park management activities.

North Luangwa Conservation Project and other Law Enforcement Support

Like South Luangwa, heavy commercial poaching eliminated rhino and almost eliminated elephant in North Luangwa National Park. In the mid to late 1980s, the Owens Foundation took on a crusade, funded largely with private money, to stop poaching. Providing a helicopter and aircraft, and grading the long-neglected roads, they actively led a paramilitary assault on poaching, largely using National Parks and Wildlife Service (NPWS) personnel. Without this effort, there is little doubt that the park would have been largely depleted of wildlife. However, militarily, the Owens operation overstepped the mark, and they left the country overnight. The vigour of two individuals made an important contribution, but failed politically, and park finances were not assured; no attempt was made to encourage tourism.

The Frankfurt Zoological Society then signed a ten-year agreement to support the park. With a highly competent field manager, the North Luangwa Conservation Project (NLCP) provided patrol equipment, logistical support (rations, vehicles), air support and training to scouts employed by government. Most impressively, they established a central control room and patrol monitoring system that enabled hourly monitoring of patrols and poaching, mapping and analysis of effort. This brought poaching under control. An indicator of success is the growing elephant population.

With law enforcement remaining in the hands of Zambia Wildlife Authority (ZAWA)[2] officers, and the project supporting this technically and logistically, the institutional structure is both effective and politically acceptable. A project review was concerned (rightly) about its financial sustainability, but (wrongly) recommended phasing out support to law enforcement and a refocus towards planning, monitoring and research, community development and public relations, which are peripheral to the core business of protecting the park from poaching. The real challenge remaining is how to fund this core business in perpetuity. There are two options: to develop some 350 tourism beds to provide the US$500,000 annually needed to manage the park, and to provide the necessary (often expensive) infrastructure; or to provide a trust fund or long-term donor support.

During the transition from NPWS to ZAWA, several donors funded NGO anti-poaching initiatives as a stop-gap measure to prevent poaching. In 2000, Zambia Wildlife Authority signed a three-year memorandum of understanding with a local NGO, the Kafue Anti-Poaching Company Limited (KANTIPO) to support anti-poaching operations in Kafue National Park. This arrangement was effective at providing logistical support. However, it fell apart for several reasons. KANTIPO tried to replace (rather than partner) ZAWA in managing one of Zambia's premier national parks without necessarily having the expertise, and was also competing directly with ZAWA for donor funds, which it ultimately failed to get. Moreover, although technically competent, KANTIPO failed to build strong enough relationships to make it a partner of choice. In Lower Zambezi National Park, 'Conservation Lower Zambezi' supplements contributions from tour operators with limited donor funds to support ZAWA's anti-poaching operations. It provided important logistical support to control poaching in the period when the emerging ZAWA was non-operational, but its long-term future also depends on negotiating and sharing responsibilities with ZAWA.

Of the three programmes, NLCP worked by far the best. It had a long-term funding base, and also employed a highly competent wildlife professional with the inter-personal skills to manage it. The Lower Zambezi project is low key, but sustainable, because of the interests of the lodge operators in supporting the park. Kantipo had too narrow a support base to survive.

Kasanka Trust and Other Initiatives in Zambia

In 1992, Kasanka Trust acquired complete jurisdiction for the management of Kasanka, a small, depleted miombo park in central Zambia, including the employment of managers and scouts and the retention of revenues. Relying on semi-volunteers rather than money, the trust has gradually developed a network of roads and built two small middle-cost game lodges. Heavily depleted wildlife populations are recovering, albeit slowly, and some re-introductions have taken place, with improvements in tourism and infrastructure. Viability is still an impediment, as tourism funds less than half the costs of managing the park, which still depends on donations. This model is cheap, and has certainly saved the park from being depleted, but more professional management and capital investment would have yielded better results. With ZAWA rightly focused on protecting and developing flagship parks (eg Luangwa, Kafue, Lower Zambezi), outsourcing the management of lesser parks to interested individuals may be the way to conserve those that are unlikely to be viable within the next ten years. The question is whether there are enough of these individuals to roll out this model more widely, and if a more commercially orientated business might not have recovered the park more quickly.

In Zambia there are currently 12 second-order parks with few resources. ZAWA has initiated negotiations with non-profit groups to manage three of these, but the general level of knowledge and financing of the potential partners remains questionable.

ZAWA has also initiated negotiations with a for-profit organization to manage a further two parks in western Zambia. Although the concept of privatizing parks is accepted and supported, several problems have emerged. A plethora of local stakeholders and authorities mean that there is no one single negotiating point, and leaves space for political intrigue and influence that play on underlying power relationships. There is also a gap between corporate culture on the one hand and government and community culture on the other. Corporates make quick decisions, negotiate linearly, and follow a western proprietary ethos in which a trade is a single transaction rather than an ongoing relationship. The transaction costs of managing complex, time-consuming relationships are a powerful commercial disincentive. Suspicion and trust are also major issues, especially when the transaction negotiations are between different races and touch issues such as the sovereignty of 'national' parks.

In a similar example in Majete National Park in Malawi, African Parks Pvt. Ltd went through two tendering processes before being finally awarded a management contract, taking three years to close this deal largely because of changing role players (namely ministers) and the need to start renegotiating with each new player. There is a lot to learn about facilitating these relationships. Challenges include the lack of precedent, the absence of information and experience to guide such deals, and the absence of park performance criteria to support the design of contracts. It does not help that the contractor is usually a white businessman, or that it is under-paid, non-commercial park agencies that are doing the outsourcing.

Similar experiences with the community–private joint ventures suggest that independent brokering, and a sound understanding of the sector backed up by solid data, are important for negotiating successful partnerships.

Marakele National Park[3]

Marakele National Park in South Africa provides a useful comparison of the performance of the private sector with one of Africa's best-run park agencies. Approximately half of the park is managed by SANParks and the other half is managed by way of agreement with Marakele (Pty) Ltd, a company that was established by a wealthy individual and which has the express purpose of assisting with the development and management of the national park. It is anticipated that a single management plan will cover the total area, but at present this is only in its draft form. As with the example of South Luangwa given below, a rigorous commercial agreement has actually supplanted the standard park management plan, and its clear targets that are aligned with budgets have ensured that it is a far more effective implementation guideline. The company has also purchased approximately 20,000ha of land,[4] representing just over one-quarter of the total park. This consolidation has effectively completed the development of the park to the extent that it is now sufficiently large and representative to meet its ecological objectives. The land purchase, fencing, restocking and rehabilitation (removal of electricity lines, 2000km of fencing, old farm infrastructure and partial clearing of invasive vegetation) has taken 2 years to complete, a process that may have taken SANParks 10–20 years, depending on resources. In comparison to the SANParks managed section, the area managed by Marakele (Pty) Ltd is properly equipped, and decision making is significantly faster, which allows management to get things done. Managing the contract with the private sector is throwing up the problem of 'how do we measure the performance of parks in general?'.

Masai-Mara Reserve[5]

The Masai-Mara Reserve in southern Kenya is owned and managed by two county councils (Narok, Trans Mara). Famous for the Serengeti migrations, this high-potential wildlife area is also infamous for poor management and high levels of financial malpractice. Recently, management of the core tourism area (Mara Triangle) was contracted out to Mara Conservancy Pvt. Ltd, with responsibility for management, a 34 per cent share of gate revenue, and moderately specific performance criteria.

Using the same staff, but with different leadership and conditions, preliminary results indicate massive improvements in infrastructure, revenue collection and visitor satisfaction. In parallel with the experience of park parastatals (Chapter 6), the relationship between the technical managers and the system of political control is messy: losing influence and patronage opportunities, members of the county council who serve on the board are not entirely committed to the change.

Community–Private Joint Ventures

In many respects, community programmes have made the transition to private partnerships far more easily than state wildlife agencies. The support provided by community-based natural resource management (CBNRM) support agencies has no doubt been important. The collation of data and, in some cases, research into the sector (eg hunting or tourism) have provided a strong factual base for negotiation. Training of communities in negotiating techniques has been important. Support agencies have acted as brokers, though with some bias towards the communities. And, finally, communities tend to accept commercial joint ventures far more readily than bureaucrats with their anti private-sector bias (see the analysis by Grindle and Thomas referred to in the previous chapter). In Botswana, 15-year agreements with tourism and hunting companies provide very significant community benefits, plus the incentive and requirement for sound conservation management. For example, Okavango Wilderness Safaris has a long-term management contract in a portion of the Moremi Game Reserve, is effectively managing the area, and is facilitating the re-introduction of rhinos. In CAMPFIRE, five-year hunting concessions provided sufficient incentive for private operators to provide management including anti-poaching and road construction. Namibia, where each community is assisted to make individual deals with private partners, is similarly effective. However, until recently, government officials in Zambia negotiated the award of five year concessions 'on behalf' of communities. This opaque and highly centralized allocation was filled with intrigue, related more to politics than performance, and the associated elite predation was an important cause retarding the transformation of the wildlife sector.

Conclusions on Outsourcing

As predicted by management theory, there are technical and financial advantages to outsourcing a range of park management activities, and even to outsourcing park management entirely. Although used as a solution where park agencies are weak, stronger park agencies design and enforce contracts better. The logical end-point is for park agencies to become contract managers, with particular strength in regulation and monitoring.

In improving these partnerships, there are two areas that are particularly challenging. The first is the setting of clear performance criteria for contract management, which we have noted is a general weakness of park management systems regardless of outsourcing. Indeed, outsourcing is likely to improve the search for clear performance indicators. The second problem is the bureaucratic disincentive for park agencies to outsource. Outsourcing internalizes costs and benefits and makes relationships more transparent. This does improve efficiency and effectiveness, However, it also reduces the opportunity for patronage or even corrupt relationships, which can be a negative incentive to the bureaucrats or politicians making the deal. As noted, mistrust and misunderstanding between the contrasting cultures of civil servants and the private sector is a common challenge.

BUILDING PARKS AND CONTRACT PARKS

Cape Peninsular[6]

The Cape Peninsular is endowed with mountains, 2200 plant species of which 100 are endemic, an endemic vertebrate fauna and a similarly biodiverse marine environment.[7] This spectacular outdoor environment is highly valued for recreation, and is set among the suburbs of Cape Town, which is growing rapidly. Public concern for its long-term protection led to several attempts to confer legal protection, the most significant of which in 1983 included 29,120ha under 14 public and 174 private authorities. This worked briefly, but coordination was never successful and the area continued to degrade.

In 1995, the provincial government of the Western Cape gave South African National Parks a tightly bound opportunity to create a national park. Although there was general support to protect the environment, and powerful support from environmental NGOs (vociferous, but representing a tiny constituency), there was also considerable public anxiety over loss of historical access, fuelled by the perception that a national park was stocked with big game and excluded people unless they paid. A critical insight was that the success of this project hinged on public opinion, which could be inexact and irrational. In short, the park managers were engaging on a political process, and the development strategy was built around this recognition, with media management and stakeholder involvement being central. Even when a court case was lost over a hotel development site, public opinion prevented this development.

The major challenge was to bring this diverse area under a single authority that had sufficient financial resources to fund conservation. Although the value of biodiversity was well recognized, the real strength of the personnel driving this process was their motivation, and understanding of stakeholder processes and commercial reality. SANParks managed to leverage foreign funding, which in turn enabled it to wrest pay-points from local authorities, notoriously averse to giving up control. Taking on staff from the three major local authorities involved, they also managed to obtain a five-year grant (R10.3 million) to bear the salary component of costs until the park became viable. By invoking imaginative pricing policies, a significant cash flow came directly to SANParks from the day it assumed responsibility, placing it in a stronger position to dictate rather than respond to events. With international visitors being price insensitive, and traditional access being an emotive local issue, the strategy was to charge tourists what they were prepared to pay, and to then provide affordable access to locals by other mechanisms.

The engagement of communities, many of which were affluent, initially had nothing to do with benefits, but with winning support for the process of creating a new conservation entity. As Daitz emphasizes, before a park can engage with communities, especially poor communities, about the delivery or real tangible benefits, it must first establish its own viability. The most important challenge was to achieve a sustainable positive cash flow independent of short-term subsidization. One can speculate that the cultural mentality shaped by this priority is the reason why the management of this park is astute, not only commercially but also in terms of public relations and biodiversity conservation: indicative is the fact that it was the first park in South Africa to have clear goals supported by management information systems. Reflecting their managerial capacity, park managers were able to solicit a large, poverty-related subsidy to employ many poor people to clear invasive alien species from the park. As with Pilanesburg and Madikwe, there appears to be a correlation between parks founded on commercial reality, imaginative park managers, and conservation success.

Using Addo Elephant National Park to Build Conservation Landscapes[8]

SANParks is mandated by national government to expand the country's formal terrestrial protected-area network from 6 to 8 per cent by 2010. This hinges on a paradigm shift from setting aside protected areas for purely preservationist reasons to encapsulating ecological patterns and processes within a broader ecosystems conservation approach, and to linking protected areas to the neighbouring land-use matrix and recognizing their potential as economic development nodes based on sustainable ecotourism growth. SANParks have embarked upon a programme to expand some of the smaller parks, and the challenge of expanding parks in landscapes that are already used is being pioneered by the Addo Elephant National Park (AENP) in the impoverished Eastern Cape Province.

The Greater Addo Elephant National Park (GAENP) project reflects national priorities to reverse land degradation and enhancing biodiversity, and to improve local livelihoods. Funding has been provided by the Global Environmental Fund in recognition of the start-up costs and biodiversity value of the area and, significantly, by the national government in recognition that a greater park diversifies tourism opportunities and holds the key to unlocking major economic growth. Tourism is recognized as a productive land-use alternative that is becoming important in many rural areas. The Eastern Cape has been identified as a prime area for government support to ecotourism. Investment is justified on economic grounds, including expanding tourism throughput and employment (one job per 100ha versus the agricultural norm of one job per 367ha).

Although the original AENP satisfied its objectives of conserving a remnant population of elephants, its small size, ecosystem degradation and loss of natural resources was beginning to impact on biodiversity. After a strategic approach based on biodiversity and economic criteria, the park was doubled in the past five years to over 135,000ha. The ultimate goal is a 372,000ha terrestrial zone covering five of South Africa's seven biomes plus a marine protected area of 120,000ha (see Note 9). The expansion is not solely focused on establishing a Schedule I protected area managed by SANParks, but it also makes provision for contractual areas within the planning boundary, and innovative conservation and development models involving private landowners, local communities and the private business sector.

Incorporating non-state land within the GAENP required SANParks to experiment with incentives to encourage landowners to convert areas of high biodiversity priority away from marginal agriculture to conservation. These incentives include legal recognition, traversing rights, management inputs, extension services, fencing support, tax exemptions, access to expensive wildlife and consumption of game. It is hoped that these incentives will help landowners to convert from low productive and often unprofitable land uses into more environmentally and financially sustainable nature-based ventures. Allowing landowners to be incorporated into the park without necessarily involving a transfer of title has several benefits: the park can be managed as an ecological whole whereas the overwhelming cost of land purchase can be reduced. Furthermore, developmental opportunities (ecotourism, hunting, game sales, etc.) for the landowner as part of a greater park are enhanced. These novel approaches have already shown results, with several areas already contracted into the park with prospective contractual partners approaching SANParks to incorporate their lands into the park. One of the conservation safeguards linked to such contractual arrangements is that they are long-term agreements that are in line with the conservation philosophy and principles laid down by SANParks. However, of critical importance remain the entry conditions of these contracting partners: Castley et al (in preparation) suggest that they need buy-in to the project concerning a percentage of revenue generation; they need to be of biological importance to the whole project; and they need to be of sufficient size to run independently of the park and so prevent small free-riders from entering the project.

Reflecting the tendency for multiple innovation, the management of this project is being outsourced, while the park's board incorporates local stakeholders. Financial sustainability is also perceived as critical. Investment alternatives, in which outsourcing to the private sector is central, have been modelled to predict a surplus of US$200,000 by 2007. The predicted increase in park revenues from US$0.4 million to US$1.4 million would normally increase direct economic impact by US$14 million to US$28 million (see Note 9). An economic goal is to transform land supporting small stock raising (US$7 per hectare) and game farming (US$8 per hectare) to multifaceted high-end ecotourism earning US$30 per hectare, with a concomitant increase in jobs and secondary economic impacts.

Communities and Contract Parks in South Africa[10]

South Africa's political transition required a transformation of society, including parks where a fortress and fences approach was no longer politically acceptable, and more innovative means of ensuring the dual goals of conservation and social justice were called for. In the build-up to a democratic order in 1994, an African National Congress (ANC) paper challenged the value of parks to local people and their previous exclusion, and suggested that they would be more relevant if used for livestock grazing. This shocked the conservation movement into change. In the land restitution process the Makuleke people received title deeds to 25,000ha of their former land in the Kruger National Park, and the Bushmen (as they call themselves) received 25,000ha in the Kgalagadi Transfrontier National Park. With the Nama people in the Richtersveld National Park, these claimants decided to maintain their land under conservation as contract parks.

The Richtersveld National Park was established on the condition that the 7000 local people would have five of the nine places on the park committee, would get an escalating lease fee (R0.50 per hectare), and would obey an upper limit to livestock grazing. Although local people are becoming increasingly aware of their rights, the powerful SANParks still dominates the arrangement. Internal community disputes also frustrate progress, and six stockowners continue to overgraze locally. Commercial development has been slow, with fewer secondary benefits than anticipated. The emergence of younger community leadership, and NGO support, is gradually improving the situation.

In 1969, under apartheid, 3000 Makuleke people were removed to enable Kruger National Park to capture the area's high biodiversity value in what is now referred to as 'pristine wilderness'! Title was returned to the Makuleke in 1998 through a Common Property Association. The land was retained for conservation as a contractual national park. Makuleke got full rights to suitable commercial development (but not gate fees) and three of the six places on the joint management board, while SANParks managed the park in accordance with a master plan. Throughout the land claim process, the Makuleke community was well supported by NGOs, donors and voluntary advisors, and the arrangement is held as innovative and fair, with clearly defined rights and responsibilities.

Although generally constructive, tensions did emerge in the relationship. When the community attempted to sell two buffalo and two elephant for hunting, entrenched park managers opposed the move as illegal. With support from NGOs and the chief executive officer (CEO) of SANParks, the hunt proceeded and earned more than half a million rand. The following year, plains game were added to the quota, but again entrenched attitudes fought this and again the CEO intervened, with R1 million being earned. In this, the third year, park managers are still opposing the quota. This division within the traditional park management authority, SANParks, also emerged in the development of a 24-bed lodge. Although SANParks participated in the bid evaluation process and award, innovation continued to be opposed by some components of the organization. Whereas the senior leadership of SANParks has been innovative and supportive, there has been a reluctance to relinquish power at the local level, and the management of this section of the park and skills transfer have been neglected, contrary to the management agreement between SANParks and the Makuleke community.

Nevertheless, conservation objectives have been met, hunting earns R2 million annually, one lodge has opened and a second is being negotiated. The cohesiveness of this community, and strong technical support from civic organizations and senior SANParks managers, have been critical success factors.

The !Khomani San claim to 65,000ha and extensive rights in an additional area (25,000ha) of the Kgalagadi Transfrontier Park is the only successful aboriginal land claim in southern Africa. Evicted from the park in 1931, this community of 1500 people had lost central coherence, and with limited civic support, remains disparate. The San received rights for traditional cultural practices and harvesting and to conduct ecotourism ventures within the contract park, and for non-commercial traditional activities in a further 4000km^2 of it.

The Mier ('coloured') people (5500 population), traditionally stockowners, were also forcibly removed from the park in the 1930s. Like the San, the Mier also received access to 25,000ha within the park, provided it was not used for residential or farming purposes.

Given the complexity of negotiating the overlapping rights of the San and Mier, little civic, financial and technical support, the low levels of literacy and organization within these communities, and some allegations of corruption within the Common Property Association, a joint management board in still being designed for the !Ae Kalahari Contract Park. Progress has been slow, with some reticence at park level to facilitate the process.

The conservation objectives of contract parks are rarely compromised, but maintaining this success depends of resolving conflicts and generating the anticipated flow of social and economic benefits. The transaction costs of brokering these agreements are also high, largely because of the historical disempowerment and dismembering of communities under apartheid. Institutional development is central to success, both for well-organized and transparently managed communities and for well-defined rights and responsibilities between the community and the park authority. In this regard, South Africa's strong legal system has been important.

Conclusions on Contract Parks

The particular circumstances of South Africa, including a relatively small parks estate, the economic value of wildlife, strong legal systems and community restitution, have forced and enabled formal alliances between park agencies and local landholders. This has ranged from the publicly desirable consolidation of Cape Peninsular National Park, to the addition of freehold land to Addo, to the retention of titled land formally returned to communities within parks. There are precursors, though of a less legalistic nature, for example where Zimbabwe and Natal informally encouraged private and communal neighbours to parks to shift their land use to wildlife through measures such as granting use rights, locating lodges outside parks, providing cheap animals for restocking, and ensuring that park pricing is not subsidized and does not undercut the provision of similar facilities by landholders. This last point seems subtle, but is actually profound.

Enabling these relationships is the fact that wildlife has been made into a competitive form of land use, and that proximity to national parks adds value to properties with wildlife enterprises.[11] But success does not only hinge on the potential to generate benefits. The institutional framework for organizing neighbours and formalizing contracts is also critical. One would expect progress to be faster where neighbours were internally cohesive, where a legal framework strengthens the ability of neighbours to work together,[12] and ultimately where landholders have the right to manage, benefit from and sell their wildlife.

MANAGEMENT SYSTEMS

Devolved Performance Management in South Luangwa

Commercial elephant and rhino poaching swept south through Africa in the late 1970s. In Zambia's Luangwa Valley, the National Parks and Wildlife Service was unable to prevent the loss of 100,000 elephants and all 6000–8000 rhinos. President Kaunda, who did not trust NPWS, asked NORAD to fund an independent Luangwa

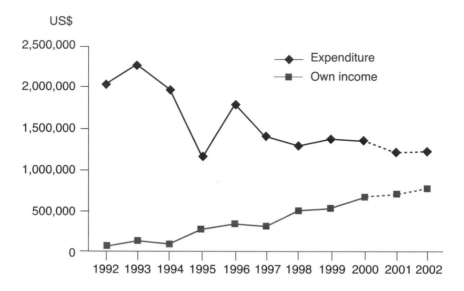

Figure 7.1 *Financing gap in South Luangwa National Park*

Integrated Resource Development Project (LIRDP) to manage the South Luangwa National Parks and surrounding communal areas. With funding of US$3 million annually, poaching was rapidly reduced from several thousand to less than 20 elephant annually. Apart from this, the LIRDP rapidly took on too many functions (more than 36), and in the nature of a budget-funded organization, did many of them poorly, especially the commercial businesses it started.[13]

In 1996, the US$1.5 million gap between income and expenditure, and imminent project closure, was used to make staff 'dissatisfied with the status quo', the first step in a change management process.[14] Thereafter, the project was re-engineered, by identifying required outcomes and building structures and procedures around these goals in a four-year process of discussion and change. Five functions (ecosystem conservation, law enforcement, tourism, roads and community-based natural resource management (CBNRM)) and four support activities (vehicles, procurement, administration and conservation education) were defined. Staffing was halved and designed around these functions, letting a few troublemakers go, recruiting two managers from the private sector, and drastically phasing out expatriate support. Budgets, financial management, targets and performance responsibility were devolved to these nine sections.

The control system was summarized by a logical framework with clear indicators, activity plans and budgets; annual workplans and budgets set by each of the nine sections, which specified targets and responsibilities; and a quarterly peer assessment of each section's performance based on a five-column matrix that, for each activity or goal, compared status with target, analysed any problems, and agreed the corrective action. This, effectively, introduced an adaptive management system. The external control mechanism was a meeting twice a year with top management and the donor that reviewed performance against articulated and quantitative targets and formally agreed budgets and workplans.

Table 7.1 *South Luangwa National Park revenue projections (2003–2006)*

Economic assessment	
	US$
Tourism income to Zambia	34,000,000
Recurrent costs	4,617,033
Capital investment (assume longer lifespan than project)	3,526,813
Net (economic) profit	**30,473,187**
Financial assessment	
Revenue projection	**4,050,000**
Tourism	3,400,000
NORAD subsidy	650,000
Core operational costs	**4,617,033**
Administration and overheads	1,103,240
Law enforcement	1,340,108
Resource monitoring	204,276
Road maintenance	860,913
Capital equipment	1,108,496
Surplus (deficit)	**(567,033)**
Capital investment	**7,053,626**
Infrastructure	5,755,700
Other (CBNRM, technical assistance, etc)	1,297,926

The results were rapid and positive, but stemmed from a simple, repeatable and clear management system rather than any superhuman leadership. Despite cutting costs by 40 per cent, performance improved in eight of the nine activities. For instance, tourism income was tripled between 1996 and 2001 (see Note 15), improving self-financing from 20 per cent to 60 per cent. The key ingredients in this improvement were a process that facilitated staff to plan for themselves, clearly defined targets, devolved responsibility and regular peer-based assessments of progress. Managerially speaking, an important conclusion from this example is that there is considerable merit in managing parks as cost centres. At this level, costs and benefits are internalized, easily perceived by managers, and therefore guide improved management. In addition, a park is at a scale of which the complexity of conservation management can be captured in well-structured performance management systems, whereas this may not be possible at agency level.

The Problematic Divergence between Financial and Economic Values

The example of South Luangwa also illustrates the challenge of reconciling the 'financial' and 'economic' sustainability of protected areas. We draw evidence from a proposal to re-fund the park for a fifth period. Moinuddin et al (2002) indicate annual expenditure for this 9050km^2 park of US$1.2 million, split into thirds between law enforcement, road maintenance and all other activities. To sustain itself financially, additional investment in infrastructure was necessary to open up the southern half of the park. Even then, financially, the park would at best break even,

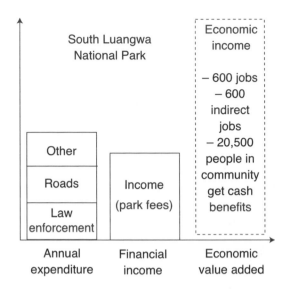

Figure 7.2 *Variance between financial and economic profitability for a savanna park*

ignoring the costs of capital development. It was safer to assume that the park would require a subsidy of about 25 per cent of total recurrent costs. Although marginal financially, this was an excellent investment seen from the perspective of society (in other words economic viability). This dichotomy is illustrated in Table 7.1 and Figure 7.2. Over four years, the US$3.4 million earned in park fees translated into some US$34 million brought into Zambia by tourists, plus about 1200 jobs. Moreover, with 5 per cent of its revenue, the park administered a community wildlife programme, which benefited 20,500 adults with cash and earned Zambia a further US$1 million. For biodiversity conservation, some 12,000km² were secured as wildlife habitats inside and outside the park, including 10,000 elephants. Unfortunately, the government policy of not funding parks was putting these benefits at considerable risk, as without money from government or a donor (in this case NORAD) the park would deteriorate steadily for lack of funding. Despite being financially marginal, there is strong justification for financial support to this park, purely on the economic grounds of value added and job creation. However, unsophisticated national economic management with priorities of health and education could not be relied on to support this investment. Park managers therefore asked donors to capitalize the park, largely through roads, calculating that this might expand tourism income sufficiently to cover recurrent costs.

We should note that this park underestimates the potential of most parks to become financially self-sustaining. Although offering an exceptional wildlife experience, achieving viability is difficult because of its remoteness, poor national infrastructure (especially roads), the high costs of operating in the uncompetitive Zambian economy, and seasonality, with the park accessible for tourism for only five months.

It is interesting to use South Luangwa to further illustrate economic issues affecting protected areas. Two of the main costs of the park relate to the provision

Table 7.2 *Relative efficiency of the performance-based patrol system (rough comparison of patrol costs)*

	Cost	Patrol days	Cost per day (US$)
South Luangwa[16]	400,000	19,128	20.91
South Luangwa	400,000	8,500	47.06
North Luangwa	300,000	10,000	30.00
Kafue patrolling	46,991	2,625	17.90

of policing and primary infrastructure (roads). For most other businesses, policing and access roads are provided as a public service so that two-thirds of park costs are related to what are normally national functions.

Paying for Service: Emergency Resource Protection in Kafue National Park

In 2002, the newly established ZAWA was in a perilous position. Most senior staff were new, and the organization could not afford salaries. Staff had been cut to one-third of former levels, and poaching was rife, with Kafue being cited as particularly bad. After years of political intrigue, donors were unwilling to invest heavily in the organization, and tended to fund conservation through other channels such as NGOs.

Only NORAD, having been involved in the sector for many years through South Luangwa, had the knowledge, flexibility and willingness to participate in a risky and unavoidably political situation. Seeing the dangers of dumping money onto a new organization with little capacity, a history of centralization and vulnerability to political manipulation, NORAD agreed to pilot a project with three critical innovations. First, it would pay explicitly for each patrol day (US$10 for pay and rations). Second, additional money would flow upwards to cover park overheads (US$5 per patrol day) and then to headquarters (US$2) in direct proportion to patrol performance. Third, performance would be the key criteria for each tranche of funding, and the development and monitoring of performance systems would be incorporated into the project with a 'backstopping' arrangement through a firm trusted by both NORAD and ZAWA.

This avoided the problems of dumping too much money centrally (ie the problems of budget-funded organizations) and allowing an organization with a highly centralized history to bloat-up without delivering real results. The programme also demonstrated the effectiveness of decentralizing operational management to cost/profit centres: given clear and simple targets, relatively weak park managers were nevertheless able to deliver highly satisfactory results (Figure 7.3). Third, external facilitation and monitoring were critical. For an additional cost of 5 per cent, consultants developed patrol monitoring and financial systems, audited performance monthly, and provided the donor and others with greater confidence in the programme.

The results were positive and informative. The pilot initiated in Kafue National Park cost US$40,000 per month. At US$18 per square kilometre, the programme was effective at controlling poaching (Figure 7.3) yet cost less than half of the best-managed systems in Zambia[16] (Table 7.2), and well under the costs predicted by

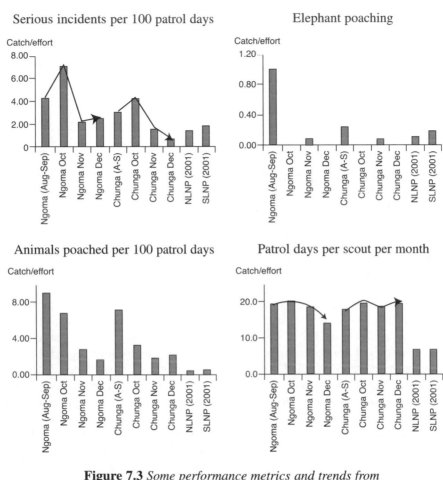

Figure 7.3 *Some performance metrics and trends from patrolling in Kafue National Park benchmarked against projects in Luangwa*

Martin[17]despite the high cost of operating in Zambia. Total direct costs were halved, yet scouts actually took home 53 per cent more pay on average; they patrolled for 20 days each month, three times the average even in 'well-managed' parks. This led to significant cost reductions in overhead and capital, with the demand for housing and other support services being halved.

Performance and motivation improved dramatically (Figure 7.3) because scouts were paid directly according to how many days they spent in the bush patrolling. This process was used as a mechanism to introduce and develop performance monitoring systems for patrolling (ie patrol monitoring forms) and also to decentralize financial management for finances, converting the park into a cost centre. The results in Figure 7.3 benchmark performance against the two Luangwa projects.[18] Poaching was reduced to one-sixth of previous levels within five months. Catch/effort indicators provided a quick and clear indicator of effectiveness, while mapping of patrols and poaching incidents enabled rapid improvements in tactics, especially the placement of patrols. These data easily doubled effectiveness. The programme also confirmed the value of intelligence. Although ground coverage will always be important, the cost of catching a poacher on patrol is expensive. However, if the information obtained from this poacher is used for follow-up operation, and intelligence is carefully managed, poaching and marketing rings can be smashed at a fraction of the cost.

If we return to the theoretical argument about accountability, this financing arrangement converted Kafue National Park from a budget-based organization to one where income was directly related to payment for value added through a clearly defined product (ie patrol days, and bonuses related to patrol targets and apprehended criminals). This effectively halved the costs of resource protection which is a major budget item in many parks. It was also an important step in changing the management culture of the park agency. At this time ZAWA's finances and decision systems were highly centralized, with all the symptoms and disfunctionality of such systems. However, to manage the US$5 overhead for each patrol day, park-level financial and management systems had to be introduced, including monthly budgets and variance analysis, purchase of supplies and equipment, and payment of scout salaries. Relatively easy to develop, fiscal devolution internalized performance accountability at park level, and ZAWA's top management immediately recognized its value. It also broke the logjam of central purchasing and administration so common with wildlife agencies.

Conclusions on Devolved Performance Management

Although the examples reflect the author's knowledge, they also demonstrate the effectiveness of simple management principles in a challenging environment, and are likely to yield even better results where managerial capacity and exposure to modern management systems is higher. Several lessons emerge:

1. Defining goals clearly, linking these to performance evaluations and financial flows and incentives, and building structures and processes around these goals (namely re-engineering) provides a high likelihood of measurable improvements in performance.
2. Devolving budgets and responsibility to cost centres at park level, and to sections, within clearly defined performance parameters (ie a loose–tight management arrangement), brings out the best in managers.
3. Paying directly for results converts a budget-driven to a value-added mentality, halves costs, and should be investigated more.

PARKS AS BRIDGEHEADS FOR BETTER LAND USE AND ENGINES FOR RURAL DEVELOPMENT AND THE ALLEVIATION OF POVERTY

CBNRM in South Luangwa

Without going in to the technical details of CBNRM programmes,[19] one component of the park's activities was supporting a community wildlife programme for 50,000 people on 4500km^2 bordering on the park. Whereas it cost US$200,000 to initiate this project, recurrent costs of supervising 45 village management committees was US$50,000, or 5 per cent of park budget. The net effects on the park were positive. With all 20,500 adults in this community receiving cash benefits from safari hunting annually, building social projects, and being well governed under park supervision, the community actively invested in wildlife management on its own land by employing 78 community scouts. Poaching in the park from this community was far lower than from others. The institutional framework and relationships established to manage the community also provided the park with easy access to leadership, and enabled many organizations to channel support to these communities. It also formed the framework for community-based land-use planning, which is important for reducing conflicts between wildlife and people.

As we have seen with SANParks' management of poverty-related financing, and with North West Parks, parks often find themselves as the most competent management authority in remote areas, and have a strong temptation to act as rural development agencies. How should they respond to this?

In our view, park agencies have a comparative advantage as rural development agencies and should seriously consider taking on this role in a carefully prescribed way. Park agencies have several critical advantages. They are the regulatory authorities for an increasing valuable resource. This gives them the power to devolve a substantial economic force to communities, but also to impose requirements for good governance. By channelling wildlife benefits through (preferably) village structures, they can encourage communities to organize themselves in situations where the lack of organization is the key factor limiting development. There is certainly an important role for wildlife agencies in devolving the authority for wildlife to communities; for clearly setting out the principles upon which devolved authority and rights are based; for monitoring procedural conformance (eg to democratic principles) and governance, for example that funds are accounted for both in the books and, critically, to the community; and for setting clear expectations for wildlife management. Thus, a wildlife agency would set policy, guidelines and procedures, according to CBNRM principles and best practice, and would mutually agree site-specific wildlife management targets (eg a combination of patrol days and poacher catch: effort ratios). It would also describe the requirements for accountable, transparent participatory democracy and monitor conformance with these conditions. In this manner the wildlife agency should forego direct natural resource management but as a regulatory and monitory agency adds real value by ensuring that key indictors of institutional performance and accountability, and wildlife conservation, are monitored. However, capacity building is an expensive activity that the wildlife agency may source and coordinate, but avoid providing. NGOs and the private sector are far better equipped in this role, which quickly absorbs much time and many resources.[20]

North West Parks, South Africa: Conservation as a Socio-economic Investment and Business Paradigm[21]

Pilansburg National Park was conceived in 1969 as a rural development strategy, with the establishment of a recreational resort and nature reserve in the site of an enormous volcano in an area otherwise marginal for agriculture. It was initiated within the Department of Agriculture and Nature Conservation in the 'independent' Bophuthatswana homeland, but was managed by a board controlled by a development agency (Agricor). From the start (1979), the park took on a business-like model, matching stocking rates to economic criteria, outsourcing non-core business activities, and emphasizing commercialization, marketing and human resource management, and thereby attracting highly qualified and innovative wildlife managers. By 1984, Bophuthatswana Parks Board was established. Trophy hunting was immediately introduced to generate income as very few visitors were interested in a park still under development, and this led management to develop models to optimize the returns from wildlife. A fundamental innovation was that game stocks were valued in the annual financial statements and therefore managed as assets. In the absence of alternative models, the board initially managed tourism developments itself. However, progress towards financial self-sustainability was slow, and in a futher innovation the private sector was contracted to develop a lodge inside the park in 1983, a move then exceedingly rare in southern Africa, where government agencies managed tourism facilities. The combination of a strong management team, operating a park along financial criteria, and recognizing the need to justify national parks in a developing country, led to the adoption of a ground-breaking philosophy, 'conservation with development'. Consequently, the board's mission statement combined economic and social criteria: 'to contribute towards improving the quality of life in Bophuthatswana by conserving wild plants, animals and landscapes for the satisfaction of people's present and future, including needs'. Not only was the economic value of the park optimized, including commercial harvesting of wildlife and outsourcing to the private sector, but the park was used actively for environmental education and recreation, with a strong emphais on new products specifically designed for and targeted at local communities. This created a supportive constituency.

By 1990, Pilanesburg had a successful tourism industry, was a quality safari hunting destination, and sold live animals into the market created by South Africa's thriving private conservation sector. It supported the highest tourism density of any protected area in Africa (400,000 per year on 48,000ha), with an average growth rate of 24 per cent and almost half the bed capacity (namely 1808 beds) of Kruger National Park.

In 1991, the government earmarked land for development through cattle grazing and arable agriculture. 'Bop Parks' commissioned a study, and was able to convince the government that wildlife, up-market tourism and hunting was a more viable option, creating significantly more jobs and income. On this basis the Bop government funded the project. For the first time, a park (Madikwe, 61,000ha) was initiated first and foremost as a development project: the project had to return a net positive financial outcome to the board and a positive economic outcome to the country. Park planning was innovative, comprehensive and built around the centrality of viable business models. Whereas the government developed wildlife production, all commercial development was outsourced. A key decision was that economic impact should be optimized at local level to develop community support.

This new park was planned, stocked and developed in less than two years. In less than ten years, reserve income (expected to double within two years) exceeds

Table 7.3 *Assessment of the merits of transforming park objectives and the means–ends relation between conservation and development*[22]

Primary goal	Biodiversity conservation	Economic development
Secondary goal (or limits to change)	If harvest, use products well	Biodiversity conservation
Impacts on society		
Economic growth and poverty alleviation	Create benefits, but unintentionally and sub-optimally	Can be used to create both institutions and economic opportunities
Land pressure	Hard-edged parks, in fact or mentally	Can promote wildlife land uses in buffer zones
Capital and infrastructure	Can deteriorate with poor financing	Higher likelihood of investment and maintenance
Alienation of people from parks		Possibilities for re-integrating parks into society
Park sustainability		
1. Ecological	Results variable, and monitoring seldom occurs, and never systematically or cost effectively	Some evidence that commercialized parks manage conservation better
2. Financial	Tends to be managed inefficiently, even if enthusiastically	Much higher probability of financial sustainability, and generally better at obtaining payments for non-market values
3. Socio-political	General neglect of parks reflects alienation from societies' needs and values	Can be brought more into alignment with societies' needs and values without sacrificing conservation

annual operating costs, with US$15 million private investment in 425 beds (28 lodges) creating 350 direct jobs. A full spectrum of wildlife has been re-introduced onto formerly degraded land, and much disruptive infrastructure removed. The economic and investment benefits are substantial (see Johnson et al, in preparation).

Based on the success of this business and development model, North West Province has commissioned a study to explore linking the two parks with an additional 167,500ha to form a protected area of 250,000ha. As an indicator of the power of this new paradigm, politicians are driving this initiative and have committed R1.5 million to investigate it. Initial models suggest the area will generate US$106 per hectare, increase employment from 93 to 1657 and wages by 53 times.

At the centre of this conservation success, is a paradigm shift that places wildlife at the centre of a business-based rural development model. Although conservation is effectively a by-product, this aspect is better managed than in most national parks: a large area of degraded land has been rehabilitated and restocked with wildlife, and conservation management is competent. Operationally, the autonomy of the board, its commercial nature, financial and business flexibility and rigour, and ability to attract and remunerate visionary staff independently of the public service, have been critical. The major challenge has been managing the tension between a complex, time-consuming multistakeholder process and the protracted nature of participatory community process, with the time constraints of a commercial approach.

Conclusions on Using Parks as Economic Engines

The reality is that many African parks have to prioritize financial sustainability if they are to survive. However, even a financially marginal park is often economically highly profitable, with substantial societal benefits in the form of economic multipliers and other values provided it supports a moderate level of tourism. However, this value is seldom monitored and quantified, losing an opportunity to create legitimate public support.

The economic value of savannah parks provides invaluable opportunities that are neither sufficiently recognized nor exploited by park agencies. Both examples given demonstrate the economic value common to, but not always exploited by, many parks. The South Luangwa example advances the notion that park agencies have a comparative advantage in improving rural governance, and hence development.[23] The examples from North West Parks suggest that there is merit is seeing parks as common pool resources that, first and foremost, serve society, and that in doing this conservation will be powerfully served. This requires a huge mental shift for park managers from one of conserving pristine wilderness to deliberately using parks to create appropriate value for society from common-pool resources, but ensuring conservation capital is maintained or improved (in other words sustainability).

As park managers we are struggling with the difficult question of who and what parks are for (see Chapter 9). What happens if we take this conclusion further and switch the primary purpose of parks to economic development (Figure 7.3), with a proviso that it should be sustainable (ie biodiversity conservation). This would:

- improve the responsiveness of parks to their constituency, thus ultimately improving political, economic and social sustainability;
- improve performance in many aspects, without necessarily threatening biodiversity.

Indeed, if parks are commercialized, and biodiversity becomes an auditable component of the balance sheet, there is a high likelihood that the monitoring and management of biodiversity will improve. A Chapter 5 demonstrates, under the current 'purist' regimes, this is not happening.

This paradigm shift is illustrated in Figure 7.3 and may form a strong basis for sustainable park management in the region. If we reverse the order of our goals, and give sustainable economic development paramountcy, it appears we will score better on most objectives, including long-term ecological sustainability. There is a strong case for changing the means–ends relationship (namely, between conservation and adding socio-economic value) that currently govern African protected areas.

CONCLUSIONS

Economically, parks are often managed as extractively, with revenues being centralized or transferred to other conservation functions, but as 'economic black holes' are politically vulnerable especially at locality level. Their societal credibility and biodiversity performance is also being undermined by the absence of clear performance parameters and management systems. As with any commodity, parks need to assess the demographic and political transitions to which they respond, and to asking the pivotal question 'What should our business be?' A proposal emerges that parks should shift their emphasis towards:

- being managed as cost/profit centres because this:
    - internalizes and improves management systems; and also
    - makes them more responsive to the local situation;
- promoting commercialization because this:
    - improves management efficiency and effectiveness;
    - improves self-sufficiency and their chances of survival;
- promoting the local economy through employment and economic growth because this:
    - encourages the expansion and consolidation of conservation-based land use in the landscape;
    - builds a political constituency for park survival.

If this approach is taken, the proviso (rather than the entry point) is that ecological systems are monitored to ensure that ecosystem health/productivity is not degraded over thresholds, or important biodiversity lost. This chapter has illustrated some of the experimentation and exciting innovations that are occurring in southern Africa. The bottom line is that these opportunities for progress are being created by a philosophy of incentive-led conservation, and by ensuring that incentives count at the level of landholders and therefore the land. The mindset is clear goals (that is, development, without compromising conservation sustainability) and alignment of institutions so that communities, farmers and park managers are incentivized to reach these goals rather than expending too much effort on the minutiae of dictating what can and cannot be done. There is plenty of evidence that if we concentrate on enabling park managers and landholders to build on the comparative advantage of wildlife, and get bureaucratic impediments out of the way, both conservation and rural development will be well served.

NOTES

1 Community concessions in Botswana earn an average of 4.5 per cent of turnover (range 4–10 per cent), Namibia 5.9 per cent (0–12.5 per cent), North West Parks 4.8 per cent (0–10 per cent) and the new SANParks concessions in Kruger and Addo 10.8 per cent (4–22.3 per cent). (Contour Project Managers, 2002). Note that many recently negotiated concessions earn 10 per cent or more of enterprise turnover for the landholder, and the lower averages above reflect a weaker negotiating position on the part of landholders in the past for lack of information and/or use rights.
2 NPWS, a government department, was transformed into a semi-autonomous parastatal (ZAWA) in 2000.
3 Based on a submission by Peter Fearnhead, Commercial Manager, South African National Parks.
4 SANParks has a call option on the land at the purchase price. This mechanism guarantees the perpetuity of the park, albeit at considerable opportunity cost to the individual.
5 Based on a submission by Agnes Kiss, World Bank.
6 Based on Daitz (in preparation).
7 Major habitat types range through semi-arid Karoo areas, fynbos, impenetrable thickets, montane forests, coastal grasslands to coastal forests, and the important marine areas of the Bird and St Croix Island groups in Algoa Bay.
8 Based on Castley et al (in preparation).
9 Based on the assumption that park fees capture 5–10 per cent of direct tourism payments.
10 Based on Grossman and Holden (in preparation).
11 Land values reflect wildlife potential. In northwestern Namibia, for example, land values (in Namibian dollars) are as follows: undeveloped, less than N$100; attractive with some game, N$101–N$300; standard game farm, N$301–N$500; game farm with good infrastructure, N$501–N$1000; fully developed with game lodge, more than N$1000 (Boonzaaier, 2002).
12 For example, intensive conservation areas in Zimbabwe, or legal conservancy arrangements.
13 These included tourism, hunting, grain milling, buses and culling for meat.
14 See Kotter (1996) for a lucid and practical account of change management.
15 Tourism was completely outsourced over this period, mostly to small, high-end operators.
16 The cheaper results in South Luangwa (US$20.91) reflect the use of temporary hires from the nearby community, and these cost reductions have to be weighed against patrolling effectiveness. There is, nevertheless, considerable merit in this option, and its addition to the Kafue system would lower costs correspondingly.
17 In fairness to Martin and his valuable paper, his calculations include all activities associated with a well-managed park, but the patrolling costs in Kafue are still much lower.
18 With slightly different monitoring systems this comparison is only indicative.
19 For CBNRM principles and some results of this programme see Chapter 4; see also Dalal-Clayton and Child (2001), and Child and Dalal-Clayton (in preparation).
20 Much capacity building is supply driven and inefficient, with donor-funded suppliers providing training according to their speciality rather than community requirements. A far better system may be to link the release of benefits to community performance criteria, and then to provide the communities with vouchers to purchase the training they need to fulfil these criteria.
21 Based Johnson et al (in preparation).
22 This comparison was conceived in open forum at the SASUSG members' meeting in Skukuza in 2003.
23 For instance, Sen (1999) advances the notion that development is linked to rights and capacities, whereas the World Bank (undated) emphasizes the centrality of untied funds in giving communities real choice, with community wildlife programmes providing cutting-edge evidence to support this claim.

REFERENCES

Boonzaaier, W (2002) *Joint Venture Decision Making Framework for Community-Based Natural Resource Management Areas*, WWF Namibia

Castley, J G, Knight, M H, and Gordon, J (in preparation) 'Making conservation work: Innovative approaches to meeting conservation and socio-economic objectives, an example for the Addo Elephant National Park, South Africa' in B Child (ed) *Parks in Transition: Biodiversity, Rural Development and the Bottom Line*, vol 2, SASUSG, Pretoria

Child, B (1995) 'A summary of the marketing of trophy quotas in CAMPFIRE areas 1990–1993', Department of National Parks and Wildlife Management, Zimbabwe

Child, B and Dalal-Clayton, B (in preparation) 'Transforming approaches to CBNRM: Learning from the Luangwa experience in Zambia', in T O McShane and M P Wells (eds) *Getting Biodiversity Projects to Work: Towards More Effective Conservation and Development*, Columbia University Press, New York

Contour 'Project Managers' (2002) presentation on joint venture decision making framework, to CBNRM in Namibia

Daitz, L (in preparation) 'Creating the Cape Peninsular National Park. An account of some of the hurdles and the strategies used to overcome them', in B Child (ed) *Parks in Transition: Biodiversity, Rural Development and the Bottom Line*, vol 2, SASUSG, Pretoria

Dalal-Clayton, B and Child, B (2001) *Lessons from Luangwa. The Story of the Luangwa Integrated Resource Development Project, Zambia*, International Institute for Environment and Development, Wildlife and Development Series No. 13

Grossman, D and Holden, P (in preparation) 'Contract parks in South Africa', in B Child (ed) *Parks in Transition: Biodiversity, Rural Development and the Bottom Line*, vol 2, SASUSG, Pretoria

Johnson, S, Boonzaaier, W, Collinson, R and Davies, R (in preparation) 'Changing institutions to respond to challenges – North West Parks, South Africa' in B Child (ed) *Parks in Transition: Biodiversity, Rural Development and the Bottom Line*, vol 2, SASUSG, Pretoria

Kotter, J (1996) *Leading Change*, Harvard Business School

Martin, R (2003) 'Conditions for effective, stable and equitable conservation at the national level in southern Africa', presented at Workshop on Local Communities, Equity and Protected Areas, TILCEP/PLASS/ART, Pretoria, 25–28 February

Moinuddin, H, Child, B, Jones, M, Dunham, K, Pope, C, Kemp, I, Sichilongo, C, Simukanze, A and Mushinge, R (2002) *Project Document for Continuing Norwegian Support to SLAMU Phase V*, Zambia Wildlife Authority

Sen, A (1999) *Development as Freedom*, Knopf, New York

World Bank (undated) 'Community Driven Development in Africa. A Vision of Poverty Reduction through Empowerment', The World Bank Group, Africa Region

WWF (1997) *Marketing Wildlife Leases*, Wildlife Management Series, WWF Southern African Regional Programme Office, Harare

Chapter 8

Does 'Commercialization' of Protected Areas[1] Threaten Their Conservation Goals?

Derek de la Harpe

with

Peter Fearnhead
George Hughes
Richard Davies
Anna Spenceley
Jonathan Barnes
Jenny Cooper
Brian Child

INTRODUCTION

Although this book has discussed the performance of parks and particularly their economic relationships with their stakeholders, the bottom line is that parks will only survive if they are financially viable. Consequently, commercialization is probably the single most important practical issue facing the management of protected areas in Africa today. Not only Africa faces these challenges. The US National Park Service is also underfunded and some authors (Leal and Lipke Fretwell, 1997) have argued that commercialization is needed even in an affluent country such as the US; certainly Reed (2002) has argued that the more commercialized state park agencies are outperforming budget-funded federal park agencies.

WHAT IS 'COMMERCIALIZATION'?

'Commercialization' is a catch-all term covering a range of measures being adopted by government agencies attempting to improve the flow of finances to, and within, their organizations. In essence, commercialization involves adopting management practices that are more closely related to those used by private-sector commercial organizations (hence the term). Implemented properly, this involves addressing both revenue and expenditure aspects. However, as we shall see, the focus is usually on the income aspects, with expenditure being neglected. In addition, proper commercialization concerns performance management and the structures and systems within these organizations.

WHY COMMERCIALIZE?

Across Africa, state funding to manage and conserve protected areas is inadequate (Martin, 2002). To some extent this has always been the case. However, the situation has been exacerbated in most post-independence countries as priorities have changed and as new governments have focused their available resources on what they consider to be higher priorities.

This underfunding of national park agencies is now probably the single most important threat to the conservation of the areas under their control. (And, unlike other threats to biodiversity such as climate change, alien species, etc, lack of funding is easier to reverse and results will visible in a shorter time frame.) Yet this is happening in an environment where the private sector has demonstrated that management of protected areas, or at least the conservation of large mammals, is commercially profitable.

There is a wide range of factors giving rise to these funding crises. Some of the more important are briefly discussed below.

The steady increase in the size of budget deficits incurred by many governments creates a crisis. This forces expenditure cutbacks or restraint, and most government functions suffer. At the same time, these governments are forced to prioritize and allocate funding. In many countries, conservation and national parks are (incorrectly, given their economic potential) considered low priorities when compared with health, education, defence and other needs. (This accords with the contention in Chapter 9 that parks do not reflect the priorities of transitional societies where economic growth and jobs are more important than outdoor recreation and intangible conservation goods and services.) Budgets are thus withdrawn or even eliminated accordingly. The 'structural adjustment' programmes being pursued by many governments have forced a number to 'downsize' state structures, and several governments have attempted to unburden themselves by offloading park agencies. Park and wildlife agencies are often disproportionately affected. In Zambia, for example, the proportion of national budget allocated to wildlife fell from 0.29 per cent in 1966 to 0.10 per cent in 2002 (ZAWA, 2002).

The loss or reduction in state funding is often exacerbated by inefficient capture of revenues by the protected-area agency. A primary cause of this is the complete loss of these revenues to the state's central treasury. Namibia is an example where park authorities get no funds from tourism and consequently discourage it. This inefficient capture of revenues is sometimes also a result of poor pricing and allocation mechanisms, with parks deriving less for their services than the market would provide. In some cases, such as the subsidization of tourism in Zimbabwe and South Africa, this has in the past pandered to a political elite. In other cases, such as the allocation of hunting and tourism concessions in Zambia (Gibson, 1999), it has been a result of corruption and patronage. In yet more cases, it is simply that government officials do not know the value of their products and services and how to position them so that this value is captured. Even the otherwise effective Zimbabwean Department of National Parks and Wild Life Management (DNPWLM) took more than 15 years to learn how to sell hunting (Figure 8.1), albeit also having to undo the public perception that the public had the right to benefit from wildlife at discounted prices.

Many African conservation agencies have for some time been supported through funding by a range of donors. This has two major disadvantages. First, it is a risky strategy because these donors' priorities change, they experience their own budget crises, they close programmes at the end of relatively short funding cycles, or they simply develop 'donor fatigue' and their funding is lost. Second, the donor process itself has many faults. Primarily, the wildlife agency is subjected to the personal preferences and value-judgements of the donor. Funding is often directed to fashionable areas rather than to core business (eg law enforcement). Donors are also cumbersome and bureaucratic. They cannot respond quickly to opportunities and are seldom allowed to be innovative. Most importantly, the project cycle is fundamentally flawed, often pumping in too

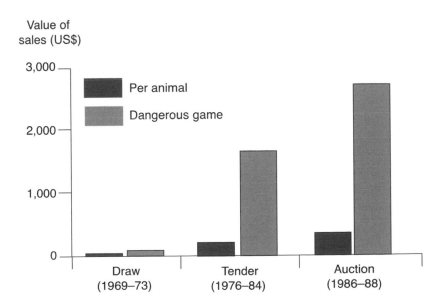

Figure 8.1 *Sale of hunting in Zimbabwe*

much money before the agency can absorb it, and then withdrawing as capacity improves. For all these reasons, reliance on donor funding is not a sustainable funding solution;

Finally, the agencies' funding crises are in many instances compounded by inefficiency and waste in the manner in which their available funds are expended. Inefficiency is a common problem: for instance, agencies that employ too many people leaving insufficient funds for implementation, or where salaries are so low that staff are constantly travelling to get allowances. Petty corruption, the retention of non-performing staff, and excessively slow purchasing are also results of poorly designed systems. Probably more serious are the effectiveness problems. These result, among other reasons, because many agencies have such a wide mandate that they focus on everything while achieving little. The net result is that wildlife agencies get less 'bang for their bucks'.

BOX 8.1
PARASTATALS AND COMMERCIALIZATION

A further cause of the rise in importance of commercialization in conservation has been the increasing number of park agencies that have been converted into parastatals. As we have seen from Chapter 6, well over half of the sub-continent's park agencies have now become parastatals. There have been several motivations for these changes:

- Management believe[2] that this will give them greater independence from central government and thus:
  - reduce bureaucracy and improve efficiency;
  - allow greater flexibility in recruitment and dismissal of staff;
  - reduce political interference in the operations of the agency and thus its use as an instrument of patronage (Gibson, 1999).
- It is also believed that parastatals have more credibility with the donor community and that this conversion will result in improved donor support to the agency.
- Most importantly, agencies have made this change in order to free themselves of the constraints associated with remaining within the government financial and accounting systems. They wish to retain all funds generated within the protected areas, instead of losing them all to central treasury, and they also want to free themselves from the government budgeting and expenditure systems. Usually, the 'price' of this conversion is that government stipulates there will be no further state funding for the new parastatal.

Zimbabwe's Department of National Parks and Wild Life Management, now the Parks and Wildlife Management Authority (PWMA), is an excellent example of a transition made with these motivations, but with the result that financial self-sufficiency is now required.

The primary justifications for parks are economic, in the broadest sense of this word, in that they are common-pool resources that provide societal rather than individual benefit. On this basis, many authors (eg Dixon and Sherman, 1990) present convincing arguments for ongoing state and other funding of protected-area systems. Although we concur with these arguments, we also recognize that this stance is largely academic and that, rightly or wrongly, most parks in Africa will only survive if they pay their own way. Moreover, we are increasingly unconvinced by the argument that commercialization, properly managed, despoils parks. Indeed, at a recent meeting[3] it was concluded that 'the trade-offs between biodiversity and socio-economic values are currently exaggerated and the synergies underestimated'. North West Parks, a provincial park agency in South Africa, has for more than a decade taken the view that parks are common property regimes that first and foremost should serve the needs of their constituent society, albeit with a proviso that ecological management should be sustainable (Davies, 2000). In reversing the normal set of priorities, they have shown that converting parks into engines of economic growth creates the welcome by-product of biodiversity conservation.

At this point, it should also be recognized that there is sometimes a further motivation for measures to increase funding. Most national park agencies realize that the long-term survival of their protected areas is contingent upon the ongoing support of local communities, especially those sharing common boundaries with the protected area, or who have historically been evicted from the area. This being the case, such agencies have been pursuing measures to increase the flow of benefits from protected areas to their constituent local communities, generally through provision of employment and through sourcing other goods and services

Box 8.2
ECONOMIC VERSUS FINANCIAL SELF-SUFFICIENCY?

It is important to recognize that economic and financial self-sufficiency are very different measures. Financial self-sufficiency is concerned with the level of the individual or agency and occurs when the organization is able to fulfil its mandate (in this case, to manage its protected area/s) with the funds available to it. Economic self-sufficiency is measured at the level of society and occurs when the impact of economic outputs from the protected area/s meet or exceed the costs of the full range of inputs. The arguments in favour of state funding of protected areas revolve largely around the economic (in the widest sense of the term) impacts of these areas. There is convincing evidence that state funding of protected-area networks is justified in economic terms, and there is a strong argument that it is thus not necessary to do so in financial terms. Unfortunately, this argument is academic as few regional governments allocate funding according to economic cost–benefit priorities: if the government cannot or will not provide the necessary funding, then the management agency may be compelled to strive for financial self-sufficiency. This chapter focuses on the tools and experiences that contribute to such sustainability.

in the local economy. Some protected areas have also facilitated access to sites of traditional importance. Others have allowed local communities to harvest resources such as thatching grass and plants needed in traditional medicine. However, the reality is that the greatest demand from these communities is for funding of various kinds. This creates additional demands on the financing of the protected-area system.[4] Such demands could undermine the financial sustainability of the park.

Faced with these situations, these agencies are being forced to adopt a range of measures that will increase the availability of funding to enable them to continue operating. The largest and most popular (and misunderstood) group of such measures is that falling under the commercialization banner.

HOW DOES COMMERCIALIZATION OCCUR?

Every agency has its own understanding and definition of what commercialization entails. Most commonly, this takes the form of the agency wanting to take on and conduct its own business ventures such as provision of accommodation, restaurants, curio shops, etc. Some have even started up their own safari hunting operations. This occurs in the belief that the private sector has been able to profitably conduct these businesses and that these profits should be applied to conservation. Africa is littered with initiatives such as the Tanzania Wildlife Investment Company (TAWICO) and Madagascar's Association Nationale pour la Gestion des Aires Protegees (ANGAP). The two main state conservation agencies in South Africa (the National Parks Board and the Natal Parks Board, now KZN Wildlife) have also been prominent in their commercialization efforts and it is interesting that the focus of both organizations (who have arguably been the most successful proponents in Africa so far) has changed substantially (see the case studies at the end of the chapter for further details).

At the other end of the scale, agencies have interpreted commercialization as merely meaning that they will ensure all revenues due are maximized through use of appropriate pricing and allocation mechanisms. In such situations, the state has recognized that the private sector is usually best placed to conduct businesses in protected areas and that the state's role is merely to 'tax' the use of these resources. Zambia is an example where all tourism operations in parks, and hunting in game management areas, have been sold to the private sector. The community-based natural resource management (CBNRM) movement has been at the forefront of the realization that the most profitable arrangements are landholder/private sector joint ventures such as those pioneered in Botswana, Namibia and Zimbabwe. The rule of thumb is to capture 33 per cent and 10 per cent of hunting and tourism turnover, respectively. In all three countries, communities have proved able to earn more money than state agencies, often from inferior resources.

The reality is that proper commercialization requires changes that are more fundamental and radical than is usually appreciated. At the lowest levels, it requires shifting from the public service mentality of providing all things to all people, regardless of cost, to carefully defining and compartmentalizing activities, focusing on those that add value and abandoning or reducing those that do not. Having defined objectives more tightly, at the second level agencies often need to be restructured around these functions. This requires the difficult task of throwing out historical precedents and norms, and redefining the agency's culture and purpose. It also requires the setting up of more rigorous management systems, be these for staff management, financial control, performance management or for the sale, outsourcing or management of commercial activities.

A further critical aspect of commercialization is frequently overlooked: one of the essential differences between most state agencies and the private sector is poor cost control by the former. The private sector is usually innovative in the methods and mechanisms that it employs to control or reduce operating costs. With the discipline of the bottom line, and the pressures of merciless competition, survival requires constant monitoring of efficiency and the ruthless elimination of activities that are not adding value. These firms are, in a way, undergoing rapid evolution in the competitive business jungle, where only the fittest survive. In its pursuit of commercialization there are many methods, already developed, that the state could adopt.

Public, budget-funded agencies are not subject to these disciplines and are poor at setting priorities and directing their limited funding to these. The common budget cut is an important example of this. In situations where funding is inadequate state agencies commonly pro-rate available funds across the full range of activities. This results in all activities affected being underfunded and therefore undermanaged.

WHAT ARE THE ISSUES ASSOCIATED WITH COMMERCIALIZATION?

There is a wide range of issues associated with commercialization of any state organization, and then fewer related specifically to conservation agencies.

Most importantly, there is the question of whether commercialization should occur at all. Many commentators have argued that conservation is such a priority that it should be funded by the state and that commercialization is potentially even a threat to conservation. The counter-point is that where park agencies have run out of money, parks have suffered badly. The massive elephant and rhino poaching that swept Africa in the 1980s is but one example, with others being settlement within 'paper parks', failure to deal with excess wildlife populations, deteriorating infrastructure, and the demoralization and loss of quality staff. On the other hand, where commercialization has occurred, the state of conservation is generally better. Despite their many problems, park parastatals have improved park management (Chapter 6), and wildlife populations are often higher near lodges than in so-called undeveloped wilderness areas. Thus, we subscribe not only to the view that commercialization is very much the lesser of two evils, but that commercialization is actually good for conservation and probably essential to its survival in transitional economies.

A further argument against commercialization of protected areas arises out of fear that it will result in increased, unsustainable levels of use (of whatever kind) of resources. Simplistically, some fear that commercialization automatically implies

Box 8.3
SELF-SUFFICIENCY: AT THE LEVEL OF INDIVIDUAL PROTECTED AREAS, OR OF THE PROTECTED AREA NETWORK AS A WHOLE?

It is frequently asked whether the self-sufficiency goal should apply for the protected-area system as a whole, or at the level of each individual area. This question arises because of the reality that some areas lack commercially exploitable resources and will thus be unable to generate adequate income to cover the costs of management and conservation. Other areas may become 'cash cows' that can be relied upon to generate surplus funding for allocation to less commercial areas that are nonetheless important from a conservation perspective.

It is necessary to recognize these realities. It is also important that the management of the more commercial areas do not lose the incentive to maximize revenues, through loss of these surpluses to the wider system. The ideal situation is one where suitable incentives exist to maximize revenues and minimize costs at the level of each individual area, but where it is possible for surpluses to be re-allocated to those other areas which are not capable of achieving self-sufficiency.

It should be noted that this situation is further complicated where there are different protected-area management authorities within the country. For example, Tanzania has the Tanzania National Park Authority (TANAPA), as well as the Wildlife Division. In South Africa, there is South Africa National Parks as well as the provincial authorities.

higher levels of usage and is thus undesirable. There are undoubtedly situations (such as Victoria Falls in Zimbabwe) where higher levels of use will result in overused resources and thus the degradation of the protected area. However, there are also many protected areas in Africa (for example, Zimbabwe's Gonarezhou National Park) that are underused and could sustain substantially increased levels of use (consumptive and non-consumptive). In these situations the argument does not hold water. More importantly, commercialization does not necessarily imply higher levels of use: it could just as easily mean securing higher (market-related) prices for the services and goods supplied by the area, while sustaining (or even reducing, perhaps using price as a rationing measure) existing levels of use.

The next most important question is who should conduct the commercial activities? There is a tendency for the agency to want to conduct these activities itself. However, this approach has many shortcomings.[5]

State agencies are generally not good at commercial business, a fact that is driving outsourcing and privatization of public functions worldwide. These agencies are not geared to the risks and rapid response times necessary in business; they tend to govern rather than service people; park agencies, with strong biological capacity, usually lack the managerial, financial and commercial skills, resources and mindsets needed to make businesses successful. Indeed, most of the efforts have resulted in the state generating less income and even incurring losses. For instance: none of the businesses managed by the Luangwa Integrated Resource Development Project (LIRDP) made money; accommodation in Kruger, Hwange and Etosha needed to be subsidized; and the private and community sector consistently outperform the state sector even in relatively simple commercial activities such as the sale of hunting and tourism.

Conduct of business by state agencies results in public funding being put at risk in these ventures. This is inappropriate, especially considering the weaknesses listed above. In addition, measures to protect public finance (eg purchasing and financial procedures) are often the very measures that prevent state agencies from operating with the necessary flexibility and speed.

One of the most important lessons learned by the private sector during the 1980s and 1990s is that it is essential for an organization to focus on its core businesses and avoid pursuing other businesses in which it does not have the necessary competencies. As Drucker (1973) points out, it is the inability to focus on core competency that bedevils the performance of public agencies. Learning from this, state agencies should focus on their core business, which is management and conservation of the protected area/s, and avoid pursuit of other aspects.

Perhaps more importantly, it puts the state in the invidious position of being both a regulator and a major participant in the industry concerned. This conflict of interest has proven difficult to manage and – particularly where the state imposes more rigorous conditions on private and community participants in the industry than it does on itself – also results in the state losing credibility among its stakeholders. A common example is the requirement for communities to have detailed land-use plans before they can begin wildlife management, when few parks have management plans to the same standard.

The fact that the state is competing with its stakeholders – often from a position of unfair advantage – also creates resentment and undermines the competing businesses. Instead of facilitating the development of private and community conservation areas, an important objective of many national conservation agencies, state agencies often see these as a threat. This is unfortunate, as it is these competing businesses that will eventually (when the allocation and pricing issues have been resolved) help to secure financial self-sufficiency. Indeed, there appears to be a correlation between the financial viability of wildlife agencies and the strength of the private sector, although this is confounded by a similar correlation between the performance of wildlife agencies and the strength, modernity and liberalization of the economies in which they are found. Although as a rule this correlation between park commercialization and the emergence of a vibrant wildlife industry is positive, there are challenges. For instance, the Zambian Wildlife Authority (ZAWA), having been partly released from the grip of government and patronage relationships, is rapidly developing a more commercial outlook, including the outsourcing of parks and the encouragement of community and private game ranches. Nevertheless, the agency has been prematurely denied public funding and to survive it is intending to extract half of the revenues from hunting business in the very community programmes it is promoting. This illustrates the dangers of imposing a requirement for financial self-sufficiency too quickly on an agency with so much power.

Especially in the early stage of experimentation there have been several unhappy experiences where contracting or leasing to the private sector has not had the desired results. The revenues have not met expectations and the state has experienced difficulty in regulating the contractor's or lessee's activities. These experiences have been quoted as reasons for not contracting to the private sector.

LESSONS LEARNED

Within southern Africa there has been a remarkable amount of experimentation with various aspects of commercialization. Having discussed the structure and accountability of park organizations in Chapter 6, we summarize here some of the key lessons relating to the income component of commercialization, namely, the earning of money.

Current low levels of funding to protected-area management agencies is probably the single most important threat to biodiversity conservation in these areas. And if these parks are unable to satisfy their ecological goals, as a result of this underfunding, then it is most unlikely that they will satisfy any social goals. If the levels of funding are to reach viable levels, commercialization is essential. This is the case virtually across Africa. There simply is no viable, practical and sustainable alternative. There are undoubtedly potential pitfalls associated with commercialization, but these risks are far outweighed by those associated with underfunding of these areas.

This being the case, the only real question is how should the commercialization be implemented and by whom? Most importantly, what should be the state's role in the commercialization process?

The state should restrict its role to that of land manager and independent regulator, and there are possibly even situations where the functions could be privatized (there have been rare exceptions to this). The state should not attempt to run the commercial businesses itself but should restrict its role to that of creating the enabling environment. The desired increased revenues should be attained through applying transparent market-related pricing and allocation mechanisms, instead of the opaque 'command'-type mechanisms that are currently in place in so many countries. In other words, the state should achieve its revenue goals through 'leasing' its resources to the private sector, instead of trying to conduct the businesses itself.

The mechanisms by which the various activities are contracted to the private sector are important and often product specific. Mechanisms range from: auctions suited to tightly defined products (eg a hunting quota); to tenders that are more flexible but less transparent and useful for selling or buying reasonably well-defined products; to individual negotiation, which creates flexibility for innovation but also scope for corruption. Where we select marketing mechanisms along the two axes of flexibility and transparency depends to a large extent on the nature of the agency. Public agencies often sacrifice flexibility for transparency because they are prone to accusations of corruption, whereas the private sector or even a well-organized and internally accountable local community have more internal integrity and would favour flexibility. The allocation process should identify the

BOX 8.4
THE IMPORTANCE OF GOVERNANCE IN THE
COMMERCIALIZATION PROCESS

Poor governance pervades many governmental and quasi-governmental agencies in Africa. This is manifested mainly in two forms, simple incompetence and more sinister corruption. Sometimes it exists in both forms, creating a 'double-whammy'.

This is an enormous subject and well beyond the scope of this chapter (in fact, even of this book). For this discussion, it should merely be recognized that poor governance results in the following hindrances to commercialization:

- Revenues are lost through poor pricing mechanisms, failure to manage contracts or collect gate revenues, as well as outright fraud.
- Costs are increased through inefficient procurement practices. This is frequently exacerbated through corrupt practices.
- Poor identification of priorities, with the result that available funding is dissipated across too wide a range of activities, including those that should be accorded low priority.

It is important to note that the opportunities for corruption – as well as the consequences of poor governance – are exacerbated when an agency embarks upon a commercialization programme.

Because of the foregoing, it will be appreciated that poor governance will be an insurmountable barrier to commercialization of any agency. This being the case, strengthened, transparent and accountable institutions are prerequisites for a successful process. This is difficult to achieve at the level of a single agency, when poor governance is widespread in the government. Recognition of this fact is sometimes an argument for creating some institutional separation between the agency and its supervising government structures.

'appropriate'[6] concessionaires, and pricing of the contract should be market based. Beyond this, it is essential that the contract entered into provides for monitoring and performance evaluation and that there are measures for remedial action (including termination) in the event that the concessionaire does not meet the targets set. At the same time, the agency must beware of the dangers of over-regulation and the imposition of non-tax disincentives.

There are still situations in Africa (Malawi and, until recently, Zimbabwe) where all revenues generated in the protected-area system revert to a central state revenue fund. The agency then obtains its funding through budget requests to the finance ministry. This situation is only defensible where the funding given to the agency is adequate. The authors are not aware of any situation where this applies. This being the case, commercialization is obviously required but this cannot work where park managers' efforts and innovations are captured by the central revenue fund with no correlation to funding allocations. This means that control of revenues generated is essential to any commercialization process.

The state's conduct should become more businesslike in both revenue and expenditure respects. Revenues generated should be market related and all revenues due must be captured (as discussed above). At the same time, allocation of funding must be to strategic priorities. Funding should be expended in an efficient manner, such that waste and inefficiency are minimized. This requires the implementation of private-sector-style financial and performance management systems.

There will be situations where commercialization involves increased volumes of throughput or extraction (more tourists, more hunters, etc). Risks exist if conservation of these areas requires that levels of extraction or use be limited (or even reduced). These risks are most pronounced where low-value bulk commodities such as mass tourism or meat are being produced and sold. High-value 'goods' such as trophy hunting and up-market tourism tend to be self-controlling and the risks are lower where these are the main products of a park. These risks are best managed through conventional (but under-used) park management and monitoring systems. Park plans should set goals and related performance measures. Use of adaptive management and 'acceptable limits to change' should identify where levels of use result in unacceptable changes and the need to limit further use.

Finally – and perhaps most importantly – it should be recognized that 'proper' commercialization requires skills, resources and managerial cultures that are in short supply in most government agencies, including those involved in conservation in southern Africa. Developing skills in the technical aspects of the agency's mandate is relatively easy and too often the focus of training and institutional development investments. Creating organizational change is far more difficult, especially in the face of interests vested in keeping things the same. The basic technical skills of developing and controlling work plans, budgets and performance in general are, in situations of change, more urgent than technical skills. This will usually lead to the bigger task of re-engineering the organization. However, the biggest challenge of all is cultural: changing the 'mindsets' of the agency staff involved. Currently, many see their roles as being to protect their areas from development and commercialization, and the private sector as untrustworthy. Many also consider themselves as authorities rather than service and value providers. Interestingly, the weaker the organization, the more it tries to grasp all functions and powers to itself and, to paraphrase the words of Marshall Murphree (personal communication), exerts its braking power rather than using its facilitating (or accelerating) influence. Countries where wildlife officials perceive their roles as facilitating and monitoring development, and harness the power of the private sector as a trusted and essential partner in the process, are likely to be the countries where the wildlife sector contributes to the economy and job creation. This will not be done by weak or failing wildlife agencies. Only strong agencies have the confidence to step back and facilitate others to make conservation work. We have seen the power of the private and even the community sector to manage conservation profitably. Yet only the public sector can unlock this potential. Thus, creating managerially strong and wise wildlife agencies is the most important challenge of all.

CASE STUDY 8.1
COMMERCIALIZATION OF
SOUTH AFRICAN NATIONAL PARKS

Peter Fearnhead

Background

Over the past century SANParks grew into one of the three largest players in South Africa's tourism industry and its largest in ecotourism or nature-based tourism. However, this was not without negative consequences. Generally speaking, the state does not have the skills, attitudes and incentives that drive successful businesses. SANParks was no exception. Some of the negative consequences included the inefficient delivery of tourism products with mediocre service standards, limited market segmentation and product differentiation; and prices that had not been determined by market forces. This has been compounded by other inefficient corporate policies and procedures, all resulting over the decades in significant opportunity cost to biodiversity conservation.

In 1999, SANParks performed an internal review of its commercial operations. This demonstrated many inadequacies in its own operations when benchmarked against similar private operations. Guided by basic economic theory that the state should be responsible for performing regulatory functions and only intervene where there is market failure, SANParks took a strategic decision to refocus its energies and resources on its core business of managing biodiversity in protected areas. Henceforth it would only provide the foundation and regulatory framework for tourism and recreation — not actually manage any commercial operations. Consequently, the management of commercial operations or aspects of commercial operations in national parks has, over time and in a responsible manner, been transferred to commercial operators who are better qualified and equipped to run these facilities. Such a fundamental shift was considered heresy by many and would not have been possible without the leadership of a chief executive who was able to see beyond the commonly accepted state-dominated model of conservation and tourism. Nonetheless, a 'cold-turkey' withdrawal from all tourism services was considered too risky for SANParks, from financial and socio-political perspectives, and so a phased approach to commercialization was adopted.

Broadly speaking, the first phase of the commercialization strategy had three components:

1 The concessioning of existing small camps in the Kruger National Park together with several new concession sites in Kruger and other national parks.
2 Outsourcing all retail and restaurant facilities in the larger rest camps in all national parks.

Case Study 8.1 *continued*

3   Outsourcing services associated with the delivery of tourism products in
     the large rest camps, eg house-keeping, garden services, laundry, security.

Results So Far of the Commercialization Strategy

A total of ten lodge concessions have been awarded to private operators, seven of
which are in the Kruger National Park, two in the Addo Elephant National Park,
and two in the Cape Peninsula National Park. In addition, an agreement has been
entered into for a private company to manage the one hotel that SANParks has in
its portfolio — the Brandwag Hotel in the Golden Gate Highlands National Park.

A typical concession allows the private operator to construct and operate
tourist facilities within the national park on the basis of a 20-year contract.
Investors have either taken over or are upgrading specified existing lodge
facilities, or they are in the process of building new ones. The contractual mechanism is a concession contract. This enables the concessionaire to use a defined
area of land, plus any buildings that may already exist on that land, in return for
payment of concession fees. Against these rights of occupation and commercial
use of the facilities, there is a set of obligations on the part of the concessionaire.
These include financial terms, environmental management, social objectives,
empowerment and other factors. Infringement of any of these requirements
carries specified penalties, underpinned by performance bonds and finally termination of the contract, with the immovable assets reverting to SANParks.

Successful construction of the ten new game lodges, with a total capacity of
383 guest beds, will result in a capital investment of R216 million in SANParks.
Under the terms of the concession contract and bidding system, it is relatively
easy to quantify the financial benefits to SANParks from the ten sites successfully tendered for. SANParks can depend, with a high degree of certainty, on a
guaranteed minimum stream of income over the concession period. This stream
amounts to 65 per cent of the actual payments of fees projected by bidders.
Starting with the guaranteed income, the Net Present Value (at a 5 per cent real
discount rate) of this stream amounts to R214 million, in constant 2000 rands.
The undiscounted, uninflated equivalent of this amount is R366 million. The
total amount forecast to be paid to SANParks (undiscounted and uninflated) over
the 20-year period is R573 million. This represents a major contribution to the
future finances of the organization. Similarly, it is estimated that – at maturity –
tax receipts will be in excess of R50 million per annum. This is equivalent to the
current state subsidy to SANParks. So far, six of the ten concessions are operational, with the remaining four still completing construction.

The primary aim of commercialization was to generate additional revenue for
SANParks. However, the process was also designed to encourage partnerships
that exhibit the correct mix of financial strength, requisite business experience and
empowerment. South Africa's history has been such that whites have been the

Case Study 8.1 *continued*

major users and enjoyers of the national park system. To encourage a constituency for conservation and support for national parks among most South African citizens, their empowerment is vital. The goal was to forge meaningful and sustainable long-term business relationships between private operators and historically disadvantaged entrepreneurs living in the locality of the parks.

Tender submissions had to include plans for tangible, quantifiable benefits to historically disadvantaged individuals and communities throughout the life of the concession. If there is a shortfall in performance in relation to accepted tender proposals, penalties of up to R1 million may be imposed and, if continual material breaches occur, the concession contract can be terminated.

All the concessions have significant percentages of black shareholding and at least two are majority black owned. This is considered an excellent result in a tourism sub-sector (game lodges) in which black ownership has hitherto been virtually non-existent. In total, the ten game lodges are projected to create 683 new direct permanent jobs, excluding employment created during the construction phase or through the multiplier effect. Bidders had to propose detailed schemes for affirmative action, undertaking to fill specified positions within an agreed timetable. In general, concessionaires have undertaken that a minimum of 79 per cent of their employees will be recruited from historically disadvantaged communities, most of which will be those living adjacent to national parks. Finally, concessionaires have undertaken to outsource minimum guaranteed rand amounts of contracts with local historically disadvantaged business people for the supply of various services. The total of these commitments is R6.3 million per annum by the third and following years.

Commercialization of the 28 shops and retail outlets and 16 restaurants was successfully concluded in August 2001. Although the process was managed successfully, the transition has been slower than anticipated and SANParks has to manage the quality of goods and services offered by a few operators. However, a recent external financial review by PricewaterhouseCoopers has shown that whereas the maximum net benefit to SANParks before commercializing the facilities was between R8 million and R13 million per annum, depending on year of comparison, the direct impact on the organization from increased turnover-related rentals and various cost savings is a minimum of R21 million per annum. This does not include the fact that the outsourced facilities are being upgraded at the operator's expense and other reverse multiplier effects on the organization's cost base.

Conclusion

These data confirm that, overall, the commercialization process will be a major success for SANParks. Needless to say, there are likely to be a few casualties among the concessionaires. But the market mechanism has been set in motion

Case Study 8.1 *continued*

and, most importantly, no public monies have been placed at risk. This is an ongoing process and the third component of the commercialization strategy – outsourcing basic services associated with delivering the tourism product in the larger rest camps – is still to be implemented.

The challenges for the future will be to ensure that monitoring mechanisms are implemented as intended, to ensure that the environmental impacts of such facilities are minimized and mitigated, that empowerment obligations are fulfilled and that SANParks receives a greatly augmented income. Perhaps, however, the greatest benefit to have emerged from commercialization is that, for the first time, SANParks has opened itself to the scrutiny of third parties and is therefore accountable to the public for the way in which it manages the national parks under its control. Moreover, the environmental regulations that apply to commercial operators are more stringent than those that apply to tourist operations run by SANParks itself, and over the course of time, SANParks will be obliged to raise its standards in this regard. This can only be to the benefit of South Africa's national parks.

CASE STUDY
8.2 COMMERCIALIZATION OF THE FORMER NATAL PARKS BOARD

George Hughes

It is unlikely that the word commercialization had any meaning for the founders of the Natal Parks Board when it was established as a parastatal in 1947. They did create an opportunity to develop a commercial thrust over 40 years later but this was not intended at the time. The primary purpose of having an organization that was semi-independent, with its own governing board, was to free it from the bureaucratic controls of direct government and to make it independent of political influence.

There are few, if any, conservation agencies in Africa that have enjoyed such excellent financial support from its local treasury department, and such excellent political support from the ruling parties, as the Natal Parks Board (NPB). From its inception there was never a time, until 1994, that adequate funds were not granted in support of conservation. This included generous support for the purchase of new conservation areas plus, normally, a generous inflation of budget to cover the start-up costs and future management of the new park or responsibility. This enabled the gradual development of an agency that was comfortable in its position, dynamic in its approach to new acquisitions and activities and ultimately attracted high-quality managers and scientists who were proud to be associated with the organization.

The year 1994 proved to be momentous for South Africa, and one negative effect was a sharp decline in funding from the Province to all departments. The

Case Study 8.2 *continued*

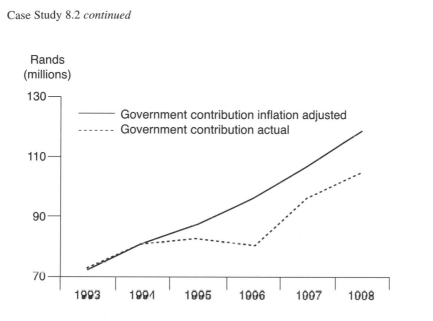

Figure 8.2 *NPB finance: declining government contributions*

board did not escape these budgets cuts, which continued until 1996 and then once again began to increase in line with inflation (Figure 8.2).

The History of Commercialization in Natal Parks Board

The first public facilities in parks in what is now KwaZulu-Natal were built in Hluhluwe Game Reserve in 1927. But it was not until 1950 that the NPB began to build camps, and a string of them followed: Hluhluwe, Umfolosi, Giants Castle, Thendele, Kamberg, etc. All were modest in size and simple in concept and structure. None were planned to make significant amounts of money but rather to provide cheap opportunities for people to visit and enjoy the parks. Over time modest little shops were also introduced. The welcoming attitude of the organization as well as the enthusiastic but non-entrepreneurial attitude of the early camp managers created a wonderful image of the Natal parks. This helped to maintain the flow of support from the Province and built a relationship with the then informed and privileged people of Natal who, to this day, remain fiercely loyal and protective of 'their' parks board.

The success of the early camps made the concept of earning money for itself widely accepted within NPB management and several dramatic developments took place over the next 20 years. During the early 1960s Midmar Dam was built and the first body to which the Province turned for development was the board. NPB recognized that Midmar would become a significant attraction for the

Case Study 8.2 *continued*

people of the region and a surprisingly large development ensued. This included dozens of chalets, a series of camping grounds, yacht and powerboat launching facilities, and for the first time a takeaway and restaurant as well as the opportunity for the private sector to participate by running specialized shops.

These were dramatic developments for a conservation agency and they attracted some comment (not all positive). The board then developed the idea of creating a separate Recreation Division within the organization. This new division's purpose was to earn significant amounts of money and create facilities on state dams and other sites that would draw the masses and theoretically spare the more important conservation parks from being overexploited and overused. It was a great idea.

The idea didn't work over the long term for several reasons. First, the vision anticipated a growing and enduring enthusiasm for water sports and activities based on sites like Midmar. This failed to transpire because by the 1980s there were changes in public taste with resulting declines in visitation. Second, when such sites were popular they were crowded to the point of discomfort and required massive staff support. These staff worked extremely hard during high days and holidays, but problems arose as a result of the fact that they were maintained as full-time permanent staff during the winters and during weeks of bad weather when there was virtually no patronage. The rising costs of these staff resulted in an ever-increasing demand to raise prices, and this was probably a contributing factor to the declines in visitor numbers over the ensuing years. These declines were sufficiently serious to convince the NPB to stop accepting the state dams for recreation areas and eventually saw the board withdrawing from several sites that it had served for up to 20 years. Eventually only Midmar, Chelmsford and Spioenkop Dams remained part of the system, and important lessons had been learned from these experiments.

While the so called 'recreation' developments were going ahead during the 1970s, it was noted that demand for accommodation in the conservation parks was growing and that serious refurbishments were required. Significant amounts of money were made available by the Province, and several camps were refurbished and enlarged but without the benefit of a business plan. As a result, NPB continued to experience the problem common to most, if not all, organizations with linkages to government, namely: the lack of recognition that all revenue-earning activities have to generate surplus revenues and that those surpluses have to be based on the real costs of building and running the facility. Despite this, the growth in gross income was favourably viewed by the Province and it continued to provide financial support, unaware that there were signs of problems within the organization. Not the least of which were strains between the Conservation and the Recreation Divisions, where the former was beginning to have fewer funds available while the latter appeared to be able to spend prolifically.

Case Study 8.2 *continued*

By the mid 1980s it had become clear that there would have to be revisions of attitude and strategy because it was equally clear that there were going to be genuine and dramatic changes in the political structure of South Africa. What is more, cognizance had to be taken of what was happening in the rest of Africa for the funding of conservation and protected areas. It appeared that virtually every state in Africa was slashing conservation budgets; therefore this was a risk that had to be taken into account in future planning.

The NPB Commercialization Strategies

The following strategies were established in recognition of these changes:

1. The Recreation Division was eliminated and all protected areas and field stations were consolidated under the Conservation Division. It was agreed that the purposes of every protected area were the same and that officers-in-charge were responsible for identical functions although the emphasis on certain functions may vary from area to area.
2. Biodiversity conservation in the Province had to become visible and relevant to every citizen (see Hughes (2002) for the development and actions taken to achieve this goal).
3. Finances had to be managed efficiently and according to generally accepted accounting practice (GAAP). This was fully supported by the board and the change to accrual accounting procedures took place over several years, reaching finality in 1993. Of course, in time this resulted in deficits appearing in the financial statements as modern accounting practice began to demand the bringing to account of future liabilities that would not have been recognized under 'normal' government accounting procedures. At the same time the board endorsed the principles of sound corporate governance as defined by the King Report (1994) and introduced audit and financial committees. This included, with the endorsement of the provincial auditor, the appointment of external auditors to the board. These changes took time and had far-reaching consequences, but they were essential to ensure the successful development of further commercial enterprises that would begin to make a significant contribution to the finances of the board.
4. All revenue-earning activities and facilities had to run on a genuine surplus (profit) basis. For the first time, in 1988, a business consultant was employed to review the individual facilities and services to ensure they were truly generating surpluses. It should be made clear that the exercise considered only the facility and not the park in which it was situated. In other words, it had no reason to doubt that the management of biodiversity assets and services was a task it carried out on behalf of the Province and that the board should be paid for that service. The survey indicated that the board was sub-

Case Study 8.2 *continued*

sidizing tourist facilities and services at a cost of a minimum of R600,000 per annum. This was considered unacceptable and a programme was instituted to review every facility and establish the real costs of providing that service or facility. Although this appears a simple and straightforward exercise it did not prove to be the case. The proper allocation of costs (especially staff) was not embraced with enthusiasm by many officers-in-charge, and it took years before the board was satisfied that each individual balance sheet was a true reflection of the situation on the ground. As clarity was obtained on each facility or service the following options were considered:

– Maintain the service or facility. Normally this decision was made because the service was already breaking even (or nearly so) or making a surplus. Business plans were then prepared to improve performance. This might require further investment, staff reductions, tariff adjustments, etc.

– Stop the service or close down the facility. This decision was made when there was such a large loss that recovery was considered impractical or undesirable.

– Abandon the area completely. The so-called 'recreation' parks suffered most from this decision and the board withdrew from Albert Falls, Vryheid and Hazelmere Dams, although some smaller conservation areas were also given up. Consideration was given to abandoning a significant number of small conservation areas but a review indicated that to make significant savings half the parks would have to be abandoned. It is noteworthy that some of the smaller biodiversity parks were found to be very important but also, because of their situation and rarity value, very expensive to run (Bourquin, 1996).

– Privatize the facility or service. One sensible result of this was the granting of concessions for the provision of catering facilities in camps. One of the most expensive experiments in the provision of a mass facility took place at Midmar over ten years. With the recorded decline in visitor use and the change of visitor values it was decided to establish a historical village adjacent to Midmar. The Province agreed to invest R750,000 per year for ten years to realize the project. Despite the enthusiasm for the project and its ultimate size, it did not achieve the success anticipated, and when the Province ceased its annual grant it was doomed. A concession was granted to a private company to manage and develop the village but after a short and difficult period the concessionaire became insolvent.

– Cease deliberate subsidies of biodiversity products. It had been general policy in order to create new populations, especially of large mammals, to either give away surplus animals (to other conservation bodies or community parks) or sell them at heavily subsidized prices (to private landowners). This policy was reviewed and it was decided to cease these practices; with few exceptions each of which would

Case Study 8.2 *continued*

require specific board approval. From 1989 the board started the annual Natal game auction (then in partnership with the Natal Game Ranchers Association) so as to allow the market to set prices. Gross income rose dramatically, especially that derived from white rhino (Figure 8.3), despite the fact that it was not necessary to increase the annual offtake of animals (Figure 8.4).

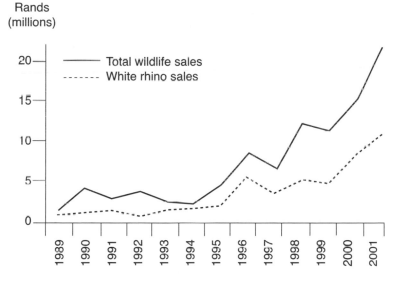

Figure 8.3 *Gross revenue from the Natal game auction (1989–2001)*

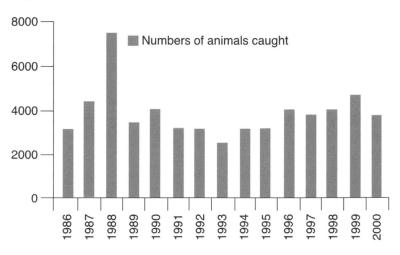

Figure 8.4 *Live large animal offtakes from Natal parks (1986–2000)*

Case Study 8.2 *continued*

- Introduce new revenue-earning activities. The introduction of hunting areas adjacent to existing parks or the re-zoning of former 'recreation' reserves that could tolerate more robust management activities such as hunting proved to be a lucrative and sensible move. (See Natal Parks Board Yearbooks for details.) The purchase of a large tour boat, the *Santa Lucia*, at St Lucia proved immensely successful (it repaid its R500,000 cost in 10 months), providing the private sector with an additional tourist attraction. The same can be said of the Centenary Game Capture Centre in the Hluhluwe-Imfolosi Park, which not only has on view the largest and most modern game capture centre in Africa but also a film auditorium, takeaway facility, a hugely successful curio market operated by the local Mpukonyoni community, and a exhibition centre designed to inform schoolchildren and visitors of the skills and expertise of southern African conservation agencies and the growing benefits of a policy of sustainable use. Funding for the Centenary Centre was obtained partly from the provincial treasury as a special grant (once again meeting its obligations to support items of a purely conservation nature (the pens and associated infrastructure)) and from donors wishing to be associated with the curio market, auditorium and exhibition centre. A similar strategy is being followed in the Ukhahlamba-Drakensberg Park, where a world-class exhibition on the wealth of rock art in the park is currently under construction.

5. Existing camps and camp grounds that had proved under evaluation to be genuinely profitable had to be expanded and upgraded to increase their financially viability. Any new camps had to be designed in accordance with market demands and to meet modern standards. To achieve this goal it was necessary to gain access to investment houses, and for the first time it was possible to overcome two major obstacles. First, until 1988 the Province would not sign as guarantor for the board in the event of it being able to borrow money, and to compound the problem the financial institutions would not consider a loan unless the Province signed as guarantor. This was an impossible situation that changed in 1988 when the Province authorized the board to borrow money (but on its own recognisance). The financial institutions, after studying the policies and cash flows, decided that the risk of lending money was tolerable. Since then, the board has borrowed R90 million to upgrade older camps and to develop new facilities. More recently, it has used as security cash flows from certain now successful camps. The practice is now well established and the substantial increase in gross revenues has justified the policy decision (see Figure 8.5).

Case Study 8.2 *continued*

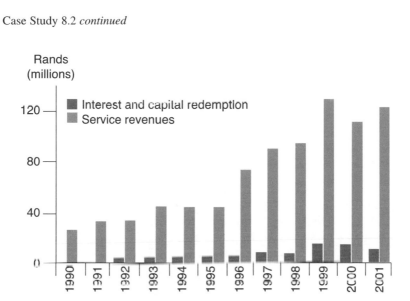

Figure 8.5 *Gross revenues and loan payments in KZN wildlife*

6. Increase donor participation. There were two legs to this strategy:
   – A joint venture scheme was created. This encouraged private individuals and corporate entities to purchase overnight facilities at a little more than cost in return for a defined number of free nights in the facility, the ability to 'swap' some of the nights allocated and the privilege of booking earlier than non-donors. Over R6.5 million was raised through this programme and it resulted in new up-market camping sites, chalets and bush lodges, all of which were marketed to the general public for the bulk of the year without NPB having to incur the capital cost of the unit. This proved to be a satisfactory arrangement for the donors and there have been several repeat investments.
   – The Natal Parks Board Conservation Trust was also created. This trust was established as an independent entity registered, appropriately, with the state and served by an independent board of trustees. Its primary purpose is to grow a capital fund from which interest may be earned and given to the formal conservation authority in the Province, originally, of course, the NPB. More recently, it has changed its name to the KZN Conservation Trust. It also raises funds to help with specific projects in protected areas. It has proved to be successful, and in its 14-year lifespan has built a capital fund of over R20 million (Figure 8.6) and made grants to conservation of

Case Study 8.2 *continued*

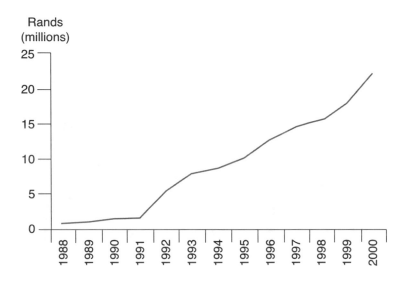

Figure 8.6 *Accumulated capital fund of the Conservation Trust (1988–2000)*

more than R7 million, to be used at the agency's discretion. It currently gives R1 million per year, a sum that would thrill many African conservation agencies.

Of course, over the years staff of the NPB and more recently KZN Wildlife have become far more active and astute in raising funds from outside sources, and significant sums have been injected into research and management.

Conclusion

It is worth reiterating that it was always NPB policy, in the final 10 years of its 50-year existence, that its commercialization programme should never replace the grant paid by the treasury each year. Instead, it was intended that surplus funds would enable the organization to do considerably more for conservation and the well-being of the people of the region. Although it was never formalized, the covenant that applied was that the board would earn R1 for every R1 paid by the Province. In the final year of its existence the board was fast progressing towards its target, earning R90 million in gross revenues compared with the grant of R110 million.

Case Study 8.2 *continued*

Entering into a commercialization programme based on proper accounting structures, sound business plans and thorough research (the board had its own resource economists and an excellent team of planners) had the following advantages:

1. It resulted in a genuine increase in additional revenues.
2. It encouraged the employment of a broader range of professional staff: hoteliers, economists, chartered accountants, etc.
3. It broadened the horizons of all staff and improved their attitudes to both customers and clients.
4. It resulted in a greater respect for the private sector as entities in their own right as well as potential partners in joint ventures.
5. It provided skills and understanding that enabled staff to better understand and negotiate with private concessionaires and visitors.
6. It greatly enhanced the image of the organization at local, national and international levels in several fields, as demonstrated by several awards.

Finally, perhaps the ultimate benefit is yet to come. There is always the risk that changes of government and political office bearers will change the excellent relationship that has always been enjoyed by conservation in Natal (and now KwaZulu-Natal) and its political patrons and thus the KZN treasury.

Perhaps KZN will follow the distressing trends seen in much of the Third World and if this does happen, which I optimistically believe it will not, no conservation body will be better prepared to survive than the parastatal that owes its existence to the skills and commitment of the staff of the NPB and the many board members who served it at no cost to the taxpayer for a period of 50 years.

References

Anon (1948–1998) *Annual Reports of the Natal Parks Board*, Pietermaritzburg

Anon (1982–1998) *The Natal Parks Board Yearbooks*, Pietermaritzburg

Anon (1988–1998) *The Policies of the Natal Parks Board*, Pietermaritzburg

Bourquin, O (1996) *The Value of Proclaimed Reserves in KwaZulu-Natal*, Natal Parks Board, Pietermaritzburg

Hughes, G R (2002) 'Democratisation: biodiversity conservation for all people – a case study from KwaZulu-Natal' in S M Pierce, R M Cowling, T Sandwith and K MacKinnon (eds) *Mainstreaming Biodiversity in Development, Case studies from South Africa*, The World Bank Environment Dept. Biodiversity Series

The King Report on Corporate Governance (1994) The Institute of Directors, Johannesburg

CASE STUDY 8.3
MADIKWE GAME RESERVE

Richard Davies

Madikwe Game Reserve covers 58,000 hectares in South Africa and incorporates game viewing including elephant, lion, leopard, black and white rhino, buffalo, wild dog, cheetah and over 18 large antelope species. The reserve was established purely on socio-economic grounds, after feasibility studies established that this would be the 'best' form of land use for the area. With this as the point of departure, it was decided to structure the reserve in the most efficient way possible. Several financial and economic models were developed to find the best approach. From this process it was identified that the state would supply the basic conservation infrastructure, including land, game, fences and support infrastructure for conservation services (dams, offices, workshops, etc) and that the private sector would supply the tourism infrastructure.

From the initial planning the state committed approximately US$2.7 million to fencing, game and other support infrastructure. Land is excluded from this and was estimated to cost approximately US$4 million. Most of this expenditure was in the early years (one to five) of the project. In addition, a further US$3.5 million has been spent on operating costs in the first ten years of operation. The project broke even (on operating costs) eight years after launch and is projected to earn double its operating requirement within 12 years of launch date.

The private sector was attracted to invest by providing a platform whence their investments could operate. The state absorbed much of the risk, by funding the conservation and land-management activities that have a long lead time to realizing the investment. The first investors completed their lodge construction within four years of launch and so far over 28 concessions with lodges have been contracted. More than 50 per cent of these projects are now operational, while the remainder are under construction or finalizing plans and environmental impact assessments. This represents a total capital investment by the private sector of over US$150 million.

There were several factors behind this early success:

1. There is a guarantee in the concession agreement, through the reserve management plan, that concession fees paid by the private sector will be reinvested in the reserve for management.
2. The concession contracts are long term, on average 45 years. This encourages fixed investment and commitment from both parties. These agreements may be ceded, with minimal restrictions.
3. The concession fees include fixed payments and percentages of turnover.
4. The state spelt out the performance criteria and provided a good contractual environment through the contracting party, the North West Parks and Tourism Board.

Case Study 8.3 *continued*

5. When structuring the agreements it was critical to allow the investors flexibility for packaging the concessions. The state tendered a large package, up to 80 beds in an area. This was then structured by an investor and parcelled off into smaller concessions. What in reality has happened is that many small concessions (10-bed lodges) have been concluded with corporate clients or small syndicates. This in essence is a small 'timeshare' type of arrangement. These pay fixed rentals with escalation formulas. The 'payments' for these smaller units provided the capital for the commercial lodges, which are inherently more risky. If a large component of the capital could be acquired relatively 'cheaply' this made the commercial investment more attractive. These lodges provide more of their rental through a turnover percentage and generally deliver better socio-economic benefits, such as training and development, direct jobs, support for small local businesses, and bringing skills and marketing to the area.

This arrangement has diversified the product and brought some stability to the park income, while still allowing for capitalizing on tourism booms. The project will provide a positive return to the state, including all costs, and does achieve significant socio-economic benefits in an otherwise economically depressed area. The game has so far proved an excellent investment and has performed financially better than initially projected.

More details on this project can be found under the North West Parks and Tourism Board website at www.tourismnorthwest.co.za. Several small booklets describing the financial and economic aspects, the community arrangements, the management plan, etc, can be accessed. Also, a more comprehensive report can be found in Davies (2000).

NOTES

1   This chapter discusses the situation pertaining to state-protected areas. Many of the principles can also be applied to wildlife management systems on private or communal land, but the focus here is on state areas.
2   And this belief is often misplaced.
3   Final Statement of the Southern Africa Workshop on Local Communities, Equity and Protected Areas, Pretoria, 28 February 2003.
4   This does not mean that the funding must come directly from the agency. KZN Wildlife have implemented a system of levies from tourists to the local communities, through a trust fund. This contributes to the communities' needs for funding without placing funding pressure on the agency.
5   Of necessity, this chapter considers the 'average' national park management agency in Africa. As such, it makes several generalizations that will not apply in every instance.
6   That is, the concessionaire that best fits the agency's objectives for the activity under consideration.

REFERENCES

Davies, R (2000) 'Madikwe Game Reserve: A partnership in conservation', in H Prins, J Grootenhuis and T Dolan (eds) *Wildlife Conservation by Sustainable Use*, Kluwer Academic Publishers, Massachusetts

Dixon, J A and Sherman, P B (1990) *Economics of Protected Areas: A New Look at Benefits and Costs*, Earthscan, London

Drucker, P F (1973). *Management: Tasks, Responsibilities, Practices*, Harper Business, New York

Gibson, C (1999) *Politicians and Poachers. The Political Economy of Wildlife Policy in Africa*, Cambridge University Press, Cambridge

Leal, D and Lipke Fretwell H (1997) 'Back to self-sufficient parks', Paper presented to 1997 PERC Forum: The Politics and Economics of Park Management. Political Economy Research Center, Bozeman, Montana

Martin, R (2002) 'Conditions for effective, stable and equitable conservation at the national level in southern Africa', In Workshop on Local Communities, Equity and Protected Areas, TILCEP/PLASS/ART, Pretoria: 25–28 February

Reed, T (2002) 'The functions and structures of protected area authorities. Considerations for financial and organizational management', World Bank Internship Program

ZAWA (2002) *Five Year Strategic Plan*, Zambia Wildlife Authority

Chapter 9

Who and What Are Parks for in Transitional Societies?

Marshall W Murphree

INTRODUCTION

A quick answer to the question posed by the title of this chapter might be, 'It depends on who you ask, and when.' Behind this seemingly flippant reply lies a fact that can be taken as axiomatic: the constituencies of parks are multiple, with their profiles and purposes subject to continuous change. Any policy on parks that ignores the dynamic dimensions of the sources, and the content of the aspirations and reactions that societies hold about parks will be sterile in its ability to deal with the future. This is the basic premise on which this chapter is based.

All societies are in transition and the premise holds true for all of them. Transitions move, however, at different paces and our title implies that in some societies the pace of transition has been so rapid and transforming in contrast to others that they can be categorized as 'transitional societies.'[1] Although they differ in important respects, all the societies of southern Africa fit this broad description on political, economic, demographic and cultural criteria. Within a single century (the 20th century, importantly the century during which most of the subcontinent's parks were established), vast changes along these dimensions have taken place, some incremental and cumulative, some episodic and convulsive. No analysis of our topic can afford to ignore them, and the following section takes up these changes in more detail.

CHANGE AND CONTINUITY IN SOUTHERN AFRICAN SOCIETIES

Political Change

This has been the most ostensible of the transitions through which these societies have passed. At the beginning of the 20th century, all of them were under the political control of colonial powers, significantly influenced by white settler populations that in some cases (eg South Africa and Zimbabwe) progressively appropriated political power through racially structured mechanisms of franchise and administration. In the second half of the century the 'winds of change' had reached the region and political power was transferred (sometimes by negotiation and sometimes by conflict) to governments legitimized on the basis that they represented the black majority populations involved. The last bastion of white minority rule fell in 1994 when the Nationalist Government in South Africa gave way to the African National Congress led by Nelson Mandela.

The importance of this transition for our topic lies in the shifting constituencies to which the pre- and post-independent governments have had to be responsive as an aspect of their continued legitimacy. Pre-independence governments marched in the main to the tune of the prevailing perspectives of their colonial metropoles on the aims of parks, which emphasized species conservation, the values of the wilderness experience and the uniqueness of Africa's 'Eden' of flora, fauna and 'pristine' landscape (Adams and McShane, 1992; Anderson and Grove, 1987; Bonner, 1993; Nash, 1967). The recreational interests of resident whites were also a consideration. More recently, the conservation of environmental service functions became a rationale for the establishment of parks and forest reserves, and with the growth of the tourism industry in the 1970s the economic contribution of parks to national economies assumed greater proportions.

Post-independent governments have had to respond to a constituency with a profile of different perspectives on parks. The largely rural component of these constituencies views parks as part of the appropriative colonial history that expelled their ancestors from the land and its resources. Pre-liberation promises to restore this land are a common aspect of local discourse (Peterson, 1991; Magome and Murombedzi, 2003). Some seek this restoration for agricultural purposes; others a restoration transferring proprietorship from the state to local regimes.[2] In either instance 'protected areas' have become 'protested areas,' and such sentiment is a powerful political factor that new governments must consider in parks policy.

Demographic Transition

This is the second change to be noted. During the 20th century the human population of the subcontinent has increased dramatically, with the percentage of this population classified as urban also rising. In Zimbabwe, for instance, the human population is now over 20 times what it was in 1900, 30 per cent of this population being urban.[3] Similar population growth is recorded for other countries in the region, although rural/urban population ratios vary more widely.

The import of these statistics for our topic lies primarily along two dimensions. First, population growth of this magnitude has greatly increased pressures on the biophysical resource base to provide for human livelihoods, even when is noted that urbanization, industrialization, technology and lifestyle aspirations modulate resource/demand ratios. This is particularly evident in areas of small-scale 'communal' agricultural production, where the cultivation of agriculturally marginal land, the compression of rotational cycles and landlessness are increasingly common. These conditions have been a powerful political dynamic in driving land redistribution movements primarily targeted at commercial large-scale land holdings but also aimed at state land, notably including national parks and forest reserves. Magome and Murombedzi note that 'National parks are conventionally viewed as sacred in global conservation,' but add 'Icons are rarely challenged, but in South Africa national parks are increasingly being challenged for land restitution purposes' (Magome and Murombedzi, 2003, p111).

The second dimension of this demographic transition important for our topic lies in the increasing urbanization of the population. There is ample evidence to suggest that the values derived from parks, and the modes of their usage, differ significantly between urban and rural populations. Urban populations tend to value parks for cultural reasons and, if they have the means, for the recreational opportunities they provide.[4] Rural cultures include intrinsic valuations of wilderness and wild flora and fauna but find less need for the recreational contexts that parks provide to urban populations. Furthermore, their livelihood means induce a more instrumental perspective on parks. For them parks may involve direct costs (opportunity costs, restrictions on movement, wildlife depredations), and if parks are perceived positively this is related to their provision of resources (fixed or fugitive) and employment. The demographic transition, with its increasingly urban population and attendant emergent class of affluence, thus has implications for the values assigned to parks in southern Africa.[5]

Economic Change

This is the third aspect of transition that has had significant impact on our topic. National economies have grown and diversified, market penetration of rural hinterlands has expanded. Healthy national economies clearly enhance the ability of governments to finance parks systems and manage them successfully. With the expansion of the international tourism industry, parks have become valuable real estate with the potential to realize significant export earnings. Conversely, poor national economic performance nullifies these potentials. Furthermore, if it results in wage labour contractions, this may cause urban/rural migration, increasing pressure on the rural/parks resource base by people for whom unsustainable modes of agriculture and natural resource use provide a livelihood strategy of last resort (Bond, 2001). The economic performance of societies in the region differs significantly; the histories of none of them show a trajectory of unilinear advancement. Thus, economic transition is a factor that must be carefully contextualized in time and place if we are to understand its impact on parks.

The commoditization of nature merits special attention. In southern Africa, trade in land and natural resource products antedates the 20th century, but the pace of its expansion has accelerated in recent times (Woodhouse et al, 2000). Commoditization brings economic estimations of wild land and wildlife more closely into line with market valuations and facilitates economically productive land-use choices. It attracts and disseminates innovation in management, as Chapter 4 illustrates. At micro levels, it can produce more equitable entitlements to revenues from common resources either by collective enterprise or through a tradable permits approach (Murphree and Mazambani, 2002; Tietenburg, 2002). It is also clear, however, that commoditization fuels competition over access rights and may exacerbate social stratification by advantaging those with entrepreneurial capital. The commoditization component of economic transition is thus one with multiple positive and negative effects on which it is difficult to generalize, beyond recognizing that commoditization has stimulated an economic interest in parks and their resources among a range of social actors to whom they were previously peripheral.

Continuities in Transition

In briefly sketching the transitions that the societies of southern Africa have experienced in the past century under political, demographic and economic sub-headings, we have in fact raised a broad range of changes which, in addition to these three, include tenurial, cultural and technological shifts. Cumulatively, they add up to a major transformation, but before leaving this summation we should also note two aspects of continuity that tenaciously retain much of the profile that they developed in the 20th century.

The first is the maintenance of state park estates by governments after independence in the face of significant constituency demands to contract them. Not only have they been maintained, they have been expanded.[6] Some see this as evidence of the commitment of governments to conservation; others more cynically regard this as a trade-off, a concession to donor country conservation sentiment in return for large aid packages. Gibson, in his work on post-independence wildlife policy in Zambia, Zimbabwe and Kenya, provides a more fine-grained political economy perspective. Arguing that extraction and redistribution lie at the heart of politics, he suggests that by maintaining extensive government control over wildlife, wildlife resources (including parks) '... became another source of goods which an incumbent party could distribute ... Political actors in all three countries regarded the primary benefits of wildlife policy to be distributive goods, and not the collective good of conservation' (Gibson, 1999, p47). In short, from this perspective, parks are for political elites and their private-sector allies, their purpose being power, patronage and accumulation. Whether this interpretation is accepted or not, the fact remains that the park estates that were established in pre-independence times are still with us today and there are strong incentives for them to remain with us in the future.

The second continuity in the midst of change lies in the persistence of an approach to governance that links positivist science and technocratic rationality to a Weberian mode of administration (Masiiwa, 2002; Chitsike, 2000; Mamimine, 2002). Formal science is expected to state facts and suggest implementation directions; the state turns these results into policy and regulations; and state agencies implement these. In a recent study of environmental policymaking in Zimbabwe, Keeley and Scoones argue that 'this technical, scientifically informed and bureaucratically managed approach remains the dominant paradigm' (Keeley and Scoones, 2000, p6). It remains so because this serves the interests of an entrenched bureaucratic-cum-scientific elite and reinforces the power of the state. The authors conclude: 'This startling continuity between pre- and post-independence settings highlights how, despite obvious shifts in politics, the embedded nature of bureaucratic attitudes and practices shaped in turn by science, provides the basis for the persistence of particular styles of state response to environmental and land management issues' (Keeley and Scoones, 2000, p15). This conclusion applies to the roots of parks policy and implementation and has implications for our topic to which this chapter later returns.

CLASSIFYING THE FUNCTIONS AND FORMS OF PARKS

The uses to which parks can be put are multiple, covering a range of values. This sentence has been carefully phrased to reflect the link between use and value. Frequently, classifications of park functions make an initial distinction between 'use' and 'non-use' functions, which obscures the fact that the designation of any area as a park is an allocative decision involving management and opportunity costs and is thus a societal use of space and resources.[7] Southern African scholarship has taken cognizance of this fact and has defined use as 'the derivation of benefit (tangible or intangible) in one or more of the following respects: economic or financial; social or cultural; political; ecological (productivity, stability and biodiversity' (SASUSG, 1996, p6).

By using this fourfold categorization, the values and benefits (actual or putative) that may be assigned to parks can be detailed as follows.

Economic and Financial Benefits

- The provision of products for subsistence use, the sustainability of such use being enhanced by parks status and management.
- The provision of goods and products traded in markets, again on a sustainable basis.
- Enhancement of the tourism industry. Parks can provide recreational and aesthetic experiences satisfying subjective values (see below) which are traded for capital. Generally, this falls within the tourism industry in various forms. It is, in effect, the 'export of nature' to use Nash's phrase (Nash, 1967). For southern Africa, parks are a lynchpin for the international tourism industry as part of a package of tourism experience sufficient to attract long-haul clients.
- The attraction of international capital from the private sector or donors. For the private sector this is usually for tourism enterprises; for donors this may be a concession to donor conservation perspectives as a lever for larger grants in other sectors. To paraphrase Nash, it is the 'exchange of nature for development goals'.
- The provision of employment across a wide spectrum, including tourism employees, parks management, bureaucrats, planners and scientists.
- The provision of reservoirs for agricultural re-introduction or expansion.[8]

Social and Cultural Benefits

- The provision of recreational sites and facilities, particularly for urban residents.
- The preservation of cultural and archaeological sites.
- The preservation of sites holding high religious significance to local populations. Some customary religions in the region are integrally linked to such sites, to the extent that they have been called 'ecological religions' (Schoffeleers, 1979).

- The satisfaction of existence values that assign intrinsic worth to landscapes and natural resources on philosophical, religious, cultural or aesthetic grounds.

Political Benefits

- The maintenance and extension of state authority and its central roles in policy and management.
- Opportunities for elite appropriation and patronage.
- Enhancement of state images as conservation stewards in the international arena.
- Opportunities for transboundary cooperation.
- The provision of sites for organizational and institutional experimentation.

Ecological Benefits

- The provision of environmental services such as watershed protection and carbon sequestration.
- The protection of rare or endangered species of flora and fauna.
- The maintenance of biological diversity, encouraging genetic diversity, natural selection and evolutionary adaptation.
- The provision of sites for scientific observation and controlled experiment.[9]
- Insurance value, ie the maintenance of ecosystem and biodiversity components that may in the future guard against currently unknown risk.

How and to what extent this long list of actual or putative functions of parks has been translated into park categories and objectives is an indication of evolving policy directions. International Union for the Conservation of Nature's (IUCN) typology of Protected Areas,[10] by category and management objective, is shown in Table 9.1 below.

With its biocentric orientation, the table shows its pedigree as the product of the World Commission on Protected Areas (WCPA), the IUCN commission that most closely resonates with members whose conservation values are primarily aesthetic and

Table 9.1 *IUCN Protected Area categories*

Category	Description
Ia	'Strict Nature Reserve': protected area managed mainly for science or wilderness protection.
Ib	'Wilderness Area': protected area managed mainly for wilderness protection
II	'National Park': protected area managed mainly for wilderness protection and recreation
III	'Natural Monument': protected area managed mainly for conservation through management intervention
IV	'Habitat/Species Management Area': protected area managed mainly for conservation through management intervention
V	'Protected Landscape/Seascape': protected area managed mainly for landscape/seascape conservation and recreation
VI	'Managed Resource Protected Area': protected area managed mainly for the sustainable use of natural ecosystems

Source: IUCN (1994)

intrinsic. It does, however, give space for livelihood and economic concerns, most explicitly in Category VI, reflecting the Union's shift towards a more anthropocentric stance at its 1996 World Conservation Congress (WCC).[11]

Table 9.1 has its shortcomings. It is a table of categories and management objectives largely tailored to authority and management by the state, although both IUCN and the Convention on Biological Diversity (CBD) now accept that protected areas may fall under non-state communal or individual regimes of proprietorship.[12] Are these necessarily spatial (see Mandondo, 1998)? If they involve agrobiodiversity where do these fit? What criteria determine their recognition, and are these necessarily formal?

LINKING THE WHAT? AND THE WHO?

More fundamentally, however, the IUCN Protected Area categories give no guidance on the critical linkages between form, function and constituency interest. Unless these linkages are articulated more tightly, the sustainability of any parks system will be problematic. The 'Who?' in our title determines function, and from function should follow form.

The range and interests of these constituencies is broad and defies attempts at detailed typologies. Certain broad profiles do, however, emerge when the question is examined through the filter of 'governance', the collectivities of interest that coalesce into collective organizational and political action.

Fortunately, the issue of governance has not escaped the attention of the WCPA. Considerable discussion and analysis has taken place. More recently a joint endeavour of WCPA and IUCN's Commission of Environmental, Economic and Social Policy (CEESP) has been initiated to examine governance and related issues under an agenda that includes, among others, the formulation of a typology of governance of protected areas across a spectrum, from totally state-managed ones through a diversity of co-managed ones to totally community or privately managed ones, suggesting criteria to judge whether they are managed through 'legal or other effective means' (see Note 12), and proposing processes by which the entire range can be included in the World Database on Protected Areas (WDPA) and the UN list.[13]

The results of this exercise were presented at the Worlds Parks Congress (WPC) in September 2003; they will hopefully give more clarity on the functions and forms that parks may exhibit in the 21st century. The exercise has already progressed to a draft governance typology that can be superimposed on the IUCN Protected Area listings, importantly including the categories of Community Conserved Areas (CCAs) and Co-Managed Protected Areas (CMPAs). If accepted, the inclusion of these two categories will be a strategic advance in policy conceptualization and the integration of form, function and constituency interest.

One must still question, however, the degree to which this classificatory approach will address the core issues that render the future of parks in southern Africa so tenuous. It may provide greater recognition to the importance of locally endogenous protected areas, it may encourage a more anthropocentric policy on parks, and it may through designation provide more aid funding for protected areas fortunate enough to be on the right list (a somewhat debatable benefit).

But detailed typologies and elaborated procedures of bureaucratic response cannot on their own provide us with directions that can address the guts of our problem. The topic 'Who and what are parks for in transitional societies?' is more than a semantic and typological question. It is a question about change in the profile and role of parks in southern Africa and their future in the 21st century. From the constellation of shifting interests and constituencies outlined in this chapter, it is clear that this future will be critically determined along the two confrontational fault lines that now characterize debate on the politics and policies of parks: conflicts over long-term conservation goals and short-term livelihood and exploitative strategies, and conflicts over centre and periphery interests. We now need new ways of thinking and acting which can turn this confrontation into congruence.

SYSTEMIC APPROACHES TO PARKS POLICY

In other words, the methodologies of the past may have been sound but the epistemologies on which they have been based have lost salience in the face of the evolutionary change. We need new conceptual approaches that address this change: less determinative and more contingent, less focused on structure and more on process, less prescriptive and more adaptive, less impositional and more facilitative. Above all, less reductionist and more systemic, viewing parks as one component in a complex socio-biological system with adaptive cycles of growth, accumulation, restructuring and renewal. Resilience rather than immutability lies at the heart of the robustness of such a system.[14]

Stemming from this conceptual stance, we conclude by suggesting that the broad and dynamic range of aspirations that parks face from their various constituencies needs a set of policies that are themselves dynamic and adaptive, and which deal centrally with four issues: diversity, legitimacy, scale and mutability.

Diversity

Diversity in function and demand is manifest in the brief survey that this chapter provides. Typological approaches attempt to deal with diversity by classification, but no typology can deal with the myriad detail of context involved. Such diversity of context renders each park or protected area unique. A more fruitful approach is to conceptually hold such entities at a generic level and examine specific profiles contextually in terms of the socio-historical, economic and ecological variables involved. The analytical constructs of common property theory take this approach, and it is somewhat curious that analyses of parks have rarely availed themselves of this body of scholarship. There is an essential affinity between 'the commons' and protected areas, in that they are both sites and bundles of collective entitlement for their constituents which require protection through controls on their use. Their legitimations may come from a variety of sources, the entitlements may be differential and the definition of their constituencies may vary, but their essence is collective and controlled access. Understood this way, the realization dawns that 'protected areas' pervade most rural landscapes, whether recognized or not. This conceptual lens drives holes through the cognitive filters that have set up false dichotomies in protected-area policy: that protected areas are confined to state management, that they are about non-use rather than use, and that they are about exclusion rather than regulated access.[15] Conceptualized in this way, a new and fruitful terrain of investigation is opened up for policy consideration. The essential task is to determine the extent of the commons in question, distinguish between the primary and secondary stakeholders involved and facilitate the emergence of regimes that, because of broad consensus, incentive and ability to influence outcomes, are best placed to provide effective management. This is not an easy task, and as the experience on conservancy formation in Namibia shows (Chapter 4) is likely to be stochastic and dynamic. Diversity in context will lead to diversity in form, which is an evolutionary strength.

Legitimacy

Legitimacy is the second important issue that policy must address. By legitimacy we mean consensual social approval, not the legality conferred by the state, which may or may not be the same. This legitimacy applies to the park or protected area concerned, its management and the system to which it is connected. Without legitimacy none of these can be effective. Legitimacy is, however, frequently contested, either because of its multiple roots or when consensual support shifts. In the first instance, state legitimacy may be legally imposed and negated by local non-compliance, or local consensual legitimacy may be rendered impotent by lack of legal authority. In the second instance, consensus may be eroded by negative performance evaluations or changes in cost–benefit equations. On this point, complex systems analysis provides certain pointers on means to promote biosocial systems with enduring legitimacy that are particularly apposite for parks policy. Among these are the use of social criteria to support the growth and spread of other valued criteria; the use of short-term fine-grained criteria of success as proxies for longer-run broader goals; and the injunction not to 'sow failures when reaping small efficiencies'.[16]

Returning to the threat to legitimacy posed by possible dissonance between that conferred legally by the state and that which arises from local consensus, common property theory again returns to give some policy pointers. The legitimacy of parks regimes is closely linked to societal perceptions of the nature and constituency of the commons involved. If these perceptions suggest that, for reasons of scarcity, uniqueness or ecosystem support functions, national common-pool resources are involved, state park jurisdictions are more likely to enjoy consensual legitimacy. If these elements are not present, state systems are more likely to be viewed as impositional and expropriative. In such cases 'the commons' are likely to be perceived more narrowly, and proximate legitimations may suggest a policy of localized non-state regimes.

Scale

Scale is an issue already addressed above in a binary centre–periphery mode. This does not, however, exhaust the scale aspects of governance that must be addressed by parks policy. Between the polar extremes of parks with full state proprietorship and local protected areas with fully devolved authority and management, lie other contexts where ecosystem characteristics dictate intermediate regimes. One may regard these as functional types, but equally important is the issue of appropriate forms of governance for such contexts. The comments on legitimacy above apply. Perceptions of whose commons is involved will critically influence the legitimacy and support given to these entities. In some cases decentralization by the state to sub-government (eg regional, district, municipal) entities may be appropriate. In other cases the aggregation of primary proprietors into larger units of collaboration may be called for. Southern Africa has several experiments of this kind (eg the intensive conservation areas (ICAs) of Zimbabwe's natural resource legislation, and conservancy formation in Namibia and Zimbabwe). These are forms of protected-area governance that are largely neglected in international policy debate and which deserve greater attention. Where such aggregations are appropriate, lines and directions of accountability are important and it has been suggested that delegated responsibility 'upward' and accountability to constituents 'downward' are critical (Murphree, 2000).

Mutability

Mutability is the forth issue that policy must address. If there is one thing that is predictable about the purposes and constituencies of parks in the 21st century, it is that they will change over time, just as they have in the 20th century. Policy must accommodate this one certainty and we have already suggested that a critical first step is to change the epistemological stance that we take. This involves a shift to a systemic science that sees emergence and evolution as central properties in the complex interactive socio-biological system that is today's world. In this world, human structures co-evolve and emerge with, and in response to, biophysical change, and those with the greatest sustainability are those that are responsively resilient. Thus policy, and the science behind it, focuses more on process and less on prescription.

Beyond this, if it is accepted that resilient human structures for the regulation and management of human–nature interactions organically emerge in specific contexts, the role of policy itself must be reviewed. It could be held that policy interventions may be more disruptive than productive. This is an issue raised by Ruitenbeek and Cartier in their analysis of the intrusions of state policy on localized non-state regimes, but if we consider that state regimes are themselves systems-within-systems the question applies equally to national park regimes. Superficially, it might appear that in such regimes the state is both designer (policy maker) and agent. The fact is that such regimes are not monolithic and their structures clearly show that design and implementation are functions assigned to different actors. The analysis that follows thus applies to all protected-area regimes, state or non-state.

Policy interventions may be appropriate when certain conditions apply: when the intervention itself generates a learning experience, when the designer has information not available to the agent, when the timing is right, and when the intervention protects conditions for the emergence of adaptive management properties (Ruitenbeek and Cartier, 2001, p30). Ruitenbeek and Cartier emphasize that the last condition of emergence is the central role of policy, and that this involves the protection of social capital against the threats of disempowerment, programmed failure and imposed distributional patterns. Policies should, they argue, also 'facilitate copying and variation. This means that options should not be unilaterally removed, and that potential avenues of investigation should not be blocked' (Ruitenbeek and Cartier, 2001, p33).

Cast in this way, the role and agenda of policy becomes considerably different to what it is today. It is likely to sit uncomfortably with a bureaucratic ethos that is directive and reductionist. It calls for a change in the thinking and actions of policy extension agents (Matose, 2002). It challenges the 'centralizing and modernizing ethic' that characterizes current conservation programmes (Murombedzi, 2003, p114). It faces the challenge of overcoming precipitate subversion by establishments 'under pressure to speed up development' that take up the trappings of participation but cut corners in the process involved, leaving 'the real things, which are people's rights and power dynamics, untouched' (Kepe, 2002, p9). It presents, however, the profile of a policy stance which can more effectively address the challenges of mutability and change that parks and protected areas now face.

CONCLUSION

Earlier in this chapter it was suggested that the issues of what and who parks are for are a subset of two major confrontational fault lines that challenge the future of southern African societies: conflicts over development and conservation goals, and conflicts over centre and periphery interests. The first of these confrontational sets pits 'long-term biodiversity goals' against 'short-term livelihood strategies' (Magome and Murombedzi, 2003, p120), conservation investments in the future against unsustainable use driven by the immediate imperatives of survival. The second set pits the interests of those living with, and dependent on, the natural resource base against the appropriative interests of centrist politics and capital. If played out as a zero-sum game, the current stasis will continue, dominated by the politico-economic centre. As Magome and Murombedzi note, 'The political environment is still hostile to local people and this is unlikely to change, particularly as the pressure of globalization intensifies. Forced to take up a "follow-the-stream" role rather than craft their own strategies, developing countries drag their own constituencies along, including rural peoples' (Magome and Murombedzi, 2003, p128). It is difficult to see how current parks policies, which seek to shore up a static system with concessionary and cosmetic forays into local participation, will contribute much to the amelioration of this condition.

Southern African societies do not, however, have to follow the stream induced by others. With insight and innovation they can seek to transform confrontation into negotiated synergies between development and conservation, between centre and periphery interests. In this chapter a new, process-oriented policy stance that focuses on enhancing the conditions for the emergence of adaptive and resilient protected-area regimes has been advocated. Such regimes would be diverse in form, function and scale, but all would seek to link benefit and responsibility with the authority of their constituents. Legitimacy and legality would be fused. This form of determinative participation echoes Ake's thoughts on participative (rather than representative) democracy in Africa. 'In this instance,' he says, 'participation is not the occasional opportunity to choose, affirm or dissent. It is rather the active involve-ment in the process, not the acceptability of the end decision that satisfies the need to participate' (Ake, 2000, p184). The system characteristics resulting from such a policy are difficult (indeed inherently impossible) to profile, other than to predict that they would be dynamic and probably produce a kaleidoscopic landscape of pro-tected areas interspersed with other land-use forms. Although uncertain, this is sure-ly a more politically and ecologically attractive situation than that which current pol-icy is likely to produce; a scenario of shrinking national parks estates serving only the interests of urban and elite segments of the societies concerned.

NOTES

1   In one sense, the term 'transitional society' can be considered a euphemism, taking its place in the lexicon of binary phrases that have sought to express a general distinction between societies char-acterized by industrialization and urbanization and those that are primarily agrocentric and rural: 'First World/Third World;' 'North/South;' 'Developed/Developing' societies. In the governance dimension, these contrasts are paralleled by distinctions on the locus of power in evolutionary analyses that go back to Weber's differentiation between patriarchal and bureaucratic societies (Gerth and Mills, 1961), and in Tönnies' distinction between Gemeinschaft and Gesellschaft (Tönnies, 1957). 'Transitional society' is broader and less invidious, emphasizing pace and process.
2   Interview notes from a recent visit to a village bordering the Gonarezhou National Park in Zimbabwe by Sandi Nielson and Hastings Chikoko are instructive on this point. The village chair-man is quoted as saying: 'Our primary concern is not the park. It is to get our ancestors' land back and benefit from its use. This land belongs to our elders and our forefathers. We believe that we should reclaim it, and there are still some elders alive who once lived here and who are now here today. This is our heritage and this is where we belong.' Nielson and Chikoko note that the coun-cillor from the same area stressed that the people do not want to destroy the area and are not opposed to conservation activities such as those under the CAMPFIRE programme. Rather, they are interested in benefits from the use of the land. 'We have not settled people in the entire conser-vation area of the park under discussion. We are only occupying a small portion so that we can reserve the remainder for Campfire projects and wildlife'. (Nielson and Chikoko, 2002, pp1, 3).
3   Statistics derived from various census reports, importantly including Government of Rhodesia (1969), Government of Zimbabwe (1992) and Central Statistical Office (1999–2002). Care should be taken not to infer that these statistics necessarily imply that before the 20th century the subcon-tinent was sparsely populated. Bell (1987) argues that there was a large build-up of populations in central and south central Africa during the Iron Age (300BC–1700AD). Citing Ranesford (1983), Curtin et al (1951), Ford (1971) and Hartwig and Patterson (1978), he suggests that after 1700 this population crashed for several reasons, including the slave trade, internecine wars, the introduction of external diseases and the re-exposure of the population to endemic disease vectors.
4   A 1989 study on the recreational patterns and preferences of urban residents in Zimbabwe showed correlations between parks use and the frequency of visits to rural homes of origin and socio-eco-nomic status. Those using parks, particularly for longer durations, were those with the means to do so and were less dependent on rural home visits for recreational and other purposes (Child and Heath, 1989). For more general analyses on correlation between socio-economic status and outdoor recreational preference, see Butler-Adam (1986) and Machlis et al (1981).
5   The links between socio-economic status and intrinsic/instrumental valuations have been noted in debates on wildlife conservation. Mordi, an opponent of sustainable use approaches, makes this observation: 'At the time of writing, no country in sub-Saharan Africa can boast of a large number of indigenous citizens who, in the light of a rapid decline in wildlife populations, feel a personal sense of loss ... Until middle class indigenous defenders of wildlife emerge, personal involvement in conservation will remain extremely low in the larger public in sub-Saharan Africa.' (Mordi, 1991, quoted in Hoyt, 1994, p218).

6   Bell, citing unpublished data states, 'The number of national parks and equivalent reserves gazetted has more than doubled since the independence of most African states in the 1960s, with a particularly rapid phase of land acquisition in the mid-1970s' (Bell, 1987, p87).

7   Other classifications make a primary distinction between 'extractive' and 'non-extractive' uses, seeing 'non-extractive' use as being less environmentally disruptive. This is, however, problematic. 'Extractive use' such as safari hunting may leave the habitat less disturbed than 'non-extractive' photographic tourism with its trail of litter, and tracks for viewing and balloon recovery.

8   This mode of 'future use' option is rarely mentioned in the literature but is often raised in local-level discussion and sometimes by land-use planners.

9   The close links between scientific interest and the establishment of parks and protected areas is examined (in the British context) by Adams (1996).

10   'Parks' and 'protected areas' are terms that tend to be used interchangeably, but there is considerable vacillation and ambiguity in this use. 'Protected areas' is the more generic term, but are all protected areas parks? Some would prefer to reserve the term 'parks' for entities managed by the state, others for areas that are primarily designed for aesthetic and recreational purposes. Thus, this terminology itself becomes a part of the typological debate.

11   Recommendation 1.35 of the WCC in 1996 asks countries to 'apply the IUCN system of protected areas categories which both provide strict protection primarily in order to protect nature and which provide for a balance of conservation and the sustainable use of natural resources to help meet the need of local people' (World Conservation Congress, 1986). A year later the (then) chairman of the World Commission on Protected Areas perceptively spoke of the 'credibility gap' produced by this recommended balancing act between strict protectionism and the satisfaction of economic and livelihood imperatives: 'On the one hand, the values of protected areas are clear, and indeed more and more such areas are being set up: on the other hand, progress is often thwarted by the ever greater pressures placed on these areas. The rhetoric which often accompanies the establishment of protected areas has to be contrasted with the reality of there being many "paper parks" — protected areas legally in existence, but not functioning in practice. This dilemma cannot be resolved by a strategy based solely on law enforcement, nor can it be dealt with only within the areas themselves. Instead protected areas must be planned and managed with, and through, local communities wherever possible, not against them; developed as part of sustainable strategies for poverty alleviation and economic and social advancement in rural areas; and encompassed within broader bioregional strategies incorporating lands around or between more strictly protected core areas' (Phillips, 1997, p55).

12   IUCN defines a protected area as 'an area of land and/or sea especially dedicated to the protection and maintenance of biological diversity, and of natural and associated cultural resources, and managed through legal or other effective means' (IUCN, 1994). The CBD defines a protected area as 'a geographically defined area which is designated or regulated and managed to achieve specific conservation objectives' (Convention on Biological Diversity, 1992, Article 2).

13   This joint endeavour has been titled the Theme on Indigenous and Local Communities, Equity and Protected Areas (TILCEPA). TILCEPA's formal agenda is to: 'With relation to the World Database on Protected Areas and the UN List, WCPA to initiate a Programme of Work on a range of protected areas or conservation areas that are outside of the officially designated or government-managed PA system. Such a Programme of Work would include (World Commission on Protected Areas, 2002):

    1. Formulating a typology of governance of PAs, including the entire range from totally government managed PAs, through a diversity of co-managed PAs, to totally community or private managed ones;

    2. Suggesting a process by which such PAs would be nominated and accepted for use in the WDPA and the UN List, including how to determine whether such areas are managed through legal or 'other effective means' (as required by the IUCN PA Category system);

    3. Providing inputs to the State of the World's Parks Report, for initial recognition and analysis of non-official PAs;

    4. Providing to the World Parks Congress, through discussion and refinement in the Governance Stream, a recommendation on the above, for endorsement;

    5. Initiating, after the WPC, the inclusion of such PAs into the World Database on Protected Areas and the UN List'.

14   Perceptive readers will recognize the provenance of these conceptual stances in complex systems theory. For an excellent summary, see Ruitenbeek and Cartier (2001).

15 For further elaboration see Murphree (2002).
16 Axelrod and Cohen (1999), quoted in Ruitenbeek and Cartier (2001, pp12–13). Ruitenbeek and Cartier, in the same work, go on to state: 'Complex systems suffer from four types of failure that can be characterized as: (i) independent failure of system parts; (ii) correlated failure of system parts; (iii) stress propagation failures; and (iv) external attacks. Systems that can avert failure are those with in-built redundancy, in-built fail-safes (precautionary failure modes) and counter-cyclical feedbacks to relieve or dissipate stress.'

REFERENCES

Adams, J S and McShane, T O (1992) *The Myth of Wild Africa. Conservation without Illusion*, W W Norton, New York
Adams, W (1996) *Future Nature: A vision for Conservation*, Earthscan, London
Ake, C (2000) *The Feasibility of Democracy in Africa*, CODESRIA, Dakar
Anderson, D and Grove, R (1987) *Conservation in Africa: People, Policies and Practice*, Cambridge University Press, Cambridge
Axelrod, R and Cohen, M (1999) *Harnessing Complexity: Organizational Implications of a Scientific Frontier*, Free Press, New York
Bell, R (1987) 'Conservation with a human face: Conflict and reconciliation in African land use planning', in D Anderson and R Grove (eds) *Conservation in Africa. People, Policies and Practice*, Cambridge University Press, Cambridge, pp79–101
Bond, I (2001) 'Campfire and the incentives for institutional change', in D Hulme and M W Murphree (eds) *African Wildlife and Livelihoods: The Promise And Performance of Community Conservation*, James Currey, Oxford, pp227–43
Bonner, R (1993) *At the Hand of Man. Peril and Hope for Africa's Wildlife*, Alfred Knoff, New York
Butler-Adam, J F (1986) *A Framework for the Social Analysis of Recreation*, Monograph Series 7/86, South African Association for Sport, Physical Education and Recreation, Pretoria
Central Statistical Office (1999–2002). 'Annual projections of population', unpublished mimeo reports, Central Statistical Office, Harare
Child, G and Heath, R (1989) 'Outdoor Recreational Pattern and Preferences Among the Residents of Harare, Zimbabwe', University of Zimbabwe, Harare
Chitsike, L T (2000) 'Decentralisation and Devolution of CAMPFIRE in Zimbabwe', Centre for Applied Social Sciences (C.A.S.S.), University of Zimbabwe, Harare
Convention on Biological Diversity (1992) 'Convention on Biological Diversity', United Nations, New York
Curtin, P, Fierman, S, Thompson, L and Vansina, J (1981) *African History*, London, Longman
Ford, J (1971) *The Role of Trypanosomiasis in African Ecology*, Oxford University Press, Oxford
Gerth, H H and Mills, C W (eds) (1961) *From Max Weber: Essays in Sociology*, Routledge and Keegan Paul, London
Gibson, C C (1999) *Politicians and Poachers. The Political Economy of Wildlife Policy in Africa*, Cambridge University Press, Cambridge
Government of Rhodesia (1969). *Census of Population*, 1969, Central Statistical Office, Salisbury
Government of Zimbabwe (1992) *Census 1992. Preliminary Report*, Central Statistical Office, Harare
Hartwig, G and Patterson, K (1978) *Disease in African History*, Duke University Press, Durham, USA
Hoyt, J A (1994) *Animals in Peril. How 'Sustainable Use' Is Wiping Out the World's Wildlife*, Avery Publishing Group, Garden City Park, New York
IUCN (1994) *Guidelines for Protected Area Management Categories*, IUCN, Gland Switzerland, and Cambridge, UK
Keeley, J and Scoones, I (2000) 'Environmental policy making in Zimbabwe: Discourses, science and politics', University of Sussex, Institute of Development Studies, IDS working paper 116
Kepe, T (2002) 'Protected area policies and commons scholarship', *Common Property Resource Digest*, no. 60: 9
Lunga, S L (1999) 'Migrants and experienced impacts to the CAMPFIRE Progamme', paper presented at the International Conference on Natural Resources Management, University of Zimbabwe, Harare, 26–29 January
Machlis, G E et al (1981) 'The human ecology of parks', *Leisure Sciences* **IV**: 195–212

Magome, H and Murombedzi, J (2003) 'Sharing South African national parks: Community, land and conservation in a democratic South Africa', in W Adams and M Mulligan (eds) *Decolonising Nature: Strategies for Conservation in a Post-colonial Era*, Earthscan, London, pp108–34

Mamimine, P (2002) 'How far the destination? Decentralisation and devolution in governance of the Commons under CAMPFIRE', in G Chikowore, E Manzungu, D Mushayavanhu and D Shoko (eds) *Managing Common Property in an Age of Globalisation. Zimbabwean Experiences*, Weaver Press, Harare, pp87–102

Mandondo, A (1998) *The Concept of Territoriality in Local Natural Resource Management and Its Implications on Livelihood in Nyamaropa Communal Land*, Institute for Environmental Studies, University of Zimbabwe, Harare

Masiiwa, M (2002) 'Common property rights and the empowerment of communal farmers in Zimbabwe: Institutional legal frameworks and policy challenges under globalisation', in G Chikowore, E Manzunga, D Mashayavanhu and D Shoko (eds) *Managing Common Property in an Age of Globalisation. Zimbabwean Experiences*, Weaver Press, Harare, pp15–30

Matose, F (2002) 'Institutional configurations around forest reserves in Zimbabwe', in G Chikowore, E Manzungu, D Mushayavanhu and D Shoko (eds) *Managing Common Property in an Age of Globalisation. Zimbabwean Experiences*. Harare: Weaver Press

Mordi, A R (1991) *Attitudes Toward Wildlife in Botswana*, Garland Publishing, New York

Murombedzi, J (2003) 'Devolving the expropriation of nature: The 'devolution' of wildlife management in southern Africa', in W Adams and M Mulligan (eds) *Decolonising Nature. Strategies for Conservation in a Post-colonial Era*, Earthscan, London, pp135–51

Murphree, M W and Mazambani, D (2002) 'Policy implications of common pool resource knowledge: A background paper for Zimbabwe', jointly published by Department of Geography, University of Cambridge, CASS Trust, UZ, Institute of Economic Growth, Delhi, Faculty of Law, University of Dar es Salaam

Murphree, M W (2000) 'Boundaries and borders. The question of scale in the theory and practice of common property management', paper presented at the Eighth Biennial Conference of the IASCP, Bloomington, Indiana, 31 May–4 June

Murphree, M W (2002) 'Protected areas and the commons', Common Property Research Digest no. 60: 1–3

Nash, R (1967) *Wilderness and the American Mind*, Yale University Press, New Haven

Nielson, S and Chikoko, H (2002) 'This part of Gonarezhou Park belongs to us', *Transborder Dialogue* 1(1), 2 3

Peterson, J H (1991) 'A proto-CAMPFIRE initiative in Mahenye Ward, Chipinge District: Development of a wildlife programme in response to community needs', Centre for Applied Social Sciences, University of Zimbabwe, Harare

Phillips, A (1997) 'Protected areas and the convention on biological diversity', in *Protected Areas in the 21st Century: From Islands to Networks*, IUCN/WCPA 1997 Conference Report, draft of 6 January 1998, IUCN, Gland, Switzerland, pp54–61

Ranesford, O (1983) *Bid the Sickness Cease: Disease in the History of Black Africa*, John Murray, London

Ruitenbeek, J and Cartier, C (2001) *The Invisible Wand: Adaptive Co-management as an Emergent Strategy in Complex Bio-economic Systems*, Center for International Forestry Research (CIFOR), Bogor, Indonesia

SASUSG (1996) *Sustainable Use Issues and Principles*, SASUSG, Species Survival Commission, IUCN, Harare

Schoffeleers, J (1979) *Guardians of the Land*, Mambo Press, Gweru

Tietenberg, T (2002) 'The tradable permits approach to protecting the commons: What have we learned?', in *The Drama of the Commons*, National Academy Press, National Research Council, Washington, DC, pp197–232

Tönnies, F (1957) *Community and Society — Gemeinschaft and Gesellschaft*, 2nd edition (translated by C P Loomis), Michigan State University, East Lansing, Michigan

World Conservation Congress (1986) World Conservation Congress, IUCN. Recommendation 1.35

World Commission on Protected Areas (2002) Steering Committee Documents, October, World Commission on Protected Areas, IUCN, Gland, Switzerland

Woodhouse, P, Bernstein, H and Hulme, D (eds) (2000) *African Enclosures? The Social Dynamics of Wetlands in Drylands*, James Currey, Oxford

Chapter 10

Parks in Transition: Biodiversity, Development and the Bottom Line

Brian Child

DEMOCRATIZING CONSERVATION

The Importance of Diversity, Experimentation and Natural Selection

In times of great change, diversity and experimentation are the ingredients of adaptation. Yet conservation, like the hegemonic civilizations of ancient China and Arabia (Landes, 1998), is not well structured to adapt. In placing biodiversity ahead of humans, and making conservation a moral issue more than an economic one, 'conservation' is in danger of prioritizing the desires of an urbanized techno-elite. This may have worked in colonial or autocratic societies, but in an age of increasing political inclusion is unlikely to succeed. Democracy and imposed conservation simply do not go together.

One of the most striking features of a recent assessment of conservation entitled *Biodiversity, Sustainability and Human Communities. Protecting Beyond the Protected* (O'Riordan and Stoll-Kleemann, 2002) is the absence of experimentation, and the tentative nature of such experimentation as there is. Although 'Protecting Beyond the Protected' is a useful barometer of the changing climate of conservation, it is also indicative of how immature our thinking still is, as well as how difficult changing the conservation mind-map from northern hemisphere animal welfarism towards a new approach based on different (southern hemisphere) value systems may be. In this same book, Norman Myers draws attention to global biodiversity being everyone's heritage but nobody's business; to the critical effect on the environment of the subsidization of agriculture, fossil fuels, road transportation, water, and forest and fish extraction; and to poverty and the impact of marginal people on marginal and biodiversity-rich environments. He asks conservationists to expand their outlook and to move from managing crises and effects to beginning to address the root causes of conservation problems. He then, to our mind, correctly identifies these as institutional roadblocks, laments the fact that institutions are perceived as a 'boring topic' and receive only a modicum of attention from conservation scientists because they are central to the causes rather than the symptoms of conservation failure.

In this we differ, finding the relationships between people, politics, values and environments not only fascinating but also critical to making conservation more effective. Old-style conservation may have already decided that nature is so important that people should not get in its way. Our starting point is that nature is important to people, and that in increasingly democratic societies it is by right their choice, not only that of techno-bureaucrats, what conservation aims for and who does it. Our optimism stems from the potential to align institutions so that the value of 'nature' encourages many ordinary people to participate in and contribute to conservation. It is the way people work with nature rather than the way nature works that will ultimately determine the future of conservation. Hence our suggestion that it is more productive to use political economics and market failure rather than ecological advocacy as the analytical frame to address conservation.

This brings us directly to the subject of sustainable use, and conservation driven by a southern, rural or landholder agenda. Highly centralized as it is, command-and-control conservation leaves little space for experimentation in which ordinary people can participate, much in the manner of the 'nationalized' assets of the Soviet socialist states. From a political–economic perspective, sustainable use has many parallels with the democratization of post-communist states, based as it is on the principles of individual rights and choice: ownership and exchange as the primary mechanisms for allocating resources. For instance, each community or landholder has rights to use wildlife and is encouraged to reinvest in its conservation by the incentives it generates. The introduction of sustainable use, which is based around the principles of revolving rights and responsibilities and therefore internalizing costs and benefits, indeed has many parallels with the political, institutional and economic challenges of transitional (post-Soviet) economies. The practical challenge is to avoid elite capture, corruption and plunder and avoid an anarchic free-for-all while the pillars of inclusionary governance are introduced: property rights, free markets, access to justice and, above all, choice and equitable local control. Devolved conservation is a direct antidote to the elite capture of the past, with the massive challenge of transferring control from a few techno-bureaucrats to hundreds of thousands of ordinary people. Devolution is a powerful but rigorous concept, and the key to this transition is highly disciplined adherence to a set of principles at the core of which are full and clear rights to benefit, manage and allocate resources.

Non-State Conservation

This book set out to examine the southern African experience in park management. This inspection is powerfully informed by the experience derived from the sustainable use of wildlife, which appears to offers the solution to both conservation and economic agendas. Indeed, it is the experience of private and, more latterly, community conservation that provides impetus for new forms of park management, and challenges the efficacy of the conventional statist park model. For example, the viability of so many of South Africa's 5000 private conservation areas gives lie to the claim that because so few parks are financially viable the quest for self-funding parks is a pipe dream. That the significant improvements in the health and diversity of ecosystems and wildlife numbers[1] on both private and community land is correlated with profitability challenges the supposed trade-off between biodiversity and development.

Perhaps one of conservation's greatest successes has been the massive conversion of land to wildlife on private land in southern Africa since the 1960s (Chapter 3), a success that is spreading to communal lands despite their challenges. We cite Zimbabwe's Communal Areas Management Programme for Indigenous Resources (CAMPFIRE) programme. Despite Zimbabwe's serious political problems, and despite a doubling of human populations in the past two decades, there were twice as many elephants and at least half again as much other wildlife in CAMPFIRE areas in 2000 as in 1990 (Child et al, 2003). The results from Namibia and Botswana, where people-pressure is lower, are even more spectacular. Moreover, in the face of cynical political upheaval, a gratifying observation was that as recently as 2003 CAMPFIRE communities were remarkably robust in following the initial principles of this programme and were even able to resist strong and corrupting political pressures. Noting that the foundation of improving capacity is secure rights, a ten-year series of hunting records showed that communities were managing their hunting quotas better than the state conservation agency. The immediate parallel that comes to mind is of the myriad street vendors and small-scale artisans that keep economies going in failing states. By dispersing the authority for wildlife to many private and community landholders, Zimbabwe's conservation system is far more robust, innovative and often better managed than had it been when entirely in the hands of the wildlife department.

An argument for centralized conservation has been that it is too important to entrust to ordinary people and certainly the vagaries of the market. This example, which is replicated across the region, suggests that (at least where conservation can pay) the opposite is in fact true: conservation is too important not to disburse responsibility.

The Price–Proprietorship–Subsidiarity Hypothesis

Southern Africa follows a conservation paradigm in which the principles of sustainable use and the importance of landholder benefit and control feature prominently. Given the rural nature of our society, there is a strong emphasis on conserving land and ecological function, rather than species alone. This pragmatic approach has translated into entrusting landholders with wildlife, and allowing and assisting it to compete in the market place, a success that has helped southern Africa's conservation reputation. At the core of this is the price–proprietorship–subsidiarity hypothesis (Chapter 3). Interpreted, this says that if a wild resource is profitable, and if these profits are controlled by landholders, the resource will be conserved, with subsidiarity introducing the managerial and moral principle that rights should never be arrogated upwards where they can be exercised efficiently by smaller and lower bodies (Handy, 1994).

A Genesis of Ideas

This book came together through the Southern African Sustainable Use Specialist Group of the International Union for the Conservation of Nature's (IUCN's) Species Survival Commission. It brings together and distils the lessons from private, community[4] and state conservation across the region. The ten chapters are a synthesis of over 50 case studies written by the people who were directly involved in them. The understanding of community conservation within the region is generally highly sophisticated, and often at the cutting edge of development thinking (see, for example, Hulme and Murphree, 2001). Despite the successes of private (that is, freehold) conservation, we found that this sphere of conservation is not well studied (Chapter 3), presumably because it is unfashionable.[5]

Instructively, and somewhat surprisingly given their long genealogy and international prominence, the philosophical understanding of the links between man and nature appear crudest for traditional state-protected areas.[6] This is a critical observation with many practical manifestations. The performance of private and community conservation is controlled by incentives. The expectation is that one will find a powerful guiding philosophy behind non-market state conservation. However, there is little evidence that this is the case. The conceptual foundations of park management (Chapters 5–10) seem raw, doctrinaire and even opportunistic. Amazingly, this includes such central issues as the definition of biodiversity and conservation goals, which is perhaps why measuring park performance is proving so elusive. The fundamental institutional and economic relationships between parks, society and management objectives are also unclear, and contain inequities and contradictions that may well make them unworkable.

These are crucial issues affecting park and conservation management. If this book does nothing more than identify this gap and encourage debate and clarity, it will have achieved an important objective. We have no hesitation is admitting that in southern Africa we are struggling collectively to grapple with these issues. We hope that this first step is useful to other park and conservation managers whom we expect are also struggling with the challenge of making protected areas sustainable and meaningful to society, two sides of the same coin.

Private and Community Conservation Provide Benchmarks and Principles

Competition and peer comparison are powerful ingredients of a learning process. Southern Africa's learning experience originates in the innovation and benchmarking provided by private and community conservation and the consequent challenge to protected areas to improve. For example, how can we justify state subsidies of savannah parks, when landholders are managing similar environments at least as well, and are also making profits and creating more economic activity and jobs?

Private conservation and sustainable use outside parks have accelerated and diversified the conceptual learning process. Private conservation has provided a much stronger understanding of financial and economic issues, and prevents us from hiding behind the false assertion that large savannah parks cannot pay for themselves and simultaneously maintain biodiversity. Community conservation has shown just how central to conservation and sustainability are political economics, power, and the alignment of institutions and societal objectives. A common lesson from all these experiences, including private conservation, community-based natural resource management (CBNRM) and the commercialization of protected areas, is structural importance of devolution to motivation and performance. A similar lesson is the importance of monitoring for efficiency and learning (in other words adaptive management). And finally, southern Africa's national parks are under tremendous pressure, creating the impetus for change and a demand to use this wealth of experience from outside parks to guide new directions in park management.

A Circle of Learning: Learning Comes Full Circle

In the 1960s, several park agencies recognized that their ultimate success lay not only in protecting parks but in modifying institutions and incentives so that wildlife became an important land use in the buffer zones around parks and in non-agricultural areas in general. After all, 90 per cent of wildlife and habitats exist outside protected areas. This proved to be both profitable and ecologically sound. The irony is that these results are now holding to account the very agencies that initiated this progress. Very few parks are financially sustainable and many suffer from ecological problems, overpopulations of elephants being an important example.

Devolving rights to wildlife on private land created spectacular results that cost the state almost nothing (Chapter 3). To repeat some statistics, South Africa's 5000 private conservation areas conserve almost twice as much land as its national parks, while Zimbabwe's wildlife population outside national parks has quadrupled in 15 years. In dry savannahs, wildlife is significantly more profitable than the livestock it has often replaced, is much less damaging to the environment at similar levels of income, and creates substantially more jobs.

Transferring these principles from private land to communities (Chapter 4) taught us a lot about the power of fiscal devolution and the intricacies of rural governance, greatly emphasizing the importance of subsidiarity. For example, the evidence is accumulating that sharing revenues and managing wildlife in public meetings at village level is an order of magnitude more powerful in terms of transparency, involvement, democratization, reduced corruption and misappropriation, and the number of projects built, than channelling benefits to higher-level representational committees, the wont of most development projects (Child, 2004). Community conservation (Chapter 4) has sharpened our thinking about governance, devolution, participation, and the design and alignment of institutions. The combination of commercial knowledge from the private sector and institutional knowledge from community development is useful for informing park agencies on how to adapt in challenging circumstances.

THE PERFORMANCE OF NATIONAL PARKS

Having been able to get reasonable data describing the progress of private and, particularly, community conservation, we then turned to the core subject of the book: parks. We were surprised at how much difficulty park agencies in the region had in answering relatively simple questions or providing data to describe their performance (Chapter 5). Several issues emerged.

Protected Areas Have a Weak Philosophical Foundation

Park conservation does not seem to be underpinned by a clear philosophical foundation. Rather, agencies are stumbling to find the correct balance between multiple, often rather unclearly defined objectives, such as: what exactly is biodiversity?; the relationship between environment and financial and economic value; how to manage the financial–economic[7] trade-off between the viability of a park and its contribution to social values?; and how to measure the performance of parks along these multiple axes. Resolution of this challenge is complicated by the fact that park norms have been established in rich countries, yet these philosophies increasingly have to respond to the demands of poorer societies.

Not surprisingly, there was little evidence of standard performance criteria, principles, or targets, and therefore of any systematic monitoring of these. Park agencies could not provide systematic records summarizing their progress in biodiversity conservation, financial information was difficult to get, and despite the legitimate claim that parks lay at the heart of a productive tourism economy, no quantitative assessment of this was available in any country.

In writing this book, one of the key tasks was to look at the ecological and socio-economic goals and performance of parks (Chapter 5), and to translate these into a set of performance criteria.[8] The fact that we produced such a range of ideas at our workshop in Skukuza in April 2003 confirmed just how unformed this area of inquiry remains (see proceedings of the workshop at www.sasusg.net/workshop2.htm). Although we have made some conceptual progress this is clearly an area that needs to be developed. Following the adage that things that don't get measured don't get done, over the next decade the Southern Africa Sustainable Use Specialist Group (SASUSG) is planning to work in tandem with regional park agencies and with communities to test and develop performance criteria by initiating a system of self-administered and peer-based learning. Two sets of criteria are key. Biodiversity performance, despite being the primary rationale for parks, is neither well defined nor anywhere systematically monitored. Equally, the emerging issues of park governance and socio-economic contribution need to be defined and measured.

Weak Regional Performance of Protected-Area Agencies

With a few exceptions, and much in line with global experience (Reed, 2002), the performance of park agencies across the region has been weak, with shrinking budgets and a loss of technical capacity. Two scenarios are common. In the least developed countries in the region, poaching has decimated wildlife, and has sometimes even been associated with settlement in parks, with the positive side that human populations are low and habitats are often intact (eg Zambia, Mozambique). Particularly towards the south, a combination of reasonably effective protection but increasingly hard edges associated with expanding human populations in wildlife dispersal areas has led to too much wildlife and the loss of biodiversity. The good news (Chapter 6) is that performance is slowly improving, through a shift towards parastatals and commercialization, and a distancing from direct political control and the problems associated with this. However, with little precedent, there is still much to learn about the structuring and management of these agencies, and commercialization itself. There appear to be considerable advantages in initiating systems of performance management, especially when this is combined with the management of individual parks as cost centres.

A central conclusion is that conventional park management systems are not responding well to changing circumstances and the pressures they are under. When we asked why, we invariably found that the objectives of parks were not aligned with those of society. This continually brought us back to the profound and fundamental question of who parks are for (Chapter 9). Park goals have previously been set by a small group of bio-techno-bureaucrats, causing misalignment between their objectives and those of society in a time of increasing scarcity and democracy. Our short answer is that parks are common property entities that must provide as much value to society as possible. In circumstances of widespread poverty, this translates into providing jobs and economic growth without damaging the productivity of natural ecosystems or losing biodiversity. Indeed, the regional experience is that we can create far more benefits from marginal lands by encouraging wildlife-based enterprises, and that this also conserves the environment. To be sure that this is the right approach, we need to monitor ecosystem productivity and biodiversity more systematically to check that these enterprises are sustainable ecologically.

Do Conservation Opportunities Flow from Emphasizing Economic Enhancement?

The experience of southern Africa suggests that the trade-offs between biodiversity and socio-economic objectives have been exaggerated and the synergies underestimated (Whande et al, 2003). Agreeing strongly that the purpose of parks is to conserve biodiversity, but not agreeing that this should excessively limit use, the starting point for making parks more meaningful to society might be a clear definition of biodiversity goals, which will also enable the design of systems for measuring it. A sensible definition involves two components: ecosystem health and biological diversity (the former being neglected of late). The goal (that is, sustainability) should be to ensure that neither ecosystem health nor biological diversity are pushed over thresholds from which recovery is difficult. These thresholds, in turn, set the bounds for maximizing economic value (and from here we follow economists in using the term 'economic' to refer to the combination of financial and non-monetary values or net social value).

Contrary to the highly conservative tenor embedded in the precautionary principles, this allows a great deal more use to occur than currently imagined. Counter-intuitively, an incentive-led approach is likely to impose less negative ecological impact than the biocentric protectionism because it addresses the institutional symptoms of conservation problems rather than their ecological effects, and because it attracts better managers which increases the likelihood that biological and socio-economic outcomes will be defined and monitored.

Is Conservation the Same as Economic Efficiency?

Taking this argument further suggests that conservation is really about getting the most value out of resources without damaging them. This is the definition of efficiency, in this case defined as the net sum of value derived (the numerator) according to limits defined by ecological thresholds (the denominator). The park manager therefore aims to maximize the net benefits that a park provides to society,[9] while ensuring that ecosystem processes or species do not degrade over thresholds by using effective, affordable and strategic ecological monitoring. Thus the performance of park management in a transitional society is equal to the net benefit generated for that society (namely the output) while maintaining the limiting factor (namely the input) – biodiversity – within acceptable limits of change.

Redefining Park Performance

Contrary as it seems to conservation doctrine, this suggests that we should use economic (which, as defined above, are fundamentally different from financial) efficiency criteria to govern the management of parks, albeit with a powerful biodiversity caveat.

Output: Net Social Benefit

This argument links well with the fundamental suggestion in Chapter 9 that because parks are a form of societal common property, we need to relate benefits to the nature of the constituent society. If we take seriously the contention that parks serve society rather than a self-selected elite who know what is good for us, this requires that parks in developed and transitional societies are managed for different economic values. In transitional societies such as southern Africa, people value jobs and economic growth, and the numerator in the efficiency criteria will tend to be more tangible. In developed societies, rural recreation is scarce and other values are paramount, so the numerator may well be highly intangible, incorporating such values as wilderness, recreation and research. This in no way implies that park policies in transitional societies will sacrifice biodiversity conservation. As we discuss below, there is mounting evidence that preference for non-consumptive and intangible uses (which appear to be related more to anthropocentric desires not to interfere with nature than a real understanding of how ecosystems work) is often more consumptive of environments than what are currently termed consumptive uses.

There is also an emerging case for giving more weight to society at park locality levels because this concentrates the impact of benefits on those having a disproportionate relationship with the park. Encouraging park policy to emphasize 'local' in management decisions is unlikely to reduce 'national' biodiversity priorities or even the upstream and downstream economic impacts of tourism. Moreover, parks embedded positively in the local economy are far more likely to provide national and global benefits. Informatively, this argument brings us back to the logic of the ancient system of parks introduced in Chapter 1, where their 1000-year survival is a result of alignment, rather than confrontation, with local societal objectives and needs.

Input: Ecosystem Diversity and Health

We turn now to the denominator: the question of ecosystem cost. As suggested, the distinction between consumptive and non-consumptive, which is common currency, is misleading. It ignores two central ecological concepts. First, ecosystems are characterized by trophic levels, and protecting or increasing one level (eg herbivores) inevitably increases the extraction of the level below. Thus, being non-consumptive of elephants means being increasingly consumptive of trees.

Second, there is a quantum energy loss between trophic levels, and the recovery half-life of trophic levels varies by orders of magnitude (Figure 10.1). Thus, damaged soil and soil–nutrient–water cycles may take 1000 years to recover, damaged habitats take decades or hundreds of years to recover, yet the large herbivore populations that we commonly emphasize usually double easily within 10 years. Measuring the 'consumptiveness' of use in terms of 10-year systems as we do is inappropriate if not dangerous.[10] We need to reject the present use of the term 'consumptive' to reflect a new concept that incorporates recovery times and the perpetuation of ecosystems rather than single species or even individual animals.

These observations have profound implications for the design of ecosystem monitoring systems. Currently, a disproportionate amount of park agency budgets is allocated to research rather than basic monitoring, as well as towards charismatic

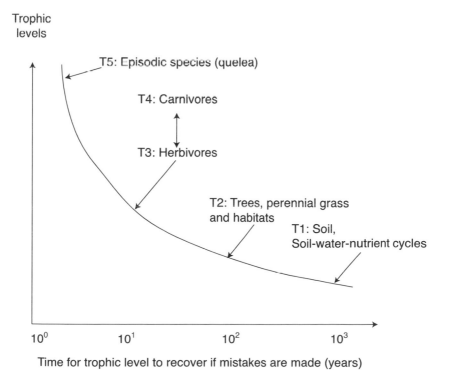

Trophic levels

T5: Episodic species (quelea)

T4: Carnivores

T3: Herbivores

T2: Trees, perennial grass and habitats

T1: Soil, Soil-water-nutrient cycles

10^0 10^1 10^2 10^3

Time for trophic level to recover if mistakes are made (years)

Figure 10.1 *Model illustrating trophic levels and recovery times as the basis for designing monitoring protocols and defining how use is consumptive*

species rather than fundamental underlying soil–water–nutrient–habitat processes. Moreover, systematic monitoring is rare. Figure 10.1 may provide a conceptual basis for the design of monitoring systems. It suggests the need to monitor several trophic layers simultaneously, and a case for linking the level of monitoring effort to recovery times and not only species and ecosystem components that are specifically threatened.

Changing the Conservation–Utility Means–End Relationship

The combination of clear societal goals and systematic ecosystem monitoring provides a mechanism for maximizing social utility from conservation areas. On the basis of this, there is a strong case for a profound change in the means–end relationship between conservation and the creation of socio-economic value, with the latter becoming the driving force. The growth in conservation areas in southern Africa demonstrates the strength of this case, which is increasingly widespread even where not explicitly stated.

The leading example is North West Parks in South Africa, which was confident enough to be explicit in its goals. State investment in the creation of new parks was justified primarily on their potential as engines of rural economic growth with biodiversity being decidedly secondary (eg Pilanesburg, Madikwe; Davies, 2000). The economic power of parks thereby provided powerful incentives for increasing conservation areas. Such examples of win–win and the experience of the private sector conservation are enabling South Africa to consider a massive increase in the area of national parks in the face of considerable demographic pressure. These pioneering examples are perhaps a precursor of where state conservation may be heading in the 21st century, at least in tropical countries.

This returns us to the ancient justification for protected areas, which is based on the net economic benefits they can generate for society, with biological health or diversity being important, but not the only value. As the governing philosophy for protected areas shifts in this direction, two challenges are likely to emerge. First, if we are to use parks effectively as an economic tool, we need to understand far more clearly how they work. We know almost nothing about how exactly this economic impact works, the number of jobs created and where these are, the nature of economic multipliers, and the geographic and distributional effects or possibilities related to conservation. Second, even a park that creates huge economic benefits is not sustainable unless the environment is healthy and a sufficient proportion of this economic impact can be retained to manage it properly. This presents park managers with three important challenges: understanding and optimizing economic impact; ensuring that parks are financially sustainable; and sustaining healthy ecosystems by monitoring and managing them.

Private and community conservation have had much clearer and narrower goals than state-protected areas – financial sustainability and ecological productivity – which is perhaps why they have been more successful. Park management is constrained by rather fuzzy conservation norms and bureaucratic and political restrictions.

This suggests the need for a far more businesslike approach to park and park agency management. Park agencies in southern Africa are, often through force of circumstance, becoming more businesslike, both in objectives and management systems. They would make faster progress if they were clearer about where they were going. Drucker (1973) emphasizes that the crucial decision to make is 'what is our business and what should it be?' Our suggestion is that protected-area agencies accept and vigorously pursue financial viability and socio-economic goals, but also define their biodiversity objectives in a way that is measurable. With three goals, there will inevitably be trade-offs. Therefore, and particularly in this early learning phase, it is imperative that they track their progress along these axes to facilitate their adaptive ability. A critical improvement in park management in southern Africa would be to clearly and consistently monitor performance in biodiversity conservation, the delivery of social value, and the underlying ability to provide these benefits as measured by technical and financial performance.

Questions of Accountability

Accountability is crucial, and in its several forms is the 'bottom line' for the range of conservation regimes discussed in this book. Private regimes have a self-evident accountability to themselves, communal regimes to their defined constituents, and public regimes to the broader public. Overlaid on these contextual types are the 'forms' of accountability: ecological, economic, organizational and political. All forms are important, and apply to all contexts — private, communal and public. However, it is with public accountability of state-protected areas that we have most to learn.

An important tenet throughout the book is that of accountability. As defined in Chapter 6, accountability as it relates to state-protected areas comes in several forms:

- The objectives of protected areas need to provide benefits that reflect values that are important to their constituency (constituency accountability).
- Park agencies and park managers need to pursue their public responsibility in an effective manner. This often requires a shift in managerial culture towards defining and focusing on outcomes that add value appropriate to their society and accepting the redundancy of past practice and norms which often do not contribute to these values although they may be accepted practice it does not specifically add value (accountability for adding value).
- The relationship and oversight between the park agency and the nations political masters, for example the Ministry of Tourism and Natural Resources (political accountability).
- The definition and achievement of specific performance goals and targets (performance accountability).

For park agencies, fundamental improvements are needed in two areas. First, the objectives set for parks need to be responsive to the needs of their constituencies, and second, park agencies need to be held accountable for performance in several ways including conservation effectiveness, socio-economic value added, and financial efficiency.

However, mechanisms for creating accountability are in their infancy (Chapter 6). The standard approach to providing public goods in the form of national parks and conservation[11] has been to nationalize and centralize control, and place it in the hands of techno-bureaucrats and, more recently, politicians. This may work where governments are accountable to citizens and where civil servants are a technical elite, but this is rare and particularly unlikely in underfunded or failing state bureaucracies. Indeed, weak accountability at several levels has emerged as a root cause of the underperformance of parks. Political leadership seldom sets goals in the service of their constituency. The misalignment between park objectives and practices and the needs of society, particularly immediate neighbours, has seldom been addressed. The relationship between park agencies and the political leadership is often dysfunctional. There is a high propensity for inefficiency, corruption, predation or patronage associated with such state-owned resources. And finally, there are few clearly articulated goals, and even fewer means of measuring performance against these, so agencies are accountable for neither efficiency nor effectiveness.

Our discussion of the transition in park objectives shows that a major challenge is making parks accountable to society in terms of their overall objectives, accountability and governance. For overall goals, the critical question is who parks are for? This will define what societal values they should provide. We have suggested that providing jobs and economic growth with a biodiversity caveat are the most suitable relationship between parks and society in southern Africa.

In terms of governance, governments have failed to fund parks or hold agencies accountable for performance. There are early indications that park parastatals are an improvement, largely because less political control reduces patronage and other distortions and because financial pressures encourage better management systems (Chapter 6). However, an emerging danger, albeit a far lesser one than total collapse, is that that park agencies are forced to focus myopically on financial survival. Ignoring their wider and real mandate to fulfil biodiversity and socio-economic goals can have enormous costs. Financial survival should be a means to this end, not an end in itself.

Many of these institutional problems are linked to monopolization of conservation by budget-funded state agencies with a lot of power, little accountability and a plethora of organizational and managerial problems. This monopoly is problematic. Having a single solution to conservation challenges is risky, leaving little space for alternative models and learning. It also lacks the selective force of competition and benchmarking so essential for long-term evolution. This is why encouraging private and community conservation initiatives was ultimately (if unintentionally) so important even for the health of park agencies.

The functions and structures of state conservation agencies can also be re-engineered to increase performance accountability. The underlying principle should be to encourage practices that add clearly articulated and measurable economic and biodiversity value. Dogmatic adherence to past norms, a symptom of dysfunctional businesses, is costly and ultimately suicidal. Devolving authority, and using market or non-commercial tests of performance that are directly linked to value, is the best way to oppose the more negative attributes associated with bureaucratic survival.

The emerging challenge is to make conservation managerially more rigorous and accountable for creating the kinds of value that are appropriate to their constituent societies. Performance accountability is built by translating a clearly articulated vision (which reflects these values) into measurable goals and by insisting on transparent reporting. There are two concrete steps that should be taken to ensure that parks are creating value. First, functions should be subjected to market tests wherever this is possible. This places more power in the hands of ordinary people, and is invaluable for rectifying the subjectivity of administrative pricing and allocation. It is one reason why the commercialization of parks is a positive development. Second, where commercial tests are not possible, functions should be submitted to clearly defined performance criteria and scrutinized regularly. Measures of biological health fit into this category.

It is obviously going to be challenging to change the way conservation is done; to shift control from a few techno-bureaucrats towards ordinary people by making conservation both more objective and more inclusive. Winning combinations are only likely to emerge with experience that invokes careful and comparative monitoring along a series of axes that include biodiversity, financial sustainability, and socioeconomic benefits and acceptability.[12] This points to the importance of peer review and learning among southern African park agencies as a mechanism of adapting to the turbulent changes affecting society and, inevitably, protected areas.

The Fallout from Weak Guiding Principles for Protected Areas

The long history of national parks has not resulted in clearly articulated underlying principles or even a clear definition of exactly what is being protected, and from whom, and for whom? Perhaps nothing is quite as important. Being unable to describe exactly what we want from parks means that performance cannot be measured and that the system lacks bottom-line accountability. This serious weakness allows some of the contradictions described below.

First, dialogue about the value of biodiversity is seldom matched by financial commitments. That national parks have survived affirms the sentiment and reality that they are of value to society. However, and this is instructive, park performance and survival appears to be far more closely related to commercial viability about which there is much denial, and far less to the laudable biodiversity conservation and public goals to which their value is usually ascribed.

Second, it may be legitimate for the state to take on responsibility for the provision of public goods such as biodiversity conservation, but is this really what is happening? In many national parks the state is providing values that the private sector is much better at (eg tourism services) and only incidentally focusing on legitimate state roles (eg biodiversity monitoring and habitat protection or recovery measures). This is a misallocation of societal resources, suggesting that performance can be improved significantly by redefining the roles and core business of state conservation agencies and the private sector.

Third, we must question if parks are providing the correct public goods. In many cases parks are, as a consequence of tradition rather than principle, providing values suited to developed rather than developing countries. The wilderness values that are still emphasized in many African park plans (often written by consultants with a different socio-economic background from most Africans) for instance, are of far lower societal value to poor people living in remote, rural areas than jobs. This reflects the locus of power and influence. The 'rules' are set by a techno-bureaucratic elite who tend to represent developed world interests and norms, where wilderness is indeed a valuable (and affordable) antidote to urban living.

Fourth, there does not appear to be consensus on what biological or social attributes parks should provide. The biological goals of protected areas are rarely defined in a manner that is measurable. One consequence is that the management of the interactions between trophic layers, for example where a herbivore is overutilizing vegetation, is decided more by politics than ecological science. Social goals are even more rudimentary.

Conservation and protected areas are expected to deliver an impressive array of outputs. Unfortunately, these goals are so general that although broadly acceptable, they paper over real misalignments and contradictions, and also enable mangers to avoid accountability. This allows all manner of weak or even self-serving management, to which public agencies are already particularly susceptible. From the way conservation is structured one can predict, correctly as it turns out, that it is likely to follow fashions; that spin-doctoring or political correctness will often be more important determinants of resource allocation than real and measurable results; and that a disproportionate amount of resources will be spent on meetings, international workshops and resolutions. Centralization also enhances the power of special interest groups to the disadvantage of all, and especially landholders and their natural resources.

Management Systems

Another area in which park agencies are weak is in understanding the managerial relationships between functions, structure and performance. Park agencies across the region are responding to rapidly changing circumstances, but still remain way behind in the adoption of modern management practice while retaining several of the worst characteristics of budget-funded state agencies: a high level of centralization, multiple and often competing goals, and the retention of functions that add little or no value and should be made redundant. Where there has been progress, it is often attributable to an ability to attract better leadership, and no amount of restructuring can replace the simple need to attract and pay the best individuals. Commercialization, and the battle for viability, is also exerting positive change in management cultures.

Managerially, two actions bring substantial and immediate dividends. The introduction of performance management systems clarifies objectives (preferably quantifiably) and provides mechanisms for systematic monitoring and corrective action. Decentralization, and the treatment of parks as cost centres, is also powerful. Critically, it internalizes costs, benefits and, ultimately, responsibility. Further, where the complexity of managing the competing goals and crises of park agencies at headquarters is usually overwhelming, at the level of a park goals can often be sufficiently simplified to provide clear guidance to task managers. The healthiest scenario is to set clearly measurable targets but also to provide managers with considerable managerial freedom provided they achieve these goals.

Bridgeheads for Economic Development

There is also a strong case for many parks to be treated as engines of economic development and bridgeheads for consolidating the use of landscapes around the sustainable use of biodiversity, especially wildlife. This seems to fit very well with the largely untested management of parks as cost centres. At this level, managers are more accountable to their local constituency and, as the cost-centre argument shows, more accountable for performance. Moreover, the local constituency is often the biggest long-term threat to the park. In this regard, not only can parks provide direct local benefits (eg job opportunities, purchase of goods and supplies) but they can be used deliberately as a tool to promote biodiversity on the land outside the parks through, for example, pricing policies, the provision of access to parks or wildlife for wildlife businesses, economies of scale and tourism infrastructure. This is obviously good for conservation. For certainly parks are not the only way to conserve biodiversity: private and community conservation is highly effective provided wildlife is allowed to pay (through the removal of artificial or bureaucratic restrictions and the development of a range of markets for wildlife products) and provided landholders are the primary beneficiary with full proprietary rights.

An important feature of successful conservation in southern Africa is that landholders have been given primacy among the wide range of possible stakeholders. This follows the belief that conservation outcome depends on the incentives faced by landholders, and leads directly to policies that maximize the return of value to landholders. This is by no means the most common situation. The combination of centralized conservation and the power of special interest groups means that so-called stakeholders (especially richer and more powerful ones) often dominate at the expense of landholders. In these cases, conservation either fails, or is inefficient with high opportunity costs. Political predation in some African countries (Gibson, 2000), the Endangered Species Act and bureaucratic management of wild resources in the western mountains and rangelands in the USA are respective examples.

KEY LESSONS LEARNED

We turn now to some of the key lessons learned:

- Although, the core purpose of parks is biodiversity conservation, this has seldom been defined or measured.
- The performance of many government park agencies has declined to low levels, with poor salaries excluding the quality of leadership needed to manage a diverse and elusive set of conservation and economic goals.
- Accountability is a fundamental problem facing protected areas. A profound decision relates to the types of value they should be providing to their constituency. The linkages between the protected-area agencies, political oversight and their societal constituency are all dysfunctional. There is a surprising absence of clearly defined goals or performance assessment in many aspects of management, causing a serious and widespread accountability problem.

- Conservation is highly centralized. Yet decentralization improves park management by internalizing decisions and reducing externalities. It improves landscape linkages between parks and the land use and communities around parks. And it creates more opportunities for people dealing with real problems to innovate.
- Private conservation on private and communal land is achieving as much biodiversity conservation as parks, and is also profitable where parks are not.[13]
- This suggests that state-run conservation mechanisms are inefficient and need to be overhauled.
- Proprietorship, price and subsidiarity are the vital ingredients of private or community conservation.
- Park management systems across the region are (and need to be) in transition. This is movement into unexplored territory in terms of institutional or management systems, performance management of biodiversity, the social responsibilities of conservation, commercialization and managing parks as cost centres. Even though many other countries must be facing similar challenges, these issues are rarely stated in the accessible literature. Comparative mechanisms are a critical learning tool that needs to be introduced.
- In reality, this transition is upending the means–ends relationship between park viability, socio-economic growth and conservation. It is better to grasp than deny this profound change.
- The relationship between commercialization and conservation is often positive. Commercialization tends to strengthen the links between management and value and therefore improve general performance (but is still very new).

CONCLUSIONS: INCENTIVES, OPPORTUNITIES AND CONTROLS

Where Does the Southern Africa Experimental Nature Originate?

If southern Africa has provided and tested a disproportionate number of new models of protected-area governance and economy, the underlying impetus stems from the switch from fortress to incentive-led conservation. The latter hinges as much on institutional innovations as on commercial possibilities. It depends, first, on scaling down to the smallest appropriate unit, and only then on scaling up according to the principles of subsidiarity. Devolving responsibility co-opts many landholders as conservationists. It is guided by the perception of value, both market and non-market, and works best where regulatory controls are minimized but tightly targeted. The global importance of southern Africa's experiences is the insights they test in a field where innovation is an exception and cautious conformism the norm (Child, 2003).

Significantly, this paradigm shifts institutions to the forefront of conservation. Making conservation a livelihood option to thousands of landholders and communities outside conventional protected areas depends on modifying institutions, laws and norms to translate wildlife's comparative advantage into real incentives for landholders to take up conservation as a business.

Enforcement Versus Non-Detriment

In the past, conservation has been a holding action against 'development', with its mechanisms heavily dependent on negative sanctions (such as Convention on International Trade in Endangered Species of Wild Fauna and Flora (CITES) and the US Endangered Species Act). The new approach is more optimistic and aims to actively extend conservation beyond the borders of protected areas. It places responsibility for conservation in the hands of many landholders, each being a potential crucible of innovation. With alignment the rationale behind this paradigm shift, it is perhaps poignant that in conserving natural selection this paradigm invokes the Darwinian struggle for the survival of the fittest as the evolutionary force driving conservation practice. Yes, there will be losses, but there will also be adaptation to change. Forces for improvement (that is, innovation, competition and selection) are much less in evidence where state agencies monopolize conservation, and where risk aversion is a predominant preoccupation. The conventional approach has the added risk of placing too many valuable conservation eggs and protected areas in the same managerial and governance basket.

Shifting paradigms to a different guiding hand – that of incentives rather than techno-bureaucratic dictate and sanction – radically alters mechanisms of accountability away from a few techno-bureaucrats. Bottom-line accountability becomes both a powerful encourager and a tough disciplinarian. Far more conservation business is achieved in the market place where adding value is the guiding hand. This releases resources once used to conserve potentially self-financing biodiversity to pay for conservation areas that are valuable but not financially viable. Importantly, the allocation of scarce conservation resources is more effective. The net result is more conservation, which is presumably why we are seeing tentative acceptance and spread of this paradigm. The US government, for example, has been recently seeking public comment on a policy[12] aimed at shifting from a cautionary 'non-detriment' approach to 'enhancement', which is built around the power of properly aligned incentives.

Self-interest

Nevertheless, there is considerable consternation with the introduction of Adam Smith's invisible hand of self-interest as the guiding force for biodiversity conservation. We present two arguments in support of this approach. First, it allows more conservation to occur. Second, it appears to have more rigorous philosophical underpinnings than conventional conservation practice such as protectionist legislation and national park philosophy.

As we have just noted, using self-interest to conserve resources that can pay for themselves frees up limited resources to pay for the biodiversity that cannot. Thus, savannah conservation can be left to private or community landholders or to parks run on business lines, and the resources released or generated by these activities might protect rare habitats or species that are less spectacular or financially viable. For example, South African National Parks is considering selling rhinos from its national parks and using the surplus to purchase land in habitats that are under-represented by the present protected-area system. If we follow this argument to its conclusion, it is irresponsible not to use wildlife efficiently (and sustainably) to generate a surplus for reinvestment in conservation.

Common Interest

Despite their longer genealogy, it is difficult to find a clear and internally consistent philosophy or values underpinning parks, much less to explain them to a deprived citizen. Indeed, protected-area philosophy appears to be politically opportunistic, and far less altruistic than is often supposed (Runte, 1987). Thus, the formation of Yellowstone National Park was linked to market development by railroad barons, almost universally it was only unusable land that was converted to parks, and today's emphasis reflects a free-riding demand for 'natural' areas by dominant elites in society. The absence of a sound conceptual basis is an important weakness that park managers need to address, and this book has initiated several suggestions in this direction: essentially arguing that parks are common property regimes, and for the maximization of societal value with a biological caveat to ensure sustainability.

The central principle is that of internalized responsibility. For instance, clear-cut tenure links incentives to performance through markets for investment or tourism dollars, while sound environmental management is increasingly factored into these performance criteria as owners and customers become more aware of the biosphere.

Correcting and Internalizing Pricing Signals

That incentive-led conservation works is no accident. The corollary is that it only works when several institutional and economic principles are strictly followed. As applied to private and communal conservation these principles are that:

- Costs and benefits are internalized at the level of the landholder. Authority, including the rights to manage, benefit and dispose (that is, sell), must be allocated to small landholder units (scaling down). The primary and controlling beneficiary of wildlife use must be the landholder as this internalizes costs and benefits at the level of the people who make the real decisions about how land will be used. Where externalities associated with fugitive resources need to be controlled, this is best done at the community level (scaling up) rather than by centralized command and control.
- Incentives reflect real values. Incentive-led conservation is powerful where wildlife and other natural resources are commercially viable, circumstances that probably pertain far more widely than we currently assume. Unfortunately, because of the way many wild resources have been governed historically, inherent comparative advantages are often masked by distorted prices, subsidies, taxes and other perverse incentives. The first and major hurdle is to allow landholders to use wild resources legally, because this is the precursor of significant benefits and the catalyst for inventing new ways of adding value. The second challenge is that the playing field is invariably biased heavily against wild resources. The taxes, charges and bureaucratic requirements

differentially imposed on wild resources need to be removed as do the subsidies for competing resources. Third, having long been extracted from the market place, a considerable amount of product development is required.[12]

- Within this framework, environmental sustainability will often look after itself because of its close link to commercial viability. For example, a tourism operator with poor-quality wildlife or degraded habitats will often be disadvantaged in the market place.
- Justice and good governance is ultimately essential for no system is sustainable without real legitmacy and support.

These principles, amply supported by experience in private and communal conservation, apply equally to state-protected areas. Private conservation, CBNRM and the commercialization of protected areas are not opportunistic or wishy-washy approaches to conservation. They require disciplined adherence to a small, increasingly articulated, set of principles that serve primarily to align incentive structures and bring into play the power of the bottom line: that is, accountability for performance. These principles echo through the chapters on private and community conservation.

Some Proposed Principles of Protected Areas

Parks in southern Africa are beginning a major realignment of values essential for their continued survival (Chapter 9). There is evidence that parks can be harnessed far more effectively to promote rural development, and that this can enhance biodiversity conservation both within parks and across the landscape (Chapter 7). However, a major problem afflicting park management is that they have no performance bottom line, and park agencies are therefore not held accountable (Chapter 6). The bottom line for protected areas ideally has several components (eg financial, biodiversity, social value added). Nevertheless, invoking even the performance pressures of the (abhorrent to some) financial bottom line has positive conservation consequences (Chapters 6 and 7), hinting at just how useful clear biological or social performance indicators might be.

Drucker's (1973) central question of defining 'what is park management and what should it be' leads to profound and fundamental questions about park conservation that have been avoided for too long:

- Who is the conservation of a park for? (Which also relates to who benefits and who pays.)
- What is conservation? As noted, this has something to do with maintaining both ecosystem health and diversity above thresholds from which normal recovery is possible.
- Only the third question brings us to 'how to do park conservation'. Although governments do have an important role in park conservation, we need to challenge the command-and-control model that so heavily dominates this field. Innovation is essential.

These questions, or at least the first two, describe the ends. To improve the means of achieving these we also reiterate Drucker's (1973) advice for the management of public institutions: use markets to guide decisions wherever this is possible and devise clear measures of performance accountability where it is not. This may profoundly change the way we organize the delivery of protected-area outcomes.

To begin with the ends – the who and the what of conservation – we offer several suggestions for clarifying the principles underlying park management:

- Who? A critical starting point is Murphree's insight (Chapter 9) that parks are common property regimes set aside for the purpose of serving a local or national constituency. This provides a philosophical foundation[13] for the question of who parks are for.
- What? Second, we suggest that, in general, parks have two objectives: ecological conservation and the provision of socio-economic value. Our innovation is to challenge the present means–ends relationship and to suggest that we aim to maximize socio-economic value within constraints imposed by ecosystems, even in protected areas.
- The biological objective of parks should be to ensure that ecosystem health and diversity thresholds remain intact (and to measure these systematically), accepting that there are cases where diversity (eg single species) or other factors may take specific and overriding priority.
- Contrary to common practice, it follows that within these limits use should be actively encouraged to maximize benefits to society, and that any socially acceptable or humane use is acceptable provided ecosystem health and diversity thresholds remain intact. In this regard, jobs, economic growth and rural development are social goals every bit as legitimate to societies where rural poverty is common, as are wilderness and science to North Americans.
- There is a third level of discussion needing a lot more debate that we have not introduced. This is the complex trade-off between producing as much value as possible and distributional issues relating to who benefits from this value.

This combination of aligning parks to provide what is appropriate to society with threshold criteria for ecological sustainability opens up many opportunities to make parks more valuable to society, as examples in this book suggest.

The emerging lesson from southern Africa is the importance and value of allowing and encouraging ordinary people and especially landholders (not only bureaucracies) to participate in conservation. Dramatic progress has occurred where incentives are aligned properly. Moreover, there is abundant evidence that public agencies are far from perfect in managing the extra-market allocation of resources (Chapter 6) that justifies their position, and also that too much responsibility has been given to them. This all suggests a major realignment not only of goals but of implementational roles. In this regard, the examples of the private and CBNRM sectors demonstrate just how effective it is for the public sector to focus on creating conditions that enable the private and community sectors to supply conservation products, rather than doing the nuts-and-bolts work themselves. Moving in this direction is likely to be the challenge of the next decade.

How Universally Applicable Are These Lessons?

There is no logical reason why the southern African approach to conservation is locality specific, although the region does have the advantages of having quality fauna in ecosystems where agriculture is ecologically difficult. However, many other regions have similar combinations of marketable wildlife and scenery in areas where agriculture is marginal. The Rocky Mountain West, east and west African savannahs, the mountains and steppes of Asia, and the tundra are examples of areas where wildlife is likely to be a competitive land use. Tropical forests still present a major question. Are the present difficulties of making forests pay inherent, or are they related to a failure of property rights, weak product development, and consequently low incentives? Forty years ago, wildlife faced similar problems. Initial hopes that it could produce more and better meat with less ecological impact never succeeded commercially, but since then the wildlife sector has diversified and added value through many product avenues.

We therefore hypothesize that the massive expansion in conservation land in southern Africa springs as much or more from the design of institutional mechanisms that promote the value of wildlife and ensure that it accrues directly to landholders as from its natural endowments. The corollary is that it is institutional constraints that limit other areas with potential from following similar trends. The centralization of control over natural resources prevents their value being internalized to landholders as conservation incentives. In poorer countries, this leads to conservation failure as in large parts of Africa and Asia. In richer countries, conservation is often imposed on landholders (eg the US Endangered Species Act) in a way that is invariably inefficient and contentious. The important lesson from southern Africa is the potential for aligning incentives to reduce conflicts and increase conservation. What is important is scaling down by devolving strong use rights to the lowest level, and ensuring that scaling up follows the principles of subsidiarity so well elucidated by Handy (1994).

Protected areas appear to have been trapped in an intellectual backwater and have not evolved in alignment with society, at least in developing or rural countries. The new concepts beginning to emerge in southern Africa probably have wider application. Two major shifts in protected-area philosophy are proposed. First, that the role of parks is deliberately responsive to the demands of society, with a greater emphasis on the creation of appropriate values coupled with more discipline in defining and measuring desired ecological outcomes. The second shift is to give particular attention to the locality through the concept of 'local' parks and the role of parks as rural economic engines. Thus, parks should be deliberately managed as a kernel from which nature-based livelihoods can spread across the landscape. Instead of reactively insisting on buffer zones, park managers can proactively create the institutional conditions to enable their neighbours to benefit by setting aside land for nature-compatible activities. There is also considerable potential to manage parks deliberately as mechanisms of rural development given that they are often the dominant economic force and source of technical capacity in remote rural areas. The potential to use parks deliberately as economic engines has widespread application, at least in rural societies. This proposal, rather than being radical or new, represents a return to the ancient concept of parks as embedded in the Arabian hemas.

One of the most valuable things that we as conservationists can contribute to effective park management is to set clear goals. However, although this is universally applicable, the fact that it is also universally ignored, confused or contradictory should sound warning bells. Those gaining from the status quo will oppose such change. Although critical managerially, obtaining such clarity of purpose may be extremely difficult politically. Imagine transferring the Pilanesburg model to Yellowstone National Park. This is a symptom of a structural cause that has its roots in the centralized, and therefore highly political, control of conservation. A hugely disproportionate number of people employed in national and international conservation organizations are based in capital cities, another symptom of the highly political nature of conservation, as is the powerful influence of special interest groups. As Mancur Olson (2002) argues so persuasively, the power of such special interest is the Achilles' heel of liberal democracies. The essence of his argument is that the 1 per cent of the population with the power or money to fight political battles is disenfranchizing the interests of the 99 per cent, creating huge economic inefficiencies and inequities.

Given how unusually centralized global conservation is, one can be pessimistic about the likelihood of change. People with power, even if they have not recognized it explicitly, will be highly reluctant to give it up. Conferences lead to conferences, and absorb disproportionate resources. Powerful forces are therefore aligned against the antidote of inclusive, decentralized conservation that features so prominently in this book. Only when most people are empowered and incentivized to conserve their land is biodiversity conservation likely to be sustainable. Fortunately, there are strong signs that ordinary people are recognizing the benefits of conservation and that democratic and economic forces will eventually overcome the hegemonization of nature. This will be good for biodiversity.

ACKNOWLEDGEMENTS

Marshall Murphree and Brian Jones provided invaluable advice on the content and structuring of this chapter.

NOTES

1   There is a lot to be said for formalizing this contribution to conservation, especially if it is held to the same (as yet absent) conservation monitoring standards as protected areas. We make this suggestion with the proviso that it is recognized that these are multiple use systems of which conservation is but one component.
2   This approach replaces highly circumscribed protected-area dogma, where we have already noted the danger of inequitable power relationships (that is, the influence of a narrow techno-bureaucratic elite).
3   This was brought home to me on a recent visit to Save Conservancy in southern Zimbabwe. When I began my career assessing game and cattle production in this very area in the mid-1980s, the landscape was red and often bare, the bush was thick with thorn scrub, and cattle and impala dominated the biomass. Cattle monocultures had eliminated or decimated many grazing wildlife species, and in several years traversing this area in the 1980s I did not see sable. On my recent trip, the grass was waist high and soil erosion obviously much reduced. I immediately saw two herds of sable (not to mention giraffe, wildebeest and impala), an obligate grazer that is a strong indicator of overgrazing.

4   Definitionally, community conservation is also private (that is, non-state) and in the CBNRM chapter we distinguish between freehold, community and state tenure.

5   Southern Africa's unfortunate racial legacy colours many aspects of life. With private landholders being predominantly white, there has been an aversion to assisting or studying them, reinforced by the inequity of supporting relatively well-off people where the demands of the poor are overwhelming.

6   We refer primarily to national parks, although several countries have different categories of state-run protected areas such as forests.

7   These terms have specific meanings in the terminology of the economist. A financial analysis is an assessment taken from the perspective of an individual or single organization and does not correct for distortions in the economy. An economic analysis uses shadow-prices to reflect real societal values rather than market prices, and is done from the perspective of society as a whole.

8   We had intended to include a chapter on ecological and socio-economic performance criteria for protected areas. However, our thinking is still too raw for this so we have instead embarked on a process of developing these criteria for state and community conserved areas through peer learning.

9   Here we have limited ourselves to maximizing benefits, and to avoid complexity have not discussed equity and distributional issues.

10 The following, apparently radical, example illustrates this proposition, asking whether we should promote the following activities in South Africa's Kruger National Park: tourism and safari hunting. This example is drawn from a policy paper prepared for South African National Parks (Child, 2002).

Tourism in Kruger generates a net profit of US$20,000, so from a financial perspective the park is marginally viable. Far more dominant economically are the several thousands of jobs created, the tourism multipliers that extend through the economy, and Kruger's importance in South Africa's tourism sector. Kruger, however, also shatters the myth that tourism is in any way non-consumptive. In terms of costs, tourism-related infrastructure (eg roads, gravel pits, impact on water flow) affects some 7 per cent of the park, and water extraction and waste disposal are other impacts. The park is fenced, so the natural process of wildlife dispersal no longer occurs. There are numerous waterholes. In the past, there were also predator control programmes. Consequently, herbivore populations are far higher than under so-called natural conditions. The effects of herbivory, plus a programme of deliberate, systematic burning (now stopped), has had a huge impact on the structure of the vegetation, which has been 'homogenized' as a bushveldt thicket. Excess elephants have knocked down woodlands, whereas overgrazing and fire have converted grasslands into thickets.

Using Kruger for safari hunting would generate a profit of at least US$2,000,000, but the multipliers in the South African tourism economy, although considerable, would be less than the tourism sector. In terms of costs, offtake rates of less than 2 per cent hardly damage wildlife populations, which increase at about 10 per cent, whereas habitats in areas that are hunted are often more healthy than in tourism areas.

So if we look dispassionately at Kruger in terms of ecological conservation or the financial viability of the park, safari hunting is a better option than tourism. It is better for the environment and generates more money to manage the park.

Economic analysis differentiates between a 'financial' assessment, which measures impact at the level of an individual enterprise, such as Kruger, and an 'economic' assessment, which values activities at the level of society. It is only when we assess Kruger economically that tourism may outperform hunting. However, as noted above, this has significant (and under-recognized) costs in terms of the environment and the park's financial survival, the latter being especially relevant as is illustrated by parks like Hwange (Zimbabwe), South Luangwa (Zambia) or Etosha (Namibia), which do not have enough money to maintain themselves.

11 Although we have challenged the assumption that park agencies are primarily providing public goods and have suggested that they focus disproportionately on providing services that can be allocated in the market place (eg tourist accommodation) and too little on providing real public goods (eg biodiversity conservation).

12 Within the region, our hope as SASUSG is to experiment with peer review to collectively improve our understanding of objectives and performance criteria, to use these comparisons to learn how to improve performance, and perhaps even as a mechanism of peer accountability. In this regard, we see relatively small differences between state, private and community conservation, and it may be wise to measure their performance with the same yardstick.

13 Fish and Wildlife Service, Department of the Interior, Draft Policy for Enhancement-of-Survival Permits for Foreign Species Listed Under the Endangered Species Act, Federal Register, volume 68, no. 159, Monday, August 18, 2003.

14 In this regard, it has taken some four decades for wildlife to become profitable. Other wild resources such as forests and natural products are often not yet viable, and perhaps it will also take investment in product development by entrepreneurs to bring this about.

REFERENCES

Child, B (2003) 'Review: Biodiversity, sustainability and human communities: Protecting beyond the protected', *Nature* **421**: 123

Child, B (2002) 'Policy for the use of natural resources by South African National Parks' (draft), Report to the Board of South Africa National Parks

Child, B (2004) *Principles, Practice and Results of Community Wildlife Management in Southern Africa*, Sand Country Foundation (in press)

Child, B (2002) 'Policy for Use of Natural Resources by South Africa National Parks' (draft), Report to South African National Parks Board

Child, B, Jones, B, Moinuddin, H, Mulolazi, A and Mazambani, D (2003) 'Final evaluation report: Zimbabwe Natural Resources Management Program – USAID/Zimbabwe', CAMPFIRE Communal Areas Management Programme for Indigenous Resources

Davies, R (2000) 'Madikwe Game Reserve: A partnership in conservation', in H H T Prins, J G Grootenhuis, and T Dolan (eds) *Wildlife Conservation by Sustainable Use*, Kluwer Academic Publishers, pp439–58

Drucker, P F (1973) *Management: Tasks, Responsibilities, Practices*, Harper Collins, New York

Gibson, C C (2000) *Politicians and Poachers: The Political Economy of Wildlife Policy in Africa*, Cambridge University Press, Cambridge, UK

Handy, C (1994) *The Empty Raincoat. Making Sense of the Future*, Arrow Books, London

Hulme, D and Murphree, M (eds) (2001) *African Wildlife and Livelihoods. The Promise and Performance of Community Conservation*, James Currey, Oxford

Landes, D (1998) *The Wealth and Poverty of Nations. Why Some Are So Rich and Some So Poor*, Abacus, London

Olson, M (2002) *Power and Prosperity. Outgrowing Communist and Capitalist Dictatorships*, Basic Books, New York

O'Riordan, T and Stoll-Kleeman, S (2002) *Biodiversity, Sustainability and Human Communities. Protecting beyond the Protected*, Cambridge University Press, Cambridge, UK, pp317

Reed, T (2002) 'The function and structure of protected area authorities. Considerations for financial and organizational management', World Bank draft paper

Runte, A (1987) *National Parks. The American Experience*, University of Nebraska Press

Whande, W, Kepe, T, and Murphree, M (2003) 'Local communities, equity and conservation in Southern Africa', Programme for Land and Agrarian Studies (PLAAS), School of Government, University of the Western Cape

Index